The Ecstatic
Poetic Tradition

D0743427

San Diego Christian College
Library
Santee, CA

809.1
M821e

The Ecstatic Poetic Tradition

A Critical Study from the Ancients through Rumi, Wordsworth, Whitman, Dickinson and Tagore

D.J. MOORES

McFarland & Company, Inc., Publishers
Jefferson, North Carolina

The following poems are reprinted by permission of the publishers and the Trustees of Amherst College from *The Poems of Emily Dickinson*, edited by Thomas H. Johnson (Cambridge, MA: Belknap Press of Harvard University Press), Copyright © 1951, 1955, 1979, 1983 by the President and Fellows of Harvard College: It is a lonesome glee (J774/F873), One joy of so much anguish (J1420/F1450), If all the griefs I am to have (J1726/F1756), Much madness is divinest sense (J435/F620).

Excerpts from *The Masnavi: Book One*, by Jalal al-Din Rumi and translated by Jawid Mojaddedi, are reprinted by permission of Oxford University Press.

LIBRARY OF CONGRESS CATALOGUING-IN-PUBLICATION DATA

Moores, D.J.
    The ecstatic poetic tradition : a critical study from the ancients through Rumi, Wordsworth, Whitman, Dickinson and Tagore / D.J. Moores.
        p.   cm.
    Includes bibliographical references and index.

    ISBN 978-0-7864-7816-3 (softcover : acid free paper) ∞
    ISBN 978-1-4766-1473-1 (ebook)

    1. Ecstasy in literature.   2. Poetry—History and criticism. I. Title.
    PN56.E27M66 2014
    809.1—dc23   2014013476

BRITISH LIBRARY CATALOGUING DATA ARE AVAILABLE

© 2014 D.J. Moores. All rights reserved

No part of this book may be reproduced or transmitted in any form or by any means, electronic or mechanical, including photocopying or recording, or by any information storage and retrieval system, without permission in writing from the publisher.

Front cover image © 2014 Shutterstock

Printed in the United States of America

McFarland & Company, Inc., Publishers
  Box 611, Jefferson, North Carolina 28640
  www.mcfarlandpub.com

To the following:
Harold Klemp, my teacher for so long.
Mom and Dad, for your support and
encouragement over the years.
Tatsiana, for your love and devotion.

Table of Contents

Preface

This book about the poetics and aesthetics of ecstasy has three points of origin: personal, incidental and academic.

Personal. When I teach ecstatic poetry I always ask my students if they have ever had an ecstasy, and I almost always hear a resounding "yes." Of course, they always ask me if I have ever had one, and my response is also always a resounding "yes." When I was fourteen years old, at a time when most people around me believed I was eventually headed for prison or worse, I had a strange, spontaneous experience that forever changed me. The details are too personal to recount here, but suffice it to say that they constituted what I call in this book an ecstasy. No drugs were involved, and although the experience occurred spontaneously, I had begun meditating a short time before it happened. I intuitively feel the two (meditation and ecstatic experience) are connected. This ecstasy, regardless of its cause, informs all of my professional work.

Incidental. After teaching ecstatic poetry for several years and hearing my good students complain when I required them to buy sometimes up to eight different books for a given course, I conceived of the idea of creating an anthology of ecstatic verse so I could put all of the poets we were studying in one inexpensive text. Before finally getting the work published—(*Wild Poets of Ecstasy*, 2011)—I received the inevitable round of rejections. In one of these Harry Keyishian, the director of Fairleigh Dickinson University Press, rejected the work because, as he said, Fairleigh Dickinson does not publish anthologies. He did say in passing, however, that he and his team of editors saw great potential in a monograph on the topic. So as I wrote the introduction to the anthology, I did so with the idea that I was setting the stage for a larger work. As I finished what ended up being a rather long opening, I realized I indeed had much more to say. The present work is a continuation of that discussion.

Academic. This book is also inspired by a collaboration with my friend James Pawelski, the executive director of the International Positive Psychology Association. I first met James in a meeting I had with him at the University of Pennsylvania, where he runs the graduate program in positive psychology. Shortly after our meeting, he and I decided to collaborate on an edited collection of essays, *The Eudaimonic Turn: Well-Being in Literary Studies* (2012). In weekly conversations that continued for about a year, James impressed me with his staggering amount of knowledge related to the new multi-disciplinary discourse on human flourishing, which Owen Flanagan has called "eudaimonics." I consequently realized, more fully than I already did, that the topic of ecstatic experience is intimately tied to the question of well-being.

Before I began engaging the findings of positive psychology, nevertheless, I intuitively located ecstatic poetry in the larger subject of well-being, particularly in my first book, *Mystical Discourse in Wordsworth and Whitman* (2006). Noticing that many of my colleagues often either dismissed the ecstatic experience as religious nonsense or interpreted it as a symptom of psychological disease or objectionable ideology, I tried to demonstrate, in a different discursive register, that the use of ecstatic language, particularly mystical language, actually enabled Wordsworth and Whitman to challenge many of the Enlightenment's jaundiced ideas: the overemphasis on reason and the marginalization of alternative ways of knowing; the reduction of human experience to cognition; the marginalization or maltreatment of affect; Cartesian subjectivity and the separation of mind from matter; mechanism and the objectification of nature; and others. I carried this challenge into my second book, *The Dark Enlightenment* (2010), arguing, from a post–Jungian perspective, for the immense psychological (and thus eudaimonic) value of the Romantic encounter with and retrieval of the unconscious "other," so often configured in the form of woman, nature, affect, irrationality, madness, childhood, and the like. This encounter is quintessentially *ekstatic*. In the present book, I try to support the same general challenge, but this time through an account of why ecstatic poetry existed almost ubiquitously in the ancient world and also why it continues to speak to us in the contemporary era.

I am grateful for having received much guidance, help, and support from multiple people to whom I am indebted: the administrative leaders at Kean University who funded generous grants and provided me with ample resources; James Cowan at the OCC library, who processed hundreds of interlibrary loans for me; Christina Walling, Amanda Foster, David Museliani, Nikiesha Hatch, Anthony Melillo, and Belinda Joyner, who helped me with the tedious but important work of transcribing notes; and Gabriella Basile, who helped me with securing permissions. Thanks to all of these good people. I would also like to thank Adam Potkay, a friend whose inspiring work, *The Story of Joy*, has changed literary studies and helped to make possible the eudaimonic turn in the discipline. Adam's work renders mine all the more relevant.

I hope you enjoy the study.

PART ONE: ECSTATIC BEGINNINGS

1. The Overture

Ecstasy is a powerfully transformative, affective experience. While it is related to joy, happiness, flow, elevation, and sublimity, it is not exactly synonymous with any of these concepts. Best described as a peak experience, as Abraham Maslow called it, ecstasy can be characterized in myriad ways and finds configuration kaleidoscopically in a variety of forms in religious and secular experience. The term is etymologically related to the Greek word *ekstasis*, which means to stand (*stasis*) outside (*ek*) of oneself, or something like self-transcendence. Willis Barnstone's insightful study, *The Poetics of Ecstasy: Varieties of Ekstasis from Sappho to Borges*, is a superb example of critical analyses of *ekstatic* forms of literature.[1] But *ecstasy*, as I explore it in Chapter 2 and the rest of the book, is a slightly different concept and contains three core characteristics: (1) the climax of *any* form of positive affect, the results of which are (2) radical self-transcendence and (3) transformative effects that significantly enhance one's sense of *eudaimonia*, another ancient Greek word that many scholars currently use to designate human well-being. This additional eudaimonic element, which has become so relevant not only in contemporary discourse across the academic disciplines but also in popular culture, business, and even government, suggests a crucial difference. Whereas Barnstone's study is an analysis of *ekstasis* in its generic form, the following is an investigation of ecstasy in its relationship to well-being.

Such a definition of ecstasy strikes a balance between the perennialist position, whose proponents maintain that ecstasies occur across time and culture, and the more recent work of historicists, who account for the role of cultural/historical forces as determinants of ecstasies. No doubt, because there are exceptions to the rule, this definition is merely a functional one and does not resolve a hermeneutic issue that has gone unresolved in philosophy and religious studies for decades—namely, whether ecstasies are the result of cultural or psychological forces. It also does not resolve the problem of how to typologically characterize ecstasies. More nuanced definitions, however, invariably seem to run the risk of overstatement and thus distortion of the elusive nature of what is ultimately a mysterious experience.

The problem of the willing self further complicates the subject. Scholars in the traditions of depth psychology and poststructuralism have called into question the nature of the self, which in many ways is without essence, its barriers permeable and its substance empty. What is the self one stands outside of in ecstatic experiences? Such a question is ultimately unanswerable. However illusory it may be, nevertheless, the self is a necessary construct without which it is impossible to function. Not to have a sense of self over a prolonged period is tantamount to psychosis, whereas to transcend the boundaries of ego in temporary forays into the psychological other is, generally speaking, extremely beneficial and serves as both a marker and facilitator of psychological health, conceived in its fullest sense as eudaimonia. To stand outside of oneself, it is necessary to hold the will, the principal instrument by which the ego asserts itself, in abeyance. By engaging in any number of ecstatic techniques, it is possible to "induce" an ecstasy, but such techniques merely serve as critical thresholds or tipping points that catalyze but do not cause the experience. Ecstasy is ultimately an elusive experience, and in some ways it is likely we will never understand its mysterious, labyrinthine complexities.

The historical record, the subject of chapters 3 and 4, attests to the human preoccupation with ecstasy in the ecstatic poetic tradition, which exists across cultures all over the globe. This tradition is rooted in ancient orality, and scholars consequently do not know precisely when it emerged. Some of the oldest texts in the Indo-European corpus bear the imprint of a poetics of ecstasy, in which the poet becomes enraptured while composing verse, and an aesthetics of ecstasy, the effects of which result in a replication of the poet's rapture in the responding reader/auditor. The Zoroastrian *Zend-Avesta* and the Hindu *Rigveda* are examples of such literature. In India these theories resulted in a rich corpus of ecstatic verse, which can be seen (in part) in the extant *Akam* poetry composed and later written down in Tamil, a non–Indo-European language. Because southern India was significantly influenced by the conquering Indo-Aryans, it is difficult to determine whether *Akam* verse is autochthonous or the result of historical influence. Other examples of ecstatic poetry in the Indian corpus are found in the Bhakti protest movement, not only in the southern Vaishnavite and Shaivite traditions, the languages of which are Tamil and Kannada respectively, but also in the northern Hindi corpus composed in honor of the deities Vishnu, Shiva, and Mahadevi. The northern Hindi tradition produced several great poet-saints, such as Mirabai, Kabir, Ramprasad, and others. Ecstatic Indian verse finds full expression in the work of Rabindranath Tagore, a Bengali writer who captured the imagination of readers across the globe.

India also spawned another ecstatic tradition in early Buddhist poetry, written in Pali, an Indo-European language. As the Buddha's teachings spread to China, there also arose a vibrant tradition of poetry in its honor. Of particular interest are the Ch'an (Zen) poets, who exerted a considerable influence on later Japanese writers. The Zen literary form known as the haiku is one of the most conspicuous examples of the poetics and aesthetics of ecstasy in its call for the dissolution of the barrier between the reading subject and the literary object. Chinese Buddhists also spread the teachings to Tibet, where the poet-saint Milarepa lived and sang ecstatic songs that have inspired countless followers.

The Indo-European poetics and aesthetics of ecstasy are seen in the mythical first poet of ancient Greece, Orpheus, whose stories suggest a shamanic role as poet-seer. The countless vase-paintings of Orpheus holding an audience spellbound with rapturous words attest to early Greek conceptions of the poet and the impact of ecstatic poetry. Such verse was rooted in music and dance, as seen in two well-known forms, the lyric and the dithyramb, both of which were sung to accompanying music and inspired movement and dancing. Images of the rhapsode from the Homeric texts and other sources also attest to the ecstatic role of those who recited the epic form.

The Greeks in part influenced the ancient Israelites, whose earliest verse, called Yahwistic poetry, is ecstatic in character. The *Nebi'im*, or bands of rapt prophets referred to in the Hebrew Bible, were likely participants in the ecstatic cult of Dionysus and other Near Eastern religions. Though originally non-priestly, shamanic outsiders, the Nebi'im were eventually incorporated into Temple life. They were also writers and quite probably authored many of the Hebrew Psalms. In addition to Biblical stories, funerary objects, coins, and other archaeological remains, the Biblical injunction against seething a kid in its mother's milk, an Orphic form of Dionysian worship, compellingly attests to the ancient Israelites' participation in the Dionysian cult.

Early Christians also took their cue (in part) from Greek Orphism and its Dionysian worship. Christian mystical poetry, therefore, can be read in such contexts. Over the centuries, there have been dozens of Christian poets who have left a legacy of rich, ecstatic verse. Many of these poets, such as Hildegard of Bingen and Juan de la Cruz, wrote verse in a state of mystical rapture or composed poetry as a result of such a state.

The Celts of the British Isles similarly created verse in a state of enraptured, divine possession. The Celtic practice of composing poetry in a darkened room attests to a much older, pre–Christian Druidic poetics in which poets were regarded as seers whose inspiration came from the gods. The Old Norse of Scandinavia and Iceland conceived of the creation of poetry in similar terms, that is, as craft or skill but also as a divine, intoxicating mead bestowed by Odin, the god of poetry.

The poetics and aesthetics of ecstasy are found ubiquitously throughout the Indo-European family of languages, but there are also autochthonous traditions, the subject of Chapter 4, that produced similar types of ecstatic verse but which had no historical connection to Indo-European culture. One example is the Sufi corpus, which later flourished in the Greek- and Christian-influenced Persian world but originally arose in a Semitic, Arabic context. Scholars generally believe that Sufism is a "homegrown" Islamic version of esoteric spirituality. The resulting poetic tradition, originally a Semitic one, is thus also not related, at least in its origins, to the Indo-European poetics and aesthetics of ecstasy. Rumi, the premier writer in Sufi literature, composed verse while whirling himself into intoxicated states of ecstasy. His poetics and aesthetics bear a striking resemblance to Indo-European conceptions and forms but cannot be directly traced to them.

Another, perhaps more compelling example of verse not related to Indo-European conceptions is found in pre–Columbian Mexico among the Nahuatl poet-kings, who generated a body of poems that can be termed ecstatic in the call for psycho-spiritual transformation. The Nahuatl conception of poets as conduits to the divine, moreover, is clearly an ecstatic poetics. Countless other non–Western, ecstatic traditions existed and can be found in ancient China, Japan, Africa, and other parts of the non–Indo-European world. The existence of such traditions points to the limitations of an account based solely on historical influence and prompts a more psychological interpretation, one that sees in all of the manifestations of ecstatic poetry the expression of underlying, psychological needs and the desire to be well, to achieve eudaimonia.

Over the centuries, most cultures have developed toward ecstatic states a kind of antagonism that has spilled over into ideas about poetics and aesthetics. In the Hellenized West, the privileging of rationalism has resulted in an Apollonian conception of poetry as the byproduct of pen, desk, and cerebral study. Yet although the Dionysian fires have cooled in Western literature, there have been frequent eruptions, an example of which is seen in the eighteenth-century compensatory aesthetics of the sublime. Romanticism, Transcendentalism, and Beat poetry are also examples of such Dionysian eruptions. The ecstatic poetic tradition persists into the contemporary era around the globe in a variety of religious and secular forms. Many contemporary poets continue to write a type of verse that stretches back into pre-history.

The individual studies that follow represent a sampling of such ecstatic poets and also a few of the many possible methods by which ecstatic poetics and aesthetics can be analyzed. The poets I have chosen by no means exhaust the tradition, and to keep the size of the study to a manageable length, I was forced to include only a few authors and exclude the rest. Of course, I chose not to write about authors who composed verse in languages in which I have no fluency. Such poets represent a rich source of scholarship for those who are so inclined and also have the requisite language proficiency. I chose to include Rumi, however, because he occupies a central position in Anglophonic culture as the best-selling poet; translations of his verse in the last twenty-five years have become a literary phenomenon, selling in the millions. I chose Wordsworth, Whitman, and Dickinson because they are major writers whose verse is quintessentially ecstatic in character, although each in a different way. The same is true of Tagore, a Nobel Prize–winning Bengali poet who translated some of his own poems into English and thus opened for Western Anglophones a window into the mysteries of Indian verse. Worth investigating are quite possibly hundreds of other ecstatic poets, or at least poets whose verse embodies some of the characteristics I list in a 20-point typology of ecstatic poetry at the end of Chapter 4. Inquiries into the global tradition offer the promise of a lifetime of scholarship and discovery. Here, I offer only a small beginning. Let me provide a brief overview of the critical studies of the selected poets.

Why is Rumi so popular in the English-speaking world? Chapter 5 represents an attempt to answer the question. Critics have faulted Coleman Barks, the individual responsible for the immense success Rumi has enjoyed over the last two decades, for lifting the poet out of his Islamic context in rather free versions that present the thirteenth-century Muslim mystic as a universal gnostic who propounds a doctrine of churchless spirituality. As I suggest, however, the "fault" lies with Rumi himself, for an examination of his verse by other translators also shows that it is equally ecumenical and carries a strong universal appeal. The chapter is focused particularly on two aspects of Rumi's aesthetics: (1) the attempt to bring readers, through subtle implication and the subversion of commonly used Sufi symbols, to a realization of non-attachment—an esoteric, spiritual idea that resonates with Western readers, many of whom crave ecstatic transformation as an alternative to traditional religious beliefs; and (2) the privileging of love, the eudaimonic effect of which is also appealing, as it calls for the ecstatic merging of subject and object. Such ideas serve as a challenge to religious legalism, in addition to other forms of religious orthodoxy, and thus account, at least in part, for why Rumi's verse resonates so strongly in the English-speaking world.

Wordsworth's poetry, the subject of Chapter 6, is also ecstatic in character and has appealed to many readers as a source of inspiration and healing. Central to the topic of ecstasy in Wordsworth's verse are several eudaimonic elements, all of which are found in a most concentrated form in "Tintern Abbey." Despite its positive nineteenth-century reception, more recent critics have faulted the poem for its complicity with various undesirable ideologies or its representation of diseased psychodynamics. My discussion of the poem's aesthetics of ecstasy questions this hermeneutics of suspicion, redirecting attention to the speaker's "wild ecstasies" and the cooling of their fires, the result of which is a mature mind characterized by the ability to enter powerful states of *ekstasis* that lead to a heightened sense of compassion, holism, eco-awareness, moral elevation, imaginative possibility, wonder, and love. With notable exceptions, Wordsworthian ecstasy is typically sober and Apollonian, a mature form of *ekstasis* that many nineteenth-century readers discerned and found to be inspiring. Despite a forceful number of detractors, scholars in the twenty-first century have also begun, once again, to recognize the eudaimonic potential in Wordsworth's aesthetics of ecstasy.

Different from Wordsworth, Whitman sang of more intoxicated, Dionysian raptures, but he was deeply influenced by his English predecessor and demonstrates a similar aesthetics of ecstasy in his poetry. What distinguishes him from his English forebear, as well as any other predecessor, however, is the intense physicality with which he invests his ideas. Inspired by the Romantic aesthetics of electricity, as it has been called, Whitman gave the nineteenth century a new vision of the electrified body—the ecstatic body—images of which he repeatedly links to eudaimonic ideas. For Whitman, the electrified body represents an *ekstatic* force that catalyzes radical self-transcendence, but such transformation can occur only through the embrace, not the denial of, corporeality. As I argue in Chapter 7, Whitman's aesthetics of the body represents a form of *anamnesis*, the retrieval of unconscious contents that analysands do in psychoanalytic work. The result is a consciousness expanded through *ekstasis* and emboldened with the audacity to declare sexuality to be inherently good and human animality to be essentially amoral. In bringing somatic energies into consciousness, Whitman violently shook the repressive, nineteenth-century value system in which the body is the othered, second member in such binaries as mind/body, reason/instinct, and psychological health/physical health. By questioning and equalizing the hierarchy implied in these conceptual divisions, Whitman challenged longstanding biases against and diseased beliefs about corporeality in Western thought. His ecstatic body also leads to the wisdom of corporeal embeddedness, eco-awareness, and embodied cognition, as well as an understanding of the profound connections between psyche and soma.

Emily Dickinson, the subject of Chapter 8, differs from Whitman in considerable ways. While he was gregarious and public, she was introverted and private; while he wanted to leave his poetry behind as a kind of new Bible, she told her sister to burn her poems when she lay on her deathbed. For all of their obvious differences, however, there are similarities between the two poets, particularly in what other scholars have recognized as a common strain of mysticism, but which is perhaps better termed an aesthetics of ecstasy. Dickinson is known, surely among popular readers but even among some scholars, almost stereotypically as a poet of disillusionment who focuses on anguish and despair.

While she indeed wrote many poems about negative states of being, she also penned hundreds of lyrics about the eudaimonic aspects of human experience. Of particular interest, of course, are her many poems about ecstasy, a word she often used along with its lexical cousins—glee, transport, rapture, inebriation, and others. She clearly suffered from some kind of psychological disorder—her mind was "cracked" as Thomas Wentworth Higginson famously observed—but perhaps her unusual psychology enabled her to see states of being, both negative, positive, and perhaps everything in between, in unique, insightful ways. An examination of her aesthetics of ecstasy reveals three observations that enable a rejection of the view that her poems suffered from the same kind of affective disorder that undoubtedly plagued her: (1) she frequently celebrates positive affect in many varieties, many of which strongly suggest eudaimonic ideas; (2) she rejects psychologically diseased, Calvinist concepts and embraces an alternative spirituality that relocates the sacred in affective experience rather than in dogma; and (3) she repeatedly expresses an urge toward boundlessness, which can be seen in other ecstatic poets. Because her work found reception in the modernist era, the poems by which she is principally known are those of despair and anguish—that is, poems foregrounding the negative states of mind that early twentieth-century thinkers privileged. But equally central to her oeuvre, however overlooked they may be, are her ecstatic poems and the aesthetics of ecstasy they suggest.

Rabindranath Tagore, the subject of Chapter 9, appealed to many early twentieth-century readers as a sort of "wise man of the East," a view many critics, particularly historicists, reject because its essentialism elides the important role of historical forces and cultural determinants in shaping a poet's work. To dismiss the wise man image entirely, however, is to overlook the nature of Tagore's initial reception in the Anglophonic world, for many readers embraced his work precisely because it seemed to offer a kind of wisdom lacking in modernist, Western culture. A brief analysis of a few early responses to Tagore's poetry will demonstrate that the aesthetics of ecstasy configured in his verse often evoked a kind of rapture in English and Irish readers. Through his poetry, Tagore seemed to liberate the ecstatic forms of affect the West had positioned itself against. Such emotions were not merely a means to aesthetic ends, however, as he seemed to use the poetic form as a way to explore and recreate strange peak experiences he had on several occasions. Of particular interest in this chapter is the catalyst that won him the Nobel Prize in 1913—*Gitanjali*—a collection of his own Bengali poems he translated into English. In *Gitanjali* Tagore explores the Indian concept of *ananda*, or bliss, a foundational concept in his poetics and aesthetics that follows a clearly discernible trajectory through ecstatic experience.

Ecstasy is by no means merely the stuff of dreamy-eyed poets, as it meaningfully signifies in other domains (the subject of Chapter 10) that extend beyond the field of literary studies. The critical implications of ecstatic states touch upon currents of thought in psychology, neurology, sociology, history, and religion, among others.

For the non-psychotic individual, moments of ego-transcendence, provided they are of the ecstatic variety, are generally conducive to psychological health and often lead to the full flourishing of the psyche. There seems to be an implicit understanding of the healing properties of ecstasy in the arts, in various religious practices, and in popular wisdom. Modern research has confirmed such intuitions by scientifically validating ecstatic techniques, for hundreds of studies support the value of meditation, one of the most effective means of triggering ecstasies. Even more compelling are the brain mapping studies that clearly show beneficial neurological changes in the brains of those who meditate or pray regularly and thus experience ecstasies more frequently. Abraham Maslow, the famous psychologist, construed ecstasy as a psychological need that, if sufficiently gratified, leads to self-actualization, or what he saw as the highest degree of psychological health.

The current paradigm shift in the discipline of psychology has resulted in an atmosphere congenial to explorations of ecstatic states, although no one, to my knowledge, has yet done so. The eudaimonic findings of Positive psychologists have rendered ecstasy a relevant subject of scientific and critical inquiry and also an essential ingredient in human well-being. Although many psychologists have been generally dismissive of ecstatic states, as quintessentially seen in Freud's reduction of "oceanic" experiences of ego-dissolution to regressive narcissism, not all of the founding figures in the discipline have ignored the value of ecstasy. Jungian, Humanistic, Transpersonal, and other psychologists have attested to its value for decades. From a psychological perspective, therefore, ecstasy is both a marker and a catalyst of the healthy psyche.

From a sociopolitical perspective, group ecstasy can affect significant numbers of people, both within the group engaged in ecstatic transformation and also in the larger culture. One of the most significant ways in which ecstatic experiences impact society is in the challenge they pose to hierarchical structures, whose more elite members generally, though not always, position themselves antagonistically against ecstasy. Such experiences find a better reception in egalitarian cultures and among the lower classes or marginalized people in stratified societies, although exceptions can always be found. Individual ecstasy also has social effects in the form of the value-shift that occurs as a result of ecstatic experiences. People who experience ecstasy are sometimes marginalized by their cultures because they embrace a different value system, sometimes one that runs against the societal grain. In ancient and current non–Western cultures, or at least in the literature of those cultures, the person who experiences ecstasy is accorded high esteem, as in the cases of the Siberian shaman, the Sufi *matzoob*, the Indian Yogi, and the African or Caribbean dancer who experiences trance-possession. By contrast, such a person is often marginalized in much of the socially stratified, contemporary world. Ecstatic experiences, nevertheless, do not inevitably result in pariah status, and sometimes they can even make an antisocial person more socially integrated. Ecstasy found a better reception in the ancient world, whose various cultures tolerated the "madness" of *ekstasis*. Perhaps not coincidentally, such madness became, as Foucault famously observed, a central preoccupation among eighteenth-century Europeans, who generally denied their ecstasy needs and demonized ecstatic practices over the centuries of their history.

Central to such denial and demonization are the anti-ecstatic religious attitudes that inform all three monotheistic faiths. Judaism, Christianity, and Islam all originated in ecstatic, pagan contexts and are also rooted in many ways in ecstatic spirituality. All three faiths are centered on the ecstatic experiences of historical figures, and all three encouraged ecstatic practices to some extent. Despite these ecstatic beginnings, however, the monotheistic faiths eventually positioned themselves in opposition to ecstasy as they developed exoteric (and thus more legalistic) forms of worship. Although the fundamentalist and mainstream varieties of each faith have come to oppose ecstasy, there are also in Judaism, Christianity, and Islam varieties of esoteric spirituality that serve as frameworks for the cultivation and interpretation of the ecstatic experience. Kabala, Sufism, Christian mysticism, Gnosticism, and some forms of Protestantism are highly ecstatic versions of monotheism and serve as a means by which some monotheists have been able to meet their ecstatic needs. Such needs also have been met outside of religious confines in the birth of the Carnival, in various counter-cultures, in New Age spirituality, and in the contemporary rave scene, all of which serve a quasi-religious function.

The monotheistic ambivalence toward ecstasy is paralleled in literary studies, the subject of Chapter 11. Literary theories generally do not sanction a rapturous response to the poetry of rapture. To the contrary, many critical strategies employed in the field call for a hermeneutics of suspicion and reading against the grain to tease out complicity in various undesirable discourses. Despite notable exceptions, in literary studies there is also a pathologizing tendency in which many aspects of human experience, even eudaimonic states of being such as ecstasy, are interpreted according to disease models, that is, theoretical frameworks that help scholars interpret various characters, authors, and forms as expressions of psychological disease but woefully fall short in their inability to enable one to shed light on aspects of well-being.

And there are other obstacles to the study of ecstasy in literature. To recognize the eudaimonic value of ecstatic poetry, for instance, is in some ways to endorse a value position—a stance that has proven to be problematic in a postmodern age in which all values are often questioned with suspicion and demystified as coded ideology or diseased psychodynamics. Ecstatic poetry also foregrounds affect—particularly positive affect—which scholars have recently observed has been neglected in literary discourse, particularly in the last three decades of the twentieth century. Some of the reasons for this neglect of affect are Roland Barthes's proclamation of the "death of the author," Jacques Derrida's statement that there is "nothing outside of the text," and Mikhail Bakhtin's dismissal of the most affective literary genre—the lyric—for its ahistorical nature. Outside of literary studies, however, scholars in several fields have demonstrated the importance of affect, particularly positive emotions and transformative, eudaimonic experiences such as ecstasy.

Yet another obstacle is the understanding of subjectivity found in literary discourse. The version of selfhood most literary scholars seem to have endorsed is based on Freud's conception of the psyche, which posits underlying neuroses as the basis of subjectivity and minimalizes the possibility of psychological health. Freud's decentering of the ego, however necessary it may be for *ekstatic* growth, has resulted in literary studies in a reveling in dissociative states and languishing in a fragmented condition startlingly similar to post-traumatic stress disorder (PTSD). The postmodern preoccupation with fragmentation and the yearning to express the ineffable, nevertheless, represent possibilities for well-being. To experience the decentering of ego, which is the essence of *ekstatic* experience, can lead to a reorganization of psychological contents and thus a higher degree of psychic health. It is necessary, however, to come back from the ecstatic experience in a more complexly organized psyche, which, according to recent research, is unitive and functions as a gestalt in which several disparate components operate somewhat independently but within a context of a unified subjectivity. Positive emotions, which always accompany ecstasies, at least as I have defined them, play a significant role in this alternative conception of selfhood. To flourish psychologically is to stand outside of oneself in dissociative moments of intense positive affect but then to reintegrate the psyche in a complex, polyphonic whole.

For all of the less-than-welcoming reception of ecstasy in literary studies, the discipline has undergone a transformation in the last decade. This eudaimonic turn, the subject of Chapter 12, is a disciplinary shift involving the work of several leading scholars that has resulted in an atmosphere much more hospitable to discussions of ecstatic states of consciousness in their poetic configurations. This turn has manifested in three interrelated ways: (1) as a growing tendency to reject suspicion as the only possible reading strategy; (2) as an aggressive search for alternative modes of critique, particularly what Rita Felski has called "positive aesthetics"; and (3) as a direct engagement with eudaimonic experience. Such a shift renders the study of ecstatic poetics and aesthetics highly credible subjects of twenty-first-century literary inquiry. Ecstasy makes the eudaimonic life possible. An examination of poetic wisdom on the subject will, I hope, support the point.

2. Ecstatic States
of Consciousness

What are ecstatic states of consciousness?[1] To define them is a nearly impossible task, since any definition will by necessity reduce an experience that transcends human understanding and ultimately restrict its range of possibilities. Scholars working in the field of mysticism studies have argued for decades over how to define the mystical state, a religious variety of the ecstatic experience. Ecstasy has myriad psychological implications, and psychological theories can thus shed valuable light on its impact on the human psyche. It would be wrong, however, to reduce the experience to a mere psychological state. Often confounding rationality, ecstasy is beyond language, no doubt, because it is beyond reason itself. The greatest ecstatic poets have left us a veritable treasure chest of verse in their attempts to capture the ecstatic experience in language, but they so frequently abandoned the difficult task of *fully* articulating what they were trying to suggest. As Whitman says in "Song of the Rolling Earth," "I swear I see what is better than to tell the best, / It is always to leave the best untold" (103–04).[2] Words, even from those with the greatest facility with language, fail to describe the ecstatic experience in its fullest sense. Scholars of mysticism have long held that one of the principal characteristics of mystical states is their ineffability. Ecstasies are beyond language and often cannot be fully put into words.

The term *description*, rather than definition, is probably better served because the latter will always be susceptible to criticism on various grounds, whereas the former will provide a functional definition, however problematic it may be, and thus allow for a greater range of configurations.

Implied in this "range of configurations" is the idea that ecstatic experiences exist on a spectrum of possibilities that spans feelings of oneness with nature, euphoria while dancing, deep contentment, being in the "zone," and the like, to life's most fulfilling moments, such as intense bliss, deep gratitude, overpowering awe, the joys of love, and the many varieties of spiritual experience. A valid objection to this spectrum of experiences is that there are genuine differences among ecstatic experiences. Indian *samadhi*, Japanese *satori*, shamanic journeys, giving birth, Christian mystical illuminations, Tantric sexual ecstasies, and a lovely day spent communing with nature in the woods are all very different experiences. The value of scholarship that points to such differences cannot be overstated in that it demonstrates nuanced variability and highlights the role of cultural determinants in conditioning ecstatic states. To hold fixedly to distinctions, however, is to miss recognizing a whole species by fixating on the differences among its members. Ecstasy is in some ways a single phenomenon with many cultural and temporal colorations.

These two approaches—one sees difference while the other sees similarity—are mirrored in the prevailing approaches to the study of mystical states. On the one hand, scholars influenced by William James, Evelyn Underhill, F.C. Happold, Aldous Huxley, and others are called perennialists because, for them, the experience crops up perennially, again and again, seemingly in every time and place throughout history. On the other hand, historicists, such as Jess Byron Hollenback, Henri Delacroix, Steven Katz, and others, emphasize the importance of history and context and the different ways in which these inform and condition the ecstatic experience. As in so many fundamental debates, both camps seem to have a measure of truth, but in raising it to absolute status, it becomes a falsehood. While the perennialists are "guilty" of essentializing the experience by overlooking important differences in cultural determinants, the historicists perhaps make so much of differences that they prevent cross-cultural connections and a fuller understanding of what is a global phenomenon. Both, however, have something valuable to contribute to our understanding.

The Problem of Words

So what is the core experience? *Ekstasis* is a Greek word that means to stand (*stasis*) outside (*ek*) of oneself. Its opposite is *enstasis*, or to remain fixed within oneself. It is possible to experience *ekstasis* in a variety of emotional states. A few years ago, a friend of mine said that when he lost his father he felt as though he were being "swallowed in a sea of grief." He was experiencing *ekstasis*, however tragic the cause, in feeling overpowered by his loss. The expression, "I was beside myself with anger," is also an example of *ekstasis*, which can characterize any moment in which people act in ways that seem contrary to their self-definitions. To be *ekstatic* in this etymological sense is simply to experience in any variety a feeling of being other than oneself. Experiences of this kind can result in horrible circumstances, as in killing one's best friend in a drunken rage. "It wasn't me," says the killer, "it was the alcohol."

Ancient Norse warriors, called *berserkers*, knew this type of violent *ekstasis* quite intimately. The trance-like states of fury they entered before battle empowered the berserkers to fight with the ferocity and savagery of wild animals, the symbolism of which was captured in the animal pelts they wore. In such moments they *ekstatically* transformed and became something other than themselves.

The term *ekstatic* can thus refer to any experience of feeling outside of one's normal bounds, the enclosure normally referred to as ego or selfhood. In many cases this self-transcendence can seem like a form of self-completion rather than the uncanny feeling of otherness. Regardless, the experience carries with it a transformation of one's sense of selfhood, however this alteration manifests.

As a term, however, *ecstasy* has evolved over time to signify a more positive experience, one accompanied by such feelings as joy, bliss, rapture, euphoria, or *any* intense positive emotion. A student recently told me of a fascinating ecstatic experience she had that speaks to the point: While in a supermarket, she had a strange moment of defamiliarization in which "the walls of the enormous store seemed to stretch away from me and I felt as though I could see everything contained within them all at once." She was consequently overwhelmed with profound feelings of wonder and gratitude for the abundance of food available for purchase. Although she did not feel joy or bliss per se, she experienced the moment ecstatically, that is, her sense of self was altered in a moment of overpowering positive affect—in this case, gratitude and wonder.[3] More compelling, the downstream effects of the experience were highly eudaimonic, as she claims to have become more of an optimist who realizes she now has a choice in how she responds to ordinary moments. She also reports a greater degree of agency in being able to overcome ingratitude, self-pity, and irritation. Ecstasy is thus not so much an emotion as it is a range of deep affective experiences or positive, affective possibilities, any one of which can catalyze, accompany, and/or immediately follow a moment of standing outside of self. It is thus necessary to distinguish between the terms *ekstatic* and *ecstatic*, the former referring to any experiences of self-transcendence— positive, negative, or neutral—and the latter signifying an *experience of standing outside of self, accompanied or at least immediately followed by an intense degree of positive affect and exerting eudaimonic, transformative effects.* The three elements—intense, positive emotion, a feeling of being outside of one's normal bounds, and eudaimonic transformation—must be present for an experience to be called an ecstasy. One without the others, as in the cases of joy with no sense of self-transcendence or feelings of otherness with no accompanying or following positive affect, is not ecstasy. While the former is simply a strong emotion, the latter is *ekstasis* but not ecstasy per se.

Such a definition is problematic, however, for it is entirely possible to cite experiences that do not fully align with these benchmarks. For instance, another student recently told me of an out-of-body experience in which he saw himself objectively in a rather strange moment of perception. Although he was able to see himself with greater clarity, he did not like what he saw, as the experience gave him a glimpse of unpleasant aspects of self he felt he needed to transform in order to be well. The *ekstasis* was accompanied by negative affect, in this case a feeling of disappointment over not having lived up to his potential. According to the definition I have articulated, this experience would not count as an ecstasy. Still, it led to highly positive downstream effects, for he locates in the *ekstatic* moment the beginnings of a highly eudaimonic self-transformation. As he puts it, "I really credit this experience—that is, the out-of-body experience and being able to see myself removed and objectively— with changing my entire life."[4] So is this an ecstasy or an *ekstatic* experience that later led to a larger and more integrated conception of self? While the experience was accompanied by negative affect, it also resulted later in a constructive reorganization of the psyche after it ended. In one sense this experience meets the criteria I have established for ecstasies, but in another sense it does not, for the presence of negative affect is a complicating factor. A definition of ecstasy that applies in all circumstances is thus an impossibility. The definition I have put forth is merely functional and will serve only as a reference point and organizational principle. Ultimately, the ecstatic experience is not representable and will always manifest in ways that confound those trying to understand it.

Varieties of Ecstatic Experience

A number of experiences can be labeled ecstatic. Ecstasies are thus not only found in religious but also in secular contexts. Many people have an ecstatic experience in the course of a lifetime. In one survey, for instance, more than 30 percent of people in a sampling of 1000 responded affirmatively to the following statement: "You felt as though you were very close to a powerful spiritual force that seemed to lift you out of yourself." Of those who responded positively, 12 percent reported having such experiences on multiple occasions.[5] Ecstasies occur very frequently, and in many cases they recur in the course of a given lifetime.

Marghanita Laski, one of the first researchers of secular ecstasies, has observed that they occur most frequently in the following domains of experience: observance of or immersion in nature, sexual love, childbirth, exercise or movement, participation in religion or spirituality, creating or appreciating art, and introspective recollection.[6] In the courses on ecstatic poetry I frequently teach, I usually ask students to brainstorm their best moments, peak experiences, most exquisite joys, most savored memories, defining experiences, optimal performances, and instances of intense positive emotion. In many cases students who first claim they never have had any ecstatic experiences begin to fill pages with brilliant examples of them. Here is one such example, taken from a student's journal:

> It came completely out of the blue and for no reason at all. It actually happened last summer on the Atlantic City beach of all places. I was walking on the boardwalk and decided to walk down by the water. At some point, completely out of nowhere, I realized that everyone I saw was beautiful, and I felt dazzlingly happy. When it hit me, no matter where I looked I saw profound beauty in every single person. It was a sudden and pure state of bliss and I knew that I loved everyone I saw and that I loved myself and loved being alive.... It was undoubtedly the most powerful (and probably the most enjoyable) experience I've known.[7]

Here are some additional examples of both religious and secular ecstasies, taken from a variety of scholarly sources:

1. Sometimes I have concentrated myself, and driven away by continued will all sense of outward appearances, looking straight with the full power of my mind inwards on myself. I find "I" am there; and "I" do not wholly understand or know—something is there distinct from earth and timber, from flesh and bones. Recognizing it, I feel on the margin of a life unknown ... on the verge of powers which if I could grasp would give me an immense breadth of existence.[8]

2. The first thing I saw when I awoke in the hospital was a flower, and I cried. Believe it or not, I had never really seen a flower until I came back from death. One thing I learned when I died was that we are all part of one big, living universe. If we think we can hurt another living thing without hurting ourselves, we are sadly mistaken.[9]

3. I realized a great scene was about to unfold within myself. I actually shook and shuddered at what I felt. A tremendous earthquake feeling was building up in me. There was a tremendous force, and I saw a glorious beauty of space unfold before me, of light, color, and of song and music, and not only of one thing good and beautiful, but of a oneness in fellowship, a wanting to belong to this greatness of beauty and goodness that unfolded before my eyes...[10]

4. I was feeling more and more peaceful and calm, and my experience seemed to acquire incredible depth and breadth. I had an increasing sense that my consciousness had a distinctly oceanic quality until I felt that I actually became what can best be described as the consciousness of the ocean.[11]

5. I sat there and knew again the oneness of all things by the sounds of the restless sea, the mournful clang of the buoy bell, the cry of the seagull as it flew ahead of the storm, but no one of these was alone. They were each part of the whole. So am I. Nothing exists anywhere which I am not a part of, and which is not part of me.[12]

6. Then and there came on me the hour of revelation.... Scents, sights, and sounds blended into a harmony so perfect that it transcended human expression, even human thought. It was like a glimpse of the peace of eternity.[13]

7. The thing happened one summer afternoon, on the school cricket field, while I was sitting on the grass, waiting my turn to bat. I was thinking about nothing in particular.... Suddenly, and without warning, something invisible seemed to be drawn across the sky, transforming the world about me into a kind of tent of concentrated and enhanced significance. What had been merely an outside became an inside. The objective was somehow transformed into a completely subjective fact, which was experienced as "mine," but on a level where the word had no meaning; for "I" was no longer the familiar ego.[14]

8. Then I was standing on the highest mountain of them all, and round about beneath me was the whole hoop of the world. And while I stood there I saw more than I can tell and I understood more than I saw; for I was seeing in a sacred manner the shapes of all things in the spirit, and the shapes of all things as they must live together like one being.[15]

These examples serve to illustrate the common elements—self-transcendence, positive affect, and eudaimonic transformation—found in ecstatic experiences. In all cases self and the world are radically transformed in a moment of intense positive emotion. In all cases, the experience culminates in a perception of cosmic unity and leaves the individual with a profoundly altered sense of self enhanced by intensified feelings of eudaimonia.

Ecstasies can also manifest in other, less spectacular forms and can occur during seemingly any activity. There are countless reports of ecstasies occurring at weddings, engagement dinners, sporting events, yoga classes, and musical performances. Ecstasies can also occur while cleaning the house, solving math equations, reading exquisite poetry, walking on a spring day, playing chess, viewing a natural wonder, stargazing, being silly, savoring a memory, doing volunteer work, relaxing after an intensely stressful period, and many other activities and moments of receptivity. There are many comical stories in Zen literature of *satori* occurring where it is least expected, that is, while cleaning the toilet, walking in the fish market, visiting a prostitute, and the like. Although Maslow distinguished peakers, or those who have frequent ecstatic experiences, from non-peakers, he believed that peak experiences characterize nearly every human life, not just a privileged few. Peakers are simply those who know how to relish and replicate the experience. Maslow also observed that peakers are found evenly distributed across the population. Ecstasies thus occur not only among artists, hippies, musicians, and New-Agers but also among dock workers, insurance executives, engineers, politicians, and scientists.[16]

Ecstasy comes in an endless number of varieties. Sometimes these involve the physical world of nature or the material world in which we live, and sometimes they offer a transcendent glimpse of the otherworldly beyond. Ecstasy can manifest in either a sober form, as in many varieties of Buddhist enlightenment, experiences amidst tranquil natural settings, and in calm moments of blissful serenity. Or it can manifest as drunkenness, as in the divine intoxication of African shamans, Dionysian revelers, whirling Sufis, and modern "ravers" gyrating to trance-dance music. Ecstasy can be an intensely personal, introspective experience, involving a journey within one's deep, mysterious interior, as in so many forms of mysticism. Or it can be shared among individuals as a collective phenomenon, as in the early Hebrew prophets, Christian Gnostics, concert goers, participants in tribal dancing rites, sports fans, and any group of people sharing an experience of self-transcendence and intense positive affect. Emile Durkheim, a pioneer in the field of sociology, called this last form of group ecstasy "collective effervescence," and he believed it was the essence of all religion.[17] Victor Turner, the famous anthropologist, called it "communitas," and he saw such group ecstasy as a form of social cement that binds members of a group or society together.[18] Ecstasies, needless to say, come in a variety of forms.

Scholars have argued extensively in their attempts to offer taxonomies of ecstasies. Such scholarship has proven to be of inestimable value in our understanding of this universal experience, bringing critical attention as it has to the nuances of what was previously regarded as a single experience. Dan Merkur's sophisticated analysis of hallucinogen-induced ecstasies is a case in point. Prior to his research, it was well known that psychedelics such as LSD-25, peyote, psilocybin, mescaline, iboga, and others often yielded profoundly meaningful religious experiences.[19] Merkur has identified no less than 24 types of unitive experiences that have been associated with such ecstasies.[20] The type of unitive ecstasy Sigmund Freud called the "oceanic" is but one of Merkur's 24 types.[21] The matter of ecstasy, it seems, is far more complex and varied than scholars previously thought.

However insightful such taxonomies may be, they are also susceptible to criticism on various grounds, not least of which is the problem of objectively identifying and analyzing what is a deeply subjective experience. Scholars working in the field of mystical studies have been at loggerheads over a variety of issues precisely because of the seemingly insurmountable problem of classifying and pigeonholing a range of experiential perceptions whose boundaries are frequently blurred. William Wordsworth saw through such artificial boundaries, when, in his famous work, *The Prelude*, he wrote

> Of that false secondary power by which
> In weakness we create distinctions, then
> Believe our puny boundaries are things
> Which we perceive, and not which we have made [2.216–19].[22]

The ecstatic experience is beyond our full comprehension, and while it may manifest differently from culture to culture, as well as from person to person, it is important to remember that the differences we see in its manifestations are due to the limitations of our own perspectives. No doubt, cultural determinants do play a significant role in shaping these experiences, but there are also several characteristics that ecstatic states share in common, and an exclusive focus on difference will surely inhibit an understanding of the experience. Scholarly inquiries, nevertheless, are highly valuable and entirely necessary if we are to characterize and better understand ecstasies.

To further complicate the matter of describing ecstatic experiences, the question of the nature of self must be addressed. If the self is transcended in moments of *ekstasis*, then is the perspective from which we perceive in such experiences not part of the self? An answer to the latter requires an explanation of the former. What is the self? The simplest answer is that no one really knows. The ultimate nature of the self is an absolute mystery whose depths we can never fully explore intellectually, since those depths contain the mind. In other words, the psyche is not simply a construct of the mind; the reasoning intellect, rather, emerges from and is a part of something larger than itself. What that *something* is, however, cannot be put into words, for to do so would be to put limits on what Martin Heidegger believed cannot be contained in language, that is, being itself.[23]

Nearly all people, nevertheless, have a sense of self, without which they could not function. Jungian depth psychology calls this sense of self "ego," which is an illusion that must, nevertheless, be protected and preserved if we are to avoid the padded room at the state mental institution. The ego is only the tip of the iceberg, as Freud famously put it, and emerges from psychological depths that transcend the conscious will. The human psyche consists of a totality of energies that includes the ego and much more. Jung argued, however, that ego-differentiation, the process by which one comes into possession of a sense of individual selfhood, is a vital component of psychological health and is responsible for consciousness itself. "The resistance of the conscious mind to the unconscious and the depreciation of the latter," he wrote, "were historical necessities in the development of the human psyche, for otherwise the conscious mind would never have been able to differentiate itself at all."[24] The opposite of ego-differentiation, ego-dissolution is healthy in moments of *ekstasis* but over a prolonged period goes by the name of psychosis. Jung claimed that the mystic and the madman both plunge into the same ocean. The difference is that the mystic knows how to swim and ultimately makes it back to shore, whereas the madman chokes on the divine waters and drowns. The self referred to in *ekstasis* thus corresponds to ego in depth psychology, and its temporary transcendence is immensely beneficial.

To let go of the willing ego and to lose one's sense of self in a moment of intense positive affect is one of the marks of a healthy psyche.

For researchers of secular ecstasies such as Maslow and Laski, as well as most scholars of mysticism, ecstatic experiences thus cannot be willed. It is not possible to decide to have an ecstasy simply because one desires it. Laski cites a number of common triggers that seem to be present in the ecstatic experience—these correspond exactly to the domains of experience I listed previously— but she also points out that these are correlative and not causal.[25] The trigger does not cause the ecstasy but is frequently present before or during the experience. In other words, it seems to serve as the tipping point, or the culminating factor in a series of elements that combine to create the experience. It is thus quite possible to desire ecstasy, to hike to a majestic mountain peak or to listen to a brilliant piece of music or to make passionate love and still not have a fully ecstatic experience. It is likewise possible to do everything wrong—as in the case of Elisabeth Kübler-Ross, who admitted that her carnivorous diet, cigarette habit, and refusal to meditate or pray made her a very strange mystic indeed—and still have a lifetime of ecstatic experiences. Triggers are by no means causal, but statistically they seem to be conducive to ecstasy.

Laski lists four "anti-triggers"— the presence of other people, reason, language, and commerce—that serve as inhibitors of ecstasy.[26] However strange it may be, some of the anti-triggers seem to contradict the triggers. People frequently report feelings of ecstasy, for instance, in the presence of other people. Although there are exceptions here in Tantric masturbatory practices and Kundalini yoga, it is unusual to have a sexual ecstasy without another person involved. Once again, anti-triggers are not causal but simply correlative. A student in one of my courses objected to Laski's anti-triggers by declaring that he once had an ecstatic moment while sitting in a noisy bookstore café amidst garrulous book buyers and reasoning intellectuals. His point was well taken, as his ecstasy occurred despite the presence of all four of Laski's anti-triggers. There are no hard fast rules in ecstasies, and the complexities of each person's state of consciousness serve as the real determinants of the experience.

In a certain sense, then, ecstasy happens to people, and people do not make ecstasy happen. It seems to come inexplicably and sometimes at random, and by no means does it ever seem to happen when one is expecting it. To the contrary, expectation, as any seasoned meditator will affirm, might reasonably be considered another inhibitor of the experience. As an aspect of the will, expectation proceeds from the willing ego, the confines of which must be expanded or outright transcended if ecstasy is to bestow its gifts on someone.

A study of ecstatic cultures and their practices, however, clearly shows a plethora of ecstatic "techniques" used to induce ecstasy. Some of these include chanting, visualizing, drumming, dancing, contemplating, whirling, fasting, enduring climatic extremes, sleep deprivation, breath manipulation, prolonged gazing, lucid dreaming, ingesting hallucinogens, praying, singing, and various spiritual exercises. All of these activities have been used by various cultures as a means to induce the ecstatic experience, but it is important to remember that inducement does not equal cause. Here, too, as in Laski's triggers, the techniques used only make someone receptive to ecstasy; they do not cause the experience but perhaps serve as catalysts in a complex reaction of a number of elements that results in ecstasy. Such experiences do not happen randomly, and they are not bestowed willy-nilly by some capricious god of ecstasy. To the contrary, a number of factors, foremost among which is the relinquishment of the will, must be present for the appropriate reaction to take place. In ecstasy, one must let go.

Ecstasy in Relation to Current Ideas on Flow, Elevation, Happiness, Joy and Sublimity

In his important research, Mihalyi Csikszentmihalyi, a founding figure in Positive psychology, rejects some of the claims of Maslow and Laski, particularly the idea that most optimal experiences happen randomly. "Happiness," he argues, "is a condition that must be prepared for, cultivated, and defended privately by each person."[27] The point is well taken, for well-being usually does not occur by accident. To the contrary, people generally must create it for themselves. The extensive reports of ecstasies, however, do seem to indicate that such experiences often occur spontaneously when people are least expecting them. The question remains whether Csikszentmihalyi's signature concept—flow—refers to the same experience I have been calling "ecstasy." I suggest both an affirmative and a negative answer. Let me explain.

Csikszentmihalyi has shown that states of flow "are reported to occur within sequences of activities that are goal-directed and bounded by rules— activities that require the investment of psychic energy, and that could not be done without the appropriate skills."[28] In other words flow requires the exertion of the will, a characteristic typically not found in ecstatic experiences. This discrepancy suggests a difference between states of flow and ecstasies: one must exert effort to enter states of flow, whereas in ecstasies the will is typically, *though not always*, in abeyance. The crucial difference between the two, nevertheless, is not determined by the matter of the willing subject but by affect, a point I will presently discuss.

What precisely is flow? People usually report it, according to Csikszentmihalyi, when no less than eight factors are present: (1) a chance of completing the task; (2) intense concentration; (3) clearly defined goals; (4) immediate feedback; (5) deep but effortless involvement that removes from awareness the worries and frustration of everyday life; (6) exercise of control over actions; (7) loss of a sense of self, which nevertheless emerges more strongly after the experience is over; and (8) alteration of time (that is, time is either lengthened or shortened).[29] Like ecstasies, states of flow can happen during a seemingly infinite number of activities, such as driving, artistic pursuits, playing chess, reading, singing, dancing, teaching, gardening, and countless others. But unlike ecstasies, in most examples of flow there is no affect present. The positive emotions associated with the experience manifest later when the sense of self re-emerges. Csikszentmihalyi does acknowledge that sometimes people report "a feeling of ecstasy for no apparent good reason."[30] In most cases of flow, however, the individual is too focused and immersed in the moment to experience positive affect, which follows after the state of flow ends. This is clearly different from the states of euphoria so often present *during* ecstasies.

Flow, therefore, differs from ecstasy in two senses: the exertion of the will and the absence of affect. Notwithstanding the issue of the will, examples of flow in which positive affect is present are difficult to distinguish from ecstasies—indeed they are ecstasies—provided they also result in eudaimonic transformation. But what about experiences in which affect does not accompany the state of flow but immediately follows it? Here the state of flow is tantamount to ecstatic technique, which can, but not necessarily always, culminate in an ecstasy. The common ground in flow and ecstatic technique is in the assertion of the will, which must be exercised to some degree in both. A close examination of the various activities used to induce ecstasies would thoroughly support this statement. The state of flow, as Csikszentmihalyi describes it, can thus be synonymous either with ecstasy or ecstatic technique, depending on the presence or absence of positive affect. If a strong degree of positive affect is present, then the state of flow is an ecstasy. If an activity and its accompanying state are affectless but then climax in an *ekstatic* feeling of otherness, catalyze an intense level of any positive emotion, and effect eudaimonic transformation, then the flow has essentially served as an ecstatic technique that successfully results in an ecstasy. If, after its completion, the activity results in no climax of positive emotion but still elicits feelings of *ekstasis,* then the state is best characterized as ecstatic technique or flow. Ecstasy is not necessarily the only optimal experience that results in well-being, for non-ecstatic states of flow and ecstatic techniques that do not culminate in ecstasy also exert eudaimonic effects. The point is that the two states—ecstasy and flow—are different.

Ecstasy is also not synonymous with joy and happiness, as Adam Potkay demonstrates in his award-winning study *The Story of Joy.* Potkay offers a helpful discussion of joy and in doing so sheds considerable light on ecstasy. While happiness can refer "either to a mental disposition or an ethical evaluation," joy "refers primarily to a mental state."[31] However, it can also be used to signify one's disposition, as in the case of a *joyous* person, a designation Potkay acknowledges is in some ways synonymous with being a *happy* person. The distinction is helpful, nevertheless, and points to the generality of happiness and the particularity of joy; the one suggests connotations of intensity and specificity that the other does not.

When joy intensifies to an extreme degree, it metamorphoses into ecstasy, according to Potkay. Given the previous discussion, however, it seems necessary to expand the definition to include the intensification of *any* positive emotion. Ecstasy is thus not an emotion in itself, although it has come to be associated with joy or bliss and understood in such terms; rather, it is a space beyond affective limits, the point at which *any* positive emotion reaches its climax, much like an affective orgasm. The difference between simple positive emotion and ecstasy, for Potkay, lies in the "fullness" of the former and the "absence" or "annihilation of embodied agency and surrender to the not–I" found in the latter—in other words, *ekstasis*.[32] "Joy, at least on this side of ecstasy," he argues, "is about return and fullness, not about standing elsewhere and hollowing out." In the ecstatic experience the "self (in some sense) is cleaved away from the body, the senses annihilated; absence becomes fulfillment."[33]

By no means faulty, Potkay's distinction between the two rests on a strictly Western understanding of ecstasy, which is informed by Orphic and Christian notions of the separation of soul and body. Ecstasy for myriad African and other non–Western cultures is fundamentally a bodily experience inseparable from its basis in physicality. Even the ancient Dionysian cult in its earliest form sought to facilitate ecstasy through a celebration of the body, not through an escape from it. In his earliest manifestation Dionysus was a vegetation and fertility god associated with the phallus, procreation, and the natural cycle of birth, death, and rebirth.[34] Sexual ecstasies, moreover, are often accompanied by feelings of self-transcendence as a direct result of erotic joy and physical union, not of bodily escape. Potkay's separation of ecstasy and joy, nevertheless, is extremely helpful because it points out the *ekstatic* nature of ecstasies, the self-transcendent aspect of which is generally not found in simple joy and other forms of positive affect, or only in an attenuated form, and proves to be problematic for happiness.

Happiness in the tradition of Aristotelian eudaimonism, as he further demonstrates, is opposed to the loss of self found in ecstasy and in some forms of intense joy. Happiness in this tradition "is a technology of the self, a fashioning and indemnification that elevates inner integrity, constancy and wisdom over external mutability, loss, and death."[35] Happiness *so defined* is protective of the self and serves to help one to resist its transcendence. The problem with Aristotle's conception, however, is that happiness is so frequently the result of ecstatic experiences; peaks in so many cases result in the quintessence of human happiness. Aristotelian notions of happiness, then, carry a self-preserving impulse and in one sense prove inimical to ecstasy, but happiness more broadly defined allows for both the protection and transcendence of the self.

Ecstasy shares significant common ground with "elevation," a term Jonathan Haidt has recently coined to designate a previously unexamined, positive emotion. The feeling of elevation is elicited by observing "acts of virtue and moral beauty," such as witnessing an act of self-sacrifice or kindness, which can motivate percipients "to behave more virtuously themselves."[36] Elevation is different from happiness in that it produces distinct physiological changes in the body, the former causing "warm, pleasant or 'tingling' feelings in the chest" and the latter causing a general sensation of being energized.[37] Elevation has been demonstrated to cause the release of oxytocin, a hormone implicated in mammal bonding, and it can even stimulate lactation in women who are breast-feeding.[38] Elevation, like gratitude and inspiration, belongs to the family of "other-praising" emotions and causes people to open up and turn their attention outward beyond themselves.[39] Simple happiness, by contrast, often energizes people to engage in private or self-interested pursuits.[40] Elevation is also different from admiration (as in witnessing athletic prowess or artistic genius) in its physiological manifestations and psychological effects. Whereas the former produces warmth in the chest and the release of ocytocin, as noted, the latter produces chills down the spine and a desire to work more diligently on one's personal goals.[41]

Such experiences of elevation are ecstatic in nature, as they seem to "push a mental 'reset button,' wiping out feelings of cynicism and replacing them with feelings of hope, love, and optimism and a sense of moral inspiration."[42] In this "inspire and rewire" conception,[43] elevation can be called a variant of ecstasy, as it meets all three of the criteria I have established. Elevation, however, is one positive emotion, while ecstasy can be the result of *any* positive emotion that transforms us by catalyzing radical transcendence and exerting eudaimonic changes. Because elevation does seem to transform feelings of selfhood, if only through lifting up and/or dilation rather than radical self-transcendence, it can be classified as an attenuated form of ecstasy. In this sense the only difference is that perhaps ecstasies are deeper experiences that climax into something more jarring to one's sense of self, whereas experiences of elevation are more subtle, though no less psychologically valuable. If elevation climaxes and causes radical changes in selfhood and one's sense of eudaimonia, then it is perhaps synonymous with ecstasy. While elevation is a form of ecstasy, however, not all ecstasies are forms of elevation. The one is a specific example, while the other is a more broadly encompassing, experiential category.

Ecstasy perhaps shares the most common ground with the sublime, an aesthetic idea with a long, complex history. Originally used by the Latin orator Longinus to signify a quality among orators, the sublime became in the eighteenth century an effect experienced by readers and viewers in response to awe-inspiring, fear-inducing objects, scenes, or textual passages. The Romantics refashioned the aesthetics of the sublime by locating it in common objects and removing, though not always, the element of fear that featured so prominently in the eighteenth-century version.

Common to all of these conceptions of the sublime is awe, which is now identified by psychologists as a valuable positive emotion. Paul Pearsall, for instance, advances a compelling argument in favor of the value of awe in his insightful study, *Awe: The Delights and Dangers of Our Eleventh Emotion.* Awe, he claims, is a highly beneficial emotion in that it challenges us to revise our conceptions of self and the world, and it intensifies the need to connect with other people.[44] The experience of awe enhances one's sense of meaning and purpose,[45] and it can also be characterized as a form of optimal experience. Sublime experiences are eudaimonic in that they foreground a positive emotion. They are also ecstatic in the effects they exert. In an important study of the sublime, James Twitchell observes that the etymology of the word implies going up and out of self but only to a point just below a threshold of complete transcendence.[46]

The sublime experience is thus quite similar to the ecstasy but differs from it in three important aspects: (1) like elevation, the sublime foregrounds only one emotion—awe—while ecstasy can be the result of any positive emotion; (2) the sublime is an aesthetic response, which is only one of the many forms of ecstasy; and (3) the sublime only goes to the threshold of complete self-transcendence, while some forms of ecstasy, particularly mystical experiences and near-death experiences, can, according to those who report them, result in a feeling of complete self-annihilation. While sublime perceptions and experiences can be ecstatic, ecstasies are not always sublime.

Ecstasy, therefore, is neither happiness nor joy, and its energies are not exhausted in the concepts of flow, elevation, and the sublime. In one sense it is all of these concepts, but in another it is so much more. Ecstasy has myriad manifestations and can be located in a variety of human experiences. As a deep, affective event that catalyzes consciousness transformation, the ecstatic experience, as I hope this study will demonstrate, is of critical importance as a means by which people in cultures past and present have achieved eudaimonia.

This eudaimonic value and importance of ecstasy can be clearly seen in the literary preoccupation with it. The ecstatic poetic tradition is one of the principal means by which human beings in various cultures have preserved the record and psychology of ecstasy (religion, of course, is another). Let us turn now to a discussion of this literary tradition by exploring its history and closely analyzing five representative poets, and then concluding with a discussion of the theoretical implications, both extra-literary and literary, of such poetry.

3. The Ancient Poetics and Aesthetics of Ecstasy

Ecstatic poetry is by no means new, rooted as it is in a tradition that extends across the globe and stretches back into the misty origins of oral verse. The poets in this tradition celebrate human beings in their best moments—"the soul at the white heat"—to use Emily Dickinson's line. Ecstatic poets often affirm the value of happiness, human connections, festivities, sexuality, and relatedness to the divine; they praise the goodness of life, the abundance of nature, and the intimate interrelation of the whole cosmos; and they configure in their verse peak states of being and eudaimonic, life-affirming emotions, such as serenity, awe, hope, wonder, rapture, gratitude, and love. In most cultures in which it is written, ecstatic poetry is born out of a poetics of ecstasy in which the poet becomes ecstatically enraptured and composes verse that replicates the same rapture in those who listen to his or her words. Throughout this study, I refer to these effects, at least as they are suggested by the various texts in which they appear, as the aesthetics of ecstasy. Such poetics and aesthetics have religious overtones, for as we shall see, poetic "possession" is often tantamount to divinity, and the various responses to this are quite similar to those people display in religious experience. The poets in many ancient cultures were considered to be seers, prophets, and wise sages. In ancient times such poets served a shamanic function, and their ecstatic transport was interpreted in a religious framework.

Ecstatic poets can be found in nearly every culture in the ancient world, and in most cultures today poets are still writing such verse. Ecstatic poetry thus represents a living tradition with ancient roots that stretch deeply through the layers of human history. A survey of this tradition will reveal its ubiquity. No doubt, the corpus is too large to be thoroughly surveyed in two chapters, and to give the subject its full due would require perhaps several volumes. What follows in this and the next chapter, therefore, is a sketch in broad outlines of the more prominently ecstatic poetry in several cultures, as well as a detailed list of characteristics, that is, a 20-point typology, of such verse.

The story begins somewhere back at the dawn of humankind when the first members of a relatively hairless, big-brained primate species realized the beauty of their own vocalizations. When these hominids began to sing, perhaps to soothe themselves after tragic encounters with big predators and to express joy over being alive in their finer moments, the tradition of oral poetry was born. Ecstatic verse gradually grew out of the rich matrix of this oral tradition. Of course, no one knows when this outgrowth took place, since writing is a relatively recent development in the cultural evolution of the human species, and literature in the form of poems and stories flourished for millennia before the invention of inscribing it symbolically on reeds and parchments. The pre-literate, oral tradition is a universal human institution, and it seems to have existed in every ancient culture.[1] Such literature is also found in all current, non-literate societies. In nearly all cultures (ancient and modern), it serves as a kind of social cement and functions to bind together members of a given society by reinforcing their values and preserving their collective history. In addition to narratives the ancient oral tradition, like the modern one, was also characterized by songs, hymns, and lyrics that served to express and induce (among others) eudaimonic emotions and states of being. Those who recited such verbal forms—minstrels, Nebi'im, shamans, *vatis*, rhapsodes, rawis, prophets, rishis, and bards—were the originators of ecstatic poetry. Their winged words, to use Homer's famous image, were sung for joy, transport, and happiness, moving both poet and auditor to rapture and ecstasy. Let us survey their traditions.

Proto-Indo-European

Such poetry was no doubt sung by the Indo-European poets who lived in Eastern Europe and Central Asia sometime between 6000–4500 BCE. Indo Europeans were a loosely related group of tribes who spoke the mother tongue, Proto-Indo-European (PIE), of nearly all Indian and European languages. The existence of PIE as the source of dozens of languages can be inferred through linguistic reconstruction and some limited archaeological evidence.

It is also possible to make some inferences about PIE poetry. Since all ancient cultures had an oral tradition in the form of poetry and song, it is safe to say that the speakers of PIE had one as well. What these poems and songs were, however, remains a bit of a mystery. One clue to their content can be seen in the theory of ecstatic possession, or poetics of *ekstasis*, found in various Indo-European cultures. For instance, the rishis, or poet-priests who wrote the Sanskrit hymns of the Rigveda, are said to have done so while in a strange state of madness. A rishi, also called a *vipra*, signifies someone who is "inwardly stirred, inspired, wise."[2] Zarathustra, the founding poet-prophet of Zoroastrianism, used the corresponding Avenstan word, *eresi*, in reference to himself. The Latin equivalent here is *uates*, which means "seer, prophet, inspired poet."[3] This term is also similar to the Gaelic word *faith* and several Germanic words that link poetry and possession, such as the Gothic *wops* (possessed) the Old High German *wuot* (frenzied), the Old English *wod* (frenzied) and many others.[4]

In these traditions the poet had two functions: (1) as a bestower of praise and (2) as a prophet or seer who was "gifted with special knowledge, perhaps through an altered state of consciousness."[5] Given this similar poetics of ecstasy among far flung, Indo-European cultures, it is thus highly likely that PIE poetry was similarly ecstatic in character and sung by a "possessed" poet-seer who moved his audience to ecstatic rapture. The poet's task was not only to embody ecstatic possession but to inspire, through an aesthetics of ecstasy, the same in his or her audience. Such poets abounded in the ancient Indo-European tradition, which contains dozens of languages that find expression in India, ancient Persia, Continental Europe, parts of the ancient Near East, the British Isles and Ireland.

Hindu

When Indo-Europeans moved into the Indian sub-continent, they brought with them, among many divinities, Soma, their god of ecstasy, as well as an eponymous juice that probably contained hallucinogens of some kind.[6] Those who imbibed soma juice experienced an ecstatic alteration in consciousness and were transported to divine heights. In the Vedas, the Sanskrit holy text of the invading Indo-Europeans, there are many references to Soma and the sacred drink imbibed in his honor. These conquering Aryans encountered in Indian culture a native ecstatic tradition in, among others, the cult of Shiva, the wild god whose ecstatic dance is the source of the creation and destruction of the universe. Over time, these two traditions melded through syncretism to become one religious teaching—Hinduism. The two religious systems proved to be fertile soil for the flowering of ecstatic verse.

The earliest extant Hindu poetry is found in the Rigveda hymns, which date from between 1500 and 1000 BCE. Other early texts are the Upanishads, the oldest of which were composed by the *rishis* mentioned above somewhere between 800 and 400 BCE, and the *Bhagavad Gita*, which was written as part of the larger *Mahabharata* in about 100 BCE. Given that the earliest poetry is inseparable from the spiritual lives of the people who produced it, Hindu verse was undoubtedly ecstatic from the beginning.

Alongside these texts, there was also from the beginnings of Hinduism a thriving tradition of lyrics sung or spoken in the many Indian languages. Such verse no doubt pre-dated but also later took its cue from the sacred scriptures. Because of the elusive nature of the non-literate, oral tradition, however, there is a paucity of preserved texts. Some of the first lyrics written down are found in ancient Tamil, a non–Indo-European, Dravidian language. The Tamil classical age known as the *cankam* predates and extends through the Christian era, spanning several centuries. This period saw the flourishing of a rich literary tradition, both oral and literate, much of which has been lost to the ravages of time. The first extant works consist of eight anthologies containing 2,381 works by 473 poets.[7] These poems are divided into two broad generic categories: *puram* and *akam*. *Puram* poems depict life outside of the family and cover a range of topics such as war, the praise of kings, suppliants' requests, mourning, ethics, and other topics. The second, more numerous, type of poems, *akam*, concern life inside the family. While the former are called "exterior," the latter are labeled "interior" because of their focus on the relations between husband and wife and their exploration of the cosmic dimensions of "human living and relatedness."[8] Because of the script in which they are written, scholars know with some certainty that the anthologies containing *akam* poems were compiled and written in the first, second and third centuries CE.[9] The poems themselves could be considerably older, but the language used in the anthologies bears a significant Sanskrit (and thus Aryan) imprint.[10] It is difficult to determine with any certainty, therefore, whether the ecstatic character of *akam* poems is attributable to Indo-European or native Dravidian influence. It is probably safe to say both traditions are accountable. Regardless, they are "bardic," "visionary," and "prophetic" in nature[11] and thus feature prominently in a survey of ecstatic poetry.

The *akam* poems are perhaps the largest corpus of verse written on a single theme—"the healthy, creative balance of the masculine and feminine principles."[12] They repeatedly show men and women living in step with the "rhythm and joy of cosmic life," but they by no means praise the otherworld and denigrate this one.[13] To the contrary, and unlike so much religious verse that devalues the material world in favor of some non-physical, transcendent realm, *akam* poems are written in honor of physical life, and they "celebrate the joy and delight of the created universe."[14] They are also highly erotically charged and read like paeans to human sexuality and its life-sustaining, fulfilling joys. A stanza from a poem by Kuruntokai illustrates the recurring eroticism in such poems:

> Fulfilled is my male quest, and
> My heart is in contentment full
> Here is the soft bed

Made of her fragrant hair
Which smells like a fresh *kuvalai* flower
On its slender stem
And I am lying on it in her embrace.[15]

This post-coital satisfaction is suggestive of the inherent goodness of sexuality, as well as the interrelatedness between human beings and the natural world, whose creative forces humans replicate in the potency and vitality of their erotic powers. Yet, for all of their eroticism, *akam* poems do not configure sexuality as an end in itself. The central aim of each one seems to be, much like the thrust of Greek Orphism, to bring the emotions and the intellect into complete harmony, the desired result of which is "the achievement of the spontaneous, creative fullness of the whole of the human personality."[16] In the spirit of healthy-mindedness, individuation, and eudaimonic psychology, *akam* poems suggest a full flourishing of the human being.

The Hindu Bhakti movement, a kind of religious reformation that gave birth to a rich tradition of "protest poets," also championed the human being in such ways. The Bhakti movement in India was a challenge to Hindu Brahmans of the priestly caste who kept a stranglehold on Hindu life and excluded certain castes from religious rites and rituals. Beginning in the sixth century CE, Indians began to rebel against the Brahman caste and their exoteric religious ideas and practices involving strict adherence to ritual, an insistence on pilgrimages to sacred cities, and the centering of religious life at temples. With the support of the Guptas, a line of kings who unified northern India, reformers turned inward and refocused Hindu religious life on bhakti, or devotion to one or more of the Hindu gods. This reformation carried with it the seeds of a new literature, for *bhaktas* (devotees) expanded upon the sacred scriptures and wrote a whole new body of religious, devotional literature. These new works, which included the famous *Puranas* (ancient stories), inspired many new devotional sects centered around Vishnu, Shiva, and Mahadevi.[17] The movement also inspired scores of poets who voiced in their works the principles of devotion and bhakti protest against Brahman orthodoxy. Bhakti verse is spontaneously written (in theory, at least) and celebratory, often accompanied by dancing and rejoicing. It is a celebration of the ecstatic union between the self and some divine figure, such as Krishna, Kali, Durga, or Shiva. Such poetry eventually found expression in several Indian languages and permeates the whole sub-continent.

Some of the oldest extant Bhakti poetry, dating from roughly the eight century, is found in the Dravidian region in the Tamil language. The poets in the Tamil tradition perpetuated the old Indo-European trend of associating the poet with divine possession. They were considered divine beings in their own right and referred to as poet-saints. Twelve of these Alvars, or Vaishnavite poets who worshipped Vishnu, were held in such high esteem as to be revered as incarnations of Vishnu's companions or attributes.[18] The Nayanmars, or Shaivite poets who worshipped Shiva, consisted of 63 known individuals who were also revered as saints because of their forcefully defiant and successful challenge to religious excess and authority. Consisting of followers of both Shiva and Vishnu, the major Tamil poet-saints left a rich corpus of ecstatic poems in praise of the Hindu gods.

Of the twelve Alvars, Antal stands out among the rest as the only female poet-saint. In her verse Antal challenged not only orthodox religious ideas but also gender constraints. Operating in the nearly global tradition of "bridal mysticism" in which the poet becomes the lover of God, she frequently used the image of plunging herself in water, also a euphemism for sexual intercourse, to describe her desire for total immersion, and thus loss of self, in Krishna's grace.[19] Such imagery in some ways echoes *Akam* poetry and its similar eroticism, with which Antal would have been familiar as the highly literate daughter of another poet-saint (her father was also an Alvar). The crucial difference here, however, is that Antal's image is strictly metaphorical and not intended to be a celebration of human sexuality. She makes it clear, in fact, that she desires not a human sexual companion but Krishna alone. In *Tiruppavai*, one of her most well-known and oft-cited works, Antal adds a bhakti coloration to the age-old rite of the *pavai* vow, a custom followed by unmarried girls who take a vow to wake early and to bathe every day in a nearby river for the whole month of Markali (mid–December to mid–January) in order to attract a husband.[20] In Antal's poem, however, the vow is to awaken from the slumber of human forgetfulness (a common theme in many Hindu parables) and to plunge oneself not in the bliss of conjugal union, despite the sexual pun, but to lose oneself in an ecstatic coupling with the god Krishna. Yet, for all of her allegorizing, Antal so frequently described her love for Krishna in erotic imagery that a well-known statue of her (the object of significant veneration) shows a curvaceous, plump-breasted, scantily-clad and thus sexually appealing, young woman. This resurfacing of eros, despite its denial in metaphor and allegory, recurs in much religious ecstatic poetry. Because it raises doubts about whether such verse is truly eudaimonic, it is a central problem that we shall return to in the course of this study, particularly in Chapter 7.

The twelfth-century movement called Virasaivism, another variant of Bhakti protest, also caused a poetic flourishing, at the heart of which are four great poets-saints—Basavanna, Dasimayya, Mahadeviyakka, and Allama Prabhu. Like the Nayanmars, these Vacanakaras were poet-saints who worshipped Shiva, but they wrote in Kannada, another Dravidian language, and they did so in a different form—the *vacana*, which means "spontaneous saying." The *vacana* form, which is characterized by free verse, arose out of the local oral tradition and represents an attempt to capture the feel of extempore expression. The *vacana* signifies a break from traditional meter, the formality of literary genres, and the arbitrary division of poetry and prose. However contradictory, some *vacanas* are clearly the result of considerable reflection, as in the case of Allama Prabhu's difficult and obfuscating "riddle poems," and others seem to embody images, symbols, and paradoxes taken from a "pan-Indian pool of symbology."[21] By and large, however, they fly in the face of "pre-meditated art"[22] and convey a felt sense of unwilled speech, as if some force beyond the speaker's conscious intentions were doing the speaking. Once again, the poetics of ecstasy seems to lie at the core of the Vacanakaras' approach to poetry, for which they saw themselves merely as mouthpieces. Such poet-saints were not craftsmen in the modern sense of the poet who labors over his work, refining and polishing it until it takes on a pleasing shape. To the contrary, they saw themselves as ecstatic vehicles through which Shiva spoke. They saw themselves as "speaking Shiva."

Central to Virasaivism is the recurring image of the opposition between *sthavara* (standing) and *jangama* (moving), as well as the favoring of the latter over the former. The privileging of *jangama* represents the Virasaiva criticism of orthodox temple culture, which was exclusionary and delineated a sacred precinct inside of which was the divine and outside of which was the profane. Such temples were fixed and thus represented *sthavara*, or the static, while the itinerant *jangama*, a Virasaivite guru, moved from village to village, carrying the sacred within himself. His wandering signified that Shiva is never static, always changing, forever fluid, ubiquitous and thus not confined to a sacred precinct such as a temple.[23] Deeply informing Virasaivite spirituality and *vacana* poetry, the opposition between *sthavara* and *jangama* is the same one between exoteric and ecstatic forms of spirituality. In some ways it is also reminiscent of the differences between *enstasis* and *ekstasis*. The *vacana* poets spoke out against Brahmanism and the various static, rigid forms it supported, such as caste, class, and gender differences, and they rejected Hindu rituals, pilgrimages, temple-going, image worship, and offerings to priests and gods.[24] Like Christian Protestants, they promulgated the idea of direct spiritual experience, championed the underclass, and advanced a doctrine of divine grace. They also proselytized like Christian Protestants, and their evangelism accounts, in part, for the pervasive influence the Bhakti movement exerted all over India.

The major Vacanakaras inspired literally hundreds of later poets who wrote, and continue to write, *vacanas* in the style of the original poet-saints. The tradition that began in the medieval era has thrived for centuries and continues to flourish well into the twenty-first century.[25] This southern Bhakti tradition also inspired many northern writers who wrote in other Indian languages. Some of these include Ravidas, Nanak, Surdas, Tulsidas, Tukaram,

Ramprasad, and many others. No doubt, in the rich Indian tradition there are too many ecstatic poets even to cite, let alone to discuss. Three of these, however, deserve special mention, since they are still widely read in India and in many parts of the West.

The first of these is the great northern saint, Kabir, a brilliant Hindi poet whose verse is popular today in America, thanks in large part to Robert Bly's versions. Kabir was born in 1440 into a Muslim family, but as an adolescent he was initiated by a Hindu guru. Although he is claimed by the Sikhs, the Muslims, the Sufis, and the Hindus, he resisted all such classifications in his verse and upheld the Bhakti resistance to exoteric, and thus limiting, forms of religious worship. Truth for Kabir was not found in books, and he is said to have been an illiterate singer of songs, though this has been a subject of debate among scholars. His poetry, nevertheless, exhibits a heart-centered spirituality and eroticism that opposes idolatry and asceticism of all kinds.

Unlike the other Bhakti poets, however, Kabir did not worship a personalized version of God. Instead, he used many images that serve to point beyond phenomenal imagery to a divine principle with no attributes. Such a conception of God requires a *via negativa,* or way of negation, for expression. Like the anonymous Christian author of *The Cloud of Unknowing* who used the images of darkness and unknowing instead of light and knowledge to signify God, the Hindus sometimes use the phrase, "neti, neti," which means, "not this, not that," to refer to the transcendent, eternal God in its non-attributable form as *Nirguna Brahman.* Whereas the Bhakti form of God, by contrast, is *Saguna Brahman*, or a personalized god with attributes, Kabir's God is beyond all such verbal description and personal characteristics. He resorted, consequently, to the use of auditory imagery, which he represented as an inner sound and called "unstruck music," that is, music not played (struck) on physical instruments such as drums or sitars but which one can hear with "inner" ears. Above all, Kabir is the premier poet of the inner sound current, or audible, mystical stream of love and wisdom that flows from a nameless, formless God.

The second major, northern poet-saint, Mirabai, is also highly revered in India and widely read in the West. Like Kabir, Mirabai was a Hindi writer whose central theme was ecstasy and its effects, or as Jane Hirshfield eloquently put it, "the consummate freedom passion calls up in us" and "the surrender of self that passion's fulfillment requires."[26] Unlike Kabir, however, Mirabai was strongly devoted to the god Krishna, whom she refers to as the "dark one," and whose presence she craves with intensely erotic longing. Mirabai is said to have been married to a husband to whom she never developed a healthy attachment, devoted as she was wholly to Krishna. According to some hagiographical accounts, she thus found herself at odds with husband and family, lost caste, and became a god-intoxicated pariah who lived, wrote, danced, and sang on the margins of society. This story strikes a resonant chord among many contemporary feminists, who see Mirabai's defiance of gender roles and social conventions as a prototype of the strong modern woman. The image of the independent young woman who scorns her husband and his wealthy family, loses caste, defies religious and secular authorities, and ecstatically sings and dances naked in celebration of the glories of Krishna's love is inspiring indeed.

The problem with this story, however, is that it comes to us from the dubious tales of hagiography, which is notorious for exaggerations and inaccuracies. The writing of saint's lives is by no means truly biographical, and thus little is known of Mirabai or even what she actually wrote. A question mark, in fact, hangs above her whole poetic corpus, according to John Stratton Hawley,[27] who notes that many poems attributed to Mirabai were actually written in the eighteenth and nineteenth centuries, not in the sixteenth century when she lived. Many of these were no doubt authored by unknown individuals who wanted to immortalize their own verse by attributing its authorship to a well-known and much revered poet-saint. "Mirabai," therefore, is more of style than an actual poet. No doubt, there was a poet named Mirabai, who lived roughly between 1498–1547 and produced a small body of poems that scholars can attribute to her with some certainty. The large body of poems bearing her name, however, such as nearly all of the "versions" in Hirshfield and Bly's popular English edition, are rather in the tradition of the *Homeric Hymns* or the *Anacreontea*, that is, they represent a school of writers who wrote in the style and spirit of the original poet. They are poems written by a whole culture, rather than one individual. Nevertheless, these poems are rife with images of drunkenness, madness, passion, spinning, dancing and ecstatic longing for a god whose presence signifies the healing power of love. Such verse quintessentially represents the ecstatic nature of the Bhakti devotional path.

The third northern poet, Rabindranath Tagore, is perhaps the most mentionable in that he is the cultural treasure not only of the Bengal region where he lived but of the whole subcontinent. He is India's most famous, and perhaps best, poet. At the height of his career, Tagore also met with significant acclaim in the West and across the globe, where he was often greeted by enthusiastic crowds frequently numbering in the hundreds and sometimes thousands. In 1913 he was the first Easterner to win the Nobel Prize in literature, which he won for a lifetime of work in several literary genres. A prolific, fecund author, he wrote plays, novels, short stories, songs, and essays, all of which fill 28 large volumes in Bengali. What captured the attention of poets such as W.B. Yeats, and then the Nobel Committee, however, was Tagore's translation of his own work, *Gitanjali*, a book of ecstatic poems inspired by Kabir and many other Bhakti poets.

Like Kabir, Tagore was not a Bhakti writer *per se*, as he was part of the movement known as Brahmo Samaj, a puritanical and somewhat sober form of Hindu monotheism that opposed caste differences, rituals, and idolatry.[28] His father, Debendranath, played a pivotal role in Brahmo Samaj as its central figure. Informing this movement was the Vedanta of the Upanishads, which Tagore, like his father, saw as the highest philosophical achievement of Indian thought.[29] Unlike his father, however, he believed the Upanishads were too cerebral and thus "incomplete in their answer to the complex longing of the human soul."[30] He conveyed in his poetry, consequently, a more heart-centered, human, devotional spirituality, the likes of which he saw in the Bhakti path, particularly in Vaishnavism and its Krishna worship, as well as in the poetry of Kabir. At a young age he heard his brother recite some ecstatic lines from the Sanskrit poet, Kalidasa, and he was moved to rapture even though he did not fully understand the language. As he developed as a poet, he began to convey in his verse a similar tone that resulted in a fiery "combination of physical passion, sensuous imagery, and verbal music."[31]

This ecstatic voice proved to be melodious music to Western ears: *Gitan-jali* went through ten editions in England between March and November in 1913 when Tagore won the Nobel Prize. Afterwards, he became a worldwide sensation. He attributed his own success with Western readers to the expression of the "vehement feelings" that never found a voice in their own literature,[32] a point to which I shall return in Chapter 8. Such readers saw reflected in *Gitanjali* the "humane spirit of Christianity, venerated in theory but ignored in practice" by so many Westerners.[33] In his writings Tagore explored many moods and states of being, and *Gitanjali* is by no means fully representative of his oeuvre. But the subject of all of his writings, as he himself claimed, was "the delight of attaining the infinite within the finite."[34] At the heart of his poetry is a molten, ecstatic core that exudes the warmth of joy, love, wonder, enchantment and innocence.

Buddhist

India has a rich tradition of ecstatic poetry, not all of which is connected to Hinduism. In the subcontinent there are many religions, each with its own literary tradition. While Hinduism is the dominant faith, India is also the land of Jainism, Sikhism, Islam, Buddhism, and several other varieties of spirituality. In each of these traditions there is a large corpus of poetry that can be labeled ecstatic. Foremost among these is Buddhism, because of its considerable influence throughout Asia and later the West, and also because of the vibrant poetic tradition it inspired. The earliest Buddhist scriptures stem from the two earliest stands of the religion, Theravada and Mahayana, each of which produced several sacred texts that were transmitted orally for centuries and then later written down in Pali, an Indo-European language related to Sanskrit. These writings include the Theravada *Tripitaka* and the Mahayana *Sutras*, among others.[35]

Alongside sacred scripture, there also developed in Buddhist circles an oral tradition of poetry. Such verse, no doubt, extends all of the way back to first *sangha*, or community of followers on the path of Buddhist enlightenment.[36] This oral poetry was passed down to followers throughout the centuries, and surely much was altered or lost along the way. Finally, in 80 BCE Pali scholars collected such poetry in two anthologies, the *Theragatha* and *Therigatha*. These early poets ecstatically sang about "their first contact with the sweet tones of the Dharma, the teachings of Buddhism,"[37] and their exhilarating conversion to the path of enlightenment. Their poetry, like Buddhist thought itself, is about the end of suffering through the relinquishment of attachment, craving, and desire, as well as the unspeakable bliss of *nirvana*, which is not a heaven or afterlife per se but a state of being that results from the *ekstatic* realization of the illusion of selfhood and the impermanence of the material world.

In the first century CE monks carried the teaching to China, where the encounter with Taoism and Confucianism produced a variety of new schools of Buddhism, each with its own distinctive understanding of the Buddha's ideas. This fertile, syncretistic marriage of religions also resulted in the birth of what some scholars have said is "the greatest unfolding of poetry in world history."[38] China's subsequent two-thousand-year cultural history has produced literally hundreds of poets, many of whom have left behind hundreds of pages of Buddhist verse. One official anthology contains 50,000 poems.[39] Foremost among these writers, based on their influence throughout China and beyond its borders, are the Ch'an poets, a group consisting of lay writers and Ch'an masters who exchanged literary and spiritual ideas with one another and subsequently created a colossal canon of poetry. Notable among this Ch'an group are some of China's most well-known poets, such as Chia Tao, Ch'i-chi, Shih-shu, Ching An, Su Tung-p'o, Wang Wei, and several others too numerous to mention.

The Chinese Buddhist schools spread their teachings throughout the Far East. In 550 CE Buddhism reached Japan by way of the Korean kings who had established cultural contact with the island.[40] Here, Buddhism commingled with the native animistic tradition, Shinto, the result of which was the birth of four major Japanese schools—Tendai, Shingon, Pure Land, and Zen (the Japanese variety of the Chinese Ch'an school). In each school a tradition of poetry also blossomed. Much like China, then, Japan also produced a large group of poets as a result of the spread of Buddhism. Most notable among these, in terms of their worldwide influence, are the Zen poets. There are several types of Japanese Buddhist poetry, the earliest of which is written in imitation of the Chinese masters. Later, however, Zen poets borrowed from the court poets' fixed courtly forms, such as the *choka*, the *tanka*, and the *sedoka*, into which they infused Zen insights. The result of this mélange of court poetry and Buddhism is the premier, Zen literary genre, the haiku, an extremely short poem with a prescribed number of syllables (often seventeen, but this can vary). The earliest of these Haiku poets are Sogi, Sokan, and Moritake, all of whom lived and wrote in the fifteenth and sixteenth centuries. The later, and much more popular, Zen writers, Basho, Buson, and Issa, carried the haiku to new heights in their mastery and perfection of the form.

Central to Zen poetics is the idea that the haiku is an object of meditation and should thus lead to something like an ecstatic perception. The form calls for "simplicity, naturalness, directness, [and] profundity,"[41] so the responding reader can see the "thing-in-itself" and have a perception unclouded by the filter of one's past associations, values, beliefs, prejudices, and emotions. Although modern neurology and postmodern theory have rendered the idea of unfiltered, direct perception of an object an ultimate impossibility, some perceptions are more direct than others. Haiku writers strive (as much as is possible) to enable the reader to experience the freshness and fullness of a given perception. This idea loosely corresponds to Victor Shklovsky's Formalist "estrangement theory," which says the purpose of literature is to free perception from habituation. Because perceptions become conditioned and automatic, good writers render the familiar in strange ways and thus enable a more original perception. Haiku poems are sparse in description, economical in their use of figures of speech, and directly focused on minute particulars because they are similarly intended to enable the reader to experience the fullness, or what Buddhists call *suchness*, of a given perception. Such *suchness* is only possible when the reader gets out of his or her own way by transcending the logical ordering of the mind and removing the mental tags one uses in lieu of full, deep perceptions.

A haiku should thus ultimately lead the reader to a sense of the utter strangeness and "irreducible mysteriousness"[42] of objects commonly perceived but rendered ordinary by habituation. For this reason, Roland Barthes saw the haiku as a supreme example of the subversion of meaning and the inherent emptiness of language. As he put it, "the work of reading which is attached to [the haiku] is to suspend language, not to provoke it."[43] The attempt to pierce the meaning of a text, a common interpretive strategy among Western readers, is a kind of self-assertion, whereas the response to a haiku should ideally be a process of self-emptying in which one stands aside and leaves "the meaning-making activity of the ego to its own devices."[44] The endpoint in reading the haiku is what Zennists call *muga*, that is, "so close an identification with the object that the unstable, mentalizing self disappears."[45] The haiku calls for the dissolution of the illusory boundaries between self and other, and it leads to a state of perception in which subject and object become one.

Shortly after Buddhism made its way into Japan, it also spread to Tibet. Here the Buddha's ideas commingled with the local Bon tradition—a religion focused on various spirits with which Shamans ecstatically communicated—and the result was the development of several schools of Tibetan Buddhism that still exist in the present day.[46] One of these strands, the Kagyu-pa, or "whispered transmission school," was the religious soil that produced the flower of Tibetan Buddhist poetry, Jetsun Milarepa. His supposed given name, Thopa Ga, or "joy-to hear," signifies Milarepa's gift of verbal eloquence, a boon many Western readers have come to appreciate in the last century. In what was a Himalayan custom, he wandered for much of his life composing and singing extemporaneous songs in return for food. He was so prolific that he is said to have left behind 100,000 poems and songs, although the figure is difficult to verify since many of these were orally transmitted and then later transcribed by individuals who interpolated additional material into the corpus and perhaps even wrote some of the poems themselves.[47] The many poems in which he praises himself and extols his own wisdom, in particular, bear the stamp of later followers and admirers. Milarepa's body of songs is thus similar to Mirabai's in that they were produced by both him and his culture.

The predominant message of these songs is also the same compassionate, loving message of Tibetan Buddhism. Milarepa has been called the "St. Francis of Tibet" because in his work there is "the same lyricism, the same tender sympathy, [and] the same earthiness..." as are found in the writings of the great Italian saint.[48] The whispered-transmission-school in which he studied Buddhism is a highly esoteric form of spirituality that required adherents to survive the initiatory rigors of a night at an extreme Himalayan altitude wearing nothing but a loin cloth. Periodically throughout the night, someone placed a wet cloth on the backs of initiates, who were required to dry it by raising their core temperature through various yogic exercises involving breath manipulation (Tibetan monks still engage in this fascinating initiation rite!). But Milarepa's Buddhism was by no means a self-focused, occult teaching designed solely for the purpose of giving the practitioner awesome powers of control over his nervous system. To the contrary, the thrust of his songs is the compassionate devoting of oneself to the service of all humankind. Such overcoming of "the demon-foe of self" (13), as he puts it, breaks "the savage fetter of suffering" (9) and enables one to dwell in the "undifferentiated void of bliss" (32). Through the transcendence of the duality of subject/object perception, one builds "the tower of ecstasy" (6), the central aspect of his teaching.[49]

Greek

The poetics of ecstasy is also found among the ancient Greeks, another people profoundly influenced by the Indo-Europeans who likely brought to the Mediterranean region a shamanic type of religion characterized by circle dancing and singing, direct spiritual experience, ecstatic journeys to the heavens and underworld, and myths of dismemberment and renewal. Such myths, rites, and techniques of ecstasy, according to Mircea Eliade, are found among all of the Indo-European peoples.[50]

Intimations of shamanic ecstasy can also be seen in the myths of the supposed first Greek poet, Orpheus, who has been called a "prototype of shamans" because of his journey to the underworld, his associations with Dionysus (the Greek god of ecstasy), and his dismemberment.[51] Although much of Orpheus' story is the stuff of myth, many scholars believe that he was likely a historical personage who lived at some point in Greek antiquity. According to the myths, he lived in the heroic age, a generation or so before the Trojan war, but this date has never been verified historically.[52] In the textual record, he is first associated with magic and religion, and the movement he inspires eventually became the mystery school called Orphism, which exerted a considerable later influence on Western religion by supplying Christianity with conceptions of the fallen self, the soul, the afterlife, and the consumption of a dismembered god. Later, Orpheus "comes to exemplify the persuasive power of speech,"[53] and countless stories extol his legendary gift of song. Despite the famous hymns bearing his name, there are no surviving poems that scholars can attribute to Orpheus. The *Mystical Hymns of Orpheus* were not authored by the poet but, like the *Homeric Hymns*, written in the style of the writer to whose name they are attributed—probably by initiates or priests of the Orphic Mysteries—and used at the opening of their secret rites.

Regardless of the lack of surviving texts, the stories of Orpheus' ability to lead an audience into an ecstatic state of rapture provide a window into ancient Greek theories of poetry and its intended effect on those who listened to it. Synonymous with song, such poetry was sung to instrumental accompaniment; it was actually called *mousike* and performed by an *aoidos*, which means singer.[54] The impact of this *mousike* on the audience was entrancing and led listeners into ecstatic states, an indication of which is seen in the etymological connection between the Greek words for song (*aoide*) and enchantment (*ep-aoide*).[55] It is also seen in countless vase paintings and other visual representations of Orpheus holding his audience spellbound in rapt wonderment.[56]

Visual depictions on other vases point to another aspect of the effect of Greek poetry—its association with rhythm and dance—for they also show

Orpheus' rapt audience physically responding to his music through movement.[57] Early Greek poetry, As A.P. David insightfully observes, is rooted in dance,[58] or more precisely, what were likely the remnants of the Indo-European, shamanic circle dance, at the center of which the poet performed by instrumentally conveying the meter while singing his enchanting song. In the Homeric epics, images of the round dance abound to such an extent that David claims Homeric verse itself "is unequivocally dance music."[59] Although some scholars might dispute this claim as an overstatement, it seems clear that early Greek poetry is inextricably linked to dance, given that poetic meter is described in "feet, or steps whose rhythm can be properly actualized by the movement of human legs."[60] The origins of Greek poetry, then, are rooted in the trance-dance, an ancient technique of ecstasy found across the globe in myriad cultures.

The trance-dance is also associated with another Greek poetic tradition—the dithyramb. Performed in honor of the god Dionysus, the dithyramb is a group song sung by a circular chorus, whose members would also engage in various accompanying dances, one of which was called the *tyrbasia*.[61] Little is known of these early dithyrambs, since only fragments of them survive. Based on textual references, scholars have said with certainty that they began as an integral part of the Dionysian rites that involved the harvesting of grapes for wine-making. The dancing associated with the dithyramb probably originally mimicked the bare-footed crushing of grapes in the wine-making process.[62] Over time, however, the form metamorphosed and became a central practice in an institutionalized religious cult. Conducted in honor of Dionysus, the god of divine intoxication, the dithyramb was performed in several ancient rites. These include the Lenaia, the Anthesteria, the Agrai, and the Eleusian Mysteries, as well as the famous *orgazein*, or Dionysian orgies, which were not sexual in nature, at least not at first, but simply involved the physical celebration of the ecstatic principle, probably through dancing in dithrambic fervor.[63] Later, the dithyramb underwent a further metamorphosis into a popular art form found throughout the many Greek city-states. Performed at the Greek dramatic contests by members of the Dionysian guilds,[64] the dithyramb was also responsible for the birth of the theatre, which grew out of these Dionysian choral performances, as scholars have long noted.

Although little is known about the early dithyramb, many scholars have commented on a form that likely grew out of it—lyric poetry. Ancient Greece had a thriving tradition of lyric poets, the most well-known of which are nine canonical writers: Alcman, Sappho, Alcaeus, Anacreon, Stesichorus, Ibycus, Simonides, Pindar, and Bacchylides. In addition to these, however, there were no doubt hundreds of others whose works were consumed by the hungry flames that famously and tragically ravaged the library at Alexandria in 48 BCE.

Lyric poems were sung, not read, and they were accompanied by the lyre, an instrument that gave the form its name, which literally means, "relating to the lyre."[65] Although today the form is associated with introspective, personal expressions of inner states of being, the lyric in ancient Greece was a public form of entertainment involving the community. As *mousike*, it also, like the epic, inspired dancing and movement. Lyric poems were performed by an ecstatic poet whose voice lay somewhere outside of himself. Such poets saw themselves as being "possessed by the power of the muse who inhabits them."[66] No doubt, it was necessary for lyric poets to achieve mastery of their various forms, but such authorial control was also accompanied by "the submersion of the will within convention."[67] Greek poetic theory thus did not call for a mindless possession of the poet who completely abandons himself to the dictates of the Muses. Rather, it required the poet to strike a careful balance between craft and inspiration, that is, between technique and ecstasy. In contemporary psychological parlance, this might be likened to Csikszentmihalyi's "flow," a state in which an individual loses self-awareness because he or she is thoroughly immersed in a challenging task. The lyric poets served as vehicles for the ecstasy of listeners and dancers by entering ecstatic states of their own.

The early, wandering rhapsodes, or those who recited epic verse, also ecstatically "sang" their verse to the accompaniment of the lyre or some other kind of harp. Homer himself refers to "harpers" on several occasions in the *Iliad* and the *Odyssey*. The term rhapsode literally means "stitcher of songs," and it signifies a poet who weaves songs together from multiple narrative sources. The *Iliad* and the *Odyssey*, with their many episodes, are clear examples of a rhapsode at work.[68] Such wandering poets were ubiquitous in ancient Greece, and their lineage stretches back into the bronze age. The early rhapsodes were associated with religious cults,[69] and their origins as poets of ecstasy is almost certain. Over time, however, they became less ecstatic. Although rhapsodes initially performed in a number of genres, at some time before the fifth century BCE, they began reciting the Homeric poems exclusively, and they did so without musical accompaniment, abandoning the origins of poetry in music and dance.[70] The divorce of poetry and its musical foundation in the form of recitation of Homeric poems unaccompanied by music is highly suggestive of the loss of the ecstatic principle. Although the rhapsodic tradition extended well into the Roman era, after the fifth-century BCE it significantly differed from how it began in the Indo-European past. Its ecstatic fires had cooled.

Along with the transformation of the rhapsodic tradition, other literary forms also underwent significant revision in ancient Greek culture. The lyric, so popular a form in early Greece, was later devalued by prominent thinkers. In his famous work, *Poetics*, Aristotle virtually ignored the lyric, focusing almost exclusively on drama. The Romans, although not without their lyric poets, privileged other literary forms and thus established negative attitudes toward the lyric that persisted until it saw a reemergence in the sonnets of the Italian Renaissance. Despite the spread of the sonnet form to England, the lyric's ancient status was not fully restored until the Romantics of the late eighteenth and early nineteenth centuries elevated the form to a prominent height.[71] When the dithyramb, once part of an ecstatic rite, became an institutionalized component of civic theatrical festivals, the wildness of its spirit significantly abated.[72] In addition to the muting of its tone, the dithyramb's subject matter also changed. Once exclusively sung in praise of Dionysus, later dithyrambs did not even mention the god at all. The theatre, which began as a celebration of this god of ecstasy, later became an ordered, civic institution, at which point its ecstatic fervor flagged. A barometer of this can be seen in the widespread performance at theatrical festivals of the paean, an unemotional, sedate poem in honor the god of reason, Apollo.

All of these transformations are in some ways attributable to the pervasive worship, both literal and figurative, of Apollo. No doubt because of multiple causes too complex to discuss here, the Greeks began to honor reason above ecstasy, and in doing so they established cultural attitudes toward ecstatic experience that have been passed down through the centuries of Western history. Plato went so far as to exclude ecstatic poets from his utopian *Republic* because he believed they were like the Sophists, or pretenders to knowledge. For Plato, the danger of poetry was that it inspired unreason and prevented the clear functioning of the rational, ordering mind.[73] To go out of one's mind and to be possessed by poetic mania by participating in a dithyramb or dancing to a sung lyric violated Plato's most sacred principle—the unfettered functioning of human reason. This anti-ecstatic spirit was immeasurably influential on the Hellenes and later Westerners.

Such Platonic logocentrism is so pervasive among Western scholars that it has actually caused some literary critics to deny the ecstatic origins of early Greek literature. Penelope Murray, for instance, has argued that inspiration in early Greek verse was strongly associated with knowledge, memory, and performance—that is, craft—and did not involve ecstasy or possession.[74] While this may have been true of later Apollonian poets, it likely does not characterize their earlier Dionysian forebears. Jennifer Wise, likewise, rejects the so called "ritual hypothesis" in accounting for the origins of the drama, arguing for the importance of writing, as opposed to Dionysian worship, as the key factor in the birth of Greek theatre.[75] Wise's point is well taken, particularly as it applies to the moment in Greek history when the theatre fully blossomed. Where the idea seems overstated is in the wholesale dismissal of the Dionysian origins of the theatre. No doubt, both critics make interesting, valuable points, but they do so through a bit of overstatement, exhibiting the characteristically Western privileging of Apollo at the expense of Dionysus. The poetics of ecstasy, as this survey has shown, is too pervasive and influential to be disregarded in such ways. To flatly deny its existence is tantamount to the kind of repressive psychological defense mechanism the Greeks themselves began using during the fifth century BCE.

Israelite

The ancient Israelites had an ecstatic poetic tradition, itself rooted in a centuries-old corpus of oral literature that existed long before the Hebrews adopted the Phoenician alphabet and began to record hymns, genealogies, historical memories, songs, and chants. The material these first writers began to inscribe on scrolls during and after the reign of David constitutes the source of the books that later became the Hebrew Bible.[76] The earliest verse in this body of literature is called Yahwistic poetry and bears the stamp of the oral tradition in that it is "devoid of the sophistication and formalism which result from centuries of theological speculation."[77] Scholars have identified such early verse in several places in the Bible: "The Song of Deborah," the victory hymn in Exodus 15, "The Oracles of Balaam," "The Lament of David," and the various "blessings" that appear throughout the Pentateuch. The language of these poems "is rich and exuberant, the imagery is picturesque, and the figures of speech extravagant."[78] Written in the same rapturous tone found in other literary corpuses, early Hebrew verse was ecstatic in character.

Of particular interest to our discussion are the earliest Hebrew prophets, or Nebi'im—groups of rapt individuals who gathered together to offer sacrifices, sing, dance, and make music at religious festivals. Their activities, which amount to ecstatic techniques, were intended to culminate in divine intoxication, a kind of possession in which one's sense of self is surrendered to God. The Nebi'im thus gathered together communally in order to "seek even greater excesses of orgiastic ecstasy."[79] In their original form they were associated with cultic festivals and served to embody and induce in spectators the madness and frenzy that characterize being rapturously filled with divine power. The Nebi'im, however, were not originally cultic functionaries but occupied the role of shaman, that is, they were not priests who conducted rituals but seers "possessed by the divine." As the tradition evolved, they became associated with Temple life and operated under the supervision of priests.

They were also writers, since writing was seen as being divinely inspired. Scholars now believe that many of the Psalms were written by this order of temple singers who composed extemporaneous hymns of praise to God. Many of these songs are the Psalms still read so widely by Jews and Christians. Later, the Nebi'im became so institutionalized that it was possible for individuals to serve both as priest and Nabi (singular). Two famous prophets, Jeremiah and Ezekiel, occupied both positions.[80] Still later, the Nebi'im became absorbed into the Levite tribe, from which all Hebrew religious functionaries emerged. At this point, however, the extemporaneous, rapturous singing died out, and the singers simply parroted previously written verses that became canonized parts of Hebrew religious life. Over time, their enthusiasm (which etymologically means to be filled with God) waned, as exoteric religious worship became more rigid and prescribed, and thus less tolerant of rapturous possession.

Sigmund Mowinckel observes that the Nebi'im were not of Israelite or Semitic origin.[81] In the extant Mesopotamian literature, however, there is no way to account for the poetics of ecstasy found among these singing prophets. Surviving Sumerian texts, which are among the oldest on the planet, were written in a broad variety of styles and genres, and there is even among this corpus a large body of hymns in praise of gods, kings, and temples. Texts claiming divine inspiration, however, are virtually non-existent in the Mesopotamian canon. As Niek Veldhuis points out, such works "do not derive their canonicity from divine sanction or divine inspiration."[82] Middle Kingdom Egypt, a literary golden age, is seemingly a more likely source of Israelite theories of poetry, since the Hebrews had significant contact with Egyptian culture during this time. Among the surviving texts, however, there are only propaganda literature and occasional poems written in praise of Pharaohs and other rulers.[83] It is important to remember, nevertheless, that the Canaanite religions with which the Israelites had significant contact—particularly the cults of Isis, Baal, Asherah, Cybele, and Anat—were characterized by ecstatic forms of spirituality. It is rather probable that Israelites participated in such cults and thus fused ecstatic spiritual ideas with their poetics and aesthetics.

Mowinckel notes that the "office of enthusiastic-orgiastic prophet" was "a common occurrence in Canaan, Syria, and Asia Minor."[84] Given the enormous cultural exchange between Greece and these areas,[85] it is likely that the Israelite poetics of ecstasy was also informed by Greek sources. The Biblical texts, moreover, strongly suggest a participation in Dionysian forms of worship—a point I will discuss more fully in Chapter 10. Saul's ecstatic encounter with the band of rapt prophets resonates with Dionysian overtones; the injunction against seething a kid in its mother's milk has been clearly shown to be a prohibition against participation in Dionysian rituals, as Radin points out.[86] Both examples, as well as many others, bear the imprint of Hellenistic culture. Early Hebrew poetic ecstasy, then, was probably informed, at least in part, by Greek and other Near Eastern conceptions.

Christian

If gone unmet, ecstatic needs will continue to insist on gratification, a point I will explore more fully in Chapter 11. The Greeks and the Hebrews may have turned their backs on ecstasy, but the ecstatic tradition lived on in a number of Hellenistic cultures, an example of which is found in the Christian mystical tradition. The early Christian world was in many ways a Greek world: the Gospels were written in Greek; many early Christians were also significantly involved with Greek pagan cults; and the Church began and came of age in Hellenistic Rome. Many Christian ideas, moreover, are found in Greek prototypes: the lapsed soul, redemption, an afterlife, a suffering god who dies and is then resurrected, wine and symbolic flesh of the god used as sacraments—all of these Greek ideas supplied the Christian Church with its spiritual foundation. The term "mysticism" itself originates in the Greek mysteries, in which people were initiated and provided with a means of divine revelation and esoteric knowledge.[87] The Christian mystics who communed directly and ecstatically with God were thus inspired, at least in part, by Greek notions of ecstasy and divine possession.

This Christian mystical tradition, like so many others, also spawned dozens of poets who wrote prolifically of their ecstatic revelations in verse forms and left a large corpus of poetical writings. Among these writers are St. Francis of Assisi, St. Theresa of Avila, St. Catherine of Siena, Pseudo-Dionysius, Hadewijch of Antwerp, John Ruysbroeck, the anonymous author of *The Cloud of Unknowing*, Thomas Merton, and many others too numerous to mention. Spanning several centuries and containing dozens of figures, the Christian mystical poets in many ways represent a continuation in the line of ecstatic bards found all over the globe (although most of them would probably cringe at the idea of being likened to a pagan). Because Christian mystical poets are legion, for brevity's sake, I will discuss only two of these writers, Hildegard of Bingen and Juan de la Cruz, both of whom wrote poetry that shines with ecstatic brilliance.

Hildegard lived in the twelfth century (1098–1179), and her worldview was hierarchical, feudal, and by no means egalitarian.[88] In keeping with this medieval *weltanschauung*, she also saw reason as God's greatest gift. In one of her songs, "Hymn to the Holy Ghost," she praised the Creator for the gift of reason and its restoration when human beings sully the divine boon: "But when reason through ill deeds lies prone / You strain and beat upon it with force / And restore it by the infusion of experience" (lines 19–21).[89] Despite this seeming paean to reason, however, she was no Platonic rationalist who fearfully dismissed ecstatic experiences. To the contrary, throughout the whole course of her life, she had powerful, possessive "visions" that she initially could not describe in words. Like many mystics, however, she later found her voice and wrote prolifically of her ecstasies, inspired by experiences with what she described as a great light from which emanated a speaking voice and highly complex, colorful sights.[90] Much like Mohamed, who is said to have dictated the Qur'an as a transcription of the voice of Gabriel, Hildegard spoke in this divine voice, or rather, it spoke through her, in all of her writings. Even in her letters, she wrote not in the first person but as "God's mouthpiece."[91] She was by no means a closeted mystic who shut out the world to commune ecstatically with God, like the famous medieval Anchorites who willingly imprisoned themselves or Indian yogis who retreat to the caves of the Himalayas. Hildegard's mystical experiences, rather, like those of so many other people who experience profound awe, led her outside of herself and supplied her with a deep concern for others. Much like the Hebrew prophets of old, she thus "castigated wrongdoing in high and low places and sought to indicate the true way which would lead the individual and the Church to its proper reward."[92] Unlike the old prophets, however, her overall message was not one of criticizing wrongdoing and the need to reform but of the ecstasy of God.

Over the last thirty years, interest in Hildegard has come to encompass every aspect of her life and work. Her visions, which she wrote about in a text called *Scivias*, have become a central concern among scholars, many of whom have tried to reduce her ecstatic experiences to her lifelong illnesses and ascribe them to some kind of neuro-physiological disorder. Sabina Flanagan refutes this reduction, arguing that "not every migraine sufferer can claim Hildegard's achievements."[93] Her point is well taken, for to liken all mystical experiences to epilepsy or some other disorder of the brain is simply bad logic. Regardless of the validity of Hildegard's visions, her poetical writings, in the form of liturgical songs of several varieties, convey a strongly ecstatic tone and configure eudaimonic emotions and peak states of experience. The majority of these songs, which she wrote in Latin in a work entitled, *Symphony of the Harmony of Celestial Revelations*, are exuberant declarations of the wonder and mystery of God. Although they clearly reflect Christian theological notions, they are heart-centered and read as though they were extemporaneously composed. Hildegard repeatedly expressed in these songs a sense of gratitude for being alive, a feeling of humility before the grandeur and glory of creation, and an affirmation of the goodness of life. And she did so in Dionysian tones and images: "O fiery spirit, praise be to You / Who work in timbrels and lutes!"[94] Perhaps most significant, her songs were intended to be sung, which is to say, they were not merely meant to be read and pondered over but, like the ancient Greek poems, lived and felt in the deeper recesses of the limbic brain where music is processed.

Juan de la Cruz (St. John of the Cross) was also a highly musical poet. In the Carmelite order in which he spent most of his adult life, singing was a central monastic activity. Carmelite nuns and friars, with the strong encouragement of St. Theresa of Avila, the founder of the order, frequently sang at liturgical feasts and also for recreation, simply for joy. John of the Cross was an avid singer who was known to break out into spontaneous song while on long journeys through the countryside amidst the beauty of nature, and on such journeys he would often create his own lyrics and accompanying melodies.[95] Theresa's Carmelite order was not characterized by austerities, which both she and John opposed. To the contrary, they both felt that the spirit of Christian joy should permeate the religious community. To this end, Carmelite nuns and friars took time out of each day to compose and sing poetry to one another. It was a perfect environment for someone with St. John's inner inspiration and poetic talents.

As I previously mentioned, accounts of saint's lives are often badly distorted and prone to ridiculous exaggeration. St. John's life is no exception. One account, for instance, says that he and Theresa were once so deeply absorbed in a conversation on the Trinity that "the two not only went into ecstasy but were seen elevated from the ground."[96] It is thus difficult to discuss his mystical visions from a scholarly perspective, since these are so deeply subjective and divorced from any kind of reference point. He was known, nevertheless, as someone capable of entering deeply meditative states in which he was "absorbed" in God.[97] Towards the end of his life, these states of ecstatic rapture became so profound that he would often lose complete consciousness of his surroundings. In some cases, if he were engaging another person, he would have to rap his knuckles against the wall to remain present in the conversation.[98] Like the others I have mentioned, he was no self-absorbed mystic and was known for the gift of humor and the delight he took in making others laugh. St. John was known for his great compassion for the poor, perhaps because of his own humble origins and his desire to help the sick and suffering. He also had a saint's forgiveness. Despite being imprisoned for nine months in a Christian monastery as a result of sixteenth century Church politics—a confinement in which he suffered considerable privation—he bore no ill will toward his captors. In others such life circumstances might have produced a pessimistic cynic, but in John they served to impel him to cultivate a deeper sense of compassion and charity toward others who were suffering.

St. John's stay in prison is of particular interest because in many ways it served as the impetus for his best poetry. While in confinement, he began composing poems in his mind in what seems to have a been a healthy defense mechanism against horrible outward conditions. Although he undoubtedly composed poetry before his imprisonment, he wrote the largest body of his verse during and after his difficult stay in the Toledo prison. Like so much mystical verse, his poetry is about divine love. Operating in the well-worn "bridal" tradition, John wrote of the union of soul and God, and he often did so, like Theresa and so many others, in erotic terms. On his death bed, interestingly, he requested to hear not prayers for the dying, which his fellow friars began to recite, but the erotic "Song of Songs."[99] A life writer, in his dying moment he preferred *eros* and its will-to-life over *thanatos*. He also frequently wrote about the value of ecstasy. In his most famous poem, "The Dark Night of the Soul," he described spiritual union with God in terms of the transcendence of self. The self-negating darkness that serves as the poem's controlling image leads him to a suspension of the senses in which he becomes the Lover who has previously laid his head on his (the Beloved's) breast: "I abandoned and forgot myself, laying my face on my Beloved; all things ceased; I went out from myself, leaving my cares forgotten among the lilies" (line 8).[100] The language here suggests Lover and Beloved have exchanged identities. While entirely unsung as a poet for at least three centuries after his death in 1591, John is today recognized not only as one of the greatest Spanish writers but perhaps the best of all Christian mystical poets. In countless critical studies scholars have demonstrated the complexity of his poetry, calling it "an artistic creation of the highest craftsmanship."[101] Although the "inspired word" and the mystical experience occupied a central place in his poetics, he was by no means a simple mystic who verbally gushed with enthusiasm for God. His eloquence, sophisticated sensibility, and impressive poetic skills rank him among the greatest of ecstatic poets.

Celtic

The poetics of ecstasy is found among another Indo-European people, the Insular Celts of Wales, Scotland, and Ireland. A central figure in Celtic culture was the bard, an inspired poet who orally recited poetry accompanied by music. Merlin and his sister, two figures from Arthurian legend, were likely Celtic bards, as scholars have claimed.[102] Researchers have gleaned a fair amount of information about the bardic mysteries from two principal sources—the writings of Latin authors and surviving bardic works, mostly later versions, from native bards and storytellers. Such sources make it clear that bards in the later tradition were rigorously trained in schools for a period of no less than twelve years, during which time they would have been carefully educated in grammar, land lore, oration, bardic law, poetic composition, and the arts of seership. They also would have been required to commit to memory a staggering amount of material: 150 Ogams or alphabets, 240 poems in various meters, and 580 tales.[103] Scholars believe these schools thrived between 200

BCE and the end of the Middle Ages, at which point they began to die out. In Gaelic Scotland, however, they persisted well into the eighteenth century.[104] The oldest surviving bardic poems show a Christian influence, which distorts any accurate view of what was originally an entirely pagan phenomenon. In some ways, then, it is impossible to disentangle the pagan and Christian elements in the bardic arts, for they are so intertwined in the surviving source texts as to be inseparable. The bardic schools themselves eventually became wholly Christianized, although they were always staffed by the laity and existed alongside the schools of the clerics.[105]

In other ways, however, it is possible to discern the non–Christian elements, for vestiges of the older pagan cult persisted for many centuries after the Christian monks succeeded in converting the Celts. Among these vestiges is the curious practice of teaching individuals how to compose verse in the dark. Students in the later schools would be locked in darkened rooms and be expected to emerge after a few hours with a poem. Scholars believe this method of teaching poetic composition was a remnant of an older Druidic rite.[106] Textual references in bardic sources suggest that in prehistoric times the poet was also something like a shaman; the bard and the Druid were one.[107] In the earlier Druidic tradition, seer-poets would be initiated by being led into caves, where they would imbibe some kind of hallucinogenic drink and then compose a poem from an altered state of consciousness. Such a method of seeking poetic inspiration, or *awen*, as it is termed in Welsh, is found not only in the method of instruction in the later bardic schools but also hinted at in surviving poems.[108] The Celtic bards were shamans of sorts, "entering the Otherworld through trance and returning with the fruits of their vision."[109] Ecstasy in the process of poetic composition, therefore, was of central importance in the bardic mysteries, for the Celts believed "verse without vision is dead, and vision is itself expressed in verse."[110]

Old Norse

Implied in this last quotation is the idea that poetry should ideally be the byproduct of both technique and inspiration, a conception of poetic composition I have already discussed in relation to the Greeks. Such a theory is similarly found among distant, linguistic cousins of the Insular and Continental Celts, the speakers of Old Norse, itself a descendant of Proto-Indo-European and the mother tongue of the Icelandic, Norwegian, and Faeroese languages. Central to Old Norse poetics was a two-fold conception of poetry: (1) as craft or skill, "with the poet represented as clever song-smith or craftsman of verse; and (2) as a gift of the gods, particularly the god Odin"[111] In relation to the first conception, the Norse conceived of a poem analogically in terms of a house or building. A good poet, then, was like a woodworker who needed to cultivate his craft as if he were building a desirable dwelling. In relation to the second, the Norse likened a poem's force to a mead (honey wine) the gods drank. Odin, the chief god in the Norse pantheon, bestowed poetic mead upon those who exhibited such an impressive level of technical skill in versification as to warrant the divine bounty. The two conceptions of verse were thus not mutually exclusive. If a poet sufficiently honed his craft, Odin would give him the sacred boon of an intoxicating mead, the effects of which resulted in greater verbal eloquence and also the powers of replicating the bestowal of a heady, divine gift in the form of inducing the same intoxication in those who listened to his rapturous words.[112]

The exceedingly high estimation in which the Norse held poetry is seen in their attributing the domain of poetic inspiration to their chief deity, who stole the poetic mead from a giant and then selectively offered it to deserving humans in the form of a regurgitated liquid.[113] The implication here is that Odin's partial digestion of the mead attenuated its potent effects and rendered it palatable to mortals. Poetic mead was thus considered dangerous because inspired verse had the capacity to stir people at deep levels, whether for good or for ill. Poetry, as the Norse insightfully discerned, could be conducive to social cohesion or serve the end of social upheaval. Divine inspiration, or what is called ecstatic possession in other contexts, occupied a problematic but central position in Old Norse poetics. The etymology of the name Odin, according to "The Online Etymology Dictionary," means "raging, mad, inspired" and stems from the base word *wet*, which means "to blow, inspire, spiritually arouse." To be so filled with Odin's boon meant that poets were sometimes seen as being troublesome and unruly, their creativity marginalizing them and pushing them to the social periphery. Still, there was generally great respect for the skilled and inspired poet in the Old Norse tradition, which valued verbal eloquence and equated it with proximity to the gods.

Based on the extant texts—the *Poetic Edda*, the *Prose Edda*, and several forms of surviving *skaldic* verse—there is no indication that the poet functioned as a shaman or prophet. It is possible, however, to discern a poetics of prophesy in the Norse belief that the gods spoke in *eddaic* meter, the implication of which is that inspired poets who recited *eddaic* verse spoke the language of the gods and thus served as a conduit through which the divine energies flowed.

This shamanic role can also be teased out of the stories about Odin, whose shape-shifting, flying, and proficiency in moving among several worlds has been interpreted by many scholars as a variant of shamanic spirituality.[114] Interestingly, Odin is said to have been a priest who lived east of the river Don in Asia,[115] not coincidentally the land in which shamanism is found. According to this euhemeristic account found in Snorri Sturlason's *Prose Edda*, Odin was a highly revered religious functionary who was sought out for his wisdom while living and then worshipped as a god after his death.[116] It is unlikely scholars will ever determine whether he actually lived, but the activities attributed to him in the myths strongly suggest a shamanic figure of some kind. Given that the Norse poetic tradition descended from Indo-European culture, which spawned a poetics of prophesy in several languages, it is not unreasonable to conclude that the Old Norse poets also once functioned in a religious capacity. The Norse ideas about the sacred character of poetry, the shamanic stories surrounding Odin, and the Indo-European influence all compellingly suggest that the Old Norse poets served at some point in the history of the ancient tradition as poet-seers in what seems to be a global phenomenon.

A Problem in the Historical Account

It is tempting to view this global ecstatic tradition strictly from a historicist's perspective and account for its ubiquity in terms of Indo-European influence. All of the traditions I have discussed thus far can be said to have been influenced, whether directly or obliquely, by Aryan ideas about ecstatic possession. Here I am referring not only to the Zen haiku, which admittedly arises in Japan but in a Buddhist context that itself originates in Indo-European influenced India, but also to Hebrew ideas, which seem to be inspired, at least in part, by Greek (and thus Indo-European) conceptions. I am also referring to the non–Aryan, Indian languages, for it has proven impossible to determine which of their ideas about poetry are autochthonous and which are attributable to the Indo-Europeans. In light of such a discussion it might seem reasonable to attribute the many varieties of the poetics of ecstasy to cultural exchange. Such a theory breaks down, however, when attempting to account for the existence of autochthonous traditions of ecstatic poetry, the subject of the next chapter.

4. Autochthonous, Non-Western and Modern Ecstatic Poetry

There are compelling examples of the poetics and aesthetics of ecstasy in cultures with no cultural contact with Indo-European ideas. The inability to account for such similarities purely through a historical approach suggests the need for a more psychological explanation of the existence of the ecstatic poetic tradition. Let us now turn to an examination of the idea and explore it in relation to other traditions.

Sufi

It might seem logical to conclude that the Greek poetics of ecstasy influenced the Sufis, the mystics of Islam, given that the Dionysian symbol of wine and the trope of intoxication are common in Islamic mystical literature. Muslims, moreover, did have significant contact with Greeks and Hellenized Christians. In its extreme form, however, this account has been discredited and shown to be a product of nineteenth-century orientalism.[1] When Western scholars first encountered Sufism in the nineteenth century, they tried to divorce esoteric Sufism from legalistic Islam by rooting its origins in Greek, Christian, and Hindu sources. Later, with the advent of racial theory, they tried to ascribe its origins to the Persians, an Indo-Aryan people who spoke Farsi, not the Semitic language of Arabic. Modern religious scholars generally agree, however, that Sufism is firmly rooted in the Qur'an and thus represents an autochthonous Muslim form of esoteric spirituality that began as a Semitic phenomenon. Although it later transformed under a Persian (and thus Indo-Aryan) influence, Sufism began as a non–Indo-European form of spirituality.

Although Sufism is actually an umbrella term covering a wide array of beliefs, practices, and spiritual lineages, there are some common features. The foundation of Sufism is the internalization of exoteric Islamic forms and the privileging of ecstatic inner revelation, the endpoint of which is the advancement to a state of such spiritual refinement that it is impossible to distinguish between self and God. The most important Sufi practices are meditation techniques that entail the recitation of Allah's 99 names (*zikr*), listening to chanted mystical poetry or music (*sama*), careful monitoring of one's inner life, observance of the Five Pillars of Islam, and engaging in spiritual study under a master. Other practices, though by no means common to all Sufi orders, include free prayer, visualization, breath control, sleep deprivation, whirling, sojourning, and fasting—all of which are ecstatic techniques employed in several cultures around the globe. In contrast to Muslim legalism, the Sufi path is a heart-centered spirituality, much like the Bhakti movement in India, and its adherents often refer to themselves as lovers of God. Love, in fact, is the central ideal in the teaching. Followers in the various orders also attempt to cultivate divine intoxication; the *majdhub*, or one who is so absorbed in God that he has lost his reason and appears mad, is accorded high esteem, if not in actual life, at least in Sufi literature. Ecstasy is the principal aim, since one cannot be full of love for God with the self obstructing the way. When the self is emptied, according to Sufism, the result is *wajd*, or ecstasy.

The Sufis exerted a considerable influence on the cultures to which Islam spread its doctrines. In addition to challenging rigid beliefs and exoteric practices (and thus functioning as a kind of reform), they also engendered, perhaps because of their ritual use of chanted poetry and music, a massive body of ecstatic verse written not only in Arabic, much of which is now lost, but also in many other languages, such as Persian, Turkish, Hindi, Urdu, Swahili, Berber, Somali, and several South Asian tongues. The first Sufi poets wrote in Arabic, the language of the Qur'an, and they took their symbols, forms, images, and poetics from a centuries-old Semitic tradition that pre-dated Islam. The pre–Islamic, Arabic poets extolled in their verse the joys of wine-drinking, the thrill of victory in war, the titillations of illicit love, and the pride of dominance, and they did so in ecstatic states of possession.[2] These *rawis*, as they were called, claimed the inspiration of the *jinn*, or nature spirits worshipped by the many Arabic tribes. Interestingly, even though Mohammed experienced several ecstatic states that transformed him into a spiritual leader, he condemned such possession, exhibiting the characteristic monotheistic response to ecstasy. Of the *rawis*, for instance, he purportedly said: "The poets are followed by the misguided. Have you not seen them raving in every valley, while they are saying what they do not do" (Qur'an 26:224–26). Despite this condemnation, the poetics of ecstasy and the images of drinking wine and enjoying illicit sex—both are taboos in Islam—persisted in early Sufi poetry, as poets simply adopted and modified pre-existing forms. Instead of being possessed by the *jinn*, they were inspired by Allah. The wine and eroticism became allegorical symbols of divine intoxication and union with God.

These first Arabic Sufi writers also drew forms and images from courtly poetry recited for the pleasure of the Muslim Caliphs and other dissolute leaders who ruled an empire that eventually stretched from the Atlantic to India. Even though Islam forbids illicit sexual liaisons and imbibing alcohol, the Muslim courts were characterized by all manner of hedonistic activities, the likes of which courtly poets celebrated in their verse. The Sufi poets adopted these images of wine, eroticism, and other transgressions as a way to shock Islamic sensibilities.[3] Ubiquitous in such verse, these images are not to be taken literally and must be read as veiled allegory. In many cases, however, there is no way to distinguish Sufi poetry from its secular, courtly counterpart. The difference is found not in the content but in the reading strategy one employs to interpret it.[4]

With notable exceptions in the verse of Rab'ia (eighth century), Mansur al-Hallah (tenth century), Ibn 'Arabi (thirteenth century), Ibn al-Farid (thirteenth century), and a few others, there is not much extant Sufi verse in Arabic; many of the early writings are lost, partly because the seat of power in the empire later shifted away from Arabia. Sufi poetry, however, flourished in Farsi, the language of ancient Persia (and modern Iran). Persian Sufi poetry was also styled after courtly models. The Sufi depictions of the Beloved (God) in Persian verse, for instance, were modeled on the ideal of youthful, masculine beauty that poets in the Turco-Iranian courts used in their poetry. The virtues Sufi poets extolled thus included "a moonlike face, skill at polo, long locks of hair, the beginnings of a moustache, a tall and slender stature, and cruel indifference to the sufferings of the lover."[5] This male model of love was homoerotic only insofar as it was a convention taken from the courtly life, which was known to be highly tolerant of homosexuality. The Sufis, like other pious Muslims, would have strongly disapproved of actual homosexuality, and they consequently used the image for its shock value, that is, for its ability to awaken readers out of their religious complacency. The persistent use of such imagery in so much Sufi poetry, nevertheless, strongly invites Queer and Freudian readings.

The Persian Sufi tradition includes many notable poets too numerous to mention; the corpus is large and represents a literary golden age. Among these are cherished writers such as Ghazali, Baqli, Saadi, Attar, and Hafiz. The one figure who stands above all of the Persian Sufis, however, is Jalal al-Din Rumi (1207–1273 CE). A traditional Muslim scholar and theologian, Rumi underwent some kind of radical transformation at the age of thirty-eight, when he met the Sufi master Shams-i Tabriz, whose presence inspired him to compose some of the most beautiful poetry ever written. After Shams introduced him to *sama*, the practice of responding meditatively to music through movement, Rumi began creating poetry in an output that was truly enormous: his *Divan-*

i Shams-i Tabriz (forty thousand verses) and *Masnavi* (twenty five thousand verses) represent the largest corpus of lyrical poetry in all of Persian literature.[6] His poetry is in verse form a mapping of the Sufi path, which ultimately involves finding God's love but not before passing through several phases of psycho-spiritual development. These include, among others, self-annihilation and the realization that one's independent existence is the barrier that stands in the way of divine ecstasy. Despite the religious content of his poetry, Rumi was by no means a heavy-handed Muslim who wrote verse simply to advance a Sufi theological agenda. No doubt, his verse reached a kind of scriptural status among Persians, and his *Masnavi* is sometimes called the "Koran in Persian."[7] His mastery of language, nevertheless, marks him as a gifted writer on par with Cervantes, Shakespeare, Tagore, Dickinson, and other greats.

What is more, Rumi's poetry was born out of ecstatic technique. Even before his time, Sufis had begun to move their bodies during mystical, musical performances (*sama*). These spontaneous movements, probably something like ecstatic dancing, were distinguished from ordinary dancing in the Sufi manuals.[8] Although in Rumi's time the subject had become something of a controversy, the great poet not only ecstatically moved but whirled in wild ecstasy. Many of his poems were born out of a practice Shams taught him—his famous whirling, which he would do sometimes for many hours. According to one story, though probably hagiographical exaggeration, he once whirled for forty hours. Regardless of the probable overstatement, it is well known that Rumi composed many of his poems while whirling himself into a state of ecstasy and then reciting inspired lines to a nearby scribe who wrote them down. Many of the poems in the *Divan-i Shams-i Tabriz* bear the marks of this method of ecstatic composition, for they read at times like unconnected lists of images and ideas. No doubt, such poems invite the reader to make deeper, less obvious connections, as scholars have maintained, but their "unfinished" state suggests they were born out of musical inspiration accompanied by movement. After Rumi's death in 1273, his son established the Mevlevi Order of Whirling Dervishes, which is today the most famous of the hundreds of various Sufi groups still in existence.

Nahuatl

Another, perhaps more compelling, example of an ecstatic poetic tradition completely unrelated to the Indo-European poetics of ecstasy is found in pre–Columbian Mexico. Despite the famous Olmec heads that seem to exhibit African racial features and the Aztec myths of the blond-haired, blue-eyed god, Quetzlcoatl, pre–Columbian Mexicans, according to anthropologists, had no significant contact with other cultures in which ecstatic poetry is found. And yet, in the Nahuatl language (a kind of lingua franca spoken by the Toltecs, the Aztecs, and earlier groups) there was a rich, vibrant tradition of poetry written in the ecstatic spirit.

This verse proved troublesome to the Spanish Friars who first encountered and then transcribed Nahuatl poetry. Some of their accounts are thoroughly in keeping with what Barbara Ehrenreich says is the characteristic Western demonization of ecstatic religions. Here is one such example from Bernardino de Sahagun:

> The Devil has provided himself here on earth with a thick wood full of pitfalls, there to hide and prepare his plans in secret as do wild beasts and poisonous snakes. This wood and these pitfalls are the songs he has inspired for his service ... which are sung without being understood except by those who have knowledge of this kind of language. The result is that they sing whatever he chooses, war or peace, praise for the Devil or contempt for Christ, and no one else can understand them.[9]

What in Nahuatl poetry accounts for the these Christian responses? Ecstatic spirituality, of course. The ecstatic tone and *ekstatic* content of Nahuatl poetry caused Sahagun significant distress, as he attributed its inspiration to the Devil and used for its description characteristically Christian images of transgression—the "thick wood" full of "wild beasts and poisonous snakes"—that is, he likens it to a dark wilderness and attributes to it animal traits, both of which Christianity positioned itself against. To be fair to the Friars who transcribed Nahuatl poetry and thus preserved it from the ravages of European greed and bloodlust, it is important to note that not all such accounts are so negative. Another Friar, Diego Duran, took a completely different view of Nahuatl verse. In his estimation Nahuatl poems at first "...seemed to me nonsense. Yet, afterward, when talking about them and discussing them, I have found them to make wonderful sense."[10] Appearing strange at first, no doubt because of their non–European packaging, the poems later revealed to the Friar the ecstatic foundation of his own religion.

Much like the verse found in so many ancient ecstatic traditions around the world, Nahuatl poetry was not concerned with secular matters and was thus intimately connected to the spiritual lives of pre–Columbian Mexicans. Written by poet-kings who believed poets were "spokesmen of the gods" and their verse a divine "revelation," such poetry "was both a panegyric and an aid to truth and goodness," according to Irene Nicholson.[11] The poet-kings had no conception of writing poetry for its own sake, and they "knew nothing of 'esthetic' theories that put emphasis on mere beauty."[12] To the contrary, their verse had a truly ecstatic function in serving as a means to teach a doctrine of self-transformation. The Nahuatl poets believed that human beings are born with a physical heart and face, but to become fully oneself it is necessary to fashion "another heart and another face which are more enduring."[13] In doing so the individual ecstatically transforms and attains a stamp of uniqueness and spiritual growth not unlike what G.M. Hopkins called "selving" and Jung termed "individuation." It is important to point out that not all Nahuatl poets suggest eudaimonic states of being, for there is also in this corpus a body of poems called "sad songs." Yet, even here, in poems seemingly about sorrow, there is an ecstatic element, for the sadness that comes from "a deep realization of man's ignorance in the face of all fundamental questions" is also "very closely bound up with ecstasy and the achievement of at least momentary glimpses of the answer."[14] Ecstasy, for the Nahuatl poets, was the answer to sorrow and the key to the transformation of the human being into something divine.

Non-Western

Still other examples of spontaneously occurring, non–Indo-European forms of ecstatic poetry abound throughout the ancient world. In the eighteenth century Japanese poets composed verse in a genre called *kyoshi*, or "wild poetry," which had literary antecedents in the "madness" of ancient Japanese and Chinese ecstatic verse forms.[15] Some of the earliest extant Chinese poetry consisted of the occult incantations of magicians who spoke magical words after entering altered states.[16] Similar "diviners," who channel a god or spirit through verse and chant for the benefit of someone seeking relief from some kind of problem or affliction, are also found still practicing in countless African cultures.[17] The festivals of the ancient Chinese featured poets singing to music and inspiring dancing and the madness of ecstasy—practices that Confucius would later condemn.[18]

Such ancient practices also still exist in Africa, where poets in the oral tradition use the power of drums and other musical instruments to achieve a hypnotic effect on their audiences.[19] Those who listen to such verse are quite familiar with ecstatic possession, which is still a widespread healing practice found in the religious rites of countless African cultures.[20] The Indo-Aryan tradition of ecstatic "wandering" poets who sang rhapsodic verse, certainly exerted influence throughout the Mediterranean, Central Asia, East Asia and the Indian subcontinent,[21] but all signs indicate that it is part of a universal ecstatic tradition found across the ancient world.

Jerome Rothenberg's landmark anthology, *Technicians of the Sacred*, attests to the existence of such a tradition. A brilliant compilation, Rothenberg's anthology features poetry written by "shaman-poets" whose sacred "techniques" enabled them to enter trance states and then sing songs inspired by the gods or alternative states of consciousness. Rothenberg identifies six characteristics of such highly complex, "primitive" poetry, by which he means verse found in oral traditions among non-literate peoples: (1) Such verse is composed to be spoken, chanted, or sung, and (2) it is characterized by an advanced degree of "image-thinking," as opposed to Aristotelian logic. (3) Such verse requires an active spectator who completes the poem through his or her response, and (4) it is thus not entirely bound by "verbal maneuvers." In other words, the effect of the poetry is achieved through a total performance involving words but also singing, intonation, visuals signs, movements, and facial expressions, all of which induce a response in the listener, who "completes" the poem. (5) Such verse has a physical basis in the human body or in an act of body and mind together, and it often openly suggests sexual imagery as a key factor in the creation of the sacred. (6) Such verse is composed by a poet who is at once shaman and artist, and who operates in a "visionary" situation prior to all "system-making," that is, exoteric religious forms.[22] This kind of poetics of ecstasy, with its accompanying verse celebrating the good life and configuring a variety of positive emotions and states of being, can be found throughout the pre–Columbian Americas as well as the myriad cultures of Asia, Africa and Oceania in the earliest oral poetry. It is truly a global tradition, not only confined to cultures influenced by the Indo-Europeans.

The Modern Era

In his famous work *The Birth of Tragedy,* Nietzsche lamented the moment in history when the Greeks eliminated the chorus from their tragedies, because it signaled to him the loss of the Dionysian principle that provided the theatre with its initial, fiery impetus.[23] Theatre, and by extrapolation much of later Western literature, became more Apollonian—that is, cooler, more rational, less exuberant, less vital, more cerebral, less ecstatic. As I discussed earlier, in addition to the theatre, other genres also underwent an Apollonian cooling, the legacy of which can still be felt in chilly winds that blow across the Western literary landscape. Despite that the four cornerstones in the foundation of Western literature—the Hebrew Bible, the Homeric texts, early Greek lyrics, and Greek drama—are entirely ecstatic in their origins, the West has produced a canon of works written primarily, but by no means exclusively, in the Apollonian spirit. Over the centuries, Westerners have come to associate literature not with the shaman-poet whose ecstatic words inspire dancing and rapture but with the brainy, mildly melancholic and/or angst-ridden, somewhat pessimistic writer who labors at his or her desk in a state of calm, introspective reflection to produce a written text.

The all-pervasive, anti-ecstatic spirit that informs the Western canon is in many ways the result of monotheism and its antagonism toward the ecstatic pagan cults, a point I will explore more fully in the Chapter 10. Another primary cause is the widespread embrace of Platonic rationalism, which reached its anti-ecstatic zenith in the eighteenth century during the great age of reason. In the spirit of Plato, Enlightenment thinkers privileged reason to such an extent that they feared and actually positioned themselves hostilely against the non-rational forces in the human psyche.

A compelling example of this hostility is seen in the eighteenth century in Italy, where Enlightenment thinking found itself pitted directly against the poetics of ecstasy. In addition to the rationalists, there was in eighteenth-century Italy a tradition of poets who performed orally in an extemporaneous manner and sang their verse to the accompaniment of a guitar or harpsichord.[24] A description by Fabi Montani of one such poet, Francesco Gianni, suggests a poetics of possession. Montani marveled at the flush that would come to [Gianni's] face and the fire in his eyes, the wild looks, the ruffled hair...." In such moments the poet would appear "in the grips of some divine force similar to that which overpowered the pythoness in the scene which Virgil has described for us...."[25] Another description of Bartolemeo Lorenzi by Silvia Curtoni Verza also captures the ecstatic nature of such performances: "[A]fter a few verses, his imagination takes fire, the voice becomes steady and resounding ... [and fills] the spectators with incredible ecstasy."[26] Though such poetry was widely admired in Italy during the age of reason, critics also frequently found fault with it on Platonic grounds, arguing against its lack of rational coherence and its *possessive* nature.

One highly successful poet, Metastasio, was actually induced to stop engaging in these kinds of performances, despite that he had won national acclaim while still very young as a result of doing so. In a letter to a friend he describes how his teacher, Gravina, compelled him to curb his ecstatic enthusiasm.

> [During these performances] my head would become feverish and my countenance flushed to a degree that was incredible.... For this reason Gravina decided to use all his teacher's authority in enforcing upon me a rigorous abstention from improvisation in the future—a prohibition which from the age of sixteen I have always scrupulously observed and to which, I am convinced, I owe what little of rational clarity and logical coherence is to be found in my writings. For, upon mature reflection ... I have become fully persuaded that the mind condemned to perform in such bold, unpremeditated fashion must of necessity take on a habit of thought that is diametrically opposed to reason.[27]

The eighteenth-century distrust of emotions and their spontaneous expression is traceable to the Greek suspicion of poetic passion that Plato so carefully articulated and then inspired countless later thinkers to adopt. Such psychologically imbalanced privileging of reason has also had a lasting impact on works of literature written after the eighteenth century.

Yet, for all of this suspicion and antagonism, the ecstatic tradition never died; it generally went underground, in the form of repression, from the time of Plato onward. In psychological repression, however, it is impossible to truly divorce oneself from psychic contents. The repressed energies may be tucked away at a safe distance, but they will always remain part of the psyche. In many cases they will serve as a compensatory other, so psychic homeostasis can be maintained. An example of this is found in the coexistence, during the eighteenth-century age of reason, of staid, orderly, unemotional, and symmetrical neoclassical art forms with other compensatory aesthetic ideals, such as the gothic, the sentimental, and the sublime. These other forms seemed to balance the eighteenth century's Platonic distrust of non-rational states of being. While the sentimental privileged feeling and the gothic offered bizarre states of consciousness, the sublime called for a "melting and elevating" of the self—a movement upward and outward beyond one's normal bounds.[28] These other aesthetics served as a stand-in for repressed ecstatic energies and compensated for the eighteenth century's psychological imbalance.

In other cases repressed energies will erupt and cause massive, psychic upheaval, as in the case of Romanticism, which began in the age of reason but ultimately served as its most forceful challenge. All three of the aforementioned compensatory aesthetics combined in Romanticism, which not coincidentally elevated the lyric the Greeks and Romans devalued to new, ecstatic heights. The Romantic aesthetic was characterized by a privileging of emotion, a return to the physical body and nature, a new appropriation of pagan imagery, spontaneity, unconscious motivation, love, eroticism, unusual states of mind, and a kind of secularized spirituality that valued consciousness transformation over belief.[29] Romantic theories of writing, moreover, called for a poetics of ecstasy, which can be seen in the most central symbol of the period—the Aeolian harp. Many Romantics believed this wind harp served as a fitting symbol of the poet as a divine instrument blown upon by the higher winds of the godlike imagination. In this sense Romanticism was an eruption of repressed, Dionysian energies. Other major ecstatic eruptions have occurred in American Transcendentalism, Beat poetry, 1960's countercultural verse, and Caribbean dub poetry. In addition to these larger movements, there are also countless individual writers who have tended the ecstatic flame, keeping it alive throughout the centuries of Western literary tradition.

As I discussed earlier, historicism cannot fully account for the existence of the ecstatic poetic tradition. There are clearly traceable influences of the Indo European poetics of ecstasy on several cultures, but as I have shown, ecstatic poetry seems to occur naturally and can be found ubiquitously across the globe. Another way to account for the persistence of such poetry, therefore, is to view it a means by which cultures all over the globe have been able to gratify the need for the eudaimonic aspects of psychological experience. Based on the foregoing discussion, it should be clear that ecstatic states are not reserved for the select few. To the contrary, any poet can experience a moment of ecstasy, or any other affective state of being for that matter, and then attempt to suggest its spirit by (re)constructing it in verse form. Poets who are not known to be particularly rhapsodic, therefore, can write ecstatic poetry. Emily Dickinson, for instance, known principally (but perhaps stereotypically) for her brooding poems about death, covered the full range of human experiences in her poems, not least of which are several dozen that depict ecstatic states of being. Several other poets similarly not known primarily as ecstatic writers have also left us with a wealth of verse in which eudaimonic states and emotions are configured. Some of these writers find representation in *Wild Poets of Ecstasy: An Anthology of Ecstatic Verse*,[30] a collection I edited principally for the purpose of demonstrating the enduring existence of a global ecstatic tradition.

A Note on the Following Studies

A principal source of inspiration for the following studies in Willis Barnstone's important work, *The Poetics of Ecstasy: Varieties of Ekstasis from Sappho to Borges*,[31] an erudite examination of *ekstasis* in its negative, positive, and neutral varieties in secular and religious literature. Barnstone discusses not only mystical transport and gnosis in Christian writers, but also the "negative" ecstasies of love in Sappho, fury in Lope de Vega and Edgar Lee Masters, and crime in Melville and Camus, as well as the more affectively neutral ecstasies of movement in Dante and memory in Constantine Cavafy. The obvious difference between Barnstone's studies and mine in the following section is that I have chosen to focus on the eudaimonic aspects of *ekstasis* that carry charges of positive affect and beneficial transformation. Published in 1983, Barstone's study saw print long before the eudaimonic turn (which I shall discuss in the final chapter of this volume) transformed many academic fields, including literary studies. A focus on eudaimonic ecstasy is justified, therefore, because there is much to be explored in discussions of its eudaimonic dimensions.

Another source of inspiration for the following studies lies in the work of James Miller, Karl Shapiro, and Bernice Slote, whose fifty-year-old landmark study, *Start with the Sun: Studies in the Whitman Tradition*, I discovered while writing my first book, a critical analysis of mystical language in Wordsworth and Whitman.[32] Miller, Shapiro, and Slote identified in their study the development of two general strands in the American poetic tradition: (1) The "New Puritanism," as they called it, is a kind of "rigorously honed intellectualism in which the old worship of the soul has been replaced by the worship of the mind," and with "the same sort of exile ... imposed on the body."[33] Writers in this tradition, which includes Eliot, Pound, Stevens, Robert Lowell, and others, have sacrificed "the song, the incantation, the magic, the passion of poetry" to "metrical essay, analysis, and exposition."[34] Their voice, moreover, is principally one of despair, fragmentation, alienation, angst, inescapable self-consciousness, and melancholy. (2) The other tradition, which Miller, Shapiro, and Slote trace back to Whitman, the Dionysian bard at its center, is a kind of "New Paganism" because it is characterized by a "pagan joy and wonder in the natural world," as well as an affirmation of the goodness of life, the holistic integration of emotion and reason, and a celebration of the body and the soul on an equal footing.[35] While the New Puritanism has come to occupy a position in high culture, so, too, has the New Paganism, which includes not only Whitman but Crane, Thomas, Lindsay, Sandburg, Williams, Roethke, and others.[36] Such a tradition demonstrates that sophisticated literature can also be about well-being.

This second tradition Miller, Shapiro, and Slote identified in American literature is, in effect, an expression of a much larger, global tradition: the "New Paganism" is a manifestation of the ancient poetry of ecstasy, which has persisted well into the twenty-first century around the world in various permutations. The persistence of such verse is seen in the widespread contemporary consumption of the older ecstatic bards—Rumi, Hafiz, Mirabai, and other poets; in the popular, fiery, spoken-word movement; in contemporary native American poetry with its insistence on "balance, reconciliation, and healing," as well as "growth and rich survival"[37]; in the countless poets who write in the Hindu, Buddhist, Sufi, Jewish, Christian, and other religious traditions; and in the work of Wendell Barry, Jane Hirshfield, Sharon Olds, Mary Oliver, and many other highly celebrated, living bards. It is also found ubiquitously around the globe whenever a poet, regardless of his or her general temperament, writes about the transformative value of intense eudaimonic experience.

It is also necessary to acknowledge Leslie Fiedler's ideas about "ecstatics" as a preferred alternative to more "academic" reading strategies. In 1970 during an address at the convention of the College English Association, Fiedler claimed the end of reading (and all art, for that matter) is not the type of sophisticated analyses in which most students of serious literature engage but the emotional response of ecstasy aroused by both canonical and popular literature. In this perspective the value of literature is found in "[...] the temporary release from the limits of rationality, the boundaries of the ego, the burden of consciousness..."[38] that affectively charged works effect in responding readers. While some critics might see such a critical approach as a mere pre-critical response that lacks rigor and sanctions an anything-goes kind of subjective reaction—and I acknowledge the shortcomings of the idea as Fiedler stated it—I suggest "ecstatics" anticipated the rise of reader response criticism. In the following study I try to honor Fiedler's ideas by analyzing the aesthetics of ecstasy found in the work of six major poets, but I do so by reconstructing the implied ecstatic response in the works in question. In employing such an approach I hope to illuminate the complexities of such responses and defend Fiedler against the charge that he was merely advocating a kind of sophomoric response to the affective dimensions of literary texts. Given the rather sophisticated work Charles Altieri has done on the affects, a topic I will discuss more fully in Chapter 11, it seems there is considerable complexity and twenty-first century relevance in Fiedler's ideas.

A Typology

So what is meant by the term "ecstatic" poetry? So far in this study I have discussed the nature of ecstatic experiences and provided a historical outline of the ecstatic literary tradition. In doing so I have characterized ecstatic verse but only implicitly. Let me close this chapter, then, with an explicit typology, extrapolated from my years of researching and teaching ecstatic verse, in the form of twenty characteristics. When I use the term *ecstatic poetry* I am referring to verse that configures

1. peak experiences, spiritual "illuminations," and ecstasies
2. moments of growth and clarity, epiphanies, and consciousness expansion
3. the life force, the inherent will-to-health, the desire for constructive change, the cultivation of potential, and well-being—in short, eudaimonia
4. intense positive affect, such as bliss, overpowering joy, intense happiness, awe, rapture, love, and the like, often in images of intoxication
5. "sober" positive emotions and states of being, such as gratitude, wonder, hope, serenity, peace, and contentment
6. a positive and optimistic *weltanschauung* but in sophisticated, mature ways that eschew naïve, misguided thinking and neurotically avoidant coping strategies
7. a turning away, in healthy and constructive ways, from the negative through psychologically mature defense mechanisms
8. an affirmation of the interconnectedness of all life

9. an affirmation of humankind's rootedness in the physical body and the joys of eroticism
10. a delight in the abundance and goodness of the natural world and its flora and fauna
11. a conception of the self that suggests unconscious depths
12. a holistic incorporation of sundered aspects of the psyche; a wholeness overcoming fragmentation
13. a replication in form or content of the "trance" states, or poetics of ecstasy, out of which it is born
14. an implied, sympathetic response from the reader and thus a formal invitation to eudaimonic experience
15. a positive orientation toward the sacred in various manifestations and generally, though not always, opposition to exoteric or legalistic religious ideas and practices
16. images that suggest and can even lead to speaking, chanting, incantation, music, and/or singing
17. images that suggest and can even lead to dance and movement
18. images of flight and outward movement, transport, soaring—the winged life
19. a celebration of festivities and hilarity
20. formal complexities that rival those found in the poetry of pessimism and despair

Of course, not all of these characteristics are ever found in one poem, but by and large they underpin, in their entirety, the ecstatic poetic tradition. To be sure, all typologies are reductive and represent generalizations of the subjects they are supposed to illuminate. This is merely a functional typology subject to deconstruction or, at the least, revision based on future research. I offer it here because it proves problematic and in many ways misguided to treat poems as ecstatic experiences, for they are actually (re)creations of experiences that are similar to ecstasies. To assess the eudaimonic effects of experiences as they are configured in such poetry is impossible, so instead I will simply appeal to the elements in this typology and highlight the eudaimonic implications of the ecstatic poetry I engage in the following studies. In other words the ecstatic experience, as I previously defined it, manifests in ecstatic poetry in the aforementioned, typological terms.

5. The Whirling Dervish: Rumi

They whirl and whirl and whirl, spinning in a counter-clockwise direction on invisible axes as their white *tannuras* rise and fall like gentle cresting waves. With heads slightly tilted, they hold their right hands to the sky and their left hands down to the earth, and their enraptured faces bespeak a sublime ecstasy in which the self is transcended and becomes something mysteriously beyond itself. As they spin in a dance that replicates the rotation of sub-atomic particles around a nucleus and the orbits of celestial bodies, the whirling dervishes of the famous Mevlevi order have for nearly eight centuries engaged in the ceremony known as *sama*, the symbolism of which suggests the progress of the soul as it strives for the realization of God's unity. Signifying musical audition or movement to music, *sama* was practiced in different varieties as early as the 800s in Bhagdad. The version the Mevlevi order adopted was inspired by Shams-i Tabriz, the mysterious teacher of the greatest poet of medieval Persia—Jalal al-Din Rumi.

At the age of 37, Rumi met Shams, a strange, itinerant holy man whose iconoclasm and esoteric ideas forever changed him. When he met Shams, whose name means "the sun," Rumi was a well-respected Muslim scholar and teacher of a Sufi order he inherited from his father. But six months in dialogue with Shams, who also purportedly taught him ecstatic practices involving whirling to music, gazing, fasting, and breath manipulation,[1] resulted in "a gushing torrent of words that pour forth from him as poetry."[2]

Until the end of his life, Rumi taught, whirled, and wrote, generating a prodigious body of verse, the total output of which represents more than that of Dante, Shakespeare, Milton, or Homer,[3] all of whom he has also roundly outsold in America in the last two decades. While Pulitzer Prize–winning poets do well if they sell 10,000 volumes, translations of Rumi sold 250,000 in 1994 alone, a level of success prompting an article on the Rumi phenomenon in *Publishers Weekly*.[4] Part of Rumi's success in America is due to previous Sufis whose mission was to promote Sufism in the West. Individuals such as Rene Guenon, George Gurdjieff, Hazrat Inayat Khan, and Indries Shah have collectively sold tens of millions of books on various versions of Sufism streamlined for the West. By the time he passed away in 1996, Indries Shah, whose works had been translated into several Western languages, had sold 15 million copies alone.[5]

The more immediate catalyst of Rumi's success in recent years, however, is Coleman Barks's "translations," or poetic renderings of existing scholarly translations. No doubt beautiful, Barks's Rumi poems are something like second generation copies, as he himself admits he does not read Farsi or Arabic, the languages in which Rumi wrote. Instead, he works with those who do so in order to render updated "versions" of the original poems. The result is a kind of gnostic Rumi, as Barks himself calls it, in some ways divorced from his Islamic context. Critics have found fault with such a version, arguing that it is necessary to preserve and to understand Rumi's religious affiliation in order to honor him as a poet. Thierry Zarcone, for instance, has complained that reading Rumi out of his context and adopting Barks's version of Sufism are tantamount to reading Meister Eckhart and converting to Christianity without ever having read the Gospels.[6]

While the point is well taken, it is important to note that Rumi in other, more scholarly, versions that I will make use of in the present chapter also speaks universal themes and voices widely shared, human concerns. In other words Coleman Barks should not be faulted with repackaging Rumi as a non–Islamic poet; the "fault" lies with the poet himself, for Rumi's spirituality contains ideas that transcend the doctrines of Islam even loosely defined. For this reason, Muslims, Christians, Jews, and Zoroastrians attended his talks and *sama* ceremonies, and followers of several faiths honored him at his funeral. As Ben Jonson famously said of Shakespeare, Rumi is "not of an age, but for all time."

What, in particular, is responsible for such an appeal? I suggest it lies in the call to human well-being that he configures in his verse. In so many of his poems Rumi invites readers to participate in psychological growth, to become aware of unconscious depths, to recall projections, to free themselves from negative and harmful thought patterns, to achieve inner peace, to co-exist peaceably in a human world, to sever growth-stymieing attachments, and to be immersed in the joys of ecstasy in all of its affectively positive manifestations. Because Rumi's verse and the construct of well-being are both far too large to treat fully in one chapter, it is necessary to focus on two particularly important aspects of the call to well-being as it appears in his ecstatic poetry—*vairag*, or non-attachment, and love—both of which are found throughout his six volume epic, *The Masnavi*, and the many lyric poems in the collection entitled *The Divan of Shams-i Tabriz*. Both themes are not only important elements in human flourishing but also intimately connected to the question of literary form, particularly the aesthetics of ecstasy.

Vairag, or Nonattachment

Hazrat Inayat Khan, an Indian Sufi who took initiation in three different orders before eventually founding the ecumenical International Sufi Movement, articulated a complex concept—*vairag*—that serves as a foundational idea in Sufism and appears throughout Rumi's *Masnavi*. A Sanskrit word literally meaning to be desiccated and without color, *vairagya* came to signify in India a drying up of the passions that bind one to material existence and thus prevent spiritual liberation. Khan discusses it in terms of unraveling the knots that ensnare human beings in the web of *maya*, the illusion of the physical world. He calls a person who has achieved such a state a "vairagi," or one who "may still be interested in all things of this life, but is not bound to them."[7] As an ideal, *vairag* is commonly mistaken and even mistranslated as indifference or detachment, but such definitions fall short of capturing the nuances of the term. The *vairagi*, in other words, is fully engaged in the world but also has the wisdom not to hold too fixedly to anything, whether it be a conception of truth, a feeling, a person, a value, an experience, or an object. William Blake's poem, "Eternity," succinctly captures the idea:

> He who binds to himself a joy
> Does the winged life destroy;
> But he who kisses the joy as it flies
> Lives in eternity's sun rise.[8]

The implication here is that holding too fixedly to a joy somehow mars it and prevents one from being able to appreciate it in its totality.

Sufis thoroughly embrace the idea of non-attachment and extend its truth to every aspect of human existence. Sometimes, particularly in early literature, the idea was taken to an almost untenable extreme. Domestic life and its many cares, for instance, were often depicted as barriers to spiritual liberation. Annemarie Schimmel, one of the premier scholars of Sufism, has noted the difficulty of finding approval of happy family life in much Sufi literature.[9] Khan and later Sufis, however, were careful to correct this idea, which they felt was a warped misinterpretation of the truth. For them, *vairag* is not a charge to live a dried up, colorless, loveless existence in which one is detached from all affect and resists deriving meaning from anything most individuals find valuable, such as love and connections to other people. In Khan's understanding of the concept, *vairag* signifies a full immersion in life—he was married and had children, much like Rumi—*and* a simultaneous consciousness of the fleeting, transitory nature of all things, including joys and even our greatest loves. In other words, he taught the necessity of kissing the joy as it flies.

Rumi never articulates *vairag* or any corresponding Persian concept in his *Masnavi*, but he strongly and repeatedly implies it throughout the narrative.

In fact, it is his unspoken but *central* concern. His esoteric narrative method suggests that *vairag* is one of the principal ideas linking all of the digressive stories in his great epic. To convey Sufi concepts, Rumi employed in the *Masnavi* an allegorical narrative strategy and adopted many of the symbols that were commonly used by Sufi writers. It is well known, for instance, that Rumi was deeply influenced by Attar's *Conference of the Birds*, a highly symbolic allegory of the soul's progress on the Sufi path. Such symbols, many of which were secular in nature and wholly violated the spirit of Sufism, required a nonliteral interpretation, as I previously discussed. Because Arabic and Persian Sufi poets took their subject matter from the decadent courtly writers who extolled the virtues of wine, illicit sex, physical beauty, pride, gold, the glories of warfare, and the like,[10] it was necessary for Sufis to distinguish their poetry from secular verse. They did so, however, principally in the interpretive strategies they brought to bear on readings of poetry. In many cases, Sufi verse is indistinguishable from its secular counterpart, the only difference being whether the imagery should be taken literally or allegorically. Given their nearly identical content, Sufi and courtly poetry were sometimes confused. Over time, however, Sufi ideas permeated the verse of secular writers in a circular return. For instance, Omar Khayyam's famous *Rubaiyat*, interestingly the best-selling poem in nineteenth-century England, was often thought to be a Sufi text, while more recent scholars have argued for a secular reading of its *carpe diem* theme. Similarly ambiguous is the poetry of Hafiz, whose "Sufism" may have been more conventional than actual.[11] In both cases the issue remains unresolved. Because of this ambiguity, Sufis before and after Rumi published handbooks in which various symbols were clearly defined in terms of their spiritual connotations and against their literal denotations.[12]

By the time Rumi began writing his verse, a number of symbols and their esoteric meanings were in common circulation among Sufis. Wine, for instance, represented the intoxication of divine love, and the drinking tavern symbolized a Sufi lodge. Lovers were Sufis themselves, while the tavern keeper and the *saqi* (one who pours the wine) could both represent the Sufi master. And there are literally hundreds of such symbols in the many volumes of Sufi verse. Sufi poets employed nearly every profane symbol the courtly writers celebrated, but they did so to advance esoteric ideas that would not be obvious to readers. As the tradition developed, however, such symbols became highly familiar to Sufis, in whose minds they became stock concepts, or reference points, that ultimately served to habituate the spiritual life. Because Sufism is an inner, esoteric spirituality, habituation of ideas is one of the worst "sins" on the path. To let one's concepts ossify in such a way is to replicate adherence to the exoteric religious forms the spirit of Sufism in many ways opposes. Sufis maintain that it is possible to study theology and outwardly observe all manner of religious customs for an entire lifetime but still lack inner, spiritual understanding, as Khan himself pointed out.[13] The ideal of *vairag* represents a freedom from attachment to ideas, even sacred concepts that serve as mental idols to which one bows.

In order to defamiliarize habituated ideas, Rumi repeatedly subverted the conventional meanings of commonly understood symbols. He taught *vairag* not by expounding upon it as a concept, the danger of which is that it would itself harden into a mental idol, but by bringing readers and those who listened to his verse recited at *sama* ceremonies to a direct realization of it. A close reading of one of the *Masnavi's* narrative threads—"How a Hare Killed the Tyrannical Lion"—will demonstrate the existence of such an aesthetics.

When Rumi wrote the *Masnavi*, the lion had become a well-known symbol of the Sufi saint, master, or sheik. Quite naturally, Sufi readers would by necessity bring such an understanding to their reading of the narrative about a lion whose dominating presence in a valley causes all of the lesser animals to run scared, the suggestion of which is the high spiritual attainment of the Sufi master whose presence strikes fear and awe into the hearts of those with lesser development and who lack the heart for self-annihilation. Rumi seemingly adopts the stock image by highlighting the lion's dominance and by attributing cleverness and trickery to the lesser animals, who concoct a scheme in which they daily select a sacrificial member from among themselves to satisfy the carnivore's voracious appetite.

At this early stage in the narrative, the machinations of the lesser animals might suggest to a Sufi reader the tricks the mind plays in preventing one from accepting the wisdom and direction of the master. Rumi reinforces such a reading in the lion's agreement to the arrangement: "... 'Alright, if you're sincere, / But I know every trick, let that be clear!'" (1.908).[14] A debate then opens up among the animals over the question of self-exertion or fate on the spiritual path. The lesser animals are fatalists who reject the role of "spiritual effort" and resign themselves to God's decrees, while the lion argues for the virtues of "self-exertion," that is, all of the activities in which Sufis engage, such as free prayer, whirling, *djikr* (reciting one of the ninety nine names of God), fasting, and the like. Such a debate also characterized discussions among esoteric Sufis and other, more legalistic, exoteric Muslims, the latter arguing for the need to resign oneself to fate, or God's will, and the former insisting on the necessity of self-exertion in the form of the aforementioned practices. The lion acknowledges the point, as any Sufi master would do, but he also adds, "...If trust will guide, okay, / But effort also is the Prophet's way" (1.916). He then quotes an Arab proverb attributed to Mohammed: "Trust God but still make sure your camel's tied!" (1.917). The debate goes back and forth, as the fatalists rebut the lion's position with compelling points, such as "...to end your plight / Annihilate your vision in God's sight" (1.925), as well as other ideas that demonstrate the virtues of resigning oneself to God's fate, a principle that lies at the heart of Islam, the etymology of which means surrender to the will of Allah.

Given the debate, the narrative does not appear to be so straightforward, as both sides seem to offer positions with which most Sufis would agree. The reader's expectations are thoroughly undermined, and it becomes unclear whether the symbol of the lion is functioning in a conventional manner. Towards the end of the debate, however, the lion seems to win the reader over by voicing a more clearly discernible, Sufi perspective. In using another conventional image—sleeping—the lion forcefully counters the compelling points the animals on the other side have previously made: "Through fatalism grace from Him will cease: / Don't doze while travelling, for if you should sleep / You'll miss His gate and court, and then you'll weep!" (1.943–44). Sufis often engaged in wandering, or traveling, which is seen positively as a severing of one's attachments. They also engaged in vigils in which they went without sleep for extended periods so as to awaken to inner spiritual realities. Sleeplessness thus registers positively both at the literal and figurative levels, while sleeping is indicative of spiritual laziness, which is implied in the lesser animals' insistence on fatalism and their opposition to self-exertion. After another rebuttal from the lesser animals and then a brief digression involving Azrael and Solomon, the implications of which clearly point to the superiority of fatalism over exertion, Rumi seems to side with the lion: "This world's a prison, we're locked up inside, / To free yourself dig all the way outside!" (1.986). The lines, which clearly suggest the Gnostic strain in Sufism and the idea that it is necessary to exert oneself to be freed from the trap of the material world, seem to win the argument for the lion. "The fatalists," according to the narrator, "grew tired of this debate; / The fox, the deer, the hare, the jackal too / Stopped answering back, abandoning their view" (1.996–97). Rumi's use of the lion symbol thus *seems* to be in keeping with convention, for although the lesser animals have voiced important insights, the lion has won the argument, as any wise Sufi master would be expected to do, by articulating superior wisdom.

The matter does not end there, however, for as the poet himself quips, "This discourse has no end..." (1.1031). The hare steps forward as the next animal selected for sacrifice to feed the hungry lion, but he concocts a clever scheme in which he will be able to avoid his self-annihilation, a reluctance that seemingly contradicts the Sufi dictum, "Die before ye die," an idea suggesting *ekstatic* self-transcendence as a necessity on the path to spiritual realization. His refusal to surrender himself to the lion also strongly suggests the *nafs*, the stubborn concupiscent self that prevents one's way on the Sufi path. The *nafs* is often symbolized in Sufi literature by the intractable donkey, so it is no coincidence the lion calls the hare an "ass-eared beast" (1.1164), an allusion that would cause Sufi readers to identify with the lion. Given the language the poet uses, Sufi readers would also see the hare's elaborate plot to evade his own self-sacrifice as the intellect's interference with the soul's development. Despite its complexity, there is in Sufi literature a markedly anti-intellectual strain. The image of breaking the inkpots and tearing the books appears throughout much Sufi writing and reinforces a commonly held distrust of intellect.[15] Although the mind can be put to good use in human life, it also ultimately must be surrendered in order to achieve the realization of God's unity. Rumi reinforces the idea of intellect stymieing spiritual progression when he associates it with the "quick-thinking hare" (1.1045) and his elaborate plot. More to the point, at the end of the description of the hare's plot, the poet reflects on a central Sufi idea about the mind:

> The intellect repeats what Gabriel said:
>   Prophet, I'll burn if I should move ahead!
> But you can still proceed towards the goal,
>   I've reached my limit, Sultan of the Soul [1.1074–75].

Much like Virgil, who, as a symbol of reason in *The Divine Comedy*, can only lead Dante to a point in purgatory and must then surrender to Beatrice, or love, Rumi is here pointing out the limitations of reason, which must yield to love if the soul is to make it back to God.[16] The hare and his plot are strongly suggestive of the negative or thwarting aspects of intellect. To reinforce the point even further, the poet draws a comparison to a fly, perched on a straw and floating in "donkey's urine" (1.1090), who thinks he is commanding a boat on a great ocean. "Narrow interpreters are like this fly," the poet declares, but "If you stop reading from your own small view, / The phoenix will grant kingdoms then to you!" (1.1096–97).

This last quotation, despite its association with the hare's plot, also marks a turning point in the narrative and serves as a subtle suggestion that readers might want to reconsider how they are interpreting the ideas the poet is exploring. Rumi interpolates a story involving Solomon and his birds, the thrust of which is that a Hoopoe—in Attar's allegory the Hoopoe represents the Sufi master—asserts his worth by claiming the ability to discern the presence of wells beneath the land, while a jealous crow, a stock Sufi symbol of the common man, insists the Hoopoe is engaging in self-praise, a Sufi transgression, and thus proving himself false. The ensuing discussion between the crow and the Hoopoe, as well as the poet's interpolated comments, are all centered once again around the question of fate and self-exertion. This time, however, Rumi seems to privilege the fatalist position, as the arguments are more strongly in favor of fate and destiny versus being able, through self-exertion, to see the traps laid before us. A reasonable conclusion at this point would be that the lion was wrong about self-exertion, particularly in light of the poet's comment: "So destiny can block the sun's bright light, / Turn lions into mice because of fright" (1.1264). The successful implementation of the hare's plot suggests as much, for it violates the reader's expectations and calls into doubt many of the lion's seemingly sound ideas. The hare's stratagem is to trick the lion into thinking that he was late for their meeting because he was delayed by another lion that blocks the road and holds another hare captive. He tells the lion that the other lion has pledged to do him harm and encroach on his territory. The hare leads him to a well in which he sees his own reflection. Seeing the image of another menacing lion, he leaps into the well and thus to his own demise. The lesser animals all begin to gather around the hare, "Happy and laughing, wild with ecstasy" (1.1366). In the end, the hare, more than the lion, seems to be a more fitting symbol of the Sufi. Rumi finishes the narrative with some comments on tyranny, not coincidentally the subject of the preceding narrative and seemingly the general point, at least on a superficial level, of the whole story.

Such closure, however, is unsatisfactory and leaves open the question of how to interpret the debate over fate and self-exertion, as well as the tension between the scheming mind and self-annihilation. Both sides in the debate represent cogent positions thoroughly in keeping with Sufi doctrine. Although Rumi seems to side with the fatalist position—if siding with the position is the same as having the hare foil the lion who opposes it—he also consciously seems to undermine himself by creating a hare who argues for fatalism but then quintessentially embodies self-exertion in his clever plot. It is important to note that the hare does not resign himself to fate like the fatalist he claims to be but insightfully frees himself through self-exertion. He embodies the lion's position, while the lion embodies his as a victim of fate. So which is the "correct" position? It seems both at once. A comment the poet makes during the exchange between the crow and the Hoopoe supports the point: "By verbal and non-verbal intimations / Our hearts give thousands of interpretations" (1.1216). The suggestion here is that he wants his readers to transcend simplistic either/or dichotomies and crude binaries that reduce the complexities of esoteric spirituality down to easily discernible truths embodied in recognizable symbols. Dick Davis has observed that Rumi's allegory is highly unstable and "resists interpretation as anything but itself." The result "is a text which simultaneously demands and resists interpretation, which points to meanings that are no sooner summoned up than they are subverted, and which remains stubbornly rooted in the vulgar complexities of untranscended human experience."[17] While such an observation is accurate and even astute, it does not account for *why* Rumi writes in such a way. Rumi's narrative technique is characterized by disorder, digression, and the lack of a *telos*, or final cause,[18] I suggest, because he can never openly state the truth he wants to convey—*vairag*. To do so would be to violate Sufism's guiding esoteric principle, which calls for individuals to achieve their own realizations through a simultaneous resignation to God's fate and a creative self-exertion. This reluctance to state a truth is seen in the Sufi insistence on silence when it comes to articulating the deepest spiritual insights. Rumi reinforces the idea when he has his hare refuse to divulge his plot to the other animals. "Keep your lips sealed," he declares, "don't mention, as a rule, / Your path, your wealth, and your religious school" (1.1051). The signature he placed on many of his lyrics—"Silence" (*Khamush*)—also suggests he cannot ultimately convey in words the truths he wants to impart.

Rumi's self-deconstructing method, then, is not intended merely to demonstrate the emptiness of language—no doubt, this is one of his goals—but rather to lead the reader to a direct realization of the constant need to destroy mental idols and to avoid exoterically relying on a set of fixed ideas and their symbolization in language. He wrote in such a way to bring readers to the realization of *vairag*, not by telling them to sever their attachments to cherished concepts but by forcing them to do so through active, self-exertion. He even hints at the concept of non-attachment through the image of a jar floating on a turbulent ocean:

> That sealed jar in the stormy sea out there
> Floats on the waves because it's full of air,
> When you've the air of dervishhood inside
> You'll float above the world, and there abide [1.991–92].

Here, the symbol seems to resonate positively, as the jar contains the air of the saintly Sufi who has severed his attachments to the world and floats safely on a nonetheless stormy ocean, or the tempest of human life. Such air enables the Sufi to be awash in the storm of life but not be affected by it. True to the concept of *vairag*, and in keeping with his self-deconstructing method, however, the poet undermines the image a few pages later:

> Our forms traverse this lovely ocean fast
> Like cups which on its surface have been cast;
> Until they're full like tubs they float on top
> But once they're filled they finally start to drop,
> Truth's sea is hidden, land is on display,
> Our forms are waves, or just the ocean spray [1.1118–20].

So as to prevent readers from too strongly identifying with the image of a jar on a stormy ocean, and to bring them to a realization of *vairag*, Rumi subverts the symbol in the same way Buddhist monks spend days creating a beautiful sand mandala only to destroy it shortly thereafter in a ceremony symbolizing the impermanence of all things.

In Sufism attachments, particularly to one's conception of self, must be severed if progress is to made on the esoteric path of God realization. *Vairag* is the means by which one is set free from the self, a point Rumi makes as he brings the story of the lion and the hare to a close: "Don't overrate the lion which can kill! / The one who breaks himself is greater still" (1.1398). Rumi's *Masnavi* is a didactic poem on the major themes of esoteric Islamic spirituality, but it is far more than theological ideas dressed as poetry. No doubt, he does preach about many Sufi concepts, foremost among which is the doctrine of ecstatic self-transcendence, but he also imbues his narrative form with a concept he refuses to name but which, nevertheless, is central to the kind of psycho-spiritual development Sufism promises. *Vairag* is his subtext throughout *The Masnavi*. By repeatedly decentering the reader's expectations and undermining interpretive strategies, he inscribes in his aesthetics an important insight about non-attachment and thus teaches the critical concept by bringing Sufis and other readers to their own realization of it.

Despite its esotericism, *vairag* is not for the select few spiritually advanced Sufis who embrace its mystical subtleties. To the contrary, it has a universal appeal and applicability. *Vairag* is implied in the states of flow that Positive psychologists have explored in the last two decades. One of the essential requirements in a state of flow is full immersion and effort accompanied by a simultaneous letting go. *Vairag* is implied in unconditional love, a non-possessive/non-binding form of love that Erich Fromm calls healthy, "mature love."[19] To live in a state of *vairag* is to avoid the trap of reducing the people we love to objects. In letting them *be*, we preserve their subjectivity and also greatly enhance our own. *Vairag* enables us to extract the deepest levels of meaning from various experiences while also avoiding letting such experiences distort the rest of our lives. What is meaningful in college may not be so significant at mid-life and may even prove to be a detriment. The ideal of *vairag* calls for us not to hold too tightly even to our guiding ideas and core values, for these too might serve the end of facilitating our well-being at one stage in our development or in particular contexts but not in others. Of course, there are limits to such an idea, and it can never be embraced absolutely. To do so is to violate the spirit of the concept. The *vairagi* is thus neither a nihilist nor a fundamentalist but someone who holds beliefs and values but not so tightly that he or she is warped by them. Although there are, to my knowledge, no studies of *vairag* in the mainstream psychological literature, its successful realization is a central aspect of human well-being.

Love, the Highest Ecstasy

No doubt, Rumi's universal popularity does not lie in *vairag* alone. I have discussed the idea simply to illustrate one highly complex aspect of the appeal to human well-being as it appears in his aesthetics of ecstasy. Although it is one of his central concerns, *vairag* alone does not have enough sex appeal to titillate the minds of so many readers. What does? Love, of course. Rumi's poetry, perhaps like none ever written, represents a foregrounding of love's power to integrate the psyche. Rumi is the foremost poet of love, which is universally accepted as the premier human value and arguably the most important aspect of human existence.

What is the support for this last assertion? Even Freud, for all of his pathologizing tendencies, admitted the value of love. As I previously noted, he dismissed oceanic experiences as pathological regression, but he also acknowledged love as the one exception to the rule:

> ... [T]owards the outside ... the ego seems to maintain clear and sharp lines of demarcation. There is only one state—admittedly an unusual state, but not one that can be stigmatized as pathological—in which it does not do this. At the height of being in love, the boundary between ego and object threatens to melt away. Against all the evidence of his senses, a man who is in love declares that "I" and "you" are one, and is prepared to behave as if it were a fact.[20]

In the experience of love, subject and object become one. The self's subjectivity is transcended and together with the other's objectivity becomes enmeshed in a mysterious, two-person fusion representing the pinnacle of human experience. Perhaps love is potent a transformative agent because it encompasses all of the positive emotions, a point Barbara Fredrickson makes in her interesting discussion of the subject. "There's a reason love is called a many-splendored thing," she observes. "It's not a single kind of positivity. It's all of the above, encompassing joy, gratitude, serenity, interest, hope, pride, amusement, inspiration, and awe."[21] No doubt, love also encompasses Haidt's "elevation," as well as any other positive emotion yet to be identified by Positive psychologists (and surely there are others not yet investigated). "What transforms these other forms of positivity into love," writes Fredrickson, "is their context. When these good feelings stir our hearts within a safe, often close relationship, we call it love."[22] Surely, there is more to the matter, but Fredrickson's idea is insightful and points to the density and complexity of love.

Erich Fromm observed that love, and only love, can solve the deepest of existential crises. While he recognized, as an answer to the question of existence, the partial value of several activities involving *ekstatic* union, such as orgiastic sexual fusion, conformity/social belongingness, and productive work, Fromm also valued love above anything else as the "most powerful striving in man."[23] He saw love as "the most fundamental passion," or the "force which keeps the human race together, the clan, the family, the society," and he argued that "[t]he failure to achieve it means insanity or destruction—self destruction or the destruction of others."[24] Without love, "humanity could not exist for a day."[25] George Vaillant has similarly argued for the centrality of love in all mammal species. He observes that if a mother hamster's neocortex is removed, she will seem feeble-minded in a maze but "still love and raise her pups" successfully. Yet, if her neocortex is left intact but her limbic system is even slightly damaged, she "can be a wizard at mazes but an utterly incompetent mom."[26] Love, it seems, is hard-wired in the brain. It is the most important experience in the lives of all mammal species. Love is, Vaillant wryly quips, "religion without the side-effects,"[27] which is to say, it carries with it the fullest eudaimonic effects of positive affect, often also the result of religious worship, but without the damaging repercussions caused by so many religious doctrines, such as guilt, conceptions of "original" sin, estrangement from the body, disconnection from nature, detachment from society, and other mind-warping ideas that many of the historical religions have covertly persuaded people to adopt.

Vaillant's quip might apply to exoteric religion, but its applicability to esoteric paths such as Sufism remains in question. The kind of love Rumi foregrounds in his verse transcends religious legalism and dogma of all kinds. Rumi speaks beyond Islamic boundaries and captures the interest of readers across the globe precisely because he does so in the universal language of love. No doubt, he repeatedly quotes from Islamic texts in his verse, and he strongly associates himself with Islam in his writings; scholars have identified roughly six thousand quotations from the Qur'an and the Hadith in his *Masnavi* alone.[28] His ideas about love, however, prove to be problematic to legalistic varieties of the Muslim faith because he does not contain them safely within Islamic confines.[29] Sufism itself has a longstanding, problematic relationship to Islam, for "its mystical wayfarers tread a path that can seem contrary to the outer law," as Llewellyn Vaughan-Lee puts it.[30] In Sufism there is a tradition of "ecstatic utterances" made by love-intoxicated "holy fools," whose ideas, however heretical, are tolerated if not always fully accommodated by legalists.[31]

In so many ways, Sufism represents the opposite pole of rigid legalism and fundamentalism. The compelling proof of such opposition is seen in the Wahhabi hostility to the Sufis in all of the lands in which al-Wahab's puritanical reforms took root. The incompatibility of Muslim legalism and Sufi ideas about love can also be seen in the story of Abu Sa'id Abi'l-Khayr, whose heart is said to have opened and flooded with love when he met a dervish who introduced him to the Sufi sheik, Abu 'l-Fadl Hasan. The next day, while listening to a lecture on the Qur'an, his teacher objected to his highly intoxicated state and ordered him to go back to the sheik because, as he complains, "[i]t is unlawful for you to come from Sufism to this discourse."[32] The story may be more myth than fact, but it clearly illustrates the legalist attitude about intoxication with divine love, which is often seen as being heterodox in the eyes of rigid fundamentalists. Interestingly, Shams seems to have had the same effect on Rumi, whose intoxication with love led to his writing verse but also had other complicating ramifications, as it raised the ire of the poet's younger son and some loyal followers who felt it was inappropriate and even unseemly for their teacher, a highly respected legal scholar, to prostrate himself before a strange, wandering dervish who taught people how to gaze, fast, chant, breathe, and spin their way into the raptures of divine love. The problem here is the universality of love itself, which cannot be contained by any system of thought. Its power can tear asunder any creed, dogma, or set of ideas—especially one's conception of self.

In poem 1759 in the *Divan*[33] Rumi demonstrates love's decentering impact on the psyche in an Islam-transcending way. "Oh, how colorless and formless / I am!" he rhapsodically intones in the opening line (1). Although it may not sound so appealing, colorlessness is a positive image Rumi frequently used to signify a level of reality beyond the physical world and its variegated forms, beyond subject/object dualism, and beyond the strictures of dogma, creed, and ritual. Here, colorlessness also seems to signify the self-emptying that results from a profound experience of love, one in which his sense of identity, even as a Muslim, is transcended. To self-identify as a Muslim or even as a Sufi, according to the poem's logic, is to privilege one possibility but to exclude others. Such a self-identification would bar access to the state of limitless being in which he revels. So the speaker simply leaves open the question of identity and ponders his mysterious subjectivity, a point the poet stresses through the phrase, "I am," which he uses as a refrain throughout the poem, and through oceanic imagery: "My sea has drowned within itself," he exclaims. "What a strange and shoreless sea / I am" (9–10). He also hints at his ecstasy through the image of "annihilation," (23) which causes him to become "inconstant like the moon," (24) as well as through the paradoxical symbol of a "sure-footed, footless runner" (25). The resulting state of being-without-being, the effects of which he attributes to Shams's wisdom and council, represents immense eudaimonic value: "Now," he concludes, "what a wondrous treasure-mine and sea of pearls I am!" (31–32). The closing image implies he is reveling in his *ekstasis*, the power of which enables him to achieve *vairag* and thus to avoid being bound by worldly attachments. "Nothing profits me," consequently, "and nothing harms; / what a wondrous useless-harmless thing / I am!" (12–13). The power of love has resulted in the eudaimonic effects of a peak experience and its attendant positive affect. In some ways this is Rumi's central theme and the central preoccupation of human beings across the planet, whether they realize it or not.

This conception of love, which is paradoxically not a concept at all but a dizzying, rapturous, mind-transcending, affective state, has a universal appeal in part because it is connected to Rumi's ideas on *ekstasis*. "Who Am I?,"[34] another lyric from the *Divan*, embodies the aesthetics of ecstasy *par excellence*. He starts by answering the question with another question: "What can I do my friend, if I do not know? / I am neither Christian nor Jew, nor Muslim nor Hindu. / What can I do? What can I do?" (1–3). The poem represents an exploration of a wholly decentered and emptied subjectivity in which all conventional markers of selfhood are erased, the result of which is puzzlement and a sense of wonder over the mystery of being. The speaker thus claims he is "Not of the East, nor of the West," (4) and he transgresses all of the boundaries held sacred by so many cultures. He belongs to no religion, no locale, and no nation, and he is neither defined by any linguistic affiliation nor by any of the traditionally conceived determinants of human existence. He even locates his subjectivity beyond land and sky, beyond "this world" and even "the next" (15). Using the *via negativa* of the mystics, he first defines himself by what he is not and consequently unties himself from the anchor points that weigh him down. But then, after transcending all of the markers by which human beings define themselves, including duality itself, he positively states that he has "embraced Oneness," the endpoint, or *summum bonum*, of Sufism. But his profound realization of oneness, which the Sufis call *tauhid*, is not simply a philosophical construct existing within a system of sober metaphysics, for he is "Drunk with love," (27) as he puts it. The poem ends on images of "drunkenness and revelry," (28) which represent the cause of his "confusion" over identity and his inability to locate his subjectivity in anything but the oneness implied in the celebratory joys of ecstatic fusion. Rumi's conception of love, as he suggests in this and so many other poems, signifies a transgression of boundaries and a subversive violation of cherished concepts. In a world segregated by divisive ideas, such a perception of *tauhid* is not possible. One cannot attain the highest Sufi truth, in other words, by filtering human experience through a Muslim/other binary. Rumi's understanding of love represents a binding universality that results in a blindness to barriers among all nations, all creeds, and even between self and other. Critics who argue for an expressly "Muslim" Rumi must account for such poems.

To be sure, the symbolism and imagery the poet uses are steeped in the Islamic tradition, but they are also not entirely confined in its enclosure. Poem 463 is a representative case in point.[35] The poet's reference to the moon being split by the "bright orb" (11) of the "Chosen One" (10) is at some level an allusion to the story of Mohammed's ascension into heaven, as Franklin Lewis notes in the helpful editorial apparatus he provides to his fine translations of some of the lyrics. An effect of the ascension was that the Prophet is said to have "cleft the moon asunder." At another level, the poem also suggests the relationship between Rumi and Shams, whom the poet refers to as "the sun in its zenith," (15) using a direct quotation from the Qur'an (93:1). As I mentioned previously, Shams' name etymologically signifies the sun, a symbol Rumi employs repeatedly throughout *The Masnavi*. At still another level, however, the poem, like all complex verse, invites readers to fill in interpretive gaps and to co-create the text in a way that transcends authorial intention and historical context. His use of the moon invites a readerly self-identification, while the sun might symbolize God or one's human beloved, or both at once. The poem is also inviting in other ways. The positive opening imagery—"With each new breath the sound of love surrounds us all from right and left"—hints at some kind of ecstatic technique, perhaps involving breath manipulation or *djikr*, the remembrance of God's name through chanting or recitation, but it also exudes a universal appeal (1). The poet implies the image of a dizzying, upward spiral, a movement perhaps reminiscent of the circling involved in *sama*, and in doing so Mohammed's ascension becomes the readers own rapture.

Rumi also involves the reader in the poem through his use of the first-person plural and by pointing out the direction of movement: "Now up we go, head heavenward."(2). In a further invitation to the reader, he attributes high divine status not only to himself but to anyone who wants to follow him on his dizzying encirclement in the skies: "We are ourselves above the skies a greater host than angels" (5). To be even more direct, he then shifts into the second-person and asks, "why do you turn your sight down from such a sight?" as if anticipating that some of those who accompany him on the journey will look earthward and thus fall short of a full realization of God (16). His enticement of the reader reaches a climax towards the end of the poem when he attributes to human beings not only the power and freedom of flight in the simile of "water-birds ... born within the sea of soul" (17) but also high status, or literally immense value, in another symbol: "...[W]e are all pearls in that sea, afloat on it, or else why wave on wave would surge all through our hearts?" (18). He closes the poem with an extension of the oceanic imagery, as he likens the effect of the great love he is suggesting to the power of an ocean wave washing over a boat, another symbol of human consciousness. "Our ship's ribs staved," he writes, "the boat will sink," the imagery of which suggests divine immersion. As he puts it in the concluding line, "our time has come for reunion, to meet with God" (20). Here, Rumi seemingly undermines the pride the reader might feel in being likened to precious pearls, free-flying waterbirds, and a species of souls greater even than angels. It is important to remember, however, that he is also pointing to the power of love and its call for *ekstatic* self-transcendence. In line 19 the image of waves breaking on the human boats floating on his cosmic sea are also accompanied by another Qur'anic allusion—"Am I not" (7:172)—a reference that nevertheless transcends Islamic boundaries. Love, in any tradition, calls for *vairag* in the form of *ekstatic* self-emptying. Rumi's invitation to the reader through an enticement with love and ecstasy is the means by which his verse transcends Islam and transgresses doctrinal boundaries. His poetry of love represents a universal language, despite its immediate Islamic context.

In poem 2214 Rumi adopts a similar strategy of speaking directly to the reader and thus bolstering his universal appeal.[36] Here, he invites the reader to participate in an intimate moment of "[b]liss ... spent seated on the terrace, me next to you, two forms and two faces with just one soul, me and you" (1). Although biography-minded, literalists will no doubt see in such imagery the relationship between Rumi and Shams, it is beyond doubt that Rumi, a poet with a highly sophisticated understanding of the multiple resonances of words, was wholly aware that his imagery would be interpreted by Muslim and non–Muslim readers alike as an invitation to join him in ecstasy and love. A subtle reference to Iraq and Khorasan later in the poem might suggest the poet intended the "me and you" he repeats throughout to signify himself and Shams, as Lewis points out in his note. Iraq might refer to Tabriz, the city with which Shams was associated, while Khorasan is the province in which Rumi was born.[37] Still, the poem cannot be reduced to the relationship between the two, since its diction and imagery also open up other, more universal planes of signification. One cannot help but to interpret the poet's use of anaphora in the repeated phrase, "me and you," as well as the second-person address in such a trope, as a direct appeal to the reader.

Other images in the poem also support the point. The speaker invites the "you" of the poem first to sit down and share "one soul" (1) with him as they listen to the "[t]he chatter of birds" (2), a symbol of the soul. After they stroll through a garden of roses, an emblem of divine love in Sufism, the poet then calls for the two to eclipse the stars that hang low to look at them by "shin[ing] like the moon" (4), which is to imply that they will receive their light from another, brighter source of luminescence—God. To reinforce his call for *ekstasis*, he erases the lines between the two: "Me and you join, beyond Me, beyond You, in joy, happy, released from delire and delusion" (5). He closes the poem not only on this appealing image of freedom from negative states but also on the pleasing promise of attaining a state of being in which they reach "dimensions where celestial birds suck sugary cubes," (7) and in which they are both "sunk in fields of sugar, me and you" (8). The ecstatic thrust of the poem suggests *vairag*, a sweet, blissful self-dissolution in love, an ego-transcending state in which "me and you," and by implication all of reality, become one. Such a realization of God's unity (*tauhid*) is the desired endpoint of Sufism, a point Rumi well knew and seems to be suggesting in the poem. At another level, however, the invitation to intimacy, bliss, love, and an oceanic experience in which the self is healed through fusion with the other, whether the other is cosmic or more terrestrial, speaks to all human concerns, not simply those of Muslims.

UNESCO and the Universality of Rumi

Given the foregoing discussion, it is important to note that I am not arguing against the valuable scholarship of historicists whose work makes possible a fuller understanding of Rumi's verse. To read Rumi severed from his Islamic roots is to miss important dimensions in his sophisticated body of verse. Still, while the point is well taken, it also does not account for the value of Barks's universal Rumi, one positive effect of which was UNESCO's designation of 2007, the 800th anniversary of the poet's birthday, as the year of Rumi. Without Barks, UNESCO's designation would have been irrelevant and perhaps even galling (given the wounds of September 11) to Westerners who previously knew little of the thirteenth-century, Muslim poet. Because of Barks, the members of UNESCO saw in Sufism a possible means of rapprochement between Islam and the West. Ahmad Jalali, then-president of the General Conference of UNESCO, has pointed out that while Kipling's famous quotation—"Oh, East is East and West is West, and never shall the twain meet"—is widely embraced, Rumi's ideas are productively connective, especially in the realm of religious thought.[38] Although there are modern examples of Sufis turning to militant extremism, as in the cases of the influential Deobandi Madrassa of India[39] and the Madhi movement in the Sudan,[40] Sufis have historically served as an ecumenical voice in Islam. For instance, they were responsible for the great spirit of tolerance that characterized Muslim culture in the sixteenth and seventeenth centuries,[41] a period in history when European Christians were burning witches and threatening other heretics with the stake in an all-pervasive spirit of religious intolerance. As Meir Hatina has demonstrated, the dialogue that emerged between Muslims and Christians at the end of the Ottoman era in Cairo, Rome, and Paris highlighted the inner spirituality of Islam as a means to diffuse Western criticism of Muslim fanaticism. In such dialogue, "Sufism shielded Islam against its assailants and stimulated cross-cultural interaction."[42] UNESCO's decision, therefore, was not the first time people in the political sphere saw in the ecumenical spirit of Sufism a means to bridge the Muslim/Western cultural divide. Barks's universal Rumi, although stripped of much of his Islamic origins, represents immense value for a global exchange of ideas and the recognition of a common humanity at a time sorely in need of cultural rapprochement.

Although Muslim legalists and historicists will no doubt find fault with such an evaluation on the grounds that Barks is transforming Islamic Sufism into a product of capitalist, Western consumption,[43] it is important to remember that Rumi is ultimately responsible for his own universal appeal. Although his poetry "does not contradict basic Quranic concepts," as Omaima Abu-Bakr observes,[44] his ideas on love do extend beyond Islamic borders. After all, he is the poet who wrote of trans-doctrinal oneness in "All Religions Are in Substance One and the Same":

> In the prayers and adorations of righteous men
> Praises of all prophets are together bound.
> All their praises mingle into a single stream,
> As the water from several cups poured in a jug.[45]

As a poet, he was ten percent Muslim and ninety percent *human*, and his international charm is rooted in his intensely human concerns, not solely in his Islamic faith. Regardless of the translation, the psychodynamics he illustrates in his poems are highly eudaimonic and speak to the universal desire to be lost in the joys of love and ecstasy through non-attachment and self-transcendence. However irrelevant such ideas may sound to pessimists and hard-boiled fundamentalists, they are deeply important aspects of human experience and central ingredients in the complex recipe of well-being. In some ways the Rumi phenomenon is a corrective to the privileging of disease, one of the legacies of modernism. Jerome Clinton has argued that the poet's popularity is due to his "earthy, joyous spiritual passion ... [which thus] fills an empty niche in the universe of modern poetry."[46] Annmarie Schimmel, yet another figure responsible for raising awareness of Sufism in the West, has likewise observed that Rumi "is anything but irrelevant, because we find in his work so many guidelines for our own life."[47] Rumi teaches us how to be well in the fullest sense. His poetry is a supreme example of the psychodynamics of well-being.

6. The Power of Imagination: William Wordsworth

He discerned and worshipped a benevolent moral force, the portal to which he located in the natural world, and in doing so he harmonized all seemingly disparate entities. He mystically communed with rocks and trees in a "wise passiveness," and he saw in them "one life," a quasi-spiritual principle that exists as both an immanent and a transcendent force connecting all animal species, all flora, all matter, and all minds in an interlocking whole. He was acutely attuned to the nuances of beauty, the depths of the sublime, the power of the imagination, and the glories of positive affect. He had measureless compassion for the convict, the idiot boy, the forsaken Indian woman, the blind beggar, the female vagrant, the innocent child, and the poor who suffer. As a young boy, he had strange, ecstatic experiences in which he found himself confused by the boundaries of himself and external objects. In such moments he merged with what he saw and reveled in the profound sense of meaning and purpose that resulted from the commingling of self and other. One of the outcomes of such commingling was that, as he later wrote, he could not accept death as a condition by which he was bound. Although he was a star pupil with considerable promise, he could not find a means to explore his strange, subjective states of being in academic discourse, and he thus turned to poetry after an usual moment of clarity in which he claimed to be compelled to do so. The result was seismic in character. He brilliantly used poetic language to explore the mysteries of human subjectivity and to demonstrate the inability of words to capture our deepest sources of being. In writing about his "wild ecstasies," as he later called them, he revolutionized poetic diction, elevated previously marginalized genres to new heights, and left a legacy that has not only profoundly influenced other poets and writers but also informed the critical practices of several interpretive communities. He became Poet Laureate of England not only because of his felicitous words but because he privileged in his verse, perhaps like no one before him in the English language, the most important of all human concerns—love. William Wordsworth, though virtually unknown outside of academe, is the central and most influential figure of Anglophonic Romanticism. Whether one adores or reviles him—and there exists today a whole spectrum of critical positions between these two poles— Wordsworth and the ecstatic dimension of his verse must be acknowledged and studied deeply if one is to understand the scope and influence of the Romantic period and its legacy.

Despite early attackers and their eighteenth-century disapprobation, nineteenth-century readers eventually came to acknowledge the value and influence of Wordsworth's verse. Even Byron, the great iconoclast who ridiculed the whole Lake School, paid his tribute to Wordsworth in Canto III of *Child Harold's Pilgrimage*. After a little prodding from Percy Shelley, Byron eventually wrote in Canto III a series of beautiful stanzas, arguably his best, in the Wordsworthian mode of attuning oneself to the rhythms of the natural world. Other nineteenth-century readers were less ambivalent about their praise of Wordsworth. Many saw eudaimonia in his verse, a means by which they could be well. In his *Autobiography* John Stuart Mill famously recalled reading Wordsworth for the first time during a deep depression:

> ...What made Wordsworth's poems a medicine for my state of mind, [*sic*] was that they expressed, not merely outward beauty, but states of feeling and of thought coloured by feeling, under the excitement of beauty. They seemed to be the very culture of the feelings, which I was in quest of. In them I seemed to draw from a source of inward joy, of sympathetic and imaginative pleasure, which could be shared in by all human beings.[1]

The result was that Mill emerged from his chronic depression and "was never again subject to it," as he claimed.[2] Many early nineteenth-century and later Victorian readers similarly took Wordsworth's complex privileging of joy and other forms of positive affect at face value, seeing in such states a secular means by which they could experience or be taught how to cultivate well-being. These readers saw him as a premier poet of human well-being.

Despite the eudaimonic nature of Wordsworth's poetry, there exists today a forceful school of critics who fault the poet's entire oeuvre as being complicit in various undesirable discourses. In her helpful overview of Wordsworth's reception history, Emma Mason demonstrates that over the last 40 years, critics in this loosely connected ideological school have charged the poet with operating from a patriarchal position, pilfering material from his sister's journals, endorsing a conservative value agenda, privileging bourgeois individualism, betraying the poor for whom he claimed to speak, attempting to escape historical and cultural forces, violating the cause of liberty, and conceiving of the Eastern other in orientalist terms.[3] Critics in the psychoanalytic camp, inspired as they are by Freudian and Lacanian notions of neurosis and the emptiness of subjectivity, have similarly faulted Wordsworth for projecting his unresolved mother complex onto the natural world and sublimating his psychic lack into religious yearnings, the psychodynamics of which are born out of unresolved anxieties, guilt, sexual frustrations, aggression, incestuous wishes, fears, and the like.

Such a demystifying tendency also finds expression in readings of "Tintern Abbey," a somewhat autobiographical poem that will serve as the basis of this chapter. Many contemporary critics have faulted the poem for various reasons: (1) Dorothy's voice is mute, a silence that betokens the subjugation of women in the nineteenth century. He is a sexist. (2) He turns his back on social ills, the French Revolution, and other problems of history in a head-in-the-sand retreat to conservatism. He is an elitist turncoat. (3) Nature is not actual nature but an imaginative creation of it used merely as a backdrop against which he paints an all-too-human portrait. His humanism denies nature and privileges the human species. (4) This portrait is of himself no less, for his version of the sublime is an egotistical one, as Keats famously called it. He is a self-absorbed egotist. (5) His self-preoccupation shows an underlying narcissism that callously ignores the oppressed and the poor who suffer. Despite his stated sympathies, he has no real regard for the disenfranchised. (6) His strong sense of individualism is a quintessential example of bourgeois subjectivity and the impossible desire to divorce oneself from culture and the real determinants of human consciousness—economics and class. He is a champion of false consciousness. (7) The "blessed mood" he discusses is a naïve illusion intended to protect a fragile, underdeveloped ego in need of resolution of various psycho-sexual neuroses. He is a neurotic. (8) The "one life" he sees among all disparate entities is similarly an illusion, a manifestation of a fixation at Lacan's mirror stage of development in which the child projects a false sense of unity onto external entities in a quest to fill his or her lack. He yearns for a wholeness he will never achieve. (9) The poet's certainty about being able to "see into the life of things" is wholly undermined by his admission that it all might be "but a vain belief," clearly the thread that, when pulled, unravels the entire construction, at the heart of which is self-doubt and anxiety. His certainty and faith belie his anxieties and uncertainties. And on it goes.

Let me challenge such suspicious hermeneutics by exploring "Tintern Abbey" in terms of the concept of *ekstasis*. To my knowledge, no one has explored the aesthetics of ecstasy found in Wordsworth's poetry. Christopher Miller comes close in an interesting discussion. Miller rejects epiphany as an appropriate conceptual framework for understanding Wordsworth's "sudden eruptions," or what he also calls "quintessentially lyric moments"[4] of consciousness transformation. In lieu of "epiphany" Miller prefers a term Wordsworth knew and often used—"surprise." Because the epiphany model has so many associations, it "tends to simplify and flatten Wordsworth's poetry" and thus slide into meaninglessness.[5] Miller's ensuing discussion is interesting and complex, as an aesthetics of surprise does seem to be more appropriate than an epiphany model in accounting for smaller moments of consciousness dilation. But what about the larger, pivotal moments—the peak experiences involving radical self-transcendence—in Wordsworth's verse? Here the surprise model itself falters, and, as I will attempt to demonstrate, ecstasy/*ekstasis* serves as a better conceptual framework.

In "Tintern Abbey" Wordsworth writes of his earlier wild ecstasies, the cooling of their fires, and the "abundant recompense" (88)[6] he receives in their stead. Such compensation is the ability to enter, through the exercise of the imagination, more profound states of *ekstasis* consisting not only of joy but also of wonder, awe, gratitude, empathy, transcendence, and love. In his mature years he is repeatedly able, through a kind of meditation involving the imaginative (re)construction of the earlier ecstasies, to experience ecstatic climaxes that lead to happiness, serenity, and resilience, all of which are psychic valuables that prove indispensable in human well-being. Wordsworth's later ecstasies represent a sophisticated response to the natural world, one that overcomes the Cartesian schism, re-orders and integrates consciousness in highly beneficial ways, alleviates depression, and instructs in the complexities of morality and positive emotion. Regardless of the suspicion with which scholars have viewed them, the ecstatic states of consciousness he implies in the poem represent the quintessence of psychological well-being, the human psyche functioning at its absolute best.

The Eudaimonic Value of Ecstasy

At the heart of "Tintern Abbey" is the idea that ecstasies are important not only in the moment when they occur but also downstream through remembrance, or, to be more precise, through imaginative (re)construction. The poem is structured around Wordsworth's return, five years later, to a natural locale that previously filled him with "aching joys" (84), "dizzy raptures" (85), and "wild ecstasies" (138), all of which he experienced through a childlike perspective (although at the time he was twenty three years old). On the previous visit he "bounded o'er the mountains" (68) in the throes of the "courser pleasures of my boyish days" (73) and their "glad animal movements" (74). He so thoroughly immersed himself in the joys of the locale that he possessed no self-consciousness, having ecstatically lost himself in nature, which he revered and loved non-reflectively, almost instinctively and viscerally. The wildness of his natural inebriation occurred to such an intensity as to reach an ecstatic pitch, the result of which was an experience etched on his brain and carrying with it the kind of clarity associated with peak experiences, as Abraham Maslow called them.[7]

More important, this experience sustains him through later, difficult times. He owes to the memory of his ecstasy a "tranquil restoration" (30) of mind that empowers him to overcome weariness, deal with loneliness, and bear "the din /Of towns and cities" (25–26). Such tranquility is the serenity that enables him to dwell at the center of calm in all storms and vicissitudes not in an emotion-denying, Stoical way but in a heartfelt peace that results in emotive connection to other people. This connection makes him a better person and results in perhaps one of the most important outcomes of the experience: "His little, nameless, unremembered acts / Of kindness and of love" (34–35). Although he does not indicate the nature of these acts, they are likely small offers of encouragement to a depressed friend, praise of a child's efforts, selfless gifts to the needy, small labors of service to those one loves, and other tokens of concern and help given out of compassion to our fellow human beings. It is also important to acknowledge the nature of the feelings the poet articulates—feelings "As have no slight or trivial influence / On that best portion of a good man's life" (32–33). Despite the poet's understatement and his use of a double negative, the implication is that the various kinds of affect that result from his admittedly colored memory of his original perception of the scene exert a significant impact on the most significant elements of a good man's life. According to such a reading, the feelings are not idealized fabrications but the result of an ecstatic state that changed the speaker's value system. All of these acts, taken together, constitute a very rewarding life indeed.

The sustenance he derives from his earlier ecstasy extends beyond a merely ethical life informed by right actions, as there is a deeper dimension that follows a trajectory ending in transcendence. He owes to the "beauteous forms" (23) that continue to haunt his imagination "another gift, / Of aspect more sublime" (36–37). This gift, despite his diction, is not sublime but *liminal*. As I previously noted, the etymology of the word sublime, according to James Twitchell, implies going up and out of self but only to a point just below a threshold of complete transcendence.[8] The *liminal* represents the limits of *sublimation*, the boundary beyond which words can no longer signify.[9] The poet, therefore, must always remain on this side of the *liminal* boundary in the subliminal realm. Still, there are times when individuals do cross over, principally through transcendent experiences, and then try to hint at the transport in language. Perhaps because he had no other appropriate term in his lexicon, Wordsworth here uses a term from eighteenth-century aesthetics, but in fact he goes over to the other side, for his gift shuttles him across the boundary between not only self and other but of material reality and the non-material realm. The state of being in question is

> ... that blessed mood,
> In which the heavy and the weary weight
> Of all this unintelligible world,
> Is lightened:—that serene and blessed mood
> In which the affections lead us on,—
> Until, the breath of this corporeal frame
> And even the motion of our human blood
> Almost suspended, we are laid asleep
> In body, and become a living soul:
> While with an eye made quiet by the power
> Of harmony, and the deep power of joy,
> We see into the life of things [37–49].

Through imaginative recollection, or a (re)construction of his earlier, wild ecstasy, the poet later experiences a more sober but subtler from of *ekstasis* in which he transcends the physical body. While such an experience is interesting for a number of philosophical and historical reasons, what is important here is the imagery, which implies the ability to still the incessant chatter of the mind; the lifting of the weight of the material world and intellectual confusion; the sleeping of the senses and the awakening of soul; a heightened type of perception that sees harmony and unity beyond the seeming discord and disunity of the world; and such empowerment through the embrace of joy that he can see into the animating principle of all things. His mental (re)contructions, which he appears to use in a kind of meditation, are indeed prodigious gifts, as they equip him with the peace of mind that approaches if not embodies a fully flourishing life. Who would not want such a blessed mood?

Still, the question of its authenticity persists. Is this mood a naïve illusion he cultivates, or is it real? As Milnes and Sinanan observe, few critics today "are inclined to accept Wordsworth's spontaneous outpouring as the fiat of 'authentic' selfhood."[10] Representative of such distrust is James Philips' discussion of Wordsworth's response to the degeneration of the hopeful French Revolution into the terror under Robespierre:

> Wordsworth offers his happiness—of which the shared life in Grasmere is the articulation—as the solution to his despair over the later stages of the French Revolution. One might be inclined to think that Wordsworth here has skipped a step, since in place of a solution to the crisis what he tenders is the happiness that follows on from a solution and practical answer to the causes of despair. The happiness of the good life has somehow survived the shipwreck of attempts to draw up a practical plan for the good life to which everyone can subscribe.[11]

Implied in Philips' reading is the idea that Wordsworthian joy is a naïve, defensive illusion.

To be sure, it is not possible to put forth any kind of convincing objective proof of the validity of his blessed, joyous mood, but it does seem to have eudaimonic downstream effects. Wordsworth presciently anticipates the objection in the stanza immediately following his description of the blessed mood when he starts but then abandons a conditional sentence structure: "If this / Be but a vain belief..." (50). It is possible that he is here expressing self-doubt, since he is surely aware that his blessed moods are strangely divorced from normal conceptions of reality. But it is also possible, perhaps even more probable, that he voices the doubt so as to deal with skeptics, since what follows the conditional is a compelling defense of the blessed moods on the grounds that they empower him with the resilience necessary to meet the challenges of difficult times and thus result in quintessential happiness. After acknowledging that he might be holding a vain belief, he refutes the doubters and perhaps assuages his own doubts by asserting that such moods have nevertheless sustained him "In darkness and amid the many shapes / Of joyless daylight" (51–52). They have inspirited him "...when the fretful stir / Unprofitable, and the fever of the world, / Have hung on the beatings of my heart" (52–54). In such moments he reconstructs his memories of the scene above Tintern Abbey, and the result is consciousness transformation: "How oft, in spirit, have I turned to thee, / O sylvan Wye! Thou wanderer thro' the woods, / How oft has my spirit turned to thee! (51–57). Toward the end of the stanza, he reinforces the point by observing that in addition to his pleasure in the current moment of his second visit "there is life and food / For future years" (64–65). Given the imaginative sustenance the first visit provided, the second no doubt offers the promise of a treasury of beauteous mental forms that will, through the active employment of the imagination, metamorphose into blessed moods that provide the strength to bear hardship, the joy to be fully happy, and the vision with which to see meaning and harmony as the basis of all reality. The truths of such moods are not demonstrably provable, but their *effects* are potent catalysts for achieving a sense of well-being amidst circumstances that would otherwise result in despair. They are truly authentic insofar as something can be judged according to its impact.

Wordsworth's blessed moods also exert other significant, eudaimonic effects, all of which are interrelated. These include the following: (1) compassion for his fellow human beings; (2) the ability to discern a deep, underlying connection among all things, or a kind of integrated consciousness in which he non-rationally intuits the presence of a connective cosmic force; (3) a heightened eco-awareness in which he sacralizes the entire green earth; (4) an internalization of natural energies from which he takes his elevated moral cue and consequently lives rightly and well; (5) the ability to overcome the mundane and the petty by continually maintaining a healthy sense of optimism and cultivating gratitude for life's many blessings; (6) a highly refined and fully developed mind rich in beautiful treasures and empowered by the forces of the imagination; (7) a deep, healthy sense of wonder about the mysteries of human existence; and (8) the clarity necessary to value the most important element in human existence—love. Let us deal with each of these effects in turn.

Further, Eudaimonic Complexities of Wordsworthian Ecstasy

Compassion. Although the poet acknowledges that the fires of his earlier ecstasy have become slow burning embers, he claims not to "mourn" (86) the cooling because "other gifts / Have followed" (86–77). Just as he justifies the loss of childhood ways of knowing and being in the famous "Intimations" ode, so does he here account for the transformation in positive terms. "[F]or such loss," he intones, there is "Abundant recompense" (86, 87). One of the gifts that follows the movement from innocence to experience is the ability to hear in nature echoes of "The still, sad music of humanity" (91), the implication of which is that his connection to the natural world instills in him a sensitivity to human suffering. In other words, nature teaches him compassion.

Here, as in *The Prelude* when love of nature leads to love of humankind, Wordsworth articulates one of the reasons why a connection to the earth is important: because it instills in him a highly complex strength of character. How does love of the earth lead to compassion for human beings? Wordsworth does not directly answer the question. One likely explanation is that connectivity with nature, a point I will discuss more fully in the next chapter, requires *ekstasis*. Recognizing that human life is embedded in nature—that is, discerning the illusory boundary between the flora and fauna "out there" and the human being "in here"—calls for a decentering of the ego. In order to see value and meaning in nature, one must overcome the Cartesian separation of mind and matter, locating the atomistic self in an interconnected web that connects the entire biosphere, perhaps even the entire cosmos. The same kind of ego decentering is required in relating to other human beings in meaningful ways, such as being sensitive to others' suffering and responding with compassion. In this sense, to feel empathy for someone else is an *ekstatic* experience. Wordsworth seems to recognize, whether consciously or implicitly, that the same *ekstatic* processes are involved in relating to both nature and other human beings.

Compassion is itself implicated in a confederation of *ekstatic* traits such as kindness, generosity, nurturance, care, and altruistic love. Christopher Peterson and Martin Seligman contrast this family of traits with solipsism, in which others are related to only in terms of how they can contribute to one's personal agenda. Compassion and its close cousins, on the other hand, "require the assertion of a common humanity in which others are worthy of attention and affirmation for no utilitarian reasons but for their own sake."[12] Wordsworth's recompense for losing his wildly ecstatic connection to nature is the *ekstatic* capability to reach out beyond the interests of self into the world of the human other. This reaching out is a highly sophisticated response. To feel empathy is to engage in an extraordinarily refined level of neurological processing, according to modern neurology.[13] The complex gift thus carries with it a universally esteemed character trait, one that can lead to noble acts of altruism and the recognition of a common substrate in human existence.

Integration of psychic components. The poet feels this substrate as a "presence that disturbs me with the joy / Of elevated thoughts" (94–95). But his elevation is not merely a mental construct, for it is "a sense sublime / Of something far more deeply interfused" (95–96). Once again, for want of a better term, he uses an older aesthetic idea in an attempt to capture an affective experience that evades encapsulation in language. The "sublime" perception that follows by no means contains the element of terror, which is so essential to eighteenth-century notions of sublimity. To the contrary, it seems to fill the poet with a profound sense of peace and the understanding of the interconnectedness of all life. It is an interfusion of all things by a kind of cosmic cement

> Whose dwelling is the light of setting suns,
> And the round ocean and the living air
> And the blue sky, and in the mind of man:
> A motion and a spirit that impels
> All thinking things, all objects of all thought,
> And rolls through all things [97–102].

What is this presence that rolls through everything, connecting all sentient creatures and the objects of their thought? Wordsworth no doubt likens it to the divine, but he does not use the term or any of its associations. And perhaps the poem is the better for it because words such as God and spirit are so clichéd as to lack meaning. In naming it a "presence" he frees the reader's perception from the tyranny of habituation and enables a clearer picture of the ultimately unnamable thing he is trying to describe. Critics seem to have sensed that Wordsworth is here trying to smuggle God into his poem, and some have faulted him for doing so. R.A. Foakes, for instance, argues that in the poem "connections are, at best, tenuous, and the associations are consciously put together in the poet's mind, with a kind of scrupulous knowledge that the evidence isn't overwhelming."[14] Such a reading, however, overlooks that the poet is indeed overwhelmed by his blessed moods and his discernment of the common, connective presence in all things. To be sure, the evidence for the existence of a unifying metaphysical force is not compelling when placed under intellectual scrutiny, but it is important to remember that the poet *feels* the presence; he does not theoretically posit its existence. He is disturbed by joy, an affective experience not bound by the rules of logic. Regardless of the question of metaphysical validity, the poet's sense of the interfusion of all life is in some ways the quintessence of well-being, for a unification of psychic contents is the polar opposite of the dissociative states linked to psychological pathologies, a point I will discuss further in Chapter 11.[15] To be well in the fullest sense, at least according to modern psychology, involves integrating psychic components and seeing the world through an integrated lens.[16] A close study of the mystical tradition also supports the point, for mystics across the globe have for centuries attested to the beneficially mind-altering properties of integrative consciousness experiences. Wordsworth's discernment of a unifying cosmic force is in many ways indistinguishable from such experiences.[17]

Eco-awareness. One of the indications that his integrated perception/construction represents well-being is that it results in a heightened eco-awareness, the manifestation of which is the nuance with which the poet describes the natural scene and its internalization. Although some ecocritics have faulted him for using nature as a mere framing device, it is important to note that Wordsworth describes the scene above Tintern Abbey with a keen eye for the details, which he captures with something approaching Hopkins' sense of *inscape*. All things in the scene—the "dark sycamore," the "plots of cottage-ground," and the "orchard-tufts—"Are clad in one green hue" (10, 11, 13). The "pastoral farms" are also "Green to the very door," (16–17) and everything—including the river Wye, the wreaths of smoke ascending to sky from chimneys, the meadows, the woods, the mountains—everything is part of "this green earth" (105). The "presence" he feels in all things exists not only out there in the world but also in the human mind. The two cannot be separated, a point Onno Oerlemans develops in his recent study, *Romanticism and the Materiality of Nature*. In one of the most recent attempts to defend Romanticism against attacks by new historicists, Oerlemans compelling demonstrates that Wordsworth's poetry is a quintessential representation of the "material sublime," or what he calls the physical ground of being in which thought and existence are embedded in the same material matrix,[18] an idea quantum theorists have also propounded in highly sophisticated terms. Wordsworth hints at the material sublime, but, as Oerlemans points out, he is always at a loss for words with which to discuss it because it is prior to and thus outside of language. It is wholly other. In locating thought and nature in the same matrix of being, nevertheless, the poet overcomes the Cartesian separation of mind and matter. Such a bridge offers the potential to overcome mechanistic conceptions and thus to heal us from a wound that has resulted in the objectification and exploitation of the earth—attitudes and practices that today represent the greatest survival challenge for the human species. Wordsworth's profound eco-awareness is more relevant and valuable today than it was in the early nineteenth century.

In *Romantic Ecology* Jonathan Bate argues for the value of Wordsworth's relationship to the earth and the states of mind that result from such an interaction. "Poems do not send people out on to barricades," he writes, "but they do have the capacity to alter mentalities," the result of which is a transformation of the politics that lead to deforestation, strip mining, carbon emissions, and other practices that harm the earth.[19] Perhaps more compelling, Wordsworth's organic conception of the earth, itself a reassertion of the previous pagan model of the world against the rise of mechanism, is also inherently valuable today in an age in which the limits of mechanism are pressing upon us and leaving us with fewer and fewer alternatives for survival as a species. To see the world as a living organism, as the poet did, places limits on how we exploit its resources and charges us with an ethics of stewardship not possible in mechanistic conceptions in which the earth is conceived of and exploited as a lifeless machine.

In an engagement with the work of Laurence Lockridge, Potkay discusses Wordsworth's "sentiment of being," as the poet describes it in *The Prelude*, in terms of a state in which one is "free of the burden of act and obligation"—an idealized "retreat from action itself."[20] Potkay, clearly sympathetic to the poet, acknowledges that such an idealization will not endear the poet to new historicists who fault him for his retreat from radical revolutionary politics, but he goes on to express the hope that Wordsworth's position might be "salvaged for a 'Green Romanticism' critical of nature's un-doing and humankind's increasingly irresponsible stewardship of the earth."[21]

Despite Potkay's hope and Bate's formidable defense, many ecocritics have received the poet with something less than warmth, more often with ambivalence. Norman Lacey, for instance, has charged the poet with merely observing nature when he claims to be a participant in its rustic ethos: "He was not in a natural relation to physical nature nor to his own nature, nor to that Nature which he extolled.... He stood in a no-man's land between town and country."[22] Other ecocritics, with notable exceptions, seem to have endorsed the complaint. As Greg Garrard argues in an introduction to ecocritical theory, "Wordsworth is, on the whole, far more interested in the relationship of non-human nature to the human mind than he is in nature in and for itself."[23] Standing behind the criticism is the politically charged idea in "deep" ecocriticism that a worthy nature poet should not merely use nature as a framing device; rather, he or she should acknowledge that nature does not need the human species for its survival. While it is important to acknowledge that the earth would likely be better off without a human presence, it seems too openly political to insist that all true eco-poets need to privilege the earth's myriad flora and fauna and thus betray their own species. No species on the planet does so, and it is reasonable for nature-minded poets to be, despite their eco-awareness, predominantly concerned with human beings. To say the poet is more concerned with human beings than he is with nature, moreover, is to operate from a faulty binary, for the greenness in Wordsworth, or, to be more precise, the internalization of greenness, fuels the human imagination. To dismiss such a sentiment as coded ideology sacrifices rare but healthy states of consciousness on the altar of (albeit important) politics.

The charge is in some ways the same as it is in other ideological readings: because the poet does not do the direct bidding of green activism by advancing its agenda in sufficient ways, he is complicit in a nature-denying ideology. But to fault a nature-poet such as Wordsworth for his human concerns is to fault him for writing poetry, which, in its best form, always contains a significant human element. Even nature poems depicting no human beings imply a human reader. Still, the point is well taken, and it is important to acknowledge that Wordsworth's principal concern is with human beings. In drawing on the lexical analyses of H.J.C. Grierson, M.H. Abrams interestingly observed that the ratio of the word "love" to "nature" in Wordsworth's poetry is 13:8.[24] Wordsworth is indeed a human poet. In "Tintern Abbey," as in so many other poems, his principal concern is undoubtedly a human one—the imagination and its power to restore, sustain, and create. To fault him for turning his back on nature is to elide the means by which the imagination derives its powers from a natural scene. Wordsworth is a human poet preeminently concerned with the growth of the human imagination, but he also teaches us that to be well in the fullest sense, we must acknowledge that both thought and corporeal life are embedded in a matrix he calls nature. His poetry implies that without consciousness of the nature-mind connection, imagination cannot reach its highest levels of development. Nature is imagination's stimulus—its informing, animating principle.

Moral instruction. Such eco-awareness is morally instructive to Wordsworth. Part of the "abundant recompense" for the loss of the earlier, wild ecstasy thus also includes something on the order of a natural cue to good living. In addition to being a "lover of the meadows and the woods" and "...all that we behold / From this green earth" (103, 104–05), or perhaps because of such reverence, the poet relates to nature as if it were a sagacious preceptor who leads him to rare treasures of wisdom. Nature is thus "the anchor of my purest thoughts, the nurse, / The guide, the guardian of my heart, and soul / Of all my moral being" (109–11). The imagery here implies that nature is a stabilizing force, the caretaker and protector of his deepest layers of being. To be sure, Wordsworth wrote "Tintern Abbey" before nature wrecked the ship on which his brother John was sailing, drowning the sibling and sending the poet into a period of dark despair. Nature, as he conceives of it in "Tintern Abbey," seems to be a benevolent force incompatible with tsunamis, earthquakes, and other natural disasters that offer no instruction in wisdom but do kill thousands and wreak horrible destruction. While this "dark" version of nature seems to contradict Wordsworth's conception of the good, helpful instructor, it is important to note that nature cannot be reduced only to its seeming indifference to human suffering. Nature is sometimes horrible to human beings, but it is also frequently beautiful, and people across the globe still find sustenance in it even after natural calamities take their loved ones. When Wordsworth claims that "Nature never did betray / The heart that loved her" (122–23), he was likely not uttering a naïve belief in nature's benevolence but pointing out that nature in its beautiful, non-threatening aspects can teach human beings to revere beauty; to cultivate serenity of mind; to be at peace with themselves and others; to live according to biologically programmed rhythms; to live ethically; and to be well in the fullest sense. While it is not clear what the poet precisely means by "moral being," the passage does suggest an ethics of responsibility towards self, others, and the environment. The cultivation of one's moral being, or at least a *sense* of one's moral being, however unstable may be the foundation on which such a construction is built, is central to the flourishing of human society.

Gratitude. Another gift Wordsworth receives is gratitude, which is not exactly a gift but more of a response to a gift, a feeling of appreciation for something that, in some cases, one can never fully repay. Yet, it is a boon and part of the poet's "abundant recompense" because gratitude broadens and builds one's positive emotional repertoire, which, if sufficiently and complexly developed, results in a greater overall sense of well-being.[25] Gratitude is *ekstatic* in that it is an other-directed emotion, its roots lying in the capacity to empathize with other people. Selfish egotists, narcissists, psychopaths, and people who expect tit-for-tat reciprocity seldom feel gratitude because they lack the ability to self-transcend.[26] Gratitude serves as a barometer and motivator of moral behavior, which it also reinforces. Its lasting benefits include personal and social development, individual health and well-being, and community strength and harmony.[27]

For Wordsworth, grateful recognition of the gifts nature has left in his imagination leads to a number of eudaimonic outcomes, as it opens him to joy and so thoroughly impresses his mind that he is able not only to survive but to prevail. Nature, according to the poet,

> .... can so inform
> The mind that is within us, so impress
> With quietness and beauty, and so feed

> With lofty thoughts, that neither evil tongues,
> Rash judgments, nor the sneers of selfish men,
> Nor greetings where no kindness is, nor all
> The dreary intercourse of daily life,
> Shall e'er prevail against us, or disturb
> Our cheerful faith, that all which we behold
> Is full of blessings ... [125–134].

Here gratitude seems to move in a circular orbit, since thankfulness for the memories of his original ecstasy at Tintern Abbey leads to a cheerful faith that life is to be appreciated for its many blessings. A cheerful faith in nature's blessings may sound naïve to the jaded and the cynical who view faith as neurotic avoidance, but such a criticism overlooks the strength that results from cultivating a sense of gratitude, for it enables Wordsworth to withstand the petty, the selfish, the backbiting, the judgmental, and even the downright hostile people of the world as well as to maintain a healthy level of optimism in spite of others' attempts to beat it out of him. Gratitude equips him with psychological resilience, one of the most critical of all human survival traits.

Instead of reading the passage as an expression of naiveté, it is perhaps more appropriate to view it as an example of the upward spirals associated with people who experience high levels of positive affect, the result of which is a continual process of growth toward optimal functioning. Positivity leads to positivity, which creates more positivity. Such upward spirals enable individuals to transform themselves and thus to become "more creative, knowledgeable, resilient, socially integrated, and healthy" in a kind of "self-sustaining" loop of well-being, as Fredrickson observes.[28] Thankfulness for the gifts of nature can lead to other, even more important, eudaimonic gifts.

Beauty and imagination. A mind so steeped in the gifts that gratitude makes possible is also receptive to the value of beauty and the healing powers of the imagination. In his address to Dorothy towards the end of "Tintern Abbey," Wordsworth offers a "prayer" (121) for her, the thrust of which is that she revel in the joys of nature and then let the images of beauty she has internalized transform and enlarge her consciousness. In the prayer he tells his sister to take delight in nature, to let "the moon shine on thee" (134–45), to let the "misty mountain-winds be free / To blow against thee" (136–37), and to revel in the wild joys that ecstasy brings. Then, when these "wild ecstasies shall be matured / Into a sober pleasure" (138–39), her mind will become "...a mansion for all lovely forms, / Thy memory be as a dwelling place / For all sweet sounds and harmonies" (139–41). A mind so enlarged by receptivity to beauty, he declares, serves as a bulwark against future loneliness, "or fear, or pain, or grief" (143). In such a hypothetical future, she can draw upon her reserves and utilize the powers of imagination, just as he has done, in order to ward off despair.

Having read and internalized Milton, Wordsworth knows that "The mind is its own place, and in itself / Can make a heaven of hell, a hell of heaven," as Satan declares in *Paradise Lost* (I.254–55). The factor determining whether one lives in heaven or hell is the imagination and its proper use of the treasures of beauty one feeds it over the course of a lifetime. Wordsworth's implication is that we have a choice in whether to be happy, and in exercising agency in making such a choice, we cultivate an important human potential.

Wonder. Part of this choice is the decision one makes between viewing the world through a utilitarian's perspective or through a profound sense of wonder. While the former constricts and reduces oneself and the objects of perception, the latter enlarges consciousness and enables a vision not otherwise possible. Wordsworth's "abundant recompense" for the sobering of his earlier, wild ecstasies includes a deep sense of wonder about self and the world. Though he never says so, the poet strongly implies that he is responding to a profound mystery about human existence in the natural world. The scene above Tintern Abbey, with all of its grandeurs and glories, is utterly strange to him. He is awed by it, and its mysterious qualities resound throughout the labyrinthine corridors of his capacious imagination. But it is also a mystery he need not attempt to solve, for to do so is to let wonder slide into utilitarian curiosity, or the "meddling intellect" that murders in its dissection of the object of inquiry. Wonder, by contrast, preserves the fascination implied in curiosity but without the need for ratiocination. An affective experience, wonder prompts us to suspend the need to discover through intellectual means and enables a "nonegoistic contemplation of the causal power that might make ... vitality, beauty, and truth possible," as Robert Fuller declares in his study, *Wonder: From Emotion to Spirituality.*[29] It is possible to get through life without a developed sense of wonder, according to Fuller, but to do so is to "lack certain sensibilities that enrich the texture of human existence."[30] One can survive without a sense of life's mystery, but to flourish one needs a deep consciousness of such mystery. Backing his claims with standard measures of psychological health, Fuller makes the bold assertion that "a life shaped by wonder is qualitatively 'better' than a life that is relatively devoid of this emotion."[31] The "intellectual, moral, and aesthetic characteristics linked to wonder," he declares, "transform personal life in ways that are, on balance, consistent with the highest levels of psychological development."[32] A sense of wonder helps us to grow, and this is no doubt why Wordsworth holds a sense of mystery about self and place close to his heart in the years after his first visit to Tintern Abbey. A significant effect of Wordsworthian ecstasies, then, is the sense of wonder they continue to foster long after they occur.

Love. The greatest gift in his cornucopia of "abundant recompense" is a clarity of mind that enables him to hold high, above all else, the supreme value of love. The poem ends with Wordsworth turning to his sister Dorothy, to whom he utters his prayer and also expresses his heartfelt devotion. In an ecstatic effusion of words, the poet calls her first "My dear, dear Friend" (116) and then "My dear, dear Sister!" (121). Despite his acknowledgement of the sibling relationship, his tone here seems more parental than fraternal, for at this point in their relationship Wordsworth was something of a caretaker to his sibling. Regardless, he clearly loves her deeply and expresses concern about her current and future well-being. His compassionate prayer is that she learn from nature in the same way he was able to do and that, should he be dead in the future, she remember him and their love with "healing thoughts / Of tender joy" (144–45). He also hopes she will empower herself with the memory of their standing together "on the banks of this delightful stream" (150) in a love bond that links the two siblings to one another and to the natural world. The poem ends with his hope that she never forget that his great love for the scene above Tintern Abbey is made more special by her presence there with him. He makes it clear to her that he brought her here not out of a sense of familial duty but with "warmer love—oh! With far deeper zeal / Of holier love" (154–55). She is the real reason for his current ecstasy.

Such are the *ekstatic* gifts that serve as compensation for the loss of youth's ecstasies. Wordsworth's blessed moods are indeed abundantly rich in positive affect, and they result in a number of markers of psychological well-being. "Tintern Abbey" is in some ways a quintessential example of healthly psychology. Wordsworth seemed conscious of trying to convey this sense of health to readers, for in his famous 1802 Preface to *Lyrical Ballads*, he wrote that, as a result of reading his poems, a reader, "if he be in a healthful state of association, must necessarily be in some degree enlightened, and his affections ameliorated."[33] Critics have claimed that his primary theme was the growth of his own mind,[34] but as Potkay points out, the "lyric 'I' in Wordsworth is often and expectedly interchangeable with a communal we, and this is particularly true when Wordsworth addresses the power of joy."[35] The poet's joy, as we encounter it in his poetry, particularly in "Tintern Abbey," is in this sense a reflection of our own.

Ecstasy Pathologized and Politicized

Given the foregoing discussion, it is puzzling to consider how we went from Mill's depression cure to undesirable ideology and diseased psychology. Are we reading the same poet? Potkay helps to shed light on the problem. In his conclusion to *The Story of Joy* he makes it clear that a number of complex developments in the twentieth century led to a deep suspicion and even outright distrust of Wordsworthian joy,[36] the result of which is that many critics today completely ignore the eudaimonic dimensions of his ecstatic verse. Even Stephen Gill, one of the poet's best biographers[37] and a highly sophisticated critic, turns the Wordsworthian aesthetics of ecstasy upside down by doubting the authenticity of the poet's transmuting of suffering into joy.[38] While ideological and psychoanalytic readings are interesting and complex, they by no means render an accurate picture of the great poet, and they consistently fail to do justice to the ecstatic dimensions of his verse, often eliding these completely or interpreting them in pathologized or politicized terms.

Yet, even though it has become almost conventional practice to level criticism against Wordsworth over the last thirty years, not all scholars hold such a jaundiced view of the poet, and I do not mean to suggest the critical reception has been entirely negative. To the contrary, many critics have recognized, whether implicitly or explicitly, the eudaimonic value of his poetry. There is even a growing tendency in this direction, one in which scholars increasingly read Wordsworth through a hermeneutics of affirmation. For instance, Richard Gravil in his fascinating work, *Wordsworth's Bardic Vocation*, approaches Wordsworth both with reverence and also an excellent scholar's critical ability to explore subtext. In justifying his approach, Gravil claims his study is "an attempt to say something responsible and holistic" about Wordsworth and to "present him whole, or as whole as can be done with a major poet of such diversity."[39] The implication here is that suspicious critics have been irresponsible in their sometimes pathologized interpretations of Wordsworth, and in doing so they leave us with a fragmented portrait. Gravil's general approach, then, is an attempt to read Wordsworth's bardic qualities affirmatively as a holism rather than as a symptom of ideological or psychological disease.

Wordsworth's eudaimonia is thus still an important element in critical discussions. Ian Dennis has astutely remarked that it is curious that so many readers have been able to spurn Wordsworth but not his joy.[40] Perhaps the reason why is that at some level critics, even those who pathologize the poet, recognize that his joy and its related aesthetics of ecstasy are implicated in the larger question of well-being, itself a centrally important human concern. In his landmark, green defense of Wordsworth, Bate challenged new historicism by recognizing value in the poet's endeavor to show readers a better way "to enjoy" and "to endure life" through a sophisticated engagement with the natural world.[41] Perhaps it is possible to take the point a step further and argue that Wordsworthian ecstasies show readers how to be well in the fullest sense; they show us how to flourish.

7. The Body Ecstatic: Walt Whitman

His prematurely gray hair and long beard suggested the kind of sagacity found in someone who exemplifies great wisdom, compassion, joy, and cosmic understanding. Although he was not without his critics, many people in his day—"Whitmaniacs," as Roger Assilineau comically called them—did discern in him a religious quality they tried to emulate. In England, America, and other parts of the Western world, he inspired followers who read his verse as a kind of scripture and saw him as a new prophet with a radical religious message.[1] He himself encouraged such ardent zeal in his actual life and in the poetic persona he constructed. As a self-appointed nurse in the Civil War camp in Washington, D.C., he compassionately gave service to his brother who lay wounded and then to hundreds of other young soldiers. He brought them not only new bandages, as a wound dresser, but also his tenderness, his wealth of cosmic insight, and, most of all, his happiness and cheer. Several close friends who knew him later in life thought he had an important religious message—some even thought he was the supreme example of cosmic consciousness—because of the wisdom he embodied. In his poetry he articulated his compassion for and identification with all people in all lands, regardless of their social status. His doctrine of the metaphysical unity of not only the human species but all material life can be found, whether implicitly or explicitly, in most of the poems in his great work *Leaves of Grass*. Walt Whitman, in some ways the greatest and most influential American poet, saw his book of verse as a kind of new Bible, a guidebook for a transformed way of living in the nineteenth century. His conscious endeavor to sing ecstatic songs about the myriad forms of physical life and the senses human beings use to discern such material forms has strong religious overtones.

What makes Whitman's spiritual ideas so unusual, however, is the intense physicality with which he invests them. He sings the body ecstatic; he galvanizes the body by imbuing it with an electrical charge that has profound implications in Western culture. David Reynolds cites mesmerism and its ideas of animal magnetism as a source of Whitman's use of the trope of electricity. The poet's concept of the electrified body was likely influenced by *The Philosophy of Electrical Psychology* (1850), in which Fowlers and Wells articulated an electrical theory as the basis of all physical and spiritual life.[2] While the influence seems highly probable, such ideas were also in circulation in mid–nineteenth-century literary discourse. The Romantic aesthetics of electricity is thus another likely source of Whitman's image. According to Paul Gilmore, Romantics on both sides of the Atlantic attempted "to imagine aesthetics as a sensual experience of the individual body, embedded in specific social situations, that somehow leads to the individual's momentary suspension in a sense of a larger whole...." In electrical aesthetics the aesthetic experience "allows one to achieve a kind of non-entity, a sense of the impersonal through the momentary disruption of dominant notions of material, political and social interests and the related conception of the atomistic self in relation to an instrumentalized, objective world."[3] L.S. Klatt has built on Gilmore's ideas by exploring how the aesthetics of electricity manifests in Whitman's poetry. As he says, "electricity becomes Whitman's metaphor of choice because it delivers a living current— magnetic, powerful, unpredictable, revelatory."[4] Such an aesthetics materializes spirituality, locating the divine in all physical and corporeal matter. The realization of the electricity of materiality has the power "to temporarily dissolve the distinctions between self and others, mind and body."[5] Conceived as such, the aesthetic experience has obvious connections to ecstasy. It is an *ekstatic* force that catalyzes self-transcendence but only through the embrace of corporeality.

This element of the body raises a number of interesting questions: How, specifically, does the body factor in such a construct? What epistemological frameworks in philosophy and literature does Whitman's electrified body challenge? Do the implications go beyond sexuality and signify in other domains? How does an electrified body relate to animality, morality, nature, and cognition? What are its psychological implications? In what ways does it manifest in Whitman's poetics? Before I offer an answer to such questions in specific detail, let me do so in a general way by making a few comments that will serve as a loose outline of the following discussion.

Whitman's image of the electrified body can be seen as a form of *anamnesis*, a term from depth psychology signifying the retrieval of unconscious contents that takes place in psychoanalytic work. In post–Jungian depth psychology, the retrieval of somatic energies is highly desirable and, through the realization of the meaningful connections between psyche and soma, results in a heightened refinement of consciousness. The poet's celebration of the body represents a significant departure from a repressive value system in which the body is the subordinated second member in such binaries as mind/body, soul/body, reason/instinct, and psychological health/physical health. In electrifying the body Whitman challenges the hierarchical order implied in such binaries by welcoming the repressed other into consciousness. He does so not by privileging the bodily other but by dissolving the hierarchy in which it is subordinated. In other words he equalizes the two members in the binary. The electrical image signifies an *ekstatic* subjectivity in which individuality and the dominating ego are subverted and forced to share space in consciousness with previously repressed psychic energies.

In retrieving the bodily other, Whitman caused a seismic shift in the nineteenth century, for his ideas about the ecstatic nature of corporeality are multiplex and manifest in the following ways: (1) a celebratory embrace of sexuality in all of its permutations; (2) a serious challenge to the moral structures of nineteenth-century America; (3) an amoral, candid perspective on animality; (4) a recognition of the embedded nature of the body, which exists as an integral part of the natural world from which it receives its electrical charge; (5) embodied cognition and an alternative epistemology that overcomes the subject/object division; (6) the spiritualization of physicality and a rejection of deeply embedded, negative Western attitudes about the body's role in religious life; (7) a heightened degree of somatic awareness that signifies eudaimonic psychological states; and (8) interesting ideas about a new poetics in which the writer is an ecstatic conduit of the body's electrical charge. Although each of these concepts can be found separately in previous authors, in Whitman they represent, if taken as a whole, a radically new conception of the ecstatic body, one in which the corporeal is no longer cast as inferior other but welcomed into consciousness as an integral component of a healthily functioning psyche.

Body and Soul, Soul and Body

In verse-chant five of "Song of Myself," a much commented upon section, Whitman discusses the union of body and soul in highly sexualized terms. The passage strongly suggests the equality of the two, as the poet places both on an equal footing, declaring, "I believe in you my soul, the other I am must not abase itself to you, / And you must not be abased to the other" (82–83).[6] This reordering of the relationship between body and soul, which is representative of the relationship between the two throughout much, but not all, of his poetry, results in ecstatic transformation, for the outcome of the union is "...the peace and knowledge that pass all the argument of the earth" (91). By recovering the body and its powerful, repressed energies, the speaker's subjectivity is profoundly transformed, as he recognizes his own sense of divinity and a connection, through love, to all other human beings and everything in the manifest universe. In this ecstatically transformed state of consciousness, all of material creation becomes sacred, including leaves in the fields, brown ants, and even scabs of moss on a fence, heaps of stones, and various types of weeds. In recognizing the value of the corporeal, all other forms of material existence seem to glow in a new light. No doubt a literary (re)construction, such a peak experience borders on the mystical. Yet, it is not the result of the transcendence of the body, as it is in so many forms of mysticism, but a direct outcome of retrieving previously repressed, somatic energies. This "inverted mysticism,"[7] as James Miller calls it, is what makes the poet's spirituality so unusual and interesting.

Elsewhere in "Song of Myself" Whitman suggests the power of bodily experience to effect ecstatic transcendence. "Is this then a touch? Quivering me to a new identity," he asks in verse-chant twenty eight (619). Such touch becomes overwhelmingly powerful, as he acknowledges at the end of the verse-chant: "you villain touch! what are you doing? my breath is tight in its throat, / Unclench your floodgates, you are too much for me" (640–41). Despite his use of the word "villain," which he clearly intends as verbal irony, corporeal sensation is a eudaimonic catalyst of self-transformation, one that results in a sense of the fluidity of human identity. This subversion of individuality recurs throughout *Leaves of Grass*. To be sure, Whitman celebrates individuality and privileges, to a heightened degree, will and subjectivity, both of which Isaiah Berlin argued are central features of all of the various Romanticisms.[8] In another respect, however, he undermines individuality, as Mark Maslan has observed,[9] by decentering the fixity of ego in myriad ways, particularly through the engagement of somatic energies that serve as inferior other to a state of consciousness in which mind and its reasoning powers dominate.

Whitman revels in the possibilities of such a manifold subjectivity, which is not unlike the poststructuralist subject in that it is "an instrument of forces external to itself."[10] Yet, such forces are not only textual and discursive, as they are in poststructuralist thought, but also material and corporeal. Like textual and discursive forces, they often exert their influence at unconscious levels of awareness. In their totality somatic energies frequently exist beyond the conscious will, which is often unsuccessful in overriding deeply ingrained, somatic habits, as Richard Shusterman points out in *Body Consciousness*, a study of the new field of somaesthetics.[11] Sometimes the body simply will not do what the will commands it to do because somatic energies are rooted in pre-verbal, non-rational unconsciousness. Although there is no doubt a link between psyche and soma, as Carl Jung and many post–Jungian scholars have made clear in so much of their work, the connection between the two exists, at least in most people, beneath the surface of consciousness. The ideal, of course, is to bring them into some kind of harmonious, conscious agreement. Whitman seems to do so. For him, bodily *ekstasis*, that is, allowing powerful somatic energies to override the conscious will, is central to his ideas about the fluidity of self. There is a direct connection between decentered subjectivity and corporeality in *Leaves*.

To be sure, the poet's electrified body should not be interpreted *solely* in terms of the retrieval of repressed somatic energies, for the image does signify in other theoretical registers. Andrew Lawson, for instance, has compellingly shown that such a conception of subjectivity is related to the notion of market exchange.[12] The poet's persistent urge to merge through sexual encounter in *Leaves of Grass*, as Lawson shows, participates in an economic discourse, an idea that clearly finds expression in Whitman's metaphor in "Song of Myself" of the orgasm as "spending for vast returns" (260). And yet, Marxist theory or any discussion of economics will fall short of a full account of human corporeality and the deeply ingrained drives with which the body is imbued because such drives preexist the cultural forces that resulted in the emergence of capitalism in nineteenth-century America. In the countless millennia of human evolution, there were sexual urges long before there were bourgeois values.

A Multiplex Sexuality

The pseudoscientists of sexuality in Whitman's time believed that sexual desires in healthy males should be periodic and infrequent, certainly enough to foster the necessary drive for copulation and reproduction but by no means functioning as a central motivating force in the human psyche.[13] Such ideas are the polar opposite of Freud's notion that libido underlies all psychic processes. Although Freud may have overstated the case, as Jung and others believed, his ideas were closer to current understanding than those of the nineteenth century. It is well-known, for instance, that humans are the most sexualized of all the great apes, and the sexual drive in healthy people is persistent and regular, although this varies across age and gender. When Whitman thus swears in "Spontaneous Me" "The oath of procreation" and celebrates "The greed that eats me day and night with hungry gnaw," he is challenging repressed nineteenth-century attitudes about the infrequency of the sexual urge (41, 42). He is making a forceful statement that the attitudes about sexuality in his day, both lay and professional, were wrong because they perpetuated psychologically repression. At least in the persona he constructed in *Leaves*, he fully embraces and surrenders to a persistent sexual drive that knows no bounds. As Klatt observes, "[h]is is a prolific and plural intercourse, oblivious to the restrictions imposed by marriage or monogamy. The erratic, spontaneous self goes where attracted. The electric pulse of the soul—sexual, social, poetic— leaps out of bounds to its receptor."[14] This electrical charge compelling the body and directing the self is a far cry from Victorian, nineteenth-century conceptions of sexuality.

In his challenge to such ideas Whitman is determined to write about the "sexual organs" and their unmentionable coupling "with courageous clear voice to prove you illustrous" ("Starting from Paumanok" 166). He sings the ecstatic joys of ejaculation and the male orgasm in the image of "Limitless limpid jets of love hot and enormous, quivering jelly of love, white-blow and delirious juice" ("I Sing the Body Electric" 60). He believes that "Sex contains all," and that it serves as a kind of cosmic cement binding not only body and soul but all material entities, all intellectual ideas, and all spiritual energies ("A Woman Waits for Me" 3). He is the poet of forbidden desires and the realization of sexual fantasies, the champion of shameful wishes and hot, wicked lusts in all of their permutations. The moral law, he believed, stood in the way of a higher truth in which soma, particularly sexuality, is vitally charged with goodness in its power to connect material entities.

According to today's understanding, there is an openly homoerotic element in the "Calamus" poems, the central image of which is a large type of sweet grass that symbolized the phallus and was even used medicinally as a libido enhancer in the folk medicine of the poet's day.[15] In such poems Whitman claims to go down "untrodden paths" in order to celebrate the "manly love" of comrades. In his paean to "adhesiveness," a type of love he distinguishes from the amativeness of the "Children of Adam" poems, Whitman speaks tenderly of "he whom I love ... holding me by the hand" ("Of the Terrible Doubt of Appearances" 11). He refers to "his friend his lover" of whom he was "fondest" ("Recorders Ages Hence" 4). He recalls happily lying face-to-face in the same bed with this friend/lover, whose "arm lay lightly around my breast" in an embrace that strongly suggests post-sexual caressing ("When I Heard at the Close of Day" 13). He also speaks of "an athlete" who is "enamour'd of me, and I of him." The nature of this relationship he describes as "something fierce and terrible in me eligible to burst forth," but which he "dare not tell ... in words, not even in these songs" ("Earth, My Likeness" 5, 6, 7). His homoeroticism can be seen clearly in such poems.

To say, however, that Whitman's homosexuality is central to his poetic vision, as Richard Tayson[16] and others have done, is problematic because it overlooks the nature of adhesiveness, which the poet describes in a "Calamus" poem as "The dear love of man for his comrade, the attraction of friend to friend, / Of the well-married husband and wife, of children and parents, / Of city for city and land for land" ("The Base of All Metaphysics" 13–15). Here, and in several other poems in the "Calamus" cluster, adhesiveness manifests not as eros between men but as *philia*, a non-sexual kind of love binding together all people, male and female. I am by no means denying Whitman's homoeroticism, which Tayson astutely observes was obscured by the previous editors of the Norton edition of *Leaves*, Sculley Bradley and Harold Blodgett, who refused to openly acknowledge the poet's homoeroticism in their footnotes.[17] Although he himself vehemently denied being a homosexual and famously boasted in a letter to John Addinton Symonds of having sired six illegitimate children, Whitman covertly imbued *Leaves* with a charge of homoeroticism that in many ways made it acceptable for future gay poets to write openly of homosexual themes. He is quantum in this regard. One reason why Whitman denied that his notion of adhesiveness involved "those semi-sexual emotions and actions which no doubt do occur between men," as Symonds put it,[18] is because his age was so intolerant of homosexual love, reducing it to sodomy, criminalizing it as a punishable offense, and pathologizing it as an unhealthy, psychological abnormality. His story of siring six children was perhaps motivated by a self-preservation instinct in a culture entirely hostile to his sexual orientation.

Another part of his motivation for rejecting Symonds' query, however, is likely due to his desire to avoid having his ideas about sexuality be reduced solely to homosexuality. As any casual reader knows, he was an inclusive poet, and he places the speakers of his poems in all subject positions. Whitman is for all people in all lands, not just for gay men. He adopted this position as a gay man who, nevertheless, wanted his ideas about sexuality to appeal to people of all sexual orientations. James Miller, consequently, characterizes Whitman's ideas about sexuality as "omnisexual," by which he means that "sexual imagery of *Leaves of Grass* does not ... fall neatly into any single category. It is autoerotic, heteroerotic, homoerotic."[19] To read Whitman's poetry solely in terms of the poet's own homosexual orientation, therefore, is to overlook the celebration of heterosexual love and female sexuality in *Leaves*. In verse-chant five of "I Sing the Body Electric," for instance, he sings a paean to the female form, which, he says, "attracts with fierce undeniable attraction" (54). In the same verse-chant he graphically describes the copulation of a bride and groom, no doubt privileging the male orgasm but also praising the vagina because it is a divine portal through which other bodies emerge into the world: "Be not ashamed women, your privilege encloses the rest, and is the exit of the rest, / You are the gates of the body, and you are the gates of the soul" (66–67). In "A Woman Waits for Me," he acknowledges his attraction to another man and "the deliciousness of his sex," (9) but he also declares his intention to copulate with receptive females: "I draw you close to me, you women, / I cannot let you go, and I would do you good" (20–21). In verse-chant eleven of "Song of

Myself" he portrays a voyeuristic, lonely woman fantasizing about joining twenty-eight young, naked men bathing in an ocean. The woman does so imaginatively and immerses herself in an ocean full of naked male bodies electrified with a sexual charge. The poet's emphasis on water imagery, wetness, streams, and sprays suggests a kind of baptismal, seminal ocean in which a lonely woman desires to achieve ecstatic transcendence through bodily embrace.

While some critics have read Whitman's amorous women as coded figures who represent his own homosexual longings, it is important to remember that his sexual vision is inclusive. Such a reading confuses Walter Whitman, the gay poet, with Walt Whitman, the Kosmos of his poetry. Other critics who do focus on the poetry have complained that in "Song of Myself" and in other poems Whitman comes up short when he claims to be representing female sexuality. While the point is well-taken, it needs qualification. As Michael Moon has observed in a discussion of the twenty eight bathers, women in Whitman's poetry are not merely a "transvestite cover" for male homosexual desire. And while Whitman may not fully represent female sexuality, particularly the female orgasm, the bathing passage and others in *Leaves* do "incorporate feminine sexuality to a considerable degree, and to a higher degree than most [contemporaneous] English-language texts...."[20] Whitman praises hetero- and homo-eroticism in *Leaves*, and to read the text solely in terms of one or the other is thus to overlook that he commingles both types of sexuality in a speaker whose bodily urges transgress all such demarcations.

The Critical Reception

In a much more openly sexual age, it is difficult to understand the radical nature of Whitman's ideas about the body and sexuality when he introduced them into the nineteenth century. The considerable extent to which he retrieves repressed somatic energies can be better seen in the responses his poetry provoked throughout the course of his career. One reviewer of the 1855 edition, for instance, called it "a mass of stupid filth."[21] Another said the work was so "beastly" that the poet deserved "no better than the lash." Charles Eliot Norton, a Harvard art historian, said the 1855 *Leaves* had redeemable traits but also contained "passages of intolerable coarseness—not gross and licentious, but simply disgustingly coarse." He was particularly concerned that the book might fall into the delicate hands of female readers who would somehow be psychologically injured by its obscenities. William Dean Howells was also concerned about the psychological welfare of female readers, confessing his urge "to delete from Whitman's poems certain lines that could offend the ladies and innocent young girls...." A Southern reviewer was downright malicious in calling the poet a "rhapsodist ... sewer-rat," referring to his cult of the body as "a monstrosity that can be classed in no geological age, nor Pliocene, nor Miocene; but in one only, of which he is the sole relic, and which by analogy to these we might term conveniently the *Obscene*." The poet Swinburne, himself a decadent poet and a bisexual with sadomasochistic tendencies, condemned the "unhealthy demonstrative and obtrusive animalism" of *Leaves* because he felt Whitman's ideas were "unnatural and incompatible with the wholesome instincts of human passion."[22] Oliver Wendell Holmes called the poet's ideas "indecent,"[23] while Charles Dana called them "uncouth," "grotesque," and "reckless,"[24] and Charles Eliot Norton called them "intolerable and disgusting."[25]

No doubt, Whitman had sympathetic readers, such as Oscar Wilde, William Michael Rossetti, the Irish critic Thomas Rolleston, the orator Robert Ingersoll, the Cuban poet José Martí, and others who saw much value in his image of the electrified body. Often, however, even readers who were sympathetic to him expressed their moral disapproval of his ideas about corporeality. In his reading of the 1856 edition, Thoreau found certain poems "exhilarating" and "encouraging," and he wrote that Whitman "has spoken more truth than any American or modern that I know." He declared that "[w]e ought to rejoice greatly in him." But Thoreau also objected to "2 or 3 pieces in the book which are disagreeable to say the least, simply sensual." Two of these, to be sure, were the openly sexual poems later titled, "Song of Myself" and "I Sing the Body Electric." Thoreau's apology for the sexual nature of *Leaves* epitomizes nineteenth-century morality: "As for its sensuality,—& it may turn out to be less sensual than it appeared—I do not so much wish that those parts were not written, as that men & women were so pure that they could read them without harm, that is, without understanding them."[26] While Thoreau acknowledged the poet's facility with language and the originality of *Leaves*, he could not countenance the poet's electrified body because it challenged the rigid, moral structures he internalized from a culture in which the body is othered.

Emerson's response was similar. In his famous letter to Whitman he praised "the worth of the wonderful gift of *Leaves of Grass*," and he greeted the poet "at the beginning of a great career."[27] In private conversation, however, he later tried to convince Whitman to excise the "filthy" passages from *Leaves*, hoping the poet would sanitize the poems by stripping them of their open eroticism. In his famous reply Whitman first complains, in effect, that literature before him is weak because writers too often denied the body. His criticism of such writers and their writing is fittingly couched in the bodily image of a flaccid penis. "There is no great author; everyone has demeaned himself to some etiquette or impotence. There is no manhood or life-power in poems.... [H]ow little [such poetry] knows Nature. Its flesh is soft." His call for a new kind of poetry is also couched in bodily images, for he articulates a desire to break from this body-denying literary tradition and thus "to be our own, to be electric, fresh, lusty, to express the full-sized body, male and female...." He then turns Emerson's "filthy" charge on its head by equating the value system in which the body and sexuality are deemed unmentionable and worthy of shame to "a filthy law [that] has to be repealed," adding, "it stands in the way of great reforms." More to the point, such a law puts a stranglehold on poetry: "I say that the body of a man or woman, the main matter, is so far quite unexpressed in poems; but that the body is to be expressed, and sex is." The touchstone of any future poets in America, he declares, "is whether they shall celebrate in their poems the eternal decency of the amativeness of Nature" and thus distinguish themselves from "the bards of the fashionable delusion of the inherent nastiness of sex...." For Whitman, no theory is of any value unless it can publicly name and accept the body's sexual charge, which is the foundation "on which all existence, all souls ... all health ... all purity, all sweetness, all friendship, all strength, all life, all immortality depend."[28] No artistic configuration in his account can be worth its salt if it does not acknowledge the determinant of corporeality. Such a stance on sexuality clearly shows his boldness and his level of commitment to challenging the rigidity of puritanical and Victorian values by bringing the question of soma into literary consciousness. With a level of courage that borders on arrogance, he wrote the letter to the most influential literary figure of his day, and at this point in his career he had only self-published a small collection of his own poems.

Whitman adopted the same stance in his poetry, challenging the filthy, moral law that destroyed the body's electrical vitality. "My call," he says in "Song of the Open Road," "is the call of battle, I nourish active rebellion" (211). In "Starting from Paumanok" he claims to "make the poem of evil also, I commemorate that part also," adding, "I am myself just as much evil as good..." (99, 100). Here, he is being more rhetorical than literal, for there is no place in Whitman's ethics for actual evils such as murder and the like. Although he called for a more open sexuality, he had a distaste for obscene language, and he strongly disapproved of the pornography of his day.[29] When he claims to be the champion of evil, as Denise Askin has pointed out, he really means *perceived* evils such as those impulses, drives, and behaviors coded filthy and rendered transgressions by nineteenth-century moral standards.[30] This stance on evil becomes clear in "Song of Myself" when he declares, "Through me forbidden voices, / Voices of sexes and lusts, voices veil'd and I remove the veil, / Voices indecent by me clarified and transfigur'd" (916–18). Whitman unclothes the body, declares it to be beautiful in its naked glory, and validates it powerful sexual urges by deeming them no longer forbidden and requiring obscurity but actually worthy of open celebration.

This challenge, at least in his non-poetic communications, is more heterosexual than homosexual, for as I have briefly discussed, he seemed ambivalent about publicly declaring his homosexuality. In his letter to Symonds Whitman strongly condemned homosexuality and rejected that his poetry suggested homoeroticism. He went so far as to call Symonds' insinuations "morbid inferences—wh' are disavow'd by me and seem damnable."[31] In an age so hostile to homosexual behavior—an age, incidentally, that did not even have "homosexual" as a category of identity, for one was either healthy and heterosexual or unhealthy and abnormal—it would have been disastrous for Whitman to position himself as an advocate for male/male sexual relations. His poetry, however, subversively suggests such a stance. As he puts it in "Native Moments," "I am for those who believe in loose delights, I share the midnight orgies of young men, / I dance with the dancers and drink with the drinkers, / The echoes ring with our indecent calls..." (5–7). To the twenty-first century reader, such homoeroticism cannot be ignored.

Regardless of this homoeroticism, such images generally went unnoticed in the nineteenth century. The readers who morally objected to Whitman's ideas about sexuality usually did not recognize his homoeroticism, as Jerome Loving points out in his biography of the poet. Not one of the "Calamus" poems, for instance, appeared on a list of offensive poems in the Boston District Attorney's office.[32] The heterosexual poems, such as the "Children of Adam" poems, "Song of Myself," and "I Sing the Body Electric," provoked the moral outcry. The reason for this blindness, as Loving observes, is that the cultural restrictions on same-sex affection were much looser in the nineteenth century. An open embrace of homosexuality had not yet caused heterosexual men to believe they were homosexual if they affectionately touched another male. Men often appeared in public arm-in-arm and frequently demonstrated non-sexual, physical affection, as they still do in many non–Western cultures where homosexuality is not tolerated. To be sure, not all readers were blind to Whitman's homoeroticism. William James, among others, "wrestled" with the poet throughout his career, at times finding profundity in his ideas about spirituality and healthy-mindedness and at others ambivalently dismissing them as effeminate byproducts of his diseased homosexuality.[33] By and large, however, Whitman's homoeroticism, which he himself publicly disavowed but which he covertly smuggled into his poems, was lost on many of the moral arbiters of his day. They often had no idea just how thoroughly he was advancing the notion of sexual freedom. What they did notice was that the poet cast sexuality in a new light, one that brought out of the darkness the animal nature of the human species. It was deeply disturbing to some but liberating to many others.

The Human Animal

In electrifying the body Whitman certainly celebrates sexuality, but he does not reduce corporeality down to the sexual impulse. His poetry suggests myriad sources of non-sexual bodily pleasure, such as eating, drinking, breathing deeply, walking, hugging, caressing, and savoring all forms of sensory experience through mindfully discerning the nuances of various sights, sounds, tastes, smells, and touches. As he says in "Song of Myself," he is "Walt Whitman, a Kosmos, of Manhattan the son, / Turbulent, fleshy, sensual, eating, drinking and breeding" (497–98). As a Kosmos, he believes in "the flesh and the appetites," and all sensory perceptions such as "Seeing, hearing, feeling, are miracles, and each part and tag of me is a miracle" (522–23). In "Miracles" he develops the idea further by cataloguing a list of sensory perceptions and designating them all to be sources of wonder. "What stranger miracles are there?" he rhetorically asks in the closing line (23). The electrified body is an animal body full of miraculous physiological processes and drives, most of which the nineteenth-century would rather not have acknowledged.

Whitman began writing before Darwin published *On the Origin of Species* in an age in which most people denied that human beings were animals, believing we are a higher life form that distinguishes itself from the animal species because we possess reason and a soul. Before Darwin, Whitman challenged such notions and brought to consciousness the animal nature of human corporeality. As Thoreau famously said of him, "[i]t is as if the beasts spoke."[34] His earliest readers—even if they missed his homoeroticism—nevertheless "understood the poet in terms that distinguish humans from animals, with Whitman enrolled squarely on the side of the animals."[35] They saw a Kosmos with wild eyes staring at them from the pages of *Leaves*, and, whether they enjoyed it or found it repulsive, his "barbaric yawp," as it rolled over their rooftops, reminded them of their own beastliness, their own animality ("Song of Myself" 1333).

Whitman strongly identifies with animal life, and he enviously longs "To confront night, storms, hunger, ridicule, accidents, rebuffs, as the trees and animals do, that is, with "aplomb in the midst of irrational things" ("Me Imperturbe" 8, 2). He claims a kinship with animals by professing to be able to understand their language. While the "*Ya-honk*" of geese flying overhead may seem like mere animalistic squawking to most people, the sensuous Kosmos listens closely and "Finds its purpose and place up there in the wintry sky" ("Song of Myself" 246, 248). This recognition of meaningful utterance goes beyond mere personification for poetic effect, as he is aligning himself with the substrate that binds all animal species. Human beings, it should be remembered, have not only a high-functioning neo-cortex capable of reasoning, planning, judgment, language, and other complex processes but also the limbic system common to all mammals and the reptilian brain found in all mammals and reptiles. The poet's discernment of meaning in honking geese is in some ways a deep, mindful recognition of such neurological commonality. Because of this kinship, he claims that he would willingly turn from human life "and live with animals, they are so placid and self-contain'd" ("Myself" 684). Given the list of images he uses in his praise of animals—they do not whine, worry about sin and duty to God, concern themselves with respectability, bow to another who lived thousands of years earlier, and become dissatisfied, unhappy, or manic—it is clear he feels human beings have allowed culture to stymie the animal bliss that lies in the body. He recovers this body-bliss for himself through long, meditative observations of animal species, the result of which is that "they show their relations to me and I accept them. / They bring me tokens of myself, they evince them plainly in their possession" (692–93). He embraces his own animality and recognizes its centrality in his subjectivity.

Despite deeply embedded attitudes and values that made people uncomfortable about their bodies and animal drives, a new discourse about the body emerged in the mid-nineteenth century America in the form of physiology, which looked at the human body amorally and openly, as if it were like any other animal body. Whitman was deeply influenced by this discourse, seeing in the popular physiology books "a healthy alternative" to the lewdness of pornographic literature and common conversation about sex and the body, as Reynolds observes. Inspired by the writings of Mary Gove, Edward Dixon, Orson Fowler, and others, the poet adopted a physiologist's attitude toward the body, viewing its animality not as a source of embarrassment but openly with a scientist's candor.[36] In "One's-Self I Sing," the first poem in *Leaves*, he thus declares, "Of physiology from top to toe I sing" (3). He delivers on the promise by acknowledging that his body smells like an animal body but declaring its smell to be good: "The scent of these arm-pits aroma finer than prayer" ("Myself" 525). He sanitizes the dirty parts by referring to the "bowels sweet and clean" ("Body Electric" 148), and he praises the nipples, teats, breast-milk, male ejaculate, the blood, the organs, and nearly *every* other part of the body. In "Pressing the pulse of the life that has seldom exhibited itself," as he declares he will do ("To a Historian" 5), he exposes "Another self," the one "skulking and hiding" beneath the surface of nineteenth-century consciousness—the othered body in all of its animal glory ("Song of the Open Road" 198).

The Embedded Body

Animal bodies do not exist independently of one another, for members of a given species are connected not only to other members of that species but also to members of other species and to the earth itself. This concept, first articulated by James Lovelock in his "Gaia" hypothesis, is a refutation of the older, atomistic conception of what constitutes a single animal. According to the "Gaia" theory, a "cow is no longer a cow ... but a collection of different organisms: from bacteria inside, to ticks on its hide, to creatures that make good homes on its dung, to the processing of its methane and carbon dioxide."[37] The human body is similarly *embedded* in an ecosystem comprising a variety of other species of both fauna and flora. Influenced by Romantic organicism and its challenge to mechanistic conceptions of the earth, Whitman recognized the embedded nature of the human body not only in its connection to other animals but in its relationship to and dependence upon the earth. The electrified body, he implies, receives its current from the earth, which is charged with its own sexual electricity: "Does the earth gravitate?" he asks, "does not all matter, aching, attract all mater?" ("I Am He That Aches with Love" 2).

In several curious passages the poet thus directs his libido toward the earth in a kind of "cosmo-erotic"[38] impulse to merge himself sexually with nature. In "By Blue Ontario's Shore" he finds himself attracted to the land on which America is being created, and thus he wants to plunge "his seminal muscle into its merits and demerits (73). He wants to fuck the continent. In "Song of Myself" he has a similar erotic encounter with the sexually inviting, "voluptuous cool-breath'd earth" (438). In gratitude for the earth's gifts, he declares his intention to repay them with penetration and semen: "Smile for your lover comes. / Prodigal, you have given me love—therefore I to you give love! / O unspeakable passionate love" (445–47). He then turns to the sea, which seductively lures him with its "crooked inviting fingers" as they wash against the shore of his receptive, charged body (449). "We must have a turn together," he avers, as he hurriedly undresses. Once again, he states his intention to show his gratitude, however bizarre and comical it may seem, with semen: "Dash me with amorous wet, I can repay you" (451, 453). Through sexual imagery, he symbolizes the union of natural and corporeal life. They are conjoined in an interdependent relationship in which the body receives its vitality from the earth and then returns such energy to the earth. Transmuting the "foul liquid and meat" of corporeal compost into the glories of "the summer growth," the earth "gives such divine materials to men, and accepts such leavings from them at last" in a reciprocity that suggests the embedded nature of corporeality ("This Compost" 13, 30, 47). In returning the body to its natural matrix and recognizing the beauty that results when it is composted, Whitman overcomes the "radical alienation between the human and the natural that our language helplessly imposes" (Outka 53). In innocently saying "my body" or "my thumb," one immediately objectifies the body by making it the object of a perceiving subject. Whitman, however, "subjectifies" the body by embedding it in a thoroughly connected matrix through sexual fusion with nature.

In *Specimen Days & Collect* he affirmed his understanding of the "pulsations in all matter, all spirit, throbbing forever—the eternal beats, eternal systole and diastole of life in things."[39] Because the human body throbs with the same force that pulses through all matter, it is connected to all things, much like his famous spider that launches its filaments out to the objects of the world or his child who goes forth and becomes everything he encounters. The body and the cosmos from which it emerges are intimately interconnected in a "vast similitude [that] interlocks all" ("On the Beach at Night Alone" 4). To view the body in an atomistic way as a separate entity is to mar the earth, for such an idea severs the connection the poet forcefully and repeatedly declares. "The earth shall surely be complete to him or her who shall be complete," he sings in "A Song of the Rolling Earth." "The earth remains jagged and broken only to him or her who remains jagged and broken" (90–91). His ideas about the connection between nature and body are informed by the natural theology of Transcendentalism, whose proponents held the belief that "the human intellect can discover truths about God by studying the natural or created world," an idea that can be traced back to Plato and Aristotle, if not farther.[40] Whitman, however, subverts this tradition in not denigrating the body as a material force that interrupts the rational discernment of non-material truths. Such truths, for the poet, are deeply embedded in the earth and the body, and they can only be ascertained through the revived animism[41] he declares and the heightened level of embodied awareness he exemplifies.

Embodied Cognition

To say Whitman's cognition is embodied is to say his perceptions result from bodily interactions with the world. "From this point of view," writes Esther Thelen, a cognition theorist, cognition depends on the kinds of experience that come from having a body with particular perceptual and motor capabilities that are inseparably linked and that together form the matrix within which reasoning, memory, emotion, language, and all other aspects of mental life are meshed."[42] A dolphin's sonar will enable it to cognitively experience the world in ways that will forever be inaccessible to humans who lack such sensory apparatus. Such a concept represents a challenge to traditional cognitive science, which sees the body as a simple house for the brain. To see cognition as being embodied is to recognize "the body as the brain's partner in the production of cognition.... The body and brain divide the labor of cognition between them, sharing in processes that neither could complete on its own."[43] According to embodied cognition theory, the body has a more prominent role in perception than it does in abstract reasoning, but one's thoughts are inevitably informed by the perceptions registered on the body. Cognition in all humans is thus in some way rooted in sensory experience.

What makes Whitman so unique is his prescient, intuitive understanding of concepts that have only recently surfaced in cognitive science.[44] In a Transcendentalist age that sought to reach beyond matter and corporeality for disembodied truths, Whitman recognized the truth-value of the sensations that registered on his body. "Mine is no callous shell," he intones in "Song of Myself." "I have instant conductors all over me whether I pass or stop" (614–15). To be sure, there are Transcendentalist and Platonic ideas in his poetry, as he was deeply influenced by Emerson and the Platonic tradition. He indeed had other-worldly concerns, a point bolstered by his many poems about death, God, the afterlife, and the like, particularly those he wrote as he aged and experienced a series of debilitating strokes and the breakdown of his body. But he also challenges what Aldous Huxley called Plato's inability to see "objects in nature as they existed in their own right."[45] As early as 1855, he articulated in a notebook that the "Great constituent elements of my poetry" are "Two, viz: Materialism—Spirituality," adding, "The intellect is what is to be the medium of these and to beautify and make serviceable there."[46] Whitman's Platonic/Emersonian spiritualism, then, represents only half of his vision. The other half is a thorough recognition of the value of sensory experience in an anti–Platonic embrace of corporeality and materiality as a means to perception and truth.

Whitman's epistemology is thus non-rational not only in the general Romantic sense of capturing levels of awareness that lie beyond the ratiocinating mind but also in that it is a celebration of the states of being that result when we stand in awe of the sensations registered on the body and consequently experience ecstatic transformation. He is the foremost poet of wonder who stands in the profoundest awe at the smallest sensory perceptions. This attribute is perhaps best seen in "Sparkles from the Wheel," in which the sight of a knife-grinder, though countless other passersby dismiss it as pedestrian, is arresting and absorbing enough for him to be thoroughly mesmerized: "The scene and all its belongings, how they seize and affect me," he exclaims (9). Unlike Plato, he sees the deepest truths in momentary perceptions of trivial, worldly things, taking immense delight in and even becoming enraptured over the sights and sounds of an old man grinding a knife. In recognizing the *suchness* of the moment, as the Buddhists would call it, he cultivates a wholly different perspective from that of the passersby who trivialize the scene as mundane and thus not worthy of attention. Instead, he looks at it in a state of wonder that rises to awe and then ecstasy. This alternative epistemology, significantly shared by the group of children he joins but lost to most of the adults passing by, represents an expanded view of an enlarged mind mindfully attentive to the sensations the body sends to it.

When Whitman denigrates book learning, as he does in "Shut Not Your Doors" (and so many other poems), he is operating from a perspective that includes both spiritual insights that elude the reasoning mind and corporeal wisdom dismissed as intellectual interference. The physicality of the spiritual knowledge he claims to bring is seen in the last two lines, in which he claims to offer "A book separate, not link'd with the rest nor felt by the intellect, / But you ye untold latencies will thrill to every page" (4–5). The latencies thrilling to every page are as much physical as they are spiritual. They are latencies because they lie dormant in the bodies and minds of the receptive reader, not on the pages of *Leaves,* a book intended to focus readerly attention on corporeal sensation. No doubt, this is why he wrote poems such as "Whoever You Are Holding Me Now in Hand" and "As I Lay with My Head in Your Lap," both of which suggest the transmutation of words to touch. Through some kind of alchemy, "words become flesh," as Karen Sanchez-Eppler observes.[47] He embodies his own book in such poems and reaches out to physically touch the reader, as if to stress that his truth lies not in poetic language but in becoming attuned to somatic sensation and ecstatically reveling in its manifold delights. After meditating on touch for three verse-chants in "Song of Myself," he makes it clear that bodily sensation is the principal route to the way of knowing he is suggesting: "Logic and sermons never convince, / The damp of the night drives deeper into my soul" (653–54). In "Of the Terrible Doubt of Appearances," he reinforces the point. "When he whom I love travels with me or sits a long while holding me by the hand, / When the subtle air, the impalpable, the sense that words and reason hold not, surround us and pervade us, / Then I am charged with untold and untellable wisdom. I am silent, I require nothing further" (11–13). The electrical charge of wisdom comes not from ascertaining some otherworldly truths—which he nevertheless did believe in—but in the corporeal sensations denied by those who narrowly focus on such truths to the exclusion of physicality. The fusion of the two is central to Whitman's spiritual understanding.

The Spiritualized Body

Although Whitman's spirituality has been explored from a number of perspectives, including Zen, Sufi, Shamanic, Taoist, and Christian, among others, his religious ideas do not fit neatly into any one of these categories for a number of complex reasons, foremost among which is his sacralization of the body. In many, but by no means all, spiritual traditions there is an antagonism towards the body, which is viewed as an obstruction to spiritual life because of its strong animal drives. Such ideas can be seen perhaps most clearly in the Christian tradition that so profoundly influenced Whitman. Although a new theology of the body emerged in Christianity during the second half of the twentieth century, the nineteen Christian centuries leading up to this development were less than kind to the body. To be sure, this antagonism of corporeality predates the Christian era and stems from several sources, such as Greek Orphism with its separation of the soul from the body, the Platonic view of the body as a hindrance to reason, and Hebrew ideas about the ritual uncleanliness of bodily fluids, intercourse, childbirth, contact with a corpse, and the like. Mary Prokes also cites Near Eastern dualism and Gnosticism as significant sources of negative Christian ideas about the body.[48] Regardless of these antecedents, over the centuries Christians developed ideas about the separation of soul and body, privileging the former and viewing the latter as somehow being incompatible with religious life. Although Christian theologians are today beginning to theorize the body in religious analyses of corporeal concepts, such as the consumption of Christ's flesh during the Eucharist and the idea of the Church as the mystical body of Christ,[49] in Whitman's Victorian culture the body, with its sex drive and strong appetites, was a fleshly burden, an embarrassment, and the means by which Satan tempted good Christians to stray from the straight and narrow path.

Whitman's electrified body challenges such ideas, of course. Although he borrows both concepts and verse forms from the Christian tradition, he also subversively undermines Christian spirituality in construing the metaphysical as "a radically different way of experiencing the physical."[50] Like Prometheus, Whitman steals heavenly fire and brings it down to the earth. He does not simply declare that the physical is the only reality, for as Reynolds points out, "an exclusive emphasis on either the physical or the spiritual misses his determined intermingling of the two realms."[51] He does, however, sacralize the body and argue for its inclusion among the things normally considered to be spiritual. Although other authors before him operated according to the same Promethean impulse in locating the divine in nature, Whitman goes a step farther by imbuing the corporeal with a spiritual charge. His esoteric spiritual ideas are informed Harmonialism, Mesmerism, Elias Hicks, and so much else,[52] but the inclusion of the body in his spiritual scheme is rather unique and represents a departure from most religious systems.

As Reynolds shows, he found a confirmation of his belief in the connection between the erotic and the spiritual in the work of Swedenborg, for he once told Horace Traubel: "I think Swedenborg was right when he said there was a close connection—a very close connection—between the state we call religious ecstasy and the desire to copulate. I find it confirmed in all my experience."[53] Erotic desire is implicated in ecstasy and manifests as a quest for self-abandonment. "It guides our religious quest for passionate connection with an ideally romanticized 'other,'" as Robert Fuller observes, "and it provides the power propelling quests to transform our mortal natures in the direction of immortality."[54] For Walt the Kosmos, the ecstasy of the body is not merely analogous to religious ecstasy; they are one and the same. As he says in "Starting from Paumanok," "Behold, the body includes and is the meaning, the main concern, and includes and is the soul; / Whoever you are, how superb and how divine is your body, or any part of it!" (187–88). Such statements, which he makes several times in *Leaves*, run against the grain of Christian dualism that informed so much nineteenth-century thought.

For all of his rhetoric about the spirituality of the body, Whitman was not a materialist. While he does locate divinity in corporeality, he also made room in his religious vision for the idea that the soul lives beyond the body. As he declares in "Song of Myself," "I pass death with the dying and birth with the new-wash'd babe, and am not contain'd between my hat and my boots" (133). In "O Living Always, Always Dying," he sings enthusiastically of his desire "To pass on, (O Living! always living!) and leave the corpses behind" (6). He wrote about such ideas even in his earliest poetry. Although he claims in "Song of Myself" to worship nothing before "the spread of my own body, or any part of it," placing his own "Firm masculine colter" above all else, even above conceptions of God, his ideas should not be reduced to materialism alone (530). As he says earlier in the poem, "I am the poet of the Body, and I am the poet of the Soul" (422). In "Paumanok" he also stressed the connection: "And I will make the poems of my body and of mortality, / For I think I shall then supply myself with the poems of my soul and immortality" (72–73). The two are holistically linked.

Throughout the course of his life, Whitman did write less enthusiastically about bodily experience. As he aged, his own bodily ailments caused him to change his rhetoric about the body, and he was less inclined to declare the spirituality of corporeality. Still, while his rhetoric may have changed, his general view of the sacredness of the body remained constant. After all, in his endless revision of *Leaves*, he let stand all of the earlier passages about the glories of the body, even though later in life his own was paralyzed, constipated, and wracked with pain and other infirmities.

Kosmic Holism

Whitman's ideas about the divinity of corporeality bring to consciousness the psychological aspects of the mind/body split. He clearly believed the soul outlives the body, so he was something of a dualist himself. But he also believed that such an idea had been driven to untenable extremes in the Western tradition, which transmuted the idea of body transcendence into tacit-but-ever-present assumptions that corporeality, particularly sexuality, is inherently bad and thus an obstacle to human well-being. His stance on the issue can be seen not only in his letter to Emerson, in which he decries the "filthy law" that renders sexuality as something dirty, but also in his poetry. In "I Sing the Body Electric" he forcefully states the idea that the animal drives of the body are inherently good and their full embrace essential to psychological well-being. In the first verse-chant he claims to "discorrupt" the bodies of those he loves and "charge them full with the charge of the soul" (4). In the second he says of the gendered body, "That of the male is perfect, and that of the female is perfect" (10). In the final verse-chant, after a detailed catalogue of body parts, he once again connects body and soul—"O I say these are not the parts and poems of the body only, but of the soul—and then proclaims their connection to be "the exquisite realization of health" (163, 162). He saw the shame about corporeality implied in mind/body dualism as being problematic, a point he states rather forcefully in "A Woman Waits for Me," where he candidly says, "Without shame the man I like knows and avows the deliciousness of his sex, / Without shame the woman I like knows and avows hers" (9–10). The genitals, he implies, are inherently good, even better when they are touched together. Whitman's electrified body implies psychological health in its fullest sense and serves as a challenge to the neurosis underlying diseased Western attitudes.

Some scholars have recognized the high degree of psychological health suggested by Whitman's poetry. As I have mentioned, William James called him the premier example of the "religion of healthy mindedness." And while he may have been ambivalent about Whitman's sexuality, in *Varieties of Religious Experience* he says healthy mindedness "is anything but absurd."[55] More recently, Leslie Jamison has psychoanalyzed the violence in Whitman's fiction, arguing that it serves as an "important catalyst for the embodied empathy that charged Whitman's poetry with such sympathetic force."[56] Doxy Hatch has also explored the poet's psychology, noting that his self-definition represents a departure from the simplistic ideal advanced by popular self-esteem literature. The poet, according to Hatch, embodies humility, balance, mindfulness, self-acceptance, non-judgmental tolerance of difference, empathy, respect for the autonomy of others, an attitude of openness and affirmation, and a nonreductionist holism—all of which signify a high level of psychological well-being.[57] Although such ideas about the psychology of Whitman are sound, it is important, once again, to distinguish between Walter Whitman and the Kosmos of his poetry. When we say there is psychological health in Whitman, we are really referring to the idealized self he constructs in his verse.

The image of the Kosmos, nevertheless, is thoroughly imbued with a sense of well-being. As Reynolds shows, the poet borrowed the image from a popular book, *Kosmos*, by the Prussian author Alexander von Humboldt, who wrote a "scientific" view of the universe as a "harmoniously ordered whole ... animated by the breath of life."[58] Whitman internalized the image, merging with it, as he does with everything, to construct a holistic self completely in tune with *all* of its own resonances and singing, in the key of cosmic life, beautiful songs about the interrelationship of matter and spirit, body and soul, self and other. This holism, as he says in "Song of Myself," is "form, union, plan—it is eternal life—it is Happiness" (1318). To be whole is to be psychologically well, to be happy, and even to be charged with ecstatic electricity, a point he also suggests in "A Song of Joys": "O the joy of my spirit—it is uncaged—it darts like lightening!" (7). Although he is here implying an out-of-body image—a bird-spirit freed from its body-cage—it is important to remember that flight from the body can manifest as a pathological symptom *and* as an indicator of well-being, depending on the circumstances. Bodily transcendence, as in the case of mysticism, can carry with it an extreme sense of well-being, while in other situations, as in tortured prisoners, diseased patients, and rape victims, it can be a self-protective measure designed to remedy a painful bodily circumstance. What prompts the release of the spirit from its cage in "Song of Joys" is an internalization of animal and natural energies, as the speaker invokes these at the beginning of the poem: "O for the voices of animals ... O for the sunshine and motion of waves in a song!" (4, 6). He may be flying from his body in a moment of ecstasy, but he does so only because he has become attuned to the electrical charge coursing through all nature and all animal life, including the one firing his own beastly body. This is well-being in the fullest sense of the word.

The sense of psychological health the Kosmos embodies presciently includes a connection to soma. Whitman seemed to know, well before Freudian discussions of psychosomatic manifestations and more recent explorations of the mind-body connection, that psyche and soma are linked in the question of well-being. To be sure, physically unwell people can be psychologically resilient, even more so because of their infirmities, but an ailing body often brings misery, as it did with Whitman as he aged. According to his journals, Whitman experienced few days of joy in his declining years, plagued as he was by a number of painful ailments.[59] The Kosmos, nevertheless, knows there is a strong link between the body and mind, each influencing the other's state of being in a circularity that signifies a totality, not two compartmentalized domains. Such compartments are cultural constructions and can be seen in the idea, held by lay people and even many psychologists, that psychological health is distinct from physical health. Despite the work of Wilhelm Reich, the father of somatic psychology and an early psychoanalyst who broke from Freud to explore his own ideas about the body, psychoanalysis is complicit with such ideas. As Perrin Elisha compellingly demonstrates, psychoanalysts tend to associate the somatic with the infantile, regressive, and pathological, and they often unwittingly collude with (and thus perpetuate) psychological disease in treatment attitudes that privilege "dissociation, alexithymia, and isolation."[60] However much Freud favored sexuality as a source of all psychic energy, he pathologized the body by locating the source of neurosis in the sexual drive.

Whitman knew better. He knew what Harry Harlowe later proved with his famously neglected, untouched monkeys—that apes and their close biological relatives need physical touch if they are to be psychologically well.[61] Without such physical connection, they become deeply neurotic. In "I Sing the Body Electric" the poet says, "There is something in staying close to men and women and looking on them, and in the contact and odor of them, that pleases the soul well, / All things please the soul, but these please the soul well" (50–51). He knew what we learned from the experiments at the sterile orphanages of the 1940s and 1950s—that if babies are not touched and loved, they will die.[62] And so he studies "long and long" a "sleeping babe nestling the breast of its mother," seeing their physical contact as the foundation and fulfillment of human life ("Mother and Babe" 2, 1). He knew, albeit only intuitively, about the powers of oxytocin, the natural hormone produced by the body that fosters mother/child bonding and compels humans and other mammals to touch and hug one another. He is a lover and worshipper of nature, but he also privileges human physicality over the natural world. In "Give Me the Splendid Silent Sun," the solar orb is beautiful, but he says "Keep your splendid silent sun" and "Give me faces and streets ... People, endless, streaming ... Manhattan crowds ... Manhattan faces and eyes forever for me" (20, 24, 36, 39, and 40). Though he has a sensibility finely attuned to the exquisite joys of nature, aesthetic beauty in its most glorious, natural form cannot compare to proximity to and contact with other human bodies. "I merely stir, press, feel with my fingers, and am happy," he sings in "Song of Myself." All bodies are beautiful and sacred for Whitman, even the body of the slave, the prostitute, the red aborigine, the diseased rheumatic, the common farmer, the ugly, the young, the old, the greasy, the pimpled—all are charged with the same electricity. "To touch my person to someone else's is about as much as I can stand" (618–19). The psychological satisfaction of physical contact with other bodies, both sexual and otherwise, is for him the *summum bonum* of human life.

As I briefly discussed, Whitman reaches out and touches the reader, not only through physically becoming his own book but also through countless tactile images. He is the "caresser of life," and "the press of [his] foot to the earth brings a hundred affections." His touch heals, and just as he tends to his wounded soldiers in the Civil War camp, so does he offer solace to an ailing reader: "I am he bringing help for the sick as they pant on their backs" ("Myself" 232, 253, 1021). He dresses wounds, both physical and psychological, and offers "To sit by the wounded and soothe them" ("The Wound-Dresser" 6). He similarly nurses readers back to psychological health through touch, through forcefully declaring the equation of body and spirit, through a celebration of sexuality, through the worship of material nature, and through an embrace of animality. He does so not only by fiat or modeling but by pointing the way for readers to become aware of their own electrical charge.

> I have no chair, no church, no philosophy,
> I lead no man to a dinner-table, library, exchange,
> But each man and each woman of you I lead upon a knoll,
> My left hand hooking you round the waist,
> My right hand pointing to landscapes and the public road
> ["Myself" 1205–09].

Physically embracing the reader with a caring, guiding touch, he points the way both to the materiality of nature and to human society, the two domains on which human well-being is so dependent.

A Corporeal Poetics of Ecstasy

Such ideas about the electrified body are not only thematic; they are also deeply inscribed in Whitman's poetics. He embraced Emerson's idea that the writer is a conductor of electricity, but he modifies the concept, as Klatt observes, taking his energy not only from the imagination, a characteristically Romantic notion, but from the world itself.[63] He also modifies it by locating the charge of inspiration in his own body, which becomes the primary source of poetic inspiration. The electrical images he sees and feels in various material entities register corporeally in him and compel his writing. As he says in "Beginning My Studies," "…these forms, the power of motion, / The least insect or animal, the senses, eyesight, love … awed me and pleased me so much, / I have hardly gone and hardly wish to go any farther, / But stop and loiter all the time to sing it in ecstatic songs" (2–3, 4–6). Given the complexity of his metaphysics and spirituality, he is clearly understating his poetic endeavor. In another sense, however, he is representing himself rather well, for the poem shows him as someone in whom there is an intense degree of somatic awareness, the electricity of which fires his writing. He is a physical writer whose poems result from bodily sensation as much as they do from the intellect and imagination. He recognizes and privileges the epistemological value of the cognitive experience that arises from his sensory perceptions. His verse exemplifies "embodied" writing.

Whitman told John Burroughs that the first edition of *Leaves* "was produced in a mood, or condition of the mind, that he had never been able to resume, and that he had felt utterly incompetent to produce anything equal to it since.—That in contemplating it," as Burroughs adds, "he felt in regard to his own agency in it like a somnambulist who is shown during his waking hours the giddy heights and impossible situations over which he has passed safely in his sleep."[64] According to his own account of the genesis of the 1855 edition, he operated from what could be called Orphic conceptions of the poet as the enraptured conduit of the Muse's inspiration. The early poetry indeed seems to have a fresh, electrical quality. As he himself admits, however, he could not maintain such an approach to writing. He published *Leaves of Grass* in nine different editions, and over the course of his life, he continually polished and revised his work. His later poems are by no means uncooked, exhibiting the refinement one does not see, by comparison, in his own earlier verse, in Saul Williams' spoken-word performances, or in the poetry of someone like D.H. Lawrence. *Leaves*, nevertheless, is imbued with a strong electrical charge that manifests in its ecstatic tone. Janice Trecker has observed this quality of Whitman's writing, identifying his "rhapshodic mysticism" as the crucial ground of *Leaves*.[65] Such an observation could not be more apt. He is, after all, "...mad with devouring ecstasy to make joyous hymns for the whole earth" ("Excelsior" 12). George Hutchinson cites "Passage to India" as an indication of the decline of Whitman's ecstatic poetry. Written in 1871, the poem signals an otherworldly shift in his focus, one in which the corporeal and material no longer play such a central role.[66] No doubt, his own declining body had something to do with why the muse of electricity abandoned him. Such is the fate of all bodies.

Regardless, Whitman's poems were to nineteenth-century America an ecstatic, electrical charge, the essence of which the poet himself claimed he did not see in Emerson, Carlyle, the German metaphysicians, or the British Romantics. All of these writers, as he put it, failed to produce "the lightning flashes and flights of the old prophets and *exaltes*...."[67] He believed literature lacked the Dionysian energies he felt coursing through his own body, so he attempted to capture these in words and to help his readers to discern the electrical charge animating all matter and all bodies.

He did so by writing in new ways. His cataloguing technique is a replication of the way animals see the world, as Killingsworth observes.[68] Animals take in sensory details, and, presumably, they do not see the forest for the trees; they see trees and more trees. Whitman definitely recognizes the totality, but he also demonstrates, through his extensive cataloguing, a keen understanding of the subtle difference among its constituent parts. His catalogues also have an incantatory quality, as critics have noted, and they can serve to transform consciousness in ways that take the reader out of the ratiocinating ego and into the rhythms of the body and the natural world. His use of free verse, which was undoubtedly inspired by Biblical forms, is an attempt on his part to recover the Dionysian element he felt was lacking in literature. As Klatt observes, "the electric line, the jagged edge of free verse ... is really as ancient as poetry itself, before the line was domesticated by fixed meters, and harks all the way back to the dithyramb."[69] He saw similarities, as he put it, in the "ancient poetry of the Hebrew prophets, of Ossian, of the Hindu singers and ecstatics, of the Greeks, of the Americans aborigines, the old Persians and Chinese, and the Scandinavian Sagas."[70] In both theme and technique, he recovered for poetry the sense of wild abandon by which it was once characterized in the ancient world. While his identification with Native Americans and other "primitive" peoples is not without its problems,"[71] he used images of such groups to invoke in the reader's mind a sense of the primal before it was layered over with Anglicized values, beliefs, morals, and behavioral codes.

Whitman saw his writing as a means to heal not only deeply internalized, diseased conceptions of the body and its relationship to nature and God but also the divisions of nineteenth-century America, wracked as it was by the pains of political, economic, and social conflict. Hutchinson reads *Leaves* as an ecstatic performance in which the poet functions precisely as a shaman does in various cultures. His ecstatic states, as they are in shamanic cultures, are a means to bridge cultural schisms and to heal psychological fragmentation. In his personal life, Whitman periodically suffered from despair, and his method of dealing with such crises was "always artistic productivity in an ecstatic mode."[72] He used shamanic techniques to heal himself and his nation. Sanchez-Eppler similarly sees his "poetics of merger and embodiment" as "his poetic goal of healing radical divisions, social and personal."[73] He hoped his book, "like grass leaves, would sprout in all regions and nourish its readers."[74] To effect such healing, he offered in *Leaves* an idealized portrait of himself as a superb physical specimen exuding vitality, despite that his genetic stock was less than perfect. The result, as Aspiz observes, was that he hoped "to establish a wonder-working electric contact with his readers, whom the very poems, the pages of the book, could charge with physical and spiritual health." In keeping with mid-nineteenth-century ideas, which called for writers to be in prime physical health,[75] he thus argued that "a sense of health may well enter into the preparation of future noble American authorship. Part of the test of a great writer should be the absence in him of the idea of the covert, the lurid, the grim estimates inherited from the Puritans...."[76] A good writer, he believed, should have a healthy body and, consequently, as healthy mind, the effects of which are good writing that helps readers to heal from the various crises that inevitably characterize human life. In imbuing his poetic persona with such images of well-being, he showed readers how to heal from diseased ideas.

The Idealism of the Body Ecstatic

The unified self Whitman celebrates in *Leaves* may thus be idealized, given the poet's own lifelong battle with an imperfect body and flawed health. Still, it should not be dismissed as a mere poetic fabrication because idealizations of self show us our potential, without which we are bereft of one of the main sources of meaning in human life. Without ideals, we drift into meaninglessness, ennui, and/or despair. The self he constructs, moreover, is likely not purely a fabrication. While it is important to recognize the difference between the man and the performing speaker, Whitman surely actualized in himself so many of the traits we associate with the Kosmos of the poetry. The claim I have made about retrieving unconscious, somatic energies must, by its logic, apply as much to the man as it does to the Kosmos. He was by no means the saint his Whitmaniacs believed him to be, but he does seem to embody so many of the characteristics we today associate with well-being.

More compelling, Whitman uses the idealized, electrified self to challenge and change several problematic values writers have internalized over the centuries of Western history. Such values manifest as conceptual metaphors through which we (mis)understand the world.[77] Whitman deconstructs, among others, such metaphors as the body as house for the soul/brain, the body as container for the mind, the body as dirty, the body as beast, the body as an object of a disembodied, perceiving subject, the body as a discrete and disconnected material entity, and the body as a temptation to stray from religious life. For him, sexual pleasure is not inherently sinful, and sexuality is not solely for the purpose of procreation. As the source of all life, it can also lead one into states of spiritual ecstasy in which one realizes the metaphysical ground of being. There is nothing immoral about frequent sexual urges, as they generally compel all human bodies, male and female. Such urges are connective and bring human beings together in meaningful ways. Animality is not a source of shame and embarrassment but a cause to celebrate and reach out to other animal species. The body and its fluids, secretions, and various parts are not ritually dirty but naturally wholesome, a potential source of well-being. The animal body is not discrete but thoroughly connected to other species and embedded in nature. It is not a barrier between self and other but a bridge that connects the two at deep levels. The body is not merely a house for the soul; it is sacred in its own right and significantly factors in spirituality.

It is not an obstacle but can be the way to the sacred. To become aware of one's somatic energies is to experience cognition in a new (deeper) way in which the body is not a mere object but endowed with subjectivity; indeed, it is perhaps *the* central determinant in human subjectivity. The result of retrieving soma and fusing it with psyche is a recognition of the value and importance of touch, sensation, and all forms of materiality and embodiment. The fusion, at least for the poet, is ecstasy.

In "A Backward Glance O'er Travel'd Roads," Whitman says *Leaves* is "avowedly the song of Sex and Amativeness, and even Animality—though meanings that do not usually go along with those words are behind all, and will duly emerge; and all are sought to be lifted into a different light and atmosphere." As I have tried to show, this new light and atmosphere are eudaimonic and, for most twenty-first century readers, highly desirable. Whitman makes having a body full of animal drives a good, sacred experience in which somatic awareness enables us to reach out beyond the self in life-fulfilling ways to connect with other animal and human bodies at the deep, soul level, with nature and the cosmos, and with the sacred, however it is conceived.

Leaves of Grass is thus a beastly book, the Dionysian howling of an animal-poet all aquiver with an ecstatic charge that connects him to the responding reader, who, in the poet's ideal conception, will interfuse with nature and all material existence and embrace a radical conception of divinity in which the physical and the spiritual are inseparably linked. For Whitman, the body ecstatic is the portal to a holistic life of happiness, which he favored and hoped his words would inspire.

8. The Cracked Mind: Emily Dickinson

She cut a strange figure. A tongue-in-cheek documentary has her looking like a nun, clad in a white, nineteenth-century dress as she runs through a cemetery, fleeing an eager reporter whose importunate request—"please Ms. Dickinson, just one word"—she vehemently refuses. Despite a gregarious, "normal" youth spent attending school, socializing, flirting with boys and girls, cultivating friendships, and meeting strangers, Emily Dickinson in her early twenties suffered from some kind of mental breakdown that would plague her for the rest of her life. At this point, she retreated to the creative silence of her Amherst room, from the windows of which the good-hearted poet would converse with neighboring children, often lowering down cookies to them, all without showing her face. When friends, sometimes even dear friends, would call upon her, she would often send down a poem or a flower on a tray rather than risk a live encounter, the likes of which she reserved solely for her nearest family members. The arrival of a social caller or some other acquaintance would send her scurrying from the parlor in a panic, as she bounded like a frightened cat upstairs to her room. Later in life, when she was suffering from what scholars believed for many years was Bright's Disease but others have more recently claimed was accelerated hypertension,[1] she insisted the family physician diagnose her by making an observation as she briefly passed by a slightly ajar door, her face turned the other way, of course.[2] Thomas Wentworth Higginson, the poet's literary mentor, initially found her presence to be disturbing. After they met for the first time in 1870, Higginson wrote: "I never was with any one [sic] who drained my nerve power so much. Without touching her, she drew from me." "The impression made upon me," he observed, "was that of an excess of tension, and of abnormal life...." Emily Dickinson appeared to him in these first impressions as being "partially cracked," as he put it.[3]

Several scholars have confirmed Higginson's initial impression, identifying psychological disease in the person of Emily Dickinson, who almost undoubtedly suffered from what today would have been called agoraphobia. At the age of twenty four, she experienced a panic attack that may have manifested as result of some kind of affective disorder,[4] whether schizotypal[5] or seasonal or bi-polar.[6] Others have made claims for a deeper psychosis,[7] but without convincingly demonstrating the point. Regardless of her psychological pathology—the exact nature of which we will probably never precisely know— Dickinson is far more than a broken mind. No doubt, most sophisticated readers would acknowledge such a point, citing her prodigious creative output and the complexity of her brilliantly original work. Many scholars, however, seem to have let their knowledge of the poet's personal psychology color their perceptions of her work in reducing it to her neuroses. No doubt, her poetry is the result of her unusual mind, but perhaps we can learn something from it if we reflect upon it in terms other than as a symptom of disease.

Let me be more precise. To pathologize her abnormal psychology fails to see the wisdom in madness and the productive truths we can learn from a "cracked" mind. In the West, madness is treated as a medical condition, but in some cultures it is held in high esteem. The Bwiti of Gabon, for instance, offer a ceremony in which initiates are given iboga, a drink containing a psychedelic bark that induces a trance lasting for over 30 hours. They refer to the ceremony as "breaking open the head" because it causes participants to go temporarily insane. It occupies a central rite of passage in their culture. Those whose minds are so cracked nearly always report a beneficial, life-enhancing experience of consciousness transformation.[8] Among the Bwiti, it is likely Dickinson would be looked upon as someone who possesses higher *gnosis*, not as a neurotic in need of treatment. Higginson seemed to sense this dimension in her psyche.

Although Higginson recognized that Dickinson was abnormal, he also wisely withheld final judgment, as he acknowledged that "[s]he was much too enigmatical a being for me to solve in an hour's interview...."[9] It is likely that he intuitively understood her famous insight: "Much Madness is divinest Sense— / To a discerning Eye—" (435).[10] Dickinson may have been "cracked," but it is important to remember that "the cracked mind ... may *let in* light which does not enter the intact minds of many sane people whose minds are closed," as R.D. Laing famously put it.[11] In the landmark anti-psychiatric work *The Divided Self*, Laing demonstrated the problems with a disease model that can only read symptoms as indicators of pathology. Such a model never renders access into the inner world experienced by the psychotic and instead functions as a way to condemn or deny the reality of this world. Laing thus believed the psychiatrist's diagnosis is one-sided. It is possible to see the behavior of a psychotic "as 'signs' of a 'disease,'" but it is perhaps more productive to interpret it "as expressive of his existence."[12] To see only signs of disease, Laing argued, is similar to seeing one image in the famous optical illusion depicting either two opposing faces or a candlestick, depending on one's focus. The disease model amounts to selective reading, as it embraces one interpretive possibility and excludes others.

Implied in this last statement is the idea that it is important to study disease not only to reduce and/or cure suffering but also to discover additional possibilities of health and well-being, for to be disease free is not the same as to be well, as Positive psychologists have taught us. Jung cultivated his method of facilitating developmental growth, which he insisted works best in healthy patients, as a direct result of working with schizophrenics. Victor Frankl derived logo-therapy from watching people suffering, surrendering to victim-hood, and dying in a concentration camp. Martin Seligman's important work on optimism is a direct result of his research on pessimism and learned help-lessness. Jonathan Haidt's fairly recent "discovery" of elevation, a previously neglected positive emotion, was born out of his work on disgust and the urge to spit. The critical element among all such thinkers is a receptivity to fasci-nating possibilities that lie beyond the reach of a disease model too-narrowly conceived.

So where is the eudaimonic value in Dickinson's poetry? In part, it lies in her poems about suffering. In an essay on the role of suffering in Dickinson's poetry, Neil Scheurich brilliantly refutes the pathologizing tendency. Dis-cussing the "possible usefulness of suffering and the implications of widespread biological treatment of distress," he argues that "pain and despair have the potential to rob us of human capacities ... but ... they can [also] be a stimulus to extraordinary creativity and insight."[13] Without directly referring to the newer discourse on posttraumatic growth (PTG), a phenomenon researchers have recently begun to explore,[14] Scheurich advances a compelling case for Dickinson's psychological distress as a source of growth, not merely as a symp-tom of underlying disease. In a sophisticated discussion, he acknowledges that Dickinson did write some poems in which she despairs of a pain too burden-some for the soul to bear. As he points out, however, she also "exults in the power of the self to lift itself beyond suffering" in many poems in which "noth-ingness and negativity are strangely empowering."[15] Scheurich is careful to note the potential dangers involved in romanticizing suffering and blinding oneself to the type of pain that does not serve as a catalyst for growth but actu-ally stymies it. He acknowledges, in other words, the sometimes blurry line between beneficial and detrimental suffering. His argument, nevertheless, serves as a compelling refutation of the disease paradigm and those who claim Dickinson as a poet of despair. To the contrary, as he shows, pain serves a gen-erally eudaimonic function in her verse, although there are exceptions. In sup-port of such a point, he makes the compelling and thought-provoking observation that if treated in contemporary psychiatry, Dickinson would surely be given an anti-depressant drug, the depression-mitigating effects of which would have prevented her from ever learning to "exult in the power of the self to lift itself beyond suffering." On Prozac, she likely would never have written great poems.

Simply because a poet writes of despair, therefore, does not mean she is a despairing poet. There is anguish in Dickinson's poetry, but it serves a *generally* constructive role, as Scheurich convincingly demonstrates. Viewed in such a light, Dickinson's despairing poetry can be compared to blues music, which, although seemingly sad, is actually intended to stamp the blues away. While the poet surely was depressive at times, her poetry evidences a sophisticated and successful attempt to deal with despair in a way that leads to psychological well-being.

In addition to the recognition of the value of certain kinds of suffering, Dickinson also strongly implies eudaimonic ideas in her treatment of ecstasy, a word she frequently uses along with its lexical cousins—glee, joy, transport, rapture, sublime, and many others. This aesthetics of ecstasy consists of two interrelated elements: (1) the complex celebration of intense positive affect; and (2) the rejection of psychologically diseased, Calvinist ideas, the result of which is the embrace of a non-dogmatic, *ekstatic* form of spirituality that manifests as frequent urges toward boundlessness, or a kind of *ekstasis* that serves to free her mind from limiting structures and enables creativity, empowerment, and further cultivation and exploration of eudaimonic states. Let us explore the construct further.

Positive Affect and the Aesthetics of Ecstasy

To be sure, Dickinson did complain of a lack of joy in several poems:

> Too few the mornings be,
> Too scant the nights.
> No lodging can be had
> For the delights
> That come to earth to stay,
> But no apartment find
> And ride away [1186].

Here she might be complaining of her own lack of receptivity to "delights," whatever these imply, or of the harshness of a world in which there is constant loss and suffering. It is important to remember, however, that she explores in her work a whole range of emotional states, from despair to love and everything in between. The despairing poems, I contend, should neither be taken as fully representative of the poet's views, nor should they be used to champion her as an anguished, tortured soul. In hundreds of other poems she writes of subtle delights, intense bliss, moments of life-affirming happiness, and a host of other positive emotions. For all of her despair, Dickinson also knew happiness and explored its complexities in complex poems. Her verse is a testament to the mysteries of love, the value of gratitude, the joys of sublime transport, the thrills of exhilaration, the strangeness of awe and wonder, the fulfillment of contentment, and so much else.

She had such a capacity for positive affect that even in moments of despair, she found herself disturbingly receptive to joy:

> One joy of so much anguish
> Sweet nature has for me
> I shun it as I do Despair
> Or dear iniquity—
> Why Birds, a Summer morning
> Before the quick of Day
> Should stab my ravished spirit
> With Dirks of Melody
> Is part of an inquiry
> That will receive reply
> When Flesh and Spirit sunder
> In Death's immediately—[1420].

Written towards the end of her life, this poem clearly shows a poet who cannot help but feel positive emotion, which, given the image, is so overpowering that it appears to "wound" her, forcing her from a despairing state that she must leave, however reluctantly, against her own anguished will. She finds her inexplicable movement from despair to joy—her transport, as she calls it in so many other poems—a mystery only death will solve. In a more famous poem she wrote of the same incapacity to remain in despair:

> I can wade Grief—
> Whole Pools of it—
> I'm used to that—
> But the least push of Joy
> Breaks up my feet—
> And I tip—drunken—[252].

Here the images suggest someone who knows grief, perhaps all too well. Her familiarity with it leaves her with a mastery over its excess, as she can traverse through whole pools of it on solid footing. Her inability to master joy, however, leaves her stumbling and shakes the foundation on which her grief is built. The drunken image suggests an intractable receptivity to positive affect. To read the poem solely in terms of her grief is to overlook its central point: while she has mastered grief, she cannot establish any kind of dominion over joy, which ecstatically pushes her against her will from despair to feelings of well-being. This receptivity to positive affect characterizes the speakers in many of Dickinson's poems and suggests a poet who was no stranger to positive emotional states.

What is of particular interest here are her ecstatic poems, or those dozens of lyrics configuring a moment of intense positive affect in which the self is profoundly altered. Although she is often considered to be a sullen writer who morbidly broods about death, she is also, however contradictorily, the poet who declared rather late in life, "Take all away from me, but leave me Ecstasy, / And I am richer then than all my Fellow Men—" (1640). Although she famously hears a fly buzz when she dies, a fly in another lyric triggers the memory of an ecstatic experience, the nature of which she leaves unstated but suggests through the image of intoxication. This other fly stirs in her "Jamaicas of Remembrance / That send me reeling in—" (1628). Many poems similarly suggest a speaker reveling in bliss and singing its praises with nuanced exuberance.

In poem 125, for instance, she writes of the relationship between ecstasy and anguish:

> For each ecstatic instant
> We must an anguish pay
> In keen and quivering ratio
> To the ecstasy.

Here, she suggests that bliss must be paid for in pain, the two states existing in a direct but unequal relationship. In the second stanza she reveals the ratio, not in numerical terms but poetically and perhaps with a different kind of accuracy: "For each beloved hour / Sharp pittances of years—" (125). Given such a poem, it might seem reasonable to conclude that the poet has experienced considerable anguish and very little ecstasy, for the speaker's tone suggests it is probable Dickinson wrote the lyric in a despairing moment of self-reflection. Such a moment by no means definitively marks her as a pessimist, however, for she wrote of the same ratio a few years later in an entirely different light: "Did Our Best Moment last— / 'Twould supercede the Heaven—" (393). Her conclusion—that such blissful moments are "A Grant of the Divine—" intended to overcome despair—affirms not pessimism but an understanding of the beneficially transformative value of the ecstatic experience, the immense power of which "...leaves the dazzled Soul / In her unfurnished Rooms," as she puts it (393). Dickinson acknowledges negative affect, but she also knows from experience the value of ecstasy, the least experience of which has the power to enable one to deal effectively with pain and suffering.

Several of her poems attest to intense ecstasies, the nature of which seems to suggest what are generally considered to be rare moments of optimal experience:

> If all the griefs I am to have
> Would only come today,
> I am so happy I believe
> They'd laugh and run away [1726].

Here and in many other such poems, the speaker revels in the power of intense positive affect to undo negative emotions, as she explores the notion that ecstasy serves as a counter-balance to grief. She recognizes the rarity of these experiences, and even savors them, knowing they will forever change her perception of states of anguish and despair:

> Oh Sumptuous moment
> Slower go
> That I may gloat on thee—
> 'Twill never be the same to starve
> Now I abundance see—[1125].

Her closing point, the image of a prisoner "unto the Gallows led— / With morning in the sky," suggests immense appreciation of rare peak experiences and the heightened perspective they give to those blessed to have them. Although in poem 1125 she claims such experiences are rare, Dickinson seems to have had them on several occasions throughout her life. In poem 326 she rather succinctly attests to their frequency and impact: "...[O]ftentimes, among my mind, / A Glee possesseth me." Here, she turns to dance imagery and suggests that if she had "Ballet knowledge," the intensity of her ecstasy "Would put itself abroad / In pirouette to blanch a Troupe—Or lay a prima mad." Though she lacks such dancing skills, her ecstasies are as "...full as Opera," which is to say, they are sublime, subtle, exquisite, deeply stirring experiences too full and too potent to articulate them in ordinary language.

Dickinson's aesthetics of ecstasy is also seen perhaps quintessentially in poem 774:

> It is a lonesome Glee—
> Yet sanctifies the mind—
> With fair association—
> Afar upon the Wind
>
> A Bird to overhear
> Delight without Cause—
> Arrestless as invisible—
> A matter of the Skies.

Because Dickinson knew the Romantic convention of associating poets with birds, a trope found in the work of Wordsworth, Coleridge, Keats, Shelley, and others, it is fair to assume that in the poem she is writing about poetry (which she frequently called singing in her letters and in other lyrics) and locating in the winged creature's song a self-projection. The Bird, the capitalization of which suggests non-literal meanings, is solitary, much like the reclusive poet, and represents a "lonesome Glee" that results from soaring to great heights in a profound isolation that "sanctifies the mind," or makes sacred her whole sense of being. Her poetry, if this lyric is a guide to her poetics, was the means by which she sang of her ecstasies, which were without cause but nevertheless deeply stirring moments of positive affect that sent her aloft on their wings.

The sanctification that resulted from such moments can be seen in other poems in which she seemingly configures a simple, positive emotion but encodes some kind of religious or spiritual perception at a deeper level of meaning. Her famous exultation in poem 76, for instance, leads her "Past the houses—past the headlands— / Into deep Eternity." Her exhilaration in poem 1118 leads to a similar kind of sacralizing of consciousness:

> Exhilaration is the Breeze
> That lifts us from the Ground
> And leaves us in another place
> Whose statement is not found—
>
> Returns us not, but after time
> We soberly descend
> A little newer for the term
> Upon Enchanted Ground—

While it is possible to read such a lyric in straightforward terms as a poetic description of a moment of excitement, the language and imagery she uses connote deeper religious implications. In likening exhilaration to a "Breeze," she is suggesting divine inspiration, the breath of God depicted in Genesis, the *pneuma* of the ancient Greeks, and the Latin *spiritus*, all of which are related to wind. The implied kinesthetic image, one of ascent and then descent, suggests the Biblical rapture in which those called to heaven at the resurrection will ascend bodily from the earth to the celestial paradise. The closing image of being returned to "Enchanted Ground" intimates consciousness expansion and the attainment of a renewed state of being in which the mundane has been transmuted into the sacred. Dickinson's ecstatic poems are intimately tied to the question of religion.

The Negative Way and a Challenge to Calvin's Disease

With this last statement I do not mean to imply that she is fundamentally a religious poet, nor am I even asserting that her ecstatic poems are essentially religious in nature. What I am suggesting is that her aesthetics of ecstasy is the means by which she partially resolved the problem she had with her family's Congregationalism, the Calvinist version of Christianity embraced by much of Amherst in the mid-nineteenth century. Critics sometimes take her satirical and critical poems about God as proof that she was a proto-modernist who rejected religion because of developments in science. Nina Baym's study, *American Women of Letters and the Nineteenth-Century Sciences*, is a compelling example of such a perspective.[16] In reading such lines as "'Faith' is a fine invention ... / But *Microscopes* are prudent / In an Emergency" (185), many critics conclude that Dickinson's position on religion was more consistent with atheism than it was with devotion.

While the point may be partially true, it is problematic to read her as a poet who entirely rejected spirituality as being incongruent with the scientific realities of a modern world. To be sure, she did take issue with certain Calvinist ideas, such as predestination and imputed sin, and she took exception to the "visions of a terrifying hell and a dour heaven" still prevalent in New England Congregationalism.[17] She also famously refused to declare herself saved by Jesus, even when her closest loved ones—her parents, her brother Austin and sister Lavinia, as well as her best friend, sister-in-law, and possible lover, Susan—did so. As Roger Lundin points out in an interesting biography, however, Dickinson's attitude toward religion was far more complex than a simple antagonism would suggest.[18] She "wrestled" with God to the end of her life.[19] Her attitude toward the Bible and Christianity, Lundin argues in a Bakhtinian interpretation, was often in the style of Medieval parody. Sanctioned on feast days as a means by which people could ridicule the serious language and ritualistic practices of the Church, parody served the productive end of fostering laughter in the congregation after "days of melancholy and fasting."[20] Dickinson's oftentimes humorous attitude toward God can be seen in the same light, according to Lundin.

Her critical stance on religion was thus similarly productive, as it enabled her to challenge the theological milieu in which she lived and wrote. A different form of spirituality than the simpler Calvinism of old, New England Congregationalism was informed by the Whig ideal of a divinely sanctioned social order and evangelical moralism, both of which Dickinson found to be objectionable.[21] More important, this challenge enabled her to arrive at deeper levels of spiritual experience than New England Congregationalism allowed. No doubt, "Calvinism functions in her oeuvre in a manner somewhat analogous to her family home," that is, as a space that provided her with "language, imagery, and a frame for experiences," as Magdalena Zapadowska observes.[22] Dickinson appropriates revivalist discourse and uses many of the tropes of a privileged genre in the Second Great Awakening—the religious hymn, which remained throughout her career a "figure for ecstatic communion," according to Daniel Manheim. In employing quasi-religious language, Dickinson was able to "draw a personal idiom out of the public language of conversion."[23]

For all of this participation in Calvinist discourse, however, she also left her Congregationalist home on several occasions in seeking out deeper levels of spirituality, the essence of which can be seen in what several scholars have called her "mysticism." Lorrie Smith observes a "curious mixture of orthodoxy and iconoclasm" in many of her post–1865 poems and concludes that this is the result of her mysticism.[24] "Her frequent use of terms like 'ecstasy,' 'rapture,' 'faith,' 'renunciation,' and 'vision,' combined with her less common, but more conspicuous use of 'saint,' 'martyr,' 'nun,' and 'communion,' evoke powerful images of sanctified revelatory life," as Angela Conrad observes in *The Wayward Nun of Amherst*.[25] Steve Carter has similarly argued that Dickinson's reclusion does not necessarily qualify her as a mystic, but "her celebration of high emotional states of bliss and ecstasy does."[26] Despite the use of such language, she is by no means a traditional mystic who communes directly with the divine, as her references to God and Jesus often "reveal a painful disillusionment."[27] For this reason I suggest the alternative "aesthetics of ecstasy" rather than mysticism.

In *Changing Rapture*, an interesting study of Dickinson's poetic development, Aliki Barnstone chronicles the poet's evolution in terms of three phases: a satirical critique of both Calvinism and Sentimentalism; an identity crisis in which she struggles with Calvinist theology; and a re-evaluation of Calvinist and Emersonian conceptions of selfhood. Out of this agon, as Barnstone argues, Dickinson developed her own narrative voice, which is characterized in part by her use of narrative gaps, or suggestive blanks that nevertheless remain "emphatically absent."[28] Aliki draws the conclusion that such gaps represent the fragmentation and disorder that later came to characterize modernism.

While it may be true that Dickinson's formal experiments prefigured those of modernism, I suggest viewing her three developmental struggles and the narrative gaps that resulted in a different light, for they can also be seen as indications of a subtler form of spirituality known as "apophatic theology," which is a negative form of belief often found in types of mysticism in which God is negated not to serve the end of advancing an atheistic position but as a means of asserting what is beyond language. According to William Franke, Dickinson's poetry, with all of its gaps, indeterminacies, fissures, silences, ellipses, and the like, is best understood as a form of apophatic poetics. Such formal omissions, Franke argues, citing Harold Bloom, "...gives her, and her authentic readers, another way to see, almost, in the dark."[29] To this discussion I would add that Dickinson's apophatic poetics represents a psychologically healthier alternative to Calvinism, that is, a spiritual position that enabled her to explore *ekstatic* states of being in which she was not bound by limiting thought structures. In such states she was able to explore the nuances of positive affect without dutiful subservience to any kind of reductive theological authority. In this regard she embodies the psychological equivalent of Keats's "negative capability," or the capacity to dwell "in uncertainties, Mysteries, doubts without any irritable reaching after fact & reason."[30] Her urges toward boundlessness and freedom from conceptual constraints in several poems can be used to support such a statement.

In poem 564, for instance, she describes an experience of "prayer," but one that leaves her with highly unorthodox perceptions. In the second stanza she "step[s] upon the North," or ascends above "Horizons," the suggestion of which is the transcendence of conceptual and perhaps even affective limits. The result of crossing this *liminal* threshold is the entrance into God's realm, a state of consciousness that cannot be articulated in verbal structures. From such a perspective, she can only use the *via negativa*, or negative way, of the mystics by affirming through negation: "His House was not—no sign had He— / By Chimney—nor by Door / Could I infer his Residence—." All she sees are "Vast Prairies of Air / Unbroken by a Settler—," which is tantamount to saying she sees nothing. She also hears nothing and describes the negation of sound simply as "Silence" that "condescended." Her response in the last two lines is a kind of speechless paralysis in which she is transfixed in a state of awe: "But awed beyond my errand— / I worshipped—did not 'pray'—." Having gone beyond her initial errand, which seems to have been to pray for repentance for some transgression, she has moved from belief and ritual into the realm of religious experience, the nature of which cannot be articulated in ordinary language but merely hinted at in a poetic form that itself offers positive assertion ultimately only through negation. Her resolution of the problem she had with Calvinism is seen particularly in the last line, in which she has discovered a deeper dimension of spirituality beyond conventional prayer— an esoteric heightening of consciousness that enables her to transcend exoteric, Congregationalist boundaries.

However liberating they were, such ecstatic experiences were profoundly disruptive for Dickinson. In a later poem, 1382, she hints at the decentering that occurs as a result of experiencing profound joy, as well as her inability to articulate this intense positive affect. Here, she calls joy "Reportless" but also "sincere as Nature / Or Deity—." She cannot express it, but locates in it a presence as sure as creation itself. She cannot contain it, as she does grief, and it leaves her with a "sumptuous Destitution— / Without a name—," an ineffable type of affect that can be described only through the oxymoronic image of a luxurious poverty that affirms itself through contradiction. Joy has "no home," as she claims, nor do those who have "inhaled it—." The ecstasy of joy leaves her homeless, as it enacts the cutting of the tethers that keep her terrestrially bound. The freedom she experiences as a consequence is implied in the closing image, for she "Thereafter roam[s]," perhaps the only possible response to an ecstatic experience in which psychic contents are radically reorganized and one is released from the anchor points that delimit subjectivity. As I will discuss more fully in Chapter 10, such forays outside of one's normal confines are inherently beneficial in the non-psychotic psyche. No doubt, they can result in a distressing decentering of ego, but they are fundamentally eudaimonic experiences that lead to a more complex conception of selfhood.

It might be a sign of pathology if the poet were to attempt to hold tightly to such experiences and their accompanying affect, but Dickinson lets go. She "kisses the joy as it flies," to use Blake's image, and in doing so, she exhibits a sophisticated understanding of the subtleties of a complex state of being. Such insight can be seen in poem 184, in which she declares, "A transport one cannot contain." Rapture is real and results in the *movement* of consciousness, although its mysterious nature is forever incomprehensible to human understanding. She conjectures what would happen if a "transport" could "lift the lid— / Unto its Ecstasy," concluding with a bit of humor that if it were diagrammed and then sold for sixpence per show, "With Holy Ghosts in Cages! / The *Universe* would go!" Indeed, such a mystery solved would be a spectacle for voyeuristic consumption, a tawdry devaluation of a highly valuable experience.

This suspicion of peering into the incomprehensible with the mind informs many of her poems, particularly those configuring or referring to the nature of intense bliss. In poem 1434 she thus warns of going too near the "House of Rose," by which she probably means both the beauty of nature and the nature of love, for to do so is to reduce the possibilities, the complexities, and the mysteries of both. She also warns of tying the "Butterfly" and climbing the "Bars of Ecstasy," and her conclusion represents a common thread of wisdom that connects many of her ecstatic poems: "In insecurity to lie / Is Joy's insuring quality." One can be certain, Dickinson avers, only of ecstasy's experiential reality, never its ineffable, irreducible nature.

She articulates a similar view of other positive emotions and aesthetic perceptions. In poem 989 she explores the nature of gratitude, which she insists cannot be captured fully in words: "Gratitude—is not the mention" of an act of "Tenderness" but the "still appreciation" that exists "Out of Plumb of Speech." The implied image suggests a plumb line used to measure depth, a measureless boundlessness she also likens to the "Sea," which seemingly has no limits and cannot be contained but still *is*. Although the "Sea return no Answer" when plumbed with "Line and Lead," the inability to reach the bottom only proves that "A remoter Bed" lies out of reach, much like the mysterious nature of gratitude, which also eludes the human capacity to understand and articulate its mystifying power. In poem 516 she explores the same concept but in relation to beauty, which she claims is "not caused" but "It Is—." To "Chase it" with a meddling intellect is to cause it to cease, whereas to let it be enables it to abide. Such a Romantic conception suggests a distrust of reason and language in accounting for the source of beauty, which is and will be if left unmolested by the ratiocinating mind. She extends this view to both poetry and love in poem 1247. Likening both to "Thunder" that crumbles "grand away" and inspires both fear and awe, she locates poetry and love in a coeval past and suggests they are equally powerful and potentially disturbing forces, the nature of which exists beyond human control. Her closing image implies a kind of Promethean warning against peering too deeply into such mysteries, for as she puts it, "We both and neither prove— / Experience either and consume— / For None see God and live—." Embedded in the image is an allusion, whether intentional or not, to Semele, mother of Dionysus and lover of Zeus, whom she tricks into revealing himself in all of his grandeur. Semele is consequently incinerated, of course, reduced to a pile of ashes, out of which Zeus snatches her womb, for it contains the god of ecstasy. The subtext says only a god can withstand godlike energies. Dickinson suggests the same powerlessness before intense positive affect. Her acceptance of the location of such perceptual experiences beyond human confines represents a refined degree of wisdom she could not have derived from a Calvinist theological matrix that only affirmed rigid dogma and narrow conceptions of spiritual experience.

Maurice Lee points out that while early critics tended to see in Dickinson's poems disjunctions between self and God, mind and nature, and subject and object, later scholars have acknowledged a more dialectical poet who entertains connections between such binaries "in loosely pragmatist and empiricist ways."[31] While I do not mean to suggest that Dickinson entirely overcame such separations, her understanding of the boundlessness of human consciousness suggests a poet with strong "mystical" proclivities. It takes courage to dwell in the uncertainties of darkness and unknowing, and only a wise soul could have the depth of insight she exhibits. As she matured, Dickinson does not seem to have merely accepted the uncertainties of decentered subjectivity but actually reveled in them. As she puts it in poem 419, "We grow accustomed to the Dark," or what she calls "Those evenings of the Brain— / When not a Moon disclose a sign— / Or Star—come out within." Although the timid may find such an absence of light distressing, "The Bravest—grope a little— / And sometimes hit a Tree / Directly in the Forehead." But after a while, they get their night vision, "And Life steps almost straight." While the poem could support a reading of the darkness as despair that results from the seemingly unjustified suffering of human life, it is likely Dickinson is suggesting a profounder truth: bumping into trees in a dark forest is an inevitability if one is to mature spiritually and stand on one's own legs. To do so requires the attainment of a rarified understanding of ecstatic states and the insight required to "see" where cultural conditioning does not allow one to do so.

The Critical Reception and Negativity Bias

It is possible, but not likely, that Dickinson's ecstasies were the result of manic episodes, or radical mood swings that manifested as a result of bi-polar disorder. Ramey and Weisberg have shown that her most productive years divide into two four-year blocks. The first of these periods (1858–1861) was characterized by seasonal affective disorder (SAD) and resulted in greater poetic output in the spring and summer than in the autumn and winter. The second period (1862–1865) was characterized by hypomania and resulted in considerably more poetic output in the Autumn and Winter than in the Spring and Summer, except in 1863. Despite their identification of psychological disorder in Dickinson during these years, Ramey and Weisberg conclude that a causal relationship between her mental state and her poetry cannot be definitively demonstrated.[32] Because her poetic output might have affected her affective life, it remains uncertain whether her ecstatic poems were the cause or the result of her mania. Simply because she had some kind of affective disorder, therefore, does not mean that her poems suffer from the same disease. At some point, the artist parts company with her art; the two stand separate and must be separately assessed.

Even among sophisticated critics who reject the literal-minded, biographical paradigm, however, there has been a tendency to focus on the negative, diseased aspects of human experience that Dickinson explores in her work. For instance, Shira Wolosky, an oft-cited, well respected Dickinson scholar whose work I greatly admire, argues that the poet's self-imposed reclusion is not a productive one in which she finds a positive substitute for what she saw as a "defective world." "Instead," writes Wolosky, "she is filled with rage at having to retreat from a world so compromised."[33] As a result of this negative metaphysical view, so the argument goes, the poet turns to poetry, which becomes "the setting for Dickinson's anguished and angry recognition that human reality is chaotic," one in which "no intelligible principle can be detected..."[34] According to such a general reading, Dickinson finds nothing redemptive in her reclusive alternative to the world's harshness: "Dickinson recluses herself not in hope of a redemption experienced as an inner state transcending the external world. Her reclusion is closer to despair—or better, to defiance of the world that makes her retreat necessary."[35] When I read such statements from critics who assume Dickinson to be predominantly a poet of anguish, I wonder if we are referring to the same writer. What about her aesthetics of ecstasy? What about all of the poems in which she explores peak moments and epiphanies? What about all of the poems in which she takes immense delight in the natural world, ecstatically celebrating its myriad flora and fauna? Perhaps Wolosky is seeing a candlestick while I am seeing two opposing faces. No doubt, Dickinson does explore a number of negative states of mind in her poems, but she also explores many eudaimonic states, simply and complexly configured. The question remains: Which voice is dominant? In her attempt to refute critics who label Dickinson a metaphysical poet, Sarah Emsley rhetorically asks, "How many metaphysical poems must a poet write in order to be called a metaphysical poet?"[36] I pose a similar question to the critics who have asserted, whether explicitly or implicitly, that Dickinson is a poet of despair: How many despairing poems must a poet write in order to be called a despairing poet? Or stated more positively: How many ecstatic poems must a poet write in order to be called an ecstatic poet?

The pathologizing tendency in Dickinson scholarship has much to do with the era in which the poet's work was first critically explored. In her compelling account of why scholars, until fairly recently, have largely ignored the influence of nineteenth-century conceptions of the sentimental in Dickinson's poetry, Maria Farland teases out the negative underlying assumptions of the critical paradigm that shaped scholarly assessments of her work. Farland observes that Dickinson's poems, though written in a Romantic/Victorian context, were not critically received until after the rise of modernism, the aesthetic canons of which were far different from, and even hostile to, the sentimental tradition of the nineteenth century:

> For those who sought to establish Dickinson's reputation as a poet, the alienation and epistemological doubt that have been the hallmarks of serious poetry since the advent of modernism became the preferred means of her recuperation and the underlying standards of aesthetic value by which the poems were re-valued.[37]

James Wilson similarly points out that Dickinson's early critics, such as Yvor Winters and others, "saw the half-understood, the obscure, and the chaotic everywhere in her poems."[38] In other words they projected upon her work the modernist sensibility that informed the critical milieu in which they were writing. Those who view Dickinson as being predominantly a depressive poet of despair—or worse, a necrophiliac whose commingling of eros and thanatos represents a psychologically diseased attempt to master an emotional loss[39]— are thus doing so through a modernist lens, one in which a work of literature can be deemed complex only if it embraces the negative philosophical assumptions that became popular after World War I. Such a view also overlooks a famous statement the poet made to Higginson: "I find ecstasy in living ...the mere sense of living is joy enough."[40] No doubt, she did not "write uncritically and joyously of human experience as if she really had given up her soul to the natural, wildly sacramental ecstasy that Emerson so famously propounded in his essays."[41] As I hope the foregoing discussion has shown, however, she did write about the ecstatic aspects of human experience in compelling and complex ways that go unaccounted for in disease paradigms and interpretations of her as a despairing proto-modernist.

9. The Wise Man of the East: Rabindranath Tagore

In her conclusion to a sophisticated essay on Tagore, Rosinka Chaudhuri articulates one of the fundamental, anti-essential ideas in historicism, Marxism, cultural studies, and postcolonial theory: "Placed in the context of modern Indian history and, more specifically, in the context of Bengali middle-class culture," she writes, "Tagore is freed from the essentialist, universal readings of his poems as repositories of wisdom and spirituality...."[1] Locating a writer such as Tagore in his context(s) is an immeasurably valuable critical practice that leads to a fuller understanding of his poetics and aesthetics. To read him out of his context(s) can lead scholars to elide the importance of the historical and cultural determinants that inform his oeuvre. All human beings, even those who live in isolated caves in the Himalayas, belong to an epoch whose cultural and ideological influences are inescapable. Living in an isolated cave in the Himalayas as an attempt to escape societal influence, in fact, is an ideologically-informed, cultural-embedded practice with historical antecedents stretching back into pre-history. Historical forces are to some extent inescapable, and to be human is to be a product of history to an arguable degree.

How far can such an idea be taken, however, and still be true? For some critics, history has become a kind of new gospel whose force is the most powerful, if not the only, determinant of consciousness and life (and thus of art and all aspects of human existence). The result has been the positioning of historical forces against various *others*, such as ahistorical formalism, aestheticism, essentialism, the transcendent subject, universal truths, grand narratives, and the like. The antagonism currently found in historicism towards such ideas represents a bit of poetic justice, since all of these concepts have been used in the past to the exclusion or at least marginalization of the question of history. This denial of history in various critical schools has come at the expense of acknowledging the vital position historical forces occupy in human existence.

The privileging of history, however, is equally problematic. To position history as the first member of such a binary as historicism/universalism comes at the expense of *othering* and thus devaluing, marginalizing, or discrediting the second member. Just as historicism has been marginalized, so have many historicists positioned themselves against ideas that prove to be not only worthy of critical investigation but also serve the end of human flourishing. In the case of Chaudhuri's concluding remark, the question remains whether there is still some value in reading Tagore's poems in universal terms as repositories of wisdom. I suggest there is.

The idea that historicism can "free" Tagore from essentialist universalism implies liberation from some kind of previous confinement, and indeed this is true. Yet, while history-denying essentialism has amounted to a kind of tyrannical repression of the role of historical forces, the opposite is also true: historicism positioned antagonistically against universalism results in a similar kind of subjugation in which Tagore's poetry, which has achieved a culture-transcending, universal appeal, is subordinated to the social forces that informed it. To be true to the spirit of "liberating" his verse, then, it is necessary to jettison both interpretive paradigms in their extreme forms because, taken to such outer limits, each has amounted to a kind of dogmatism that reads selectively and foregrounds a valuable insight at the expense of *others*. Just as essentialists have denied history, so do historicists sometimes ignore universal forces that transcend cultures.

To be sure, I am not making a case to stop historicizing poets and their verse but simply suggesting that in Tagore's case historicism should not be used as a demystifying antagonist of his "wisdom," which indeed has a universal appeal and value. Though Tagore lost his cachet with his Western audience because of some bad translations and his critical stance on nationalism and colonialism, he has outlived his context. Sixty years after his death, he is still the crown jewel of Indian literature, and readers still read him in the West and around the globe, where he is viewed not necessarily as a Bengali writer but as an author whose rich wisdom carries a universal value. Why does focusing on Tagore's global appeal necessarily amount to a "faulty" or "confined" interpretation? No doubt, there are dangers in viewing him *solely* in essentialist terms as a "wise man of the East," but surely there is something to be said for an author whose ideas can reach across cultural and temporal boundaries to capture the imaginations of later generations and foreign readers who do not have a sense of his historical reference points.

Recent critics have generally dismissed the universal appeal of his poetry as so much essentialism that does no justice to the truly important issues of history. In an otherwise insightful postcolonial reading, for instance, Michael Collins laments that the stir Tagore caused among the Anglo literati had nothing to do with the problem of colonialism. As he points out, writers such as Yeats and Pound showed little interest in Indian politics or the problem of British imperialism. For them, the poet's image served "as a reminder of a forgotten European past"[2] that was once steeped in the kind of mysticism and spirituality Tagore represented. Such essentializing, according to Kalyan Sircar, another historicist, amounts to a denial of "the existence of a separate history and culture different from their own, something new, something they do not have."[3] The point is well taken, for both Yeats and Pound were not as sensitive to the issue of imperialism as were Marxists and other anti-colonial writers.

A total dismissal of the Anglo response to Tagore as a kind of narcissistic insensitivity to India's plight, however, is problematic on at least two grounds. First, its logic implies that people who know nothing of an author's milieu but respond eudaimonically to a text read out of context, that is, one written outside of the reader's cultural or temporal sphere, are doing so in a kind of self-absorption and thus injuring the writer's art in some way. Surely, those who read Shakespeare in translation or know little or nothing of his biography and his Elizabethan context but still find his work beautiful and inspiring are not necessarily self-absorbed. It is also possible that such readers have good taste and refined sensibilities, recognize genius-level facility with language, and discern a highly nuanced understanding of psychology—all of which one can detect in Shakespeare's work, even when it is read out of context or in translation.

Second, dismissing Tagore's Anglo reception as an essentialist denial of history also completely overlooks the nature of that reception, which was so enthusiastic in part because readers saw in his poetry "the passionate outbursts" that English society "kept severely in check," as Tagore himself put it.[4] They saw it, in other words, as a guide to well-being. Their reactions bolster the point: Yeats claimed that Tagore's poems stirred him "as nothing had for years."[5] He would often become so enraptured while reading them that he would have to close the volume, "lest some stranger would see how much it moved me."[6] C.F. Andrews claimed an even deeper ecstasy, something on the order of a peak experience, while listening to Tagore read his ecstatic poems:

> They flooded my whole mind and soul and body ... I was literally intoxicated. I hardly knew what was happening to me, or what was going on around me ... I went out onto Hampstead Heath alone. It was a clear, soft moonlit night ... and I remained out under the sky long into the night, almost until dawn was breaking.[7]

In an initial reaction published in *The North American Review*, May Sinclair wrote of being so moved at hearing Tagore recite his poems that she could not put her rapture into words: "The thing was an experience too subtle, too profound, and too personal to be readily translatable into language."[8] Dutta and

Robinson, two of the poet's recent biographers, account for Tagore's appeal by noting that "western [*sic*] admirers saw [in it] the humane spirit of Christianity, venerated in theory but ignored in practice, reflected back at them ... in pure form."[9] Such responses may have little to do with Indian history and British imperialism, but given the foregoing discussion of the value of the ecstatic experience, they should not be dismissed as mere essentialism or reduced to a universalist's desire to deny history. To do so is to support the untenable notion that to experience intense positive affect in a moment of *ekstasis* that leads one to see the world with new eyes is of no consequence. Surely, eudaimonic responses to Tagore deserve a more thorough consideration.

Indeed, Tagore's positive, later global, reception outside of his historical context was due, at least in significant part, to the eudaimonic elements in his poems. Many readers saw his verse as speaking their own desire to be well. As Yeats said, "...we are not moved because of [their] strangeness, but because we have met our own image, as though we had walked in Rossetti's willow wood, or heard, perhaps for the first time in literature, our voice as in a dream."[10]

To be fair, it is necessary to acknowledge Collins's conclusion, in which he faults poststructuralists for causing "rigid divisions" that have resulted in the marring of Tagore's humanism, cosmopolitanism, and internationalism, all of which he admits, however reluctantly, "might still have some mileage."[11] Historicists, however, are also partly responsible for their own rigid divisions. To construe the poet's universal appeal as the other of the more important concerns of history and culture is equally divisive and problematic. The embedded attitude in his image proves the point: Tagore's universalism is like an old car that, nevertheless, still has a few miles before it is consigned to the junkyard of ideas. A more appropriate image, I suggest, recognizes the poet's culture-transcending appeal as the driving engine of our humanness.

The historicist *othering* of Tagore's universalism thus seriously destabilizes highly valuable psychodynamics, permutations of which are seen in *Gitanjali*, a collection of poems that Tagore himself translated into English from three previously published, Bengali works. *Gitanjali* captured the interest of the British literati in 1913, and within several months, as noted, it served as the tipping point that won him the Nobel Prize. The result of such an accolade was international recognition and a rock-star's reception in nearly every country he visited, as he was often greeted by crowds of hundreds and sometimes thousands of enthusiastic readers. The first Easterner to win the Nobel, Tagore achieved universal appeal, as I will attempt to demonstrate, in part because his ecstatic poems illustrate the construct of well-being in a variety of interesting ways. Perhaps most relevant to our discussion is his foregrounding of the Indian concept of *ananda*, which means something like ultimate bliss. In

Gitanjali Tagore's aesthetics of ecstasy suggests a kind of *ekstatic* joy that most Westerners had never before encountered, particularly in the decadent verse of the late Victorian age and in the poetry of the early twentieth century. To such readers, Tagore's bliss was utterly strange and indeed seemed to suggest a wisdom lacking in the West.

Ecstatic Experience and Tagore's Theory of Art

An Indian, Tagore was raised in a culture in which ecstatic experiences were recognized as being somewhat common. Over the course of his life, he himself experienced several peak moments that directly affected his art. In the essay entitled "Sahite Aitihasikata," he wrote of three such moments he recalled from childhood. In the first of these he describes gazing on a garden, in which "light fell on the trembling coconut fronds and the dewdrops burst into glitter." The perception leaves him with a "strange joy" that he had never before felt. In the second instance he recalls seeing "a blue cumulous suspended high over the third storey of our house," an image he describes as a "marvelous spectacle." In the third instance, which followed shortly after the second, he recalls being profoundly moved by what he calls the "amazing spectacle" of a cow licking a donkey, the sight of which he views "with enchanted eyes."[12] At the age of eighteen, he had an even profounder epiphany in which

> ... a sudden spring-breeze of religious experience for the first time came into my life and passed away, leaving in my memory a direct message of spiritual reality. One day while I stood watching at early dawn the sun sending out its rays from behind the trees, I suddenly felt as if some ancient mist had in the moment lifted from my sight, and the morning light on the face of the world revealed an inner radiance of joy. The invisible screen of the commonplace was removed from all my things and all men, and their ultimate significance was intensified in my mind, and this is the definition of beauty.[13]

In his *Reminiscences* he recalled a similar instance of rapture that occurred at the age of twenty-one:

> One morning I happened to be standing on the verandah looking that way. The sun was just rising through the leafy tops of those trees, As I continued to gaze, all of a sudden a covering seemed to fall away from my eyes, and I found the world bathed in a wonderful radiance, with waves of beauty and joy swelling on every side.[14]

At the age of 46, he had something like of an out-of-body experience while tending his dying son:

> When his last moment was about to come I was sitting alone in the dark in an adjoining room, praying intently for his passing away to his next stage of existence

in perfect peace and well-being. At a particular point of time my mind seemed to float in a sky where there was neither darkness nor light, but a profound depth of calm, a boundless sea of consciousness without a ripple or murmur. I saw the vision of my son lying in the Infinite and I was about to cry to my friend, who was nursing the boy in the next room, that the child was safe, that he had found his liberation.[15]

Such experiences were frequent and profound enough as to leave Tagore with a sense of certainty about their value and validity. "I am sure that there have come moments," he wrote, "when my soul has touched the infinite and has become conscious of it through the illumination of joy."[16] His ecstasies radically changed him and, perhaps more relevant to our discussion, they informed his art.

When Tagore spoke of art serving to free one from "the mere machinery of life," he did so in part because of his many ecstatic experiences, which left him with the feeling of having transcended the aspects of his culture that served as bonds of perception. Today, scholars have discredited the idea of free, unmediated perception, which, in fact, is an active construction rather than a passive recording of direct experience. Tagore's sense of having been freed from social constraints as a result of his peak experiences, nevertheless, is not entirely at odds with current neurological and poststructuralist ideas on the impossibility of unmediated perception. Human beings, no doubt, see things in ways in which they are taught or conditioned to see them. Tagore's theory of art, however impossible it may ultimately be, nevertheless calls for us to awaken from such conditioning and to resist it *to the extent that such resistance is possible*. The poet's sense of having transcended his own culturally embedded position during his strange experience while tending his son, for instance, may ultimately still be in some ways rooted in Indian metaphysical ideas on the nature of death and reality, but the experience also transformed him by freeing him from his culturally-bound ideas about grief and leaving him with a new perceptual construct about death that cathartically enabled him to accept its inevitability.

Regardless of their ultimate metaphysical validity, Tagore's ecstatic experiences profoundly touched his poetics and aesthetics, which are deeply informed by the sense of joy he seems to have experienced in several peak moments. His interpretation of the epiphany he had at age eighteen—"[t]he invisible screen of the commonplace was removed from all my things and all men, and their ultimate significance was intensified in my mind, and this is the definition of beauty"—clearly supports S.K. Nandi's observation that Tagore took immense delight in all of creation and tried to replicate such joy in his writing, particularly in his poetry.[17] His conception of artistic beauty was inextricably linked to the intense experiences of bliss he had variously throughout his life. He saw in the principle of expression, that is, in all forms of artistic creation, a kind of ubiquitous, intense joy—that is, *ananda*—which pervades the universe.[18] Poetry was for him a way not only to simulate and replicate such ecstasy but to effect a similar state of being in the reader.

Poetry and Ananda

The first poem in Gitanjali illustrates Tagore's conception of poetic inspiration as bliss. Here he likens himself to a "frail vessel" that God empties and fills repeatedly with "fresh life" (1),[19] the implication of which suggests not only humility and egolessness but an endlessly renewed vibrancy that serves as a fount of creativity and also a source of all organic animation. In the second line he calls himself "[t]his little flute of reed" that God has carried "over hills and dales, and hast breathed through it melodies eternally new" (2). As a flute through which the Eternal blows melodies, he is an instrument of that which causes joy. The image of breath suggests not only physical but divine life, as it calls to mind the Hebrew *adhama*, a verb meaning "to breath life into" and the etymological root of the name Adam, as well as the Greek *pneuma*, which means life or spirit but literally signifies wind or breath. To be enthusiastic in both the Latin and Greek etymologies, is literally to be filled with this divine wind. Here, however, the breathing is musical life—the sacred, celebratory tones of which can be heard throughout the peaks and valleys of material existence, that is, in both pain and happiness. In being so played upon, the poet-as-flute is taken ecstatically beyond himself: "At the immortal touch of thy hands my little heart loses its limits in joy and gives birth to utterance ineffable" (3). The bliss he feels, caused by an allegorical (but by implication sensual) touch by divine hands, moves him beyond intellectual conceptions of selfhood and also across the boundaries of affective experience. It enables him to articulate a kind of impossible speech, conceived organically as giving birth, or new life, to that which is beyond language. May Sinclair's attempt to articulate her reaction to hearing Tagore's poems, which produced an effect that struck her as being "too subtle, too profound, and too personal to be readily translatable into language," is here heard (however impossibly) as utterance ineffable. Intense joy certainly can be described in words, but because it is processed in parts of the brain not directly associated with the linguistic function, it is better captured in song and poetry. It is easier to sing or write suggestive poems about joy, as George Vaillant observes,[20] than to clearly articulate the emotion in communicative utterances. Tagore's poems represent an attempt to capture through suggestion this ecstatic power of intense bliss, which lies beyond the pale in ineffable speechlessness.

In several other poems in *Gitanjali* Tagore similarly configures *ananda* in terms of a divine gift, the effects of which are not entirely cognitive but also affective. In poem 46, for instance, he likens the inspiring bliss to the soft "footsteps" of a divine "messenger" he hears secretly walking in his own heart (2), the message of which is a eudaimonic disorientation of his normal, waking state of consciousness: "I know not why to-day my life is all astir," he intones, "and a feeling of tremulous joy is passing through my heart" (3). Here poetic inspiration causes a stirring of positive affect that disrupts his conception of self and leaves him apprehensively joyful. His choice of the adjective "tremulous" suggests at once timidity and vibration, as if he were coming to consciousness of an emotion that has the potential to decenter one's will, beliefs, and values and in doing so to reorganize psychic contents. In poem 57 inspiring *ananda* becomes light, or "world-filling," "eye-kissing," "hearty-sweetening light" (1) that permeates not only the center of his being but the whole world as a dancing luminescence, a musical light that plays "the chords of my love" (2). This luminescent *ananda* is a "wild" light whose playful "laughter passes over the earth" like an overflowing sea on which "butterflies spread their sails" and whose cresting waves toss up beautiful "lilies and jasmines" (2). He closes the poem quite fittingly with a mixed metaphorical picture of the light of *ananda* as "heaven's river," which has "drowned its banks" and left a "flood of joy ... abroad" (5).

This watery, oceanic image also finds expression in poem 69, in which he calls *ananda* a "stream of life that runs through my veins night and day" (1). This bliss serves as his lifeblood and also "runs through the world and dances in rhythmic measures" (1). It represents a vitality that renders possible not only corporeal but material existence, and its metrical effect results in celebratory affect, dynamic movement, and jubilation. Such an animating principle "shoots in joy through the dust of the earth in numberless blades of grass and breaks into tumultuous waves of leaves and flowers," (2) and it is also found in "the ocean-cradle of birth and death" (3). As the poem closes it is clear that *ananda* manifests not only as a world-transcending spiritual energy but also as erotic vitality, the touch of which he feels in his "limbs" and in the "life-throb of ages dancing in my blood this moment" (4). The oceanic bliss of *ananda* is at once this-worldly and other-worldly—a powerful vitality that manifests musically as rhythm and inspiration and represents an unstoppable, dynamic force that floods beyond conceptual and affective limits. In poem 70 he is thus "tossed and lost and broken in the whirl of this fearful joy" (1). In its oceanic grandeur and force *ananda* knows no boundaries, and its inexorable and "restless" (3) push causes all things to "rush on" in "endless cascades" of "abounding joy that scatters and gives up and dies every moment" (3). The result of his apprehension (which etymologically means both fear and understanding) of *ananda* is a perception of the "music" of life, the song of joy that pervades the universe and can be heard in both happiness and suffering, or as he puts it in poem 71, in "the poignant song ... echoed through all the sky in many-coloured tears and smiles, alarms and hopes" (3). The culmination of his auditory wisdom is a transference of musical power in the form of poetic inspiration: "The great pageant of thee and me has overspread the sky," he avers in the closing lines. "With the tune of thee and me all the air is vibrant, and all ages pass with the hiding and seeking of thee and me" (5–6).

It is important to note that his privileging of joy is not some kind of neurotic avoidance of the unpleasant aspects of life—that is, suffering, inequality, cruelty, and the like—but more likely a mature, healthy coping strategy intended to facilitate a successful adaptation to life's inevitable hardships. He was from an upper class family, no doubt, but he had his share of tragedies. In the years before he published *Gitanjali*, for instance, he experienced the tragic deaths of his father, wife, son, and daughter. Despite such losses, throughout his life he "maintained good health, high spirits, a cheerful outlook, and a childlike spirit of wonder."[21] He also preserved a strong sense of hope and a belief in the ubiquitous presence of joy, and he did so not in avoidance of the unpleasant but in light of it. Kalyan Sen Gupta observes that Tagore "fully recognizes the existence of evil in the world, and not as some accidental accompaniment to our life, but as something pervasive and central to it."[22] His writings, particularly *Gitanjali* but many others, "attest to the belief that the existence and experience of evil cannot override our faith in beauty, goodness, and harmony."[23] The poet saw death holistically as part of life, not as its tragic interruption. To be sure, he experienced grief and thus a sense of the tragic after he lost loved ones, but he always recovered his perspective that death is located in a continuous cycle and does not represent a break or interruption in that cycle but its fulfillment or completion. Gupta claims Tagore's ideas on the rightness and propriety of death are the result of an "aesthetic distance"[24] the poet was able to achieve after loss or hardship. If we set aside the negative connotations of "aestheticizing" as ignoring the real and instead view it as a form of psychological agency exercised to assert the right to determine how events affect us, then Tagore's "aesthetic distance" immediately emerges as a valuable means of well-being. To focus on the tragic aspects of life, Tagore wrote, represented "a form of mental dipsomania that disdains healthy nourishment," for such a perspective interprets the world selectively by ignoring that life also offers goodness, beauty, joy, and love.[25]

For Tagore, art originates from his sense of "the wholeness of life,"[26] as Andre Dommergues puts it, by which is meant an understanding that all opposites and separate entities are linked. This idea of wholeness pervades his entire oeuvre. Dutta and Robinson go as far as to claim that "faith in the unity of man and nature inform [not only his copious writings but] everything he did."[27] In poem 72 the poet feels this holism physically in God's "deep hidden touches," (1) which result in a new kind of visual wisdom in which he sees with enchanted eyes through the web of *maya*, or illusion. He also likens God to a musician who "joyfully plays on the chords of my heart in varied cadence of pleasure and pain" (2) and thus locates the joyful perception not only in sight and physical touch but also in profoundly powerful affect, the effects of which are a delight he takes in the "rapture of joy and sorrow" (4). This reveling in contrary states of emotion lends a complexity to Tagore's verse and serves as a forceful refutation of the image of the poet as a Pollyanna who elides the unpleasant.

To the contrary, all aspects of life are subsumed in this conception of the totality of life, or what he calls in poem 78 "the picture of perfection! the joy unalloyed!" (1). Here, he entertains the notion of a "break in the chain of light" in the form of a lost star, (2) perhaps a symbol of the human soul. The implication of such a loss is that perfection has become imperfect, and the realization temporarily halts the gods' celebration of their creation. "Yes," cries a divinity, "that lost star was the best, she was the glory of the heavens!" (3). The pronouncement has consequences for human beings and results in a quest for the soul. Even though human beings feel as though "in her the world has lost its one joy" (4) and the search for her thus continues unceasingly, there never truly was a discontinuity in the metaphysical wholeness but only a charge by the gods for human beings to search within to discover the hidden depths they have lost touched with and perceived from the perspective of limited awareness as constituting a break in the cosmic chain. The stars themselves know that such a perception is illusory and thus faulty: "Only in the deepest silence of the night the stars smile and whisper among themselves—'vain is this seeking! Unbroken perfection is over all!'" (5). As he suggests, it is possible to catch a glimmer of the grand cohesion of all things phenomenal and numinous in the emptiness implied by darkness.

Because his conception of wholeness implies a kind of boundlessness with no divisions, and because he resists the myth of finality and closure, as Anupam Nagar recently put it,[28] Tagore often chose to capture the essential qualities of the grand unity in images of night and darkness, both of which have profound religious implications. As scholars have demonstrated, there are a number of influences on Tagore's conception of the divine, including not only the "protestantism" of his family's Brahmo Samaj[29] but also the Upanishads,[30] the tradition of the mad, wandering Bauls of Bengal,[31] and Buddhism.[32] Foremost among such influences is the Bhakti reform tradition, whose many groups advanced either the *saguna* or *nirguna* conception of God. In the Indian tradition God is conceived of in terms of having attributes but also transcending them. As in the cases of Judaism and Christianity, God can be described and at least partially understood in human terms as having charac-teristics, but ultimately God exists beyond all attributes and can never be fully comprehended by human reason or articulated in speech. Indians refer to the first conception (God with attributes) as *saguna brahman* and the second (God without attributes) as *nirguna brahman*. Tagore seems to have adopted both versions of the divine. The celebratory images in his verse, such as danc-ing, inebriation, and joy, stem in part from Vaishnavism, or worship of Vishnu, particularly but not exclusively in the form of Krishna as a manifestation of *saguna brahman*. Such Bhakti ideas seem to have originated in the medieval period, and they profoundly affected Indian religious life, particularly during the five hundred years leading up to the twentieth century.[33] Images of dark-ness, which might be traceable to the medieval *Virasaiva* worship of Shiva as *nirguna brahman*, also find expression in *Gitanjali* in several poems.

Despite the ultimate impossibility of comparing *nirguna brahman* to anything, Tagore, like Dickinson, uses the image of night/darkness as a kind of *via negativa* in which several possibilities are suggested. In poem 15, for instance, the darkness of night serves as the means by which he is ecstatically emptied and then transformed by being filled with musical inspiration. In the first verse the poet is sitting not in a prominent position in "this hall of thine" but humbly in a "corner seat" (1) from which he contemplates his "useless" position as a singer who "can only break out in tunes without a purpose" (2). In the third verse he anticipates finding his purpose "[w]hen the hour strikes for thy silent worship at the temple of midnight," at which point he will "stand before thee and sing" (3). The affective thrust of the poem seems to lie in the sense of renewal the poet locates in the darkness, which he sacralizes by likening to a temple of midnight, and in the movement from sitting and languishing to standing and flourishing. The emptiness of darkness represents an exteri-orization of the emptying of ego, the little *enstatic* self that blocks the way and renders his life purposeless by preventing the renewal necessary for arriving at a sense of meaning. He prays for such ecstatic renewal in the closing verse: "When in the morning air the golden harp is tuned, honour me, commanding my presence" (4). The sensory appeal to the freshness of morning air is also a subtle externalization, but here he has ecstatically self-transcended and found meaning in a conception of himself as a well-tuned, golden harp, an image suggesting immense value, stirring vibrations, rapturous music, and the vacuity of ego. Like the Romantic Aeolian harp, he is now an instrument played upon by a more potent force lying outside of the confines of the *enstatic* self.

The same pattern of movement from languishing to rejuvenation through darkness appears elsewhere in *Gitanjali*. In poem 25 the speaker finds himself mired in "the night of weariness," longing for the oblivion of restful sleep so he can renew his "flagging spirit" (2). The image of darkness here has a twofold aspect, at once suggesting negative and positive connotations. In the opening image darkness is clearly a symbol of suffering, but as the poem closes the poet has transmuted the darkness into some kind of purifying, renewing agent with the power to restore happiness: "It is thou who drawest the veil of night upon the tired eyes of the day to renew its sight in a fresher gladness of awakening" (3). The veil of night drawn over tired eyes signifies a mollification of suffering that leads again to the renewal of the day, an exteriorization of his inner, rejuvenating happiness. In poem 24 he similarly welcomes the coming of dusk, which he describes suggestively through the image of swaddling a baby: "If the day is done, if birds sing no more, if the wind has flagged tired, then draw the veil of darkness thick upon me, even as thou hast wrapt the earth with the coverlet of sleep and tenderly closed the petals of the drooping lotus at dusk" (1). Darkness here also signifies negatively and positively. On the one hand it is suggestive of death and weariness, as seen in the first verse in the image of the end of day and in the second as the effete traveler "whose sack of provisions is empty" and whose "garment is torn and dust-laden" (2). But on the other hand darkness is nurturing and caring, like a parent whose attentive tenderness has the gentle power to restore and to heal. The closing image bolsters the point, for the speaker yearns to "renew his life like a flower under the cover of thy kindly night" (2). The flower simile intimates the beauty of ecstatic transformation found in the darkness of the benevolent night.

Tagore's use of night in its twofold aspect is interesting because it calls upon readers to dissociate themselves from previously held, negative associations related to darkness. In locating the divine in darkness and attributing the conventionally fearful night with benevolence and the power to effect highly beneficial transformations, Tagore has enabled readers to respond to his poems in new, complex ways. His defamiliarization of darkness results in an image that at once induces fear (because of conventionally negative past associations) and serves as a seductive invitation to embrace the unknown and to cultivate potential through the purifying blackness of night. In a stroke of genius, the poet has suggested matter through manner, effecting a response in readers not by fiat but by inscribing in his form the nonverbal affect he hopes to induce. He is a master of hinting at the unspeakable. Donald Tuck has observed that Tagore's poetry is highly "non-verbal" in the sense that it "throbs with ... suggestive ideas" about the divine, ideas that can never be fully expressed in language by either poet or critic.[34] A strict focus on thematic and/or cognitive content would ignore the connections between form and content, text and reader. As Anupam Nagar has said of Tagore's poetry, "a hermeneutic attached only to the meaning of the words misses the emotional movement of the music."[35] The poet thus locates the divine in darkness to suggest affective, non-rational possibilities that transcend language.

In poem 23 he revels in such possibilities, even though they are disturbing and decentering. "Art thou abroad on this stormy night on the journey of love my friend?" he asks of God (1). Here, the stormy darkness causes a stirring of apprehension and anticipation, both of which he projects outward: "The sky groans like one in despair" (1). Despite the conventionally negative imagery, which is also found in the second verse as a restless sleeplessness, the affective thrust of the poem is positive. In the third verse he claims he can "see nothing" (3) except darkness, but he also strongly implies a sense of excitement and awe over the possibilities: "I wonder where lies thy path!" (3). He also wonders about the "dim shore of the ink-black river" and the "far edge of the frowning forest," configuring the darkness as a fear-inducing, overpowering mystery whose force is located in a "mazy depth of gloom" (4). The language he uses clearly suggests what Rudolph Otto called in *The Idea of the Holy* the *"mysterium tremendum et fascinans*," a response to the presence of the divine in the form of fear and awe coupled with a kind of compelling fascination.[36] But Tagore does not merely say so; he implies the response, rather, in a mixed, complex tone of excitement and awe coupled with images of conventionally negative affect (fear and despair) and in a disturbing atmosphere one does not normally associate with God (mazy depth of gloom, frowning forest, stormy night)—all of which nonetheless suggest eudaimonic possibilities of consciousness transformation, or ecstatic renewal through the emptiness implied by darkness. In using such a technique to describe what is ultimately a eudaimonic experience of anticipating the coming of some kind of divine ecstasy, Tagore once again suggests content through formal effect. By estranging the love of God and casting it as darkness, storm, and despairing groans, the poet subverts and decenters the reader's perception, the result of which, at least in the implied response, is the same sense of reveling in possibilities in the same disrupted state of being.

Ananda and Eudaimonia

Tagore's sense of wholeness of *ananda* is a refutation of the tragic view of life as a disparate set of random events. Kaiser Haq has called such a view "vague nonsense,"[37] and he cites it as an example of how Tagore "often lived happily beyond the bounds of common sense."[38] Haq does at least acknowledge that, because Tagore took wholeness seriously and because it significantly informs his work, the idea should factor in some way in critical analyses. Still, there is a belittling tone in the remark, for Haq implies that although Tagore held a "nonsensical" view, scholars must nevertheless tolerate its senselessness because it was important to the poet and recurs throughout his work. Some early critics similarly found Tagore's ideas to be "preposterously optimistic,"[39] as Thomas Sturgis Moore did when he heard the poet read. Some contemporary scholars also feel the same way. In his study, *The Inner World: A Psychoanalytic Study of Childhood and Society in India*, Sudhir Kakar reduces Indian ideas on metaphysical unity to a "loss of symbiotic relationship to the mother," the result of which is a "narcissistic injury of the first magnitude" and the consequent yearning to seek out a substitute, which manifests in the form of "mystical proclivities."[40] Such critical reductions entirely miss the mark, however. In light of what psychologists have recently concluded about the constructive benefits of optimism, they completely overlook the immense *value* of having a sense of wholeness and a holistic view of life, both of which are characteristics of psychological health and thus of well-being. Although Tagore's views on the unity of life are informed by unproven, untested, and widely devalued metaphysical ideas, they result in a healthy sense of optimism about the interconnections and meanings in a seemingly random world. Who can argue with that?

It is important, therefore, not to dismissively deal with Tagore's ideas about *ananda* as an absurd little indulgence that nevertheless warrants analysis because they are found throughout his work. As I discussed previously, religious dogma may not be relevant in the contemporary secular world, but religion is still highly important because it is an instrument through which eudaimonic traits, emotions and states are cultivated, as George Vaillant argues in *Spiritual Evolution*.[41] To dismiss Tagore's spiritual ideas as essentialist is to ignore the value they compellingly imply. His conception of God as *nirguna brahman,* as I have shown, suggests a number of ideas that bear directly on well-being: darkness functions as a space in which possibility itself becomes possible and thus serves as the impetus for the realization and cultivation of potentials; the image suggests a universally valued character trait, humility,[42] in which self-emptying results; it implies the kind of self-renewal necessary for happiness and optimal experience; it is a means of healthy self-expansion in the sense that the speaker is made more complex through the healthy assimilation of ecstasies; it results in the estrangement of perception in both the speaker and the reader and thus implies a new, more complex view of life; it expresses the inexpressible through suggestion and thus results in bringing to consciousness previously unconscious affect, the effects of which are an enriched sense of self; the response it evokes—*mysterium tremendum et fascinans*—has been shown to be immeasurably valuable in optimal psychological functioning; and it enables the speaker (and perhaps the reader) to move from sitting and languishing to standing and flourishing. Clearly, all of this value is lost in the dismissal of his conception of the divine as vague nonsense lying outside the bounds of common sense. His conception of God, it seems, contains considerable wisdom.

It is equally important not to other Tagore's universal appeal by interpreting it as an apolitical, anti-historicist denial of the cultural moment in which the poet wrote. As I have tried to demonstrate, there is considerable value in the poet's universalism, which served the end of simulating in verse forms and inducing in the reader eudaimonic psychodynamics. His peak experiences left him with a strong sense of joy, permutations of which he explored in his poetry. His experience of *ananda* impelled him to configure intense joy as a ubiquitous force that connected the "inner" and "outer" worlds. Such holism resulted in a metaphysics of unity in which all disparate entities are bound together. Even death, in this conception, is not a tragic interruption of life but a natural and necessary completion of a unified cycle. Particularly compelling is the strong sense of hope and optimism his poems convey. For Tagore, joy was so overpowering that it also forced an ecstatic self-transcendence that resulted in a high degree of psychological health, indications of which are seen in the profound sense of self-renewal that recurs throughout *Gitanjali*. Other such indications include a celebratory tone and jubilant images of festivities, dancing, rhythm, and music. Still others include the mature healthy defense mechanism he adopts in acknowledging the unpleasant side of life, as well as the aesthetic distancing through which he is able to see beauty and value in hardship and suffering. His successful endeavor to intimate what cannot be articulated in language, moreover, suggests a poet who profoundly felt the beauty of ecstatic experience but also well knew the limits of language and the dangers of attempting to fix in words what will always finally evade linguistic encapsulation. *Gitanjali* served as the tipping point that won him the Nobel prize and then international recognition because it spoke to the desire to be well, and it continues to do so universally. The historicist dismissal of Tagore's "wisdom" completely overlooks these dimensions of his verse.

Eudaimonic Wisdom and the Problem of Historicism

Tagore himself found historicism irritating, as Chaudhuri herself notes, and he wrote that it was "difficult to put up with the pedantic historian when he tries to force me out of the center of my creativity as a poet."[43] He emphasized this irritation more forcefully in the same essay: "To hell with your history!"[44] he exclaimed in exasperation. Admittedly, he seems to be protesting too much, and his comments perhaps belie a frustration over the (ultimately) inescapable forces of history. His irritation, nevertheless, was consciously driven by a reaction to vulgar Marxist critics who viewed his writing from a perspective that interpreted him as a bourgeois author whose aesthetic ideas could be crudely reduced to his class-based values. To the contrary, his view of art and his conception of himself as a poet were informed by society-transcending ideas, and whenever he spoke or wrote about art, he never ascribed a sociological origin to it.[45] He actually saw art as a means by which one can transcend culture: "True art withdraws our thoughts from the mere machinery of life and lifts our souls above the meanness of it. It releases the self from the restless activities of the world and takes us out of the noisy sick-room of ourselves."[46] Implied in this perspective is the idea that society—"the mere machinery of life" and "the restless activity of the world"—is stifling and confines us to an *enstatic* and unhealthy psycho-spiritual space. For Tagore, art serves a liberating function by enabling an *ekstatic* release from society and the socially bound self. No doubt, such an aesthetics posits the Cartesian subject of liberal humanism, but the question of its transcendent aspects remains. While it is impossible to fully transcend one's culture, it is possible to awaken from one's cultural hypnosis and to become conscious of previously unconscious, socially determined values and ideologies. This awakening, however contradictory it may seem, is one of the tacit goals of most historicists. Such an awakening, or liberation, to use Tagore's image, does in some respects amount to a "transcendence" of the social and thus historical. I would suggest this is what Tagore implied in his aesthetics, which, therefore, should not be reduced to a kind of society-denying urge to escape the forces of history. As an activist, he was deeply involved in politics at various points in his career, serving as Ghandi's most forceful critic and lecturing the East and the West on the perils of nationalism (and thus tacitly supporting the cause of universalism). For Tagore, art can serve as a challenge to the cultural and historical forces that threaten to stifle human beings and prevent well-being; art in its transcendent aspect, in other words, can serve to facilitate agency.

Although I have spilled considerable ink in refuting the historicist othering of Tagore's universalism, I am not simplistically calling for a return to the essentialism of old. Such a blind essentialism is dangerous because it entirely elides important cultural determinants that can enable a better understanding of a given writer. In her landmark work, *Formal Charges: The Shaping of Poetry in British Romanticism*, Susan Wolfson has called for "an historically informed formalist criticism" that will serve to redeem formalism from its image as being "naively idealistic, or worse, complicit with reactionary ideologies."[47] Although Wolfson advances the call in the context of Romanticism studies, her "new formalism" has utility in all areas of literature.

In the case of Tagore, for instance, it is important to note that his poetry is in some ways an "ecstatic performance" rooted in dramatic *Rasa* theory,[48] which itself strongly influenced the Bhakti movements that inform Indian spirituality. As Sailaza Pal observes, temple life was inextricably linked to the dramatic arts in the Bhakti tradition.[49] Temple functionaries were well acquainted with the techniques of achieving dramatic effects and the various emotional responses with which *Rasa* theory is concerned. Tagore's ecstatic, celebratory music and dance imagery, then, likely originates in the context of the *Rasa* ideas that permeated Indian religious life. Like the poets Mirabai and Mahadeviyakka, who took their cue from the *devidasi* tradition of temple dancers, Tagore was also influenced by "temple ritual arts, especially dancing and poetry, [which] were deeply enmeshed with one another."[50] Other images of divine dancing Tagore would have known include the "Maha-Ras," in which Krishna, Radha, and the Gopis rapturously gyrate themselves into states of ecstasy, as well as Shiva's "laysa" and "tandava" dances that serve as courtship of Parvati and end in divine copulation and the destruction of the world.[51] I leave it up to other scholars, perhaps historically aware formalists or formally attentive historicists, to explore this connection. The point is simply that in the older conception of essentialism, such informing influences would be entirely ignored. To focus on them would involve mitigating a deep understanding of the text itself. In a historically aware formalism, however, it becomes possible to acknowledge such determinants without elevating them to an absolute status that warps one's view of Tagore's poetry. His "ecstatic performance," in other words, can be located in a historical context of cultural influences without reducing it to such determinants.

This last statement implies at once cultural connection and cultural transcendence. Gupta points out in his valuable study that Tagore believed the self expands through social intercourse, and he also rejected, particularly in his later work, the idea of an essential self standing apart from nature and culture.[52] Despite this seeming anti-essentialism, the poet also maintained a steadfast belief in the necessity of self-creation through removal to a private space in which the possibilities of the imagination might be explored and cultivated. As he himself put it, "[w]e could not truly live for one another if we cannot claim the freedom to live alone, if our social duties consist in helping one another to forget we have souls. To exhaust ourselves completely in mere efforts to give company to each other, is to cheat the world of our best."[53] This divorce from society and culture should not be interpreted as a kind of narcissistic withdrawal, for Tagore also believed that a complete separation from society is wrong. As Nandi points out, the poet believed that "[w]hen man is selfishly alone and separated from the rest of creation by his narrow self-gratificatory pursuits," he is deprived of possibilities that require other people for their actualization.[54] To discover the imagination's potentials, one of Tagore's preoccupations as both artist and educator,[55] it is necessary to remove oneself from human society in the solitude of creative exploration, but to actualize such potentials one needs other people. Tagore seems to strike a balance between self and society, between the imagination and cultural determinants. To identify with one over the other is faulty and leads either to narcissism or the loss of creative vitality.

The question remains whether such an idea, which calls for a kind of "soft essentialism," can be supported beyond Tagore's belief. I suggest an appeal to the work of the philosopher Martha Nussbaum can render the poet's universalism highly relevant. In a landmark essay, "Social Justice and Universalism: In Defense of an Aristotelian Account of Human Functioning," and in a later work, *Sex and Social Justice,* Nussbaum articulates a cogent defense of culture transcending universals. She points out the negative aspects of rigid, "politically correct" anti-essentialism, which has resulted in a kind of relativistic paralysis that prevents any kind of positive assertion of the value of any position, even those supporting the causes of women, postcolonial subjects, and other marginalized constituencies. She also notes the "odd phenomenon" of anti-essentialists taking up ideologically suspect positions that prove to be ironically complicit in the reactionary views anti-essentialism is intended to reject. An extreme embrace of anti-essentialism, as she demonstrates, prevents one from being able to introduce the smallpox vaccine in Indian villages in which there is worship of a smallpox goddess, for to do so would be to foist Western essentialist notions of medicine on an ancient culture. Anti-essentialism also prevents one from condemning the ancient belief that because menstruating women ritually pollute the atmosphere, they should be banned during menses from the kitchen, the temple, and the workplace. Anti-essentialism results in an intellectual quagmire because in destroying essence it also renders impossible *any* position and prevents any positive assertion of values beyond a given culture. If all cultures are correct in the politically correct version of anti-essentialism, and if no culture has a right to impose its values on another, then all cultural practices can be justified, including Nazi death camps and forced female circumcision.

Nussbaum solves this dilemma by positing the existence of ten universals that do indeed transcend cultures: mortality, corporeality, cognitive capability, early infant development, practical reason, affiliation with other human beings, relatedness to other species and to nature, humor and play, separateness, and strong separateness.[56] She anticipates objections from cultural relativists and social constructionists by admitting that such universals "never turn up in ... [such a] vague and general form ... but always in some specific and historically rich cultural realization."[57] In other words they are always informed by the contexts in which they occur, but they also transcend those contexts in being found across the globe in thousands of culturally distinct manifestations. Nussbaum also articulates what amounts to a universal standard of what it means to be well in her conception of "basic human functional capabilities," all of which are related to her universals. These include (1) living a full live span;

(2) having good health, proper nourishment, shelter, sexual satisfaction, and mobility; (3) being able to avoid non-beneficial pain and enjoying pleasure; (4) using the five senses and the mind; (5) having other-directed attachments to things and people beyond ourselves, the result of which is grief, love, longing, and gratitude; (6) being able to form a conception of the good and planning one's life around such a concept; (7) engaging in familial and social interaction; (8) having concern for and relatedness to animals, plants, and the natural world; (9) laughing, playing, and enjoying recreational activities; (10) living one's own life and nobody else's; and (10*a*) living one's life in one's own surroundings and context.[58] To bolster her concept of universals, Nussbaum argues that such human functional capabilities can be judged according to whether they fall above one of two possible thresholds: "a threshold of capability to function, beneath which a life will be so impoverished that it will not be human at all, and a somewhat higher threshold, beneath which those characteristic functions are available in such a reduced way that, though we may judge the form of life a human one, we will not think it a *good* human life."[59] Stated positively, living above the second threshold implies flourishing, a good life conceived in terms of actualizing potentials through exercising functional capabilities. Without such standards, however vague they may be, "we have no adequate basis for saying what is missing from the lives of the poor or marginalized or excluded, no adequate way of justifying the claim that any deeply embedded tradition we encounter is unjust."[60] Nussbaum's universals and basic functional capabilities amount to a kind of "soft essentialism," the implications of which make it possible to discuss well-being as both a culture-bound and culture-transcending construct.

In *Gitanjali* are found every one of Nussbaum's universals and the basic human functional capabilities[61] she posits as a kind of marker of the good life: Tagore's ecstatic poetry speaks to the question of bodily existence and death, to the value of using the mind imaginatively, to connections to other people and the natural world, to play and festivities, and to a private space, however it is conceived, in which one individuates and thus discovers the "self." His poetry also speaks to living a full lifespan in good physiological and psychological health, to the joys of pleasure and play, and, above all, to the fulfillment found in love and connectedness not only to family and friends but the whole divine cosmos.

Gitanjali appealed to the Anglo literati and then the whole world (and continues to do so) because its concerns are so universally relevant, not in the vague way of old essentialism but in a specific Indian context as an ecstatic performance in the Bhakti tradition of Rasa aesthetics. Still, it is not necessary to be familiar with such a context to recognize that Tagore's poetics of ecstasy represents highly valuable psychodynamics in its appeal to human well-being.

10. Extra-literary Implications

Now that I have described ecstatic states, established the existence of the ecstatic poetic tradition, and analyzed five representative poets in this corpus, the question of the relevance of such poetry rises to the forefront.[1] One might be compelled to ask: "So what?" Given the longstanding tradition of ecstatic poetry, which existed ubiquitously in the ancient world and extends into the present century, it is possible to infer that its implications signify well beyond the literary domain. The poetics and aesthetics of ecstasy do not represent mere literary posturing, the stuff of dreamy poets whose lyrics belie the realities of a much harsher, real world. To the contrary, ecstatic experiences and their poetic (re)constructions signify in many significant domains, three of which I will discuss here: ecstasy is (1) an important psychological need that has posed profound (2) sociopolitical and (3) religious problems and implications. Let us explore each of these in turn.

The Ecstatic Cure

Ecstasy bites deeply into the soul, sometimes leaving those who experience its joys forever transformed, forever unable to return to their previous lives. The ecstatic experience, however it comes about and whatever form it takes on, quite often leaves people with radically altered perspectives. As a result, their values, ideologies, and even conceptions of selfhood transmute, usually for the better. The work of Elisabeth Kübler-Ross, the physician known for codifying the grieving process and founding the hospice movement in America, supports such an idea. Kübler-Ross spent much of her later career investigating the near-death experience (NDE), by which is meant the phenomenon of returning to life from actual, clinical death. In her analysis of some 30,000 such cases, she found that those who are resuscitated often report experiencing such profound bliss that they are sorry to be brought back to life.[2] Regardless of the question of the validity of NDEs, when these people do reintegrate with the world, they often undergo a sea-change in their values and report a richer, fuller human experience. One previously aggressive, competitive, and materialistic man who had such an ecstasy, for instance, began growing day lilies by the hundreds simply to give them away as gifts.[3] The experience of *ekstasis* can transform the psyche. It can function as a catharsis that expunges diseased psychological patterns and induces growth. Ecstasy both heals psychological wounds and serves as a catalyst for human well-being.

Human beings seem to sense at an intuitive level these transformative properties of ecstasy. In Toni Morrison's *Beloved*, for instance, the character Baby Suggs organizes ecstatic gatherings for newly freed slaves as an attempt to mollify the traumas of being subjected to racial hatred and the horrid material conditions of enslavement. These "whoops," as they are called, involve festive singing and dancing in a circle. Although appearing in a work of fiction, Baby Suggs' whoops are a replication of the ring-shouts that often took place in early African American culture. A ring-shout is an ecstatic activity in which participants often beat time with a broom stick and dance in a circular formation, sometimes for hours, while repeating some inspirational word or phrase. This use of ecstatic practice for healing purposes is very ancient and can also be found among the *Orpheotelestae* of ancient Greece. The *Orpheotelestae*, adherents of the Orphic mysteries in which people were taught how to make ecstatic out-of-body journeys,[4] offered cures by performing circle dances around the afflicted. Native Americans, the !Kung of Africa, Moroccans, Christian Ugandans, and many others engaged in a similar ecstatic activities to heal the afflicted.[5]

Andrew Newberg, a researcher at the University of Pennsylvania medical center, has conducted some interesting neurological research on the brains of groups of people who engage in such ecstatic practices. His conclusions support what people seem to have intuitively known: ecstasy is good for us. Among those whose brains Newberg has mapped are praying nuns, meditating Buddhist monks, and Pentecostal Christians who engage in an old ecstatic practice called *glossolalia*, or speaking in tongues. This fascinating research shows observable differences in the types of brain states resulting from each ecstatic activity.[6] Ecstasy is not merely "in the imagination." The common thread in all of these practices, moreover, is neurologically, psychologically, and physiologically beneficial states that enhance well-being and thus optimize human experience. The altered brain waves that result from such states, as he concludes, lead to positive beliefs, which themselves not only stimulate the immune response but also result in lower levels of cortisol, a hormone related to stress.[7] Such states also result in a sense of the loss of time, the result of which is a central ingredient in human happiness—losing oneself through total immersion in the moment.[8] Given the well-known mind-body connection, which today finds the clearest endorsement in what is called *integrative* medicine, Newberg's findings highlight the value of cultivating ecstatic states of being. Ecstasy positively alters the brain and beneficially impacts the body.

Other studies of the brains of people who engage in ecstatic techniques such as meditation and visualization scientifically support the value of ecstasy. In one study, for instance, practitioners of Yoga Nidra, a form of meditative visualization, exhibited a 65 percent increase in dopamine levels over non-meditating controls.[9] The neurotransmitter dopamine, a chemical produced naturally in the brain, is responsible for feelings of well-being. When such levels are low, human beings are often miserable. Even in monkeys, low dopamine levels result in a "multifaceted misery that in human beings is labeled neurotic."[10] Responsible for inducing observable optimal states of mind, ecstatic techniques help people to achieve high levels of positive affect. In another study meditants were shown to have a decreased activation of the autonomic nervous and endocrine systems, both of which are intimately involved in stress management.[11] The same study also observed significantly better attentional control and lower emotional reactivity in meditators. When shown a violent movie clip, meditants exhibited lower levels of emotional arousal than non-meditating controls, the implication of which is that they have better control over their emotions.[12] Several other studies show that meditants often demonstrate lower levels of negative emotion, higher levels of positive affect, increased neural response, increased immune response, enhanced endurance to affective challenges, and improved psychological coping.[13] A recent meta-analysis confirmed that there is a large body of scientific literature attesting to the value of meditation, which has been demonstrated to be an effective treatment for depression, anxiety, psychosis, borderline personality disorder, and attention deficit hyperactivity disorder.[14] The same meta-study also points to irrefutable evidence of immediate and long-term changes in the brain as a result of meditation. Most compelling is the brain mapping research that clearly shows a greater cortical thickness in the brains of meditants, particularly in the regions responsible for processing positive emotions.[15] Those who meditate, simply put, are happier than those who do not.

This positive effect of ecstasy is no wonder, given the affective content of the experience, which is often described in such highly positive terms as joy, transport, rapture, euphoria, elation, exhilaration, bliss, exultation, felicity, jubilance, glee, mania, excitement, intoxication, and overpowering happiness. An encounter with such an intense concentration of positive emotion is a call to growth and also facilitates psychological development, a refinement of one's values, attitudes, and relationships, and a clearer sense of one's goals and purpose in the world. To stand outside of oneself in the experience of ecstasy, then, is highly beneficial and generally conducive to growth.

What is more, there is a need for ecstasy in the human psyche. Findings from research on the importance of love, the greatest ecstasy, have validated this last statement. It is well known that married people are healthier and live longer than their single counterparts. Cardiac patients who own dogs have significantly fewer additional heart attacks than those who have no canine companionship during their recovery.[16] Love, says modern neurology, is responsible for the creation of important neural circuitry, without which humans could not adapt and survive. Children deprived of love will often simply die, or if they do survive they will display serious psychological and even physiological disturbances. Researchers have learned this truth from a variety of sources: (1) Friedrich II famously attempted to ascertain the natural language he stupidly believed all human beings would naturally speak if they were not spoken to at birth. The basic needs of the babies he enlisted in his horrible study were met, but the children themselves were never spoken to or verbally interacted with. They all died. (2) The sterile nurseries of the 1940s and 1950s—orphanages that provided for basic needs but denied children any kind of loving touch out of fear of disease—reported a mortality rate of 75 percent to 100 percent. The majority of their children simply died unloved and emotionally abandoned. (3) Feral children who are raised in the wild or locked in a closet and denied all human contact seem to be developmentally stymied for their whole lives, and they are further beset by other challenges, such as learning disorders, speech problems, and social ineptitude. (4) Monkeys separated from their mothers display all of the characteristics of human neurosis.[17] Given such reports, the idea that love is a central ingredient in the recipe for human development seems indisputable.

The kind of *ekstasis* that love makes possible, moreover, is responsible for one of the most sophisticated processes in which the human brain can engage—feeling empathy for someone or something outside of ourselves. This kind of empathic reaching out of ourselves into someone (or something) else's world, says neurologist Gerard Huther, "requires a tremendously refined level of perceiving and processing."[18] It is this capacity, he claims, "that sets the human brain apart from all other nervous systems."[19] The need for ecstasy, then, is explainable in such terms, for its gratification results in a sophisticated level of neurological development. Ecstasy, it seems, completes us by facilitating our growth.

Maslow's famous "hierarchy of needs" thoroughly bolsters the assertion that human beings have a developmental need for ecstasy. Maslow argued that we have a number of inherent psychological needs that, if gone unmet, result in neurosis and psychological disease. He arranged such needs in a hierarchy because he also claimed that higher needs such as the urge to express oneself creatively and the desire for social recognition are not activated until the lower needs for physiological sustenance and safety are met. In other words, human beings are not even aware of the higher needs if the lower ones are not gratified. We cannot be cognizant of our need for social acceptance if we are hungry or physically imperiled. Maslow's hierarchy, then, is a prioritization of human needs, and it says that certain needs (the lower ones) have stronger claims over others (the higher ones). The higher ones must be met, however, if we are to reach our full human potential. At the top of his hierarchy, Maslow placed "self-actualization," or the need for personal growth and the cultivation and fulfillment of potential. What led him to value self-actualization as the highest need were his investigations into the peak experiences of what he called psychologically super-healthy people.[20] Maslow observed that super-healthy people often reported states of intense bliss or joy in moments when the boundaries that divide the self from the other are dissolved. He used the words "ecstasy" and "peak" synonymously to describe such experiences, and their investigation occupied a prominent position in his research throughout most of his career.

"The term peak experience," Maslow wrote, "is a generalization of the best moments of the human being, for the happiest moments in life, for experiences of ecstasy, rapture, bliss, of the greatest joy." Such peaks are often associated with but not limited to "profound aesthetic experiences such as creative ecstasies, moments of mature love, perfect sexual experiences, parental love, experiences of natural childbirth, and many others."[21] Maslow believed human beings became fully human when, once their lower needs were met, they could allow themselves to become conscious of their need for ecstasy and begin moving towards a full cultivation of their potential. Peak experiences were for Maslow both indicators and facilitators of mature psychological health.[22] The circularity of this last point is not tautological, for it says that peaks are not only effects but also causes. To experience an ecstasy causes a realization or further activation of the need for such states of being, which, once experienced, enable human beings to function optimally.

The assertion that ecstatic states of being represent a need and serve as inducements to psychological growth also finds support in contemporary psychology. In the last decade the discipline of psychology has undergone a seachange in its new focus on eudaimonia. In the field called Positive psychology, scores of researchers have now begun rigorously examining the impact of positive affect on psychological development. One of the leading figures in Positive psychology, Martin Seligman, a researcher at the University of Pennsylvania and one-time president of the American Psychological Association, has made the forceful claim that positive emotions are not mere *epiphenomena*, or effects of some prior cause.[23] They are, rather, phenomena, or causal agents that exert a beneficial impact on psychological growth. According to Seligman, who bases his assertion on the brilliant work of Barbara Fredrickson, positive emotions "broaden our abiding intellectual, physical, and social resources, building up reserves we can draw upon when a threat or opportunity presents itself."[24] In other words, they undo all of the harmful effects of negative emotions, they serve as a healthy, mature defense against unhappiness and the potentially hazardous internalization of the world's many woes, and they also serve as a creative resource that broadens our perspectives and builds our emotional repertoires. Positive emotions make us more complex beings.

This current acknowledgment of the value of positive emotion is a long time in the making, coming as it does after a century-long focus on psychological disease. Most of the dominant schools in psychology have fixated on pathology and have even pathologized eudaimonic states of being, a tendency for which Freud is at least partly responsible. Despite his brilliant contribution to the discipline of psychology in providing the first systematic codification of the unconscious and its dynamics, Freud seems to have established a pattern from which psychology has only recently begun to free itself. His model of the psyche was entirely disease-focused, and he interpreted nearly all psychic states and traits in terms of underlying neuroses and unresolved, unconscious complexes. Freud's crude reduction of "oceanic" experiences is a case in point. When asked by a friend, Romain Rolland, to explain spiritual experiences in which the ego seems to dissolve and flow outside of itself, Freud first declared that he could not discover this oceanic feeling in himself. He then went on to interpret such experiences as symptoms of neurosis, claiming that "pathology has made us aware of a great number of states in which the boundaries between ego and the external world become uncertain."[25] For Freud, the oceanic feeling is merely the result of a narcissistic regression to an earlier phase of psychological development before ego had fully dissociated itself from the objects of its perceptions. His theory, focused as it was on what was wrong with the human psyche, could make no sense of ecstatic experiences, nor could it enable him to recognize their value.

With his negative focus on disease, Freud seems to have set the twentieth-century standard for most of mainstream psychology, or what Seligman calls "business-as-usual psychology," by which he means the type of research that focuses exclusively on disease and ignores well-being and positive states of being such as those found in and resulting from ecstatic experiences. What is more distressing is the tendency in such scholarship to interpret highly beneficial, eudaimonic states and experiences through the lens of disease. One example of such reductive interpretations is found in the work of scholars who have pathologized shamanic experiences, classifying as schizophrenic what is perhaps human consciousness at its absolute best. Mircea Eliade, the famous scholar of religion and myth, forcefully refuted this interpretive paradigm and argued for trying to understand shamanic experiences with a more open mind.[26] Another example is found in the similar diagnoses by some twentieth-century psychiatrists of C.G. Jung, Freud's greatest student and later rival, as a psychotic. Just as many of Jung's peers could not understand him, so have even modern scholars suggested that his bizarre, *ekstatic* states of consciousness were symptoms of an underlying psychological malady. In a thorough but rather negative biography, for instance, Ronald Hayman implies that Jung was a borderline schizophrenic whose visions could be explained in terms of psychiatric models of disease.[27] Such assertions do no justice to ecstasy, born as they are out of ignorance, fear, and a tendency to interpret any abnormal state of consciousness as a symptom of pathology.

A meta-analysis cited in the *New York Times* on the types of studies published in psychology journals proves the point that there has been little focus on healthy states of mind: from 1968 to 1998 researchers published over 45,000 articles on depression and only 400 on happiness.[28] There is something clearly wrong with this ratio, which amounts roughly to 100:1, as it speaks volumes about where our focus has been and where it needs to be. As Seligman and other Positive psychologists argue, it is undoubtedly necessary to investigate psychological pathology, but it is equally necessary to learn about optimal states of psychological well-being by identifying and studying models of health. The new Positive psychology does not call for an end to the study of pathology, as this would prove disastrous for human development. It does point out the woeful imbalance in our focus on disease states, however, and it calls for a redirection of scholarly energies through the careful examination of the optimally functioning psyche. Seligman's tenure as the APA President has inspired a whole new wave of researchers, and the brilliant work he has catalyzed has caused a major paradigm shift in psychology and thus legitimized the value of studying states of mind associated with the ecstatic experience.

The positive turn thus represents the latest major transformation in the discipline of psychology. This turn towards the eudaimonic is in one sense only a decade or so old, but in another sense it is a natural outgrowth of a whole series of developments in psychology. As Christopher Peterson observed before his recent, untimely death, several individuals set the stage for Positive psychology. These include Rogers, Maslow, Neill, Albee, Cowen, Bandura, Winner, Gardner, Sternberg, Levitt, Hogan, and Bucosky.[29] Not all of the pioneers of psychology were entirely pessimistic and disease-focused.

For instance, William James, the father of American psychology and a contemporary of Freud's, recognized the value of what he called "healthy-mindedness," or the refusal to embrace a negative emotion or state of mind. In his study, *The Varieties of Religious Experience*, a foundational work in the fields of religious studies and the psychology of religion, James expressed admiration for those who consciously reject unhappiness and embrace an optimistic outlook on life. He claimed that the "religion of healthy-mindedness," or the loose confederation of self-help groups and ecstatic spiritualisms that existed in his day, was "anything but absurd" and actually systematized the strategy all humans use to a greater or lesser degree to protect their happiness.[30] This refusal to succumb to despair—or stated more positively, the deliberate choice to preserve positive states of emotion in the face of negative outward circumstances—is a survival strategy human beings have used for time immemorial:

> We find such persons in every age, passionately flinging themselves upon their sense of the goodness of life, in spite of the hardships of their own condition, and in spite of the sinister theologies into which they may be born.... It is probable that there never has been a century in which the deliberate refusal to think ill of life has not been idealized by a sufficient number of persons to form sects, open or secret, who claimed all natural things to be permitted.[31]

Human beings intuitively seem to know that in order to preserve their sanity, they must (to some extent) shut out the miseries of the world and take refuge in their own self-cultivated, inner bowers. To function optimally as a human being, it is necessary not to give in to despair and to cultivate in consciousness the eudaimonic states and emotions that characterize happiness. The most potent weapon against unhappiness, it seems, is happiness itself.

This last statement is deceptively simple, but a closer look at its implications suggests an oft-overlooked profundity: happiness is not something that simply happens to us; happiness does not come by happenstance but by cultivation and effort. The experience of Victor Frankl, another precursor to Positive psychology, attests to the notion of choice in happiness. Frankl was a Jewish doctor and researcher—interestingly, one of the first investigators of the out-of-body experience—who survived the horrors of Auschwitz. While in the camp, Frankl realized that the Nazis could take everything from him, as they did, but they could not take from him what he came to regard as the most prized human possession—his freedom to choose how he let the outer circumstances of his confinement and the loss of nearly all of his loved ones affect him. He observed that when his fellow inmates relinquished this freedom by succumbing to victimhood and despair, they would die almost invariably within forty-eight hours. Frankl developed a whole new type of psychotherapy called logo-therapy as a result of his observations at Auschwitz.[32]

Jung, much like Frankl later did, rejected Freud's narrow focus on pathology and his reduction of all psychological states to neurotic sexuality, and he eventually adopted a more eudaimonic approach. Jung accepted many of the psychodynamics of the Freudian model of the psyche, but he also believed the unconscious was not merely a repository of disagreeable traits and socially unacceptable impulses. To the contrary, the unconscious for Jung represented the promise of growth and the possibility of self-renewal through *ekstasis*, or ego's engagement with the mysterious, unconscious depths of the human psyche. In his work with clients, Jung discerned that an encounter with the collective unconscious, or the deeper psychic levels beyond the Freudian personal unconscious, usually carried with it a numinous[33] quality. The *numinosum* for Jung is the mysterious aspect of the unconscious, the *imago dei* (God-image) in the human psyche, the part of the unconscious that seems spiritual to those who experience its joys and terrors. Although he made no professional claims to the absolute validity of the spiritual aspects of the unconscious, he did recognize the transformative value of an encounter with their numinous depths:

> No matter what the world thinks about religious experience, the one who has it possesses the great treasure of a thing that has provided him with a source of life, meaning and beauty that has given a new splendour to the world and to mankind. He has pistis[34] and peace. Where is the criterion by which you could say that such a life is not legitimate, that such experience is not valid and that such pistis is mere illusion?[35]

Jung valued numinous experiences so highly that he encouraged his clients to cultivate religiosity, not simply by attending church services but through an experiential engagement with a spiritual path. Jungian psychotherapists thus encourage a deep involvement with spirituality because psychotherapeutic methods can only take one so far. As part of their therapy, many Jungian analysands become intimately engaged with various types of experiential spirituality such as Buddhism, Yoga, Sufism, Christian Gnosticism, Kabbala, and the like.

Erich Fromm similarly foreshadowed the eudaimonic turn in psychology, theorizing about the most important of all ecstasies—love. For Fromm, the need to overcome, through *ekstasis*, the isolation of the ego is the central drive in the human psyche:

> This awareness of [man] as a separate entity, the awareness of his own short life span, of the fact that without his will he is born and against his will he dies, that he will die before those whom he loves, or they before him, the awareness of his aloneness and separateness, of his helplessness before the forces of nature and society, all this makes his separate, disunited existence an unbearable prison. He would become insane could he not liberate himself from this prison and reach out in some other form with men, with the world outside.[36]

This reaching beyond the self is achieved, according to Fromm, in mature, unconditional love, not only in its erotic forms but also in its non-sexual varieties. The ecstasy of love, in its manifestations as *epithumia, eros, philia, storge,* and/or *agape*, represents the completion of human development and signifies the meaning of human life. Only love, according to Fromm, can heal the neurosis of *enstasis*.

Yet another important school of psychologists who studied eudaimonic states of being was the Humanistic branch. Carl Rogers and Abraham Maslow in some ways provided the first layer in the foundation of Positive psychology. Although humanistic psychology was generally distrustful of the scientific method—the accepted modus operandi in contemporary psychology—as a viable means of uncovering important insights about the human psyche, its privileging of health over disease provided a model that Positive psychologists have thoroughly embraced. Peterson acknowledges that there is considerable overlap in the general programs of Positive and Humanistic psychology, but he distinguishes the new psychology from the older variety in that the former is still firmly committed to the scientific method, an emphasis on statistical reliability, and the need to replicate findings.

Positive psychology thus did not originate in a vacuum, and many important thinkers in the twentieth-century have made possible the exploration of its signature premise—namely, that "what is good about life is as genuine as what is bad and therefore deserves equal attention from psychologists."[37] Thanks to some daring and forward thinking individuals, there is now a new psychology in the new century, a field of legitimate academic inquiry that sees immense value in eudaimonic states of being and even says that we have a choice in their creation. Csikszentmihalyi, as I discussed in Chapter 2, thoroughly endorses the idea of a willful cultivation of eudaimonic states. The key, according to his theory, is how we utilize our attention. Csikszentmihalyi claims that "the information we allow into our consciousness becomes extremely important; it is, in fact, what determines the content and quality of life."[38] According to this idea, our state of being is determined by the thoughts we allow into our minds and by the emotions we cultivate as a result. The value of ecstasy here rises immediately to the foreground. Intense bliss is not just so much fluff, as twentieth-century cynicism and pessimism would have it, but proves to be of inestimable value as both a marker of and a catalyst for psychological development. Nevertheless, no one in contemporary psychology, to my knowledge, has engaged in any kind of serious research of ecstatic states.

The Uncontrollable Madness

Given that ecstasies have been reported for time immemorial and occur across cultures, it is safe to say they are not only a private, psychological affair but also a social issue. What, then, is the relationship between ecstasy and society? This is a difficult question to answer, since it depends entirely on the values, mores, and structures of the society in which the ecstasy occurs. Another element to complicate the matter is whether we are referring to individual or collective ecstasy, since both have social ramifications but in different ways. Regardless, for a number of reasons I shall explore in the rest of this chapter, ecstasy has by no means found a welcoming reception in modern societies.

One of the functions of group ecstasy, according to Barbara Ehrenreich, is to keep the structure of a society "from becoming overly rigid and unstable by providing occasional relief in the form of collective excitement and festivity."[39] In her downright fascinating book *Dancing in the Streets*, Ehrenreich explains the function of group ecstasy in terms of Turner's concept of *communitas*, or "the spontaneous love and solidarity that can arise within a community of equals."[40] *Communitas* is highly effective in fostering social cohesion and can thus be considered, from a strictly anthropological perspective, the endpoint of ecstatic rites in tribal and egalitarian communities. By serving as a kind of pressure relief value that eases tensions and restores social balance, collective ecstasy binds people together. In overly rigid, hierarchical, or dogmatic societies, however, ecstasy does not fare too well. "Hierarchy," Ehrenreich observes, "is antagonistic to the festive and ecstatic tradition."[41] Individuals who have a vested interest in maintaining the social stratifications in a given culture will find ecstasy to be problematic and even position themselves hostilely against it. The Nilotic Nuer of Africa, for instance, regard trance possession as "punishment for one's sins" and see it as a serious threat to self-mastery.[42] In *Ritual Cosmos* Evan Zuesse discusses the widespread practice among sub–Saharan Africans of ecstatic "possession trance," an activity he claims people of the lower classes often engage in because it serves as an escape from a conception of self too rigidly prescribed. This kind of social rigidity is precisely what drives many people in African cultures to engage in ecstatic possession, since it enables a reinterpretation of selfhood and an expansion beyond one's limited or restricted bounds.[43] Collective ecstasy, in the forms of carnival celebrations, Roman bacchanalia, music festivals, and the like can pose a challenge to authority, since it levels class distinctions and dissolves ethnic, racial, and gender boundaries. In communal ecstasy, everyone is the same and belongs equally to the same collective social body, a serious problem in a society too conscious of its social divisions.

In *Ecstatic Religion*, a study of the phenomenon of ecstasy in dozens of non–Western cultures, I. M. Richards analyzes the widespread use of ecstatic states as a means, however paradoxical, of self-assertion by individuals and groups, particularly those on the periphery of a given culture. Although he acknowledges that the social functions of ecstasy do not exhaust the concept's meaning and significance, Richards compellingly demonstrates that ecstatic possession is often a means by which women in patriarchal societies and marginalized men in others are able to challenge rigid social structures and redress psychological wrongs inflicted upon them by such structures.[44] Within limits, ecstatic possession is tolerated in many cultures and provides the marginalized with a means by which they can protest social inequalities and assert themselves in the face of oppression. A clear example of this use of ecstatic possession as a means of social protest is found in the Indian Bhakti tradition, which I discussed in Chapter 3. Those on the periphery of Indian society, particularly those who were outright excluded from religious activities, used ecstasy to reshape Hinduism in one of the most radical transformations in religious history.

Another example of group ecstasy as a challenge to hierarchy is found in the American counter-culture of the 1960s. Today, America has more or less become tolerant of hippie subculture, however marginalized it still is. But in the formative days it was a major social problem precisely because of its ecstatic nature. Characterized by non-courtship trance dancing, wild hair whipping, egalitarianism, communal joy, and loss of self in highly rhythmic music, the counter-culture replicated many of the features of ecstatic rituals and practices found in cultures all over the world, as Ehrenreich observes. Its values questioned authority and called for the liberation of the oppressed and a re-examination of social distinctions based on race, ethnicity, class, gender, and sexual orientation. The counter-culture adopted as its chemical agent of choice a drug not coincidentally called "ecstasy" and later renamed "acid" (LSD-25), which was the vehicle through which nearly a generation of people defied the roles prescribed to them by what they saw as an overly rigid hierarchy and outdated value system. LSD, with the ecstatic experience it offered, was for the counter-culture the path to self-transformation and societal re-configuration.

How did the hierarchy respond to such group ecstasy? In some ways precisely how other hierarchies have responded—that is, with extreme violence in many cases. More relevant to our discussion, in 1968 LSD was rendered illegal in America and most other parts of the West. Why did the hierarchy ban a well-studied, relatively benign drug, the derivative of which occurs naturally in flora all over the world, causes no chemical dependency, and poses no overdose dangers, when a toxic drug such as alcohol continues to be legal and thus responsible for some 50,000 deaths annually in America alone? No doubt, a thoughtful answer here would require more space than I have the luxury to fill, and I do not mean to ignore that recreational use of all mind-altering substances poses challenges to any society. At least part of the reason for the ban on LSD is that the ecstatic values of the counter-culture that used it challenged the materialistic foundation of American society. One of the value-shifts that often seems to occur as a result of ecstatic experiences, whether they are chemically or naturally induced, is the favoring of a more meaningful human experience through deeper emotional bonds and self-fulfillment, neither of which the acquisition of material goods and status markers can provide. Given this value shift, various hallucinogens have even been used as a treatment for alcohol and narcotic addictions.[45] Maslow speculated that LSD's efficacy in helping alcoholics recover from addiction lay in its ability to induce, by chemical means, a peak experience.[46] Its possible benefits notwithstanding, LSD posed a threat to the social hierarchy because those who ingested it often came to reject the shallowness of materialistic living, the foundation of American life.

The subtext here is that we can tolerate the alcoholic who destroys his own life, ruins the lives of family members, and even accidentally kills a few people on the highway because he poses no danger to foundational American values. But if young people begin ingesting a harmless, naturally-derived synthetic agent that causes them to see through the rigidity of social stratification and the hollowness of societal values, then the drug must be banned, which indeed it was. It is important to state that I am by no means making a plea for recreational drug use of any kind here; Albert Hoffman, the chemist who created LSD, and several other researchers have decried the problems posed by the recreational abuse of LSD and other hallucinogens as well as the obstacles this placed in the way of valuable research. To the contrary, I am merely pointing out the politics of ecstasy as a social phenomenon,[47] as well as the utter irrationality of allowing the use of a toxic, addictive, harmful drug (alcohol) that annually ruins the lives of tens of thousands of people and banning a benign agent that offers, through carefully designed research controls, an interesting window into the mysteries of human consciousness. Incidentally, the U.S. Government has recently approved clinical trials involving psychedelics, and in the last few years there have been several studies conducted in places around the country, including Harvard University, the institution that fired Timothy Leary and Richard Alpert back in 1963 for their undisciplined research on hallucinogens.

Group ecstasy is thus a problem if a hierarchy is too rigid or too insecure about its foundational values. In some cases the ecstatic experience will prove to be such a problem to certain hierarchies that it will be deemed madness and banned. The Romans, for instance, for all their enthusiastic embrace of Greek culture, could not tolerate the Dionysian festival called the *Bacchanalia*, outlawing it in 186 BCE, an early date in the development of the empire. To be sure the ecstatic festival would not continue, the Romans killed roughly 7000 Dionysian worshippers in one of the bloodiest crackdowns in religious history.[48] The Romans found the Bacchanalia threatening in part because its energies represented a madness that challenged the state. Personal religious experience was actually rendered illegal in Rome. This accounts for the curious lack of mystics in Roman culture.

Madness is a fitting label in some ways. Ecstasy, after all, is also a synonym for insanity. This connection can be traced back to the god of ecstasy, Dionysus, who was also the god of madness. The experience he bestowed, depending on whether one accepted or rejected the god, was either a blissful, divine intoxication in which the soul might even leave the body in joyous flight or a horrible and sometimes violent loss of all restraint. In either case, however, the resulting experience was to go temporarily out of one's mind—that is, to go mad. The ecstatic experience renders access to deep layers of the psyche that normally remain inaccessible to the illusory self we call ego. If a person is unprepared for an engagement with the unconscious *other* self, it is entirely possible he or she can end up temporarily or even permanently mired in a psychotic state. According to Jung, an encounter with unconscious depths should only occur "if [one's] conscious mind possesses the intellectual categories and moral feelings necessary for their assimilation."[49] Otherwise, the result is likely madness, an experience that can so thoroughly destabilize and decenter a person's inner landscape as to render him or her unfit to return to society.

Even if the individual does not go clinically insane, it is possible that he or she could become at least incongruous with mainstream society. The Sufi poets and masters, for instance, often spoke of the *matzoob*, one who directly experiences the ecstasy of Allah. The *matzoob* in Sufi literature is a social outcast, a pariah who has glimpsed God-realization and thus can no longer function in society. In India, as well, there is a tradition of the wandering yogi who renounces all ties to normal life to seek the state of *samadhi,* or blissful intoxication in which the perceiver cannot distinguish himself from the objects of his perceptions. The attainment of such intense, ego-dissolving bliss renders the yogi unfit for societal re-integration, and he thus spends his days wandering on the fringes of life.

In most cases, however, ecstatic experiences do not result in an individual being banished to the far cliffs, condemned to live a life of solitude because he or she has dared to speak the unintelligible language of joy. Nor do they usually result in incarceration in the state mental hospital, though this is a real possibility. They do leave one with social challenges. Maslow observed that transcenders, or self-actualizers who experienced multiple ecstasies, seem less happy in some ways because their peaks leave them with radically altered perspectives. Such transcenders "can be more ecstatic, more rapturous, and experience greater heights of 'happiness,'" he wrote, "but they are as prone or maybe more prone to a cosmic-sadness ... over the stupidity of people, their self-defeat, their blindness, their cruelty to each other, their shortsightedness."[50] In other words, because they see the lack of actualization of potential in most people, self-actualizers often no longer fit well into society. No doubt, they can and frequently do adapt and adjust to the stupidity, blindness, self-defeat, and shortsightedness of others, but they often spend their lives feeling as if they are in some ways fringe-dwellers.

Ecstasy thus often has a problematic relationship to societal structures. To be a functioning member of society is to be well adjusted, but as Freud observed in his seminal work, *Civilization and Its Discontents*, social adjustment often requires that we turn our backs on parts of ourselves. This is in some ways the essence of socialization itself. The problem here is that it is thoroughly possible to be well adjusted, to make lots of money, to have a family, and to embody all of the markers a given society values but also be utterly miserable and neurotic. In the "The Unknown Citizen," W.H. Auden brilliantly explores this idea in his description of a deceased man whom the "bureau of statistics" says had everything that should result in happiness. As the speaker claims, the man "was fully sensible to the advantages of the Installment Plan / And had everything necessary to the Modern Man" (19–20). The poem's closing irony, however, drives home the point that the appearance of social markers of happiness does not equal happiness itself: "Was he free? Was he happy? The question is absurd: / Had anything been wrong, we should certainly have heard" (28–29). Jung once saw a client who closely resembled Auden's subject, a successful, well-adjusted engineer with a family and all of the outward appurtenances of a successful life. When he began analyzing the man's dreams, however, Jung discontinued therapy because he saw in them a latent psychosis. He was afraid that if he continued prompting the man to engage the unconscious through dream work, he would end up in an irreversible psychosis. The man's social adjustment was compensatory to a potentially destabilizing, latent psychosis.

Maslow similarly lamented that our older ideals of the sage, the knight, the prophet, the hero, and the like have all given way in the modern age to the mere "well-adjusted man." But adjustment does not equal psychological health, as Auden's poem and Jung's anecdote both demonstrate. Depending on society or at least one's immediate environment (spouse, family, friends, teachers, co-workers, etc....), sometimes being well adjusted can mean turning one's back on ecstasy, which is tantamount to closing the door on psychological health and self-actualization. The key element here is the social group to which one belongs and whether it is conducive or hostile to ecstatic states. In a brilliant poem Emily Dickinson captured this idea of the role a given society or social group plays in determining reason and madness:

> Much Madness is divinest Sense—
> To a discerning Eye—
> Much Sense—the starkest Madness—
> 'Tis the Majority

In this, as All, prevail—
Assent—and you are sane—
Demur—you're straightway dangerous—
And handled with a Chain—

If ecstasy is deemed valuable by the collective, as it was in so many ancient cultures, then it will be considered divine sense. If, however, society finds ecstasy problematic, as is the case in so much of the modern world, then it will be seen as the starkest madness. The mob rules on this issue.

In his famous work, *Madness and Civilization*, Michel Foucault traced the history of madness from the Renaissance through the eighteenth-century and offered a detailed analysis of the central idea found in Dickinson's poem: madness is in some ways a social construct and changes according to a society's values and needs. According to Foucault, the specter of *unreason*, reason's other, begins to bulk large on the European horizon at the end of the Middle Ages. Madness and the madman "become major figures" in this period, and how they are treated (first sent away from society in the famous ship of fools and then later confined in the hospital) signifies Europe's desire to distance itself from and to repress unreason.[51] Foucault never explains why madness becomes such a central concern from the Renaissance onward, focusing principally on its cultural manifestations in the eighteenth century. One way to account for this phenomenon is to interpret it as a symptom of the West's troubled relationship with ecstasy. According to Robert Johnson, a Jungian analyst who argues for the value of *ekstasis*, unless we temporarily go out of ourselves in the healthy madness of ecstasy, we will go insane, or at least become neurotic as a result of denying ourselves moments of self-transcendence. The uneasiness over and preoccupation with madness from the Renaissance onward is thus in some ways reflective of the West's problematic encounter with and denial of ecstasy over the centuries.

Central to the issue is an all-pervasive, Western suspicion of ecstasy and ecstatic practices. This suspicion informed the attitudes of many European Christians who, in their missionary and imperialistic endeavors, encountered countless ecstatic practices in Africa, Oceania, and aboriginal North, Central, and South America. The bringers of Christian light to the shadowy recesses of far flung, darker-skinned parts of the world often encountered the ecstatic practices that had once been a central feature of their own religion, a subject I will presently discuss. Their response, however, was to demonize and often attempt to eradicate such practices in countless acts of religious chauvinism. As Ehrenreich observes, "*grotesque* is one word that appears again and again in European accounts of such events; *hideous* is another."[52] An example of this response is found in *Heart of Darkness*. In his famous nouvelle Joseph Conrad wrote of the "midnight dances" and "unspeakable rites" (75) in which his protagonist, Kurtz, participates. Kurtz is a European "emissary of light," who, nevertheless, is seduced and seemingly destroyed by the allure of dark, ecstatic rites performed in the jungle. Marlow, the narrator through whom Kurtz's story is filtered, himself speaks of the allure of the "weird incantations" of ecstatic practices, which he ultimately resists, likening them to "the responses of some satanic litany" (101). He also notes the "narcotic effect" (96) produced by the big African drums, the hypnotic "throb" (99) of which he similarly resists. This ability to retain one's European sense of self-consciousness and self-possession in the face of rituals that serve as an alluring call to ecstasy is not confined to Conrad's work of fiction. To the contrary, the encounter, as it is configured in *Heart of Darkness*, is highly characteristic of the whole history of European confrontation with and refusal of ecstatic rites and experiences.

In general, therefore, the West has not recognized the need for ecstasy, even antagonistically positioning itself against ecstatic experiences. An example of such antagonism is found in the suppression of the so called Black Mass, or Witches' Sabbath, of the Middle Ages. Until fairly recently, scholars believed the Black Mass—a supposed nighttime gathering of witches and Satan worshippers who fly to the woods on broomsticks or animals, conjure the dead, kiss a goat on the anus, renounce the Christian faith, and engage in dancing and a sexual orgy—was merely an imaginative fiction created by overly zealous inquisitors. To a great extent, the elements of the Black Mass were imaginative colorings offered by cruel, Catholic inquisitors whose creative tortures would encourage confession to the most outrageous of scenarios. But in his book, *Ecstasies: Deciphering the Witches' Sabbath*, Carlo Ginzburg makes a sophisticated case for modifying the total dismissal of the Black Mass as fiction. Some of the activities were, in fact, actual practices—remnants of older ecstatic forms of pagan spirituality. Through an exhaustive analysis of historical documents, Ginzburg compelling demonstrates the presence of shamanic and/or ecstatic elements in various versions of the Black Mass, particularly the flight, coded fertility rituals, nighttime dancing, and orgies—all of which strongly indicate the persistence of ancient ecstatic practices that predate the Christian era.[53] The witch hunts, it seems, were in some ways the result of the West's problematic stance toward ecstasy.

Another example of this Western antagonism can be seen in its internalized devaluation of the wildness of ecstatic celebrations and states of mind. The physical world correspondent of the ecstatic state of mind is the *wilderness*—a wild, untamable, natural locale beyond the strictures of society and its values, morality, prohibitions, and hierarchies. As Jung and the post–Jungians have made clear, the wilderness in the Western psyche is a source of anxiety, intimations of which can be seen in a variety of sources. Ancient Hebrews in their scapegoating practices would ritually load all of the tribe's sins onto two goats, offering one as a sacrificial slaughter to Yahweh and sending the other away from the tribe into the wilderness where it could scatter the Israelites' transgressions.[54] The psychological subtext here is that untamed nature, or wildness not contained by boundaries, is associated with sin and transgression, an idea that finds repeated expression in Western literature. So many of the pagan, Canaanite divinities who represented the natural wilderness in various manifestations became demons in the Hebrew Bible and later New Testament. Christians demonized two of these ecstatic, pagan goat-gods, Pan and Dionysus, amalgamating them and using the image as a visual representation of Satan himself. In the *Divine Comedy* Dante's Pilgrim thus strays from the "True Way" of the Christian path into the "Dark Wood of Error" and needs a journey through hell in order to be cleansed of his transgressions.

This anxiety over wilderness, with its threat to societal order and morality, is in some ways well founded, for early humans by necessity needed to recognize the dangers of the natural wild and thus band together to form rudimentary societies for the sake of survival. In another sense, however, the demonization of the wild comes at the expense of an estrangement from one's own nature, that is, the body. Ecstasy, although it can take on the form of transcendent, otherworldly visions, is also a corporeal experience of the flesh and the senses, as Robert Johnson observes.[55] One of the implications of the repression of ecstatic forms of worship, therefore, is that physicality, or the sensuous life of the body, is also denied. This association between the body and ecstasy can be seen in countless ecstatic cults, such as those of Dionysus, Asherah, Shiva, Tantrism, and many others, in which sacred sexuality in the form of female fertility or phallus worship features prominently. The much-commented-upon mind/body split in Western consciousness clearly indicates that the body, despite its powers of effecting *ekstatic* renewal, is a source of anxiety in the collective Western psyche.

Ehrenreich also cites Calvinism, with its profound distrust of direct spiritual experience and its reliance on blind faith, as a highly influential and pervasive force that greatly contributed to the widespread Western prejudice against ecstasy. The fullest expression of Calvinism, Puritanism proved to be a relatively joyless form of spirituality that H.L. Mencken comically defined as "the haunting fear that someone, somewhere, may be happy."[56] The Puritan legacy, with its cold sneer at joy and its version of an angry, punishing God who frowns on human sinners, still stares America and parts of Europe angrily and disapprovingly in the face. Despite ecstasy's place at the top of Maslow's hierarchy of needs, the West has not proven to be very conducive to ecstatic experience. The problem is not Calvinism per se but monotheism in general, a subject to which we now turn.

The Devil's Work

Across the ancient world, people practiced ecstatic forms of spirituality, either individually or collectively, by losing themselves in divine intoxication. In rural China, even in the sober Confucian era, there were festivals in which people worked themselves into a state of ecstasy while dancing "to the sound of clay timbrels." Those who took part in such activities, according to Marcel Granet, "were all like madmen."[57] The Aryan invaders of India brought to the sub-continent the worship of their god of ecstasy, Soma, whom they honored by imbibing a hallucinogenic drink by the same name. The Aryans encountered in India the cult of the ecstatic dancing god, Shiva. Scholars have not agreed on a date for the origin of Shaivite worship, but the evidence suggests that it predates the Indo-European invasions and probably stretches back at least to the Indus Valley civilization of Mohenjo-Daro (2600 BCE and probably beyond).[58] The cult of Shiva, as some scholars have maintained, might be the ultimate origin for the Dionysian practices found all over the ancient Mediterranean world.[59]

Other influences on the Greek form of ecstatic worship include multiple Near Eastern cults, such as those of Isis, Baal, Asherah, Cybele, and Anat. Characterized by ecstatic practices, these cults, along with the Greek Dionysian variant, are possibly responsible for the ecstatic character of early Hebrew worship, which was marked by celebratory dancing and singing the praises of God. In Africa ecstatic drumming and dance was, and still is in many parts of the continent, an inseparable component of religious life. In Oceania the historical record attests to countless varieties of ecstatic forms of spirituality. The archeological remains of the pre–Columbian Americas suggest ecstatic practices used for healing and religious rites. In Europe ecstatic practices bearing a shamanic character can be found among the Celtic, Druidic, and Norse cultures. In Central Asia and Siberia, religious life centered around the shaman, whose primary function was to engage in out-of-body journeys to the heavens or to the underworld either for the purpose of healing, retrieving a lost soul, and securing a revelation, or simply for joy alone. Ecstatic spirituality, it seems, is the oldest form of religion and can be found nearly everywhere in the ancient world.

For all its ancient ubiquity, however, ecstasy has found a hostile reception in the modern era, particularly in the West but also in other parts of the globe, including Africa, the Middle East, and Asia. In China the older ecstatic rites were eventually prohibited, likely because civic authorities and priests of the state religious cult saw them as a challenge to the hierarchy. By the time of the great ancient empires, "all orgiastic elements were strictly eliminated," according to Max Weber, because religious authorities deemed them "as dangerous as the Roman nobility once considered the cult of Dionysus."[60] In the Near East the advent of monotheism, with its later global impact, proved to be a fatal blow to ecstatic spirituality, serving as a mean of repression of ecstasy in nearly every culture where it spread its doctrines.

The relationship of monotheism to ecstatic spirituality is not simple and clearly defined, however, and it certainly cannot be viewed strictly in the terms of former's outright hostility to the latter. After all, the three monotheistic faiths—Judaism, Christianity, and Islam—were founded as a result of ecstatic experiences. The ancient Hebrew patriarchs, Abraham and Moses, communed ecstatically and thus directly with God. Jesus experienced the divine during his baptism, when the spirit came to him as a white dove. Muhammad, during his famous meditations in his mountain cave, Gare Hira, heard a voice whose words he later dictated to scribes, who wrote them down as the Qur'an. Muhammad also made his famous night journey from the Dome of the Rock in Jerusalem through the heavens, a shamanic sojourn, according to David Leeming,[61] that rendered Jerusalem the third holiest city in Islam (after Mecca and Medina). All of these pivotal founders had some kind of ecstatic experience that served as the foundations of their respective faiths. Monotheism, in some ways, would not be possible without ecstasy.

What is more, all three monotheistic faiths tolerated and even participated in ecstatic spiritual practices. As I discussed in Chapter 3, the oldest Hebrew prophets operated in prophetic guilds, or bands of holy men, who, with the help of music and dancing, would work themselves into a "form of collective, self-induced ecstasy" and lose themselves in a "sea of divine intoxication."[62] The ecstatic prophetic guilds exerted such a considerable influence over the Israelites that they played a pivotal role in the transformation of Saul from man to first king of Israel. The prophet Samuel tells Saul that before he can become king, he must endure the kind of ecstatic transformation the guilds effected in people. Samuel sends Saul on a journey and prophesies that he will meet "a company of prophets coming down from the shrine, led by lute, drum, fife, and lyre, and filled with prophetic rapture." Then, says Saul, "the spirit of the Lord will suddenly take possession of you, and you too will be rapt like a prophet and become another man" (1 Sam. 10: 4–6). Saul becomes king as a result of his ecstasy, an experience Israelites so thoroughly cherished that their participation in ecstatic cults was widespread.

Although Muhammad and his followers destroyed the many ecstatic cults that worshipped at the sacred Kaaba stone in Mecca, Moslems retained some features of the pagan cults they positioned themselves against, foremost among which is the circumambulation around the Kaaba in a counterclockwise direction. The *tawaf*, as it is called, seems clearly to be a sober variant of the circle dance found throughout so many ecstatic cultures, as Ehrenreich observes.

Islam also spawned a rich ecstatic tradition in Sufism, the mystical variant of Muslim spirituality that honors, as a kind of first principle, the ecstasy of knowing God directly.

Early Christians were so influenced by the ecstatic Dionysian cult that their version of Jesus was a variant of Dionysus. Scholars have long noted the striking similarities between the two gods: both are sons of a major deity; both are born of virgin mothers; both survive being killed as infants; both perform miracles to inspire faith; both battle evil forces; both return to their birthplaces only to be rejected; both are strongly associated with wine and turning water into wine; both suffer wounding, death, and resurrection; both descend into the underworld; both attain to immortality; both evangelize their messages and establish cults; and both pose challenges to social barriers and class/gender distinctions.[63] Such similarities attest to the pervasive influence of the Greek form of ecstatic religion—after all, the early Christian world was a Greek world—and thus the ecstatic character of early Christian spirituality.

For all of this participation in ecstatic spirituality, however, monotheists also found ecstasy to be a troubling challenge. Early Hebrews participated heavily in ecstatic religious cults, both Near Eastern and Greek, to such an extent that later priestly and prophetic reformers saw this as a violation of the first four commandments. The Hebrew Bible is rife with the pattern of the Israelites breaking their covenant with Yahweh and then being punished for bowing down to other gods. Foremost among these was the Greek god, Dionysus. The origins of the prophetic guilds is unclear but points to both Near Eastern and Greek sources. Coins, funerary objects, and building ornaments found in Palestine (modern day Israel), nevertheless, confirm the Greek influence, showing that ancient Israelites worshipped Dionysus, sometimes alongside Yahweh, despite Biblical prohibitions.[64]

A detail in the story of Saul's transformation also indicates a connection to Dionysus: Samuel tells Saul that before he meets the band of prophets he will encounter three young men carrying, among other things, *three goats* (1 Sam. 10:3). The goat was strongly associated with Dionysus and served as the god's ritual stand-in during rites. A baby goat, or kid, in particular, was often boiled in its mother's milk at the sacred meals of Dionysian and Orphic rituals. Such practices, as Max Radin points out, shed light on the mysterious injunction (which appears three times in the Bible) against seething a kid in its mother's milk. Radin notes that it appears twice in Exodus (23:19 and 34:26), along with a list of other *ritual* prohibitions, and once in Deuteronomy (14:21) as a *dietary* prohibition. The prohibition against boiling a goat in its mother's milk is, in effect, a ban on Dionysian worship.[65] The Deuteronomist, however, a priestly reformer, misunderstood the injunction and placed it in a list of dietary regulations, perhaps because by the time he wrote Dionysian participation had been significantly curtailed. It seems that a foundational element in Jewish dietary regulations—the prohibition against having meat and dairy in the same meal—is based on a misunderstanding of a Biblical injunction, which was itself based on an attempt to prohibit participation in an ecstatic pagan cult.

Robert Johnson sees the Biblical injunction against seething a kid in its mother's milk as the pivotal moment when the Hebrew religion turned its back on ecstasy.[66] His point about the loss of the ecstatic principle in Judaism is bolstered by the curious practice by many Jews who desire spirituality of continuing to culturally identify with Judaism but also turning to Buddhism, Sufism, Vedanta, or the New Age for the promise of direct ecstatic experience. It is necessary to point out, however, that Judaism has not entirely closed the door on ecstatic experience. The Jewish mystical tradition, informed by the many ecstatic cultures Jews encountered over the centuries, stretches back to well before the Christian era and has persisted throughout the ages in the form of esoteric Judaism, or *Kabbala*. Today, there is even a resurgence and popularization of Kabbala, particularly in America, with many non–Jewish adherents turning to its ecstatic doctrines. In general, however, ecstatic spirituality has not fared too well in mainstream Judaism.

Islam, too, has received ecstasy problematically. To be sure, Muslim mysticism, or what is called Sufism, the essence of which is the cultivation of ecstatic inner experiences, has a long history stretching back to the beginnings of Islam. With its ecstatic practices of meditation, recitation of God's many names, fasting, sleep deprivation and the like, Sufism, particularly its later forms, is a clear example of ecstatic spirituality. Although Sufism is still alive today as a rich and vibrant worldwide movement, Sufis have been marginalized in many parts of the Muslim world.

Sufism fully blossomed in ancient Persia, an area comprising present-day Iran and parts of Afghanistan, but the Shi'a of present-day Iran have looked upon Sufi practices with considerable suspicion. Ironically, the Ayatollahs of the fundamentalist government are well known for their mystical writings; the Ayatollah Khomeini even penned a book of Sufi poems before his death, and Iranians claim the rich tradition of Sufi writing as their own. The poetry of Rumi and Hafiz has achieved a kind of scriptural status in Iran, valued as it is just beneath the Qur'an and the Hadith. The theological narrow-mindedness and intolerance of the Iranian Shi'a, however, have driven practicing Sufis out of Iran. To be called a *dervish*, a once revered title used to designate a follower of a Sufi order, is now pejorative in Iran and signifies "a term of contempt suggesting idleness, drug use, immorality, and every other sort of evil."[67] While "expelling living dervishes, Iranian Ayatollahs claim the cultural mantle of safely deceased Sufi saints."[68] Such distancing enabled "the religious hierarchy of Iran to eliminate possible rivals to their authority while appropriating those Sufi doctrines which they admired."[69] The legalistic fundamentalists of Iran, it seems, identify with a non-legalistic esotericism that poses no threat because it exists at a safe temporal distance.

The Sufis of Afghanistan have not fared much better. The type of spirituality that today characterizes much of Afghanistan, as well as many other parts of the radicalized Muslim world, is called Wahhabism, named after the fiery and puritanical eighteenth-century reformer, Abd al-Wahhab, who believed the ecstatic Sufis were infidels. Wahhab's legacy is the violent persecution of Sufis in the form of the destruction of shrines and tombs and the elimination of Sufi worship in much of the Muslim world. Wahhab was something like the John Calvin of Islam, as Ehrenreich observes. He interpreted the ecstatic variety of Muslim spirituality as "a rivalry between competing authorities"—a problematic power struggle that stood in the way of his version of a "pure" Islam—and he reacted violently to Sufism.[70] In 922 CE in a similarly intolerant, fundamentalist climate, the famous Sufi teacher Mansur al-Hallah was crucified and then beheaded for daring to challenge the religious authorities of his day by sharing directly with the people the Sufi concept of cultivating ecstatic inner experiences. Wahhab's crackdown was thus by no means unprecedented and served as a resurfacing of the ongoing tension between exoteric and esoteric spirituality that has characterized much of the world's religious history.

Despite Wahhabism, the Sufis enjoyed a safe haven in Turkey, the final resting place of the great poet Rumi, until Mustafa Kemal Ataturk rose to power in 1920. In his attempts to secularize and Westernize Turkey and free it from Ottoman models of governance, Ataturk replaced Muslim laws with secular legal codes, closed religious schools, and restricted the building of mosques. Because the Sufis were quite influential in Turkey, they bore the brunt of Ataturk's reforms, which resulted in the confiscation of all Sufi meeting places and the banning of all Sufi activity. The most significant blow came with the illegalization of Sufism. To the present day, Sufis are legally restricted from operating in Turkey. It is still possible to see the famous whirling dervishes in Turkey, but only in "cultural performances," not in actual religious worship.

The ecstatic variety of Muslim spirituality has proven to be problematic for the two major forces at odds in the world today—fundamentalism and secularism. But the Sufis do enjoy significant freedom to operate in the rest of the secularized Western world, Turkey notwithstanding. Today, Sufism is more of a Western phenomenon than a Middle Eastern one. Rumi's immense popularity in the Western world, particularly in America, where he is one of the best-selling poets more than 800 years after his birth, attests to the enthusiastic embrace of Sufi doctrines in the largely Christian West.

The turn to Sufism by many former Christians has much to do with Christianity's own troubling relationship with ecstatic spirituality. Christianity does have a rich tradition of mystics whose experiences are quintessentially ecstatic. However, like the Iranian mullahs who claim Sufi doctrines from a safe distance but then distance themselves from actual Sufis and their practices, so have Christians proudly claimed their mystics but also found them a challenge. St. Theresa of Avila, for instance, was almost brought up on heresy because of her "diabolical" ecstatic visions. Shortly after her death, however, she was canonized as a saint and later named a Doctor of the Church, two very high honors indeed. Meister Eckhart, with his ecstatic doctrine of the soul's interchangeability with God, was also almost charged with heresy in his day. Today, however, he is fondly claimed by Christians as a much revered, mystical theologian. This after-the-fact praise suggests that there needs to be a safe enough temporal distance between the ecstatic experience and the Church hierarchy for a given mystic to be brought into the fold. Because the Catholic Church serves as a mediator between God and believer, mystics and their claim of direct experience prove to be a highly problematic challenge that threatens the authority of the priesthood, liturgy, and sacred texts—elements that serve as the foundation on which the Church authority rests. During the medieval period, the Church wanted to control religious experience so directly that its leaders vehemently opposed, persecuted, and sent to the stake many individuals who attempt to reveal the secrets of the Bible by translating it from Latin into local vernaculars. Despite the tradition of the mystics, Catholicism thus has effectively turned its back on ecstasy in its attempt to build and then preserve the ecclesiastical structures erected on the foundation of Christ's own ecstatic experience.

The antagonism among early Christians, characterized in part by the debate over the selection of books that would later be called the New Testament, was centered in some ways around the issue of ecstatic experience. Whereas the Gnostics advocated the cultivation of direct spiritual experience, suggesting an allegorical (thus non-literal) reading of the Gospels and claiming in various texts that all people could attain the states of consciousness Jesus experienced, the more ecclesiastical Christians favored texts that supported the importance of mediators of spiritual experience, such as the papacy, the priesthood, and the liturgy.[71] The latter group won the day, obviously, and Gnostic texts were banned from the Biblical canon, in some cases lost in obscurity until the rediscovery of some of them in 1945 at Nag Hammadi in Egypt.

The early Church did tolerate some vestiges of ecstatic practices in allowing, as part of the mass, wine drinking, circle dancing, speaking in tongues, and *enthusiasmos*, or becoming filled with God.[72] Over the centuries, however, the Church began to sober up and became much less tolerant of such

Dionysian elements. At the end of the fourth century, this sobriety found its fullest expression in the words of John Chrysotom, whom Ehrenreich calls the "fiery and intolerant" archbishop of Constantinople. Chrysotom's pronouncement on the matter of dancing in the Church serves as a barometer of the age: "For where there is a dance, there is also a Devil."[73] In 400 CE this verbal venom was accompanied by the wholesale destruction of Eleusis in Greece and the killing of its priests by Romans who had by now formally adopted Christianity as its official and only religion.[74] Eleusis—long the seat in the ancient Mediterranean world of the Greater Mysteries that provided an initiatory experience culminating in a mystical revelation induced by the ecstatic practices of fasting, dancing, and imbibing an elixir that may have been laced with a hallucinogen—proved to be a threat to Christian church authorities who saw themselves alone as mediators between God and the soul.

From this point onward the Church grew increasingly more hostile to ecstatic techniques. While the practice of ecstatic dancing in Catholic churches continued through the late Middle Ages, in the thirteenth century the Church could tolerate no more. "Catholic leaders," according to Ehrenreich, "finally purged the churches of unruly and ecstatic behavior" by banning dancing inside churches and listing it as a "confessable sin" in a directory of sins published in 1317.[75] Christianity, like Islam and Judaism, found ecstatic practices too problematic and purged them from the list of admissible behaviors within the confines of a house of God. What was once sacred activity for people in so many ancient cultures thus became unacceptable to the sober Church fathers, who so sufficiently demonized it that to this day direct spiritual experience is viewed by many Christians suspiciously and skeptically. Despite a few notable exceptions, such as tongue-speaking Pentecostals, rapturous Baptists, ecstatic Evangelicals, Born Again believers, Quakers who meditate on the inner light, and Catholics who fuse Christianity with African and Native American religious practices, ecstasy has come to be synonymous with the devil's work in the collective Christian psyche.

The Aching Need

Although these negative attitudes about ecstasy permeate Western culture, in large part because of monotheism, the need for ecstasy in the human psyche continues until it is met in one form or another, whether constructively or destructively. As Robert Johnson points out, ecstasy needs can be met through high-grade forms, such as cultivating the state of consciousness necessary for the *ekstasis* of joy; through attenuated forms, such as sporting events and political rallies; or through low-grade forms such as drug-use.

Another example of the manifestation of the psychological need for ecstasy is found in the birth of the European Carnival. Ehrenreich observes that almost precisely when the Catholic Church banned festivities in the fourteenth century as a worship activity and sent them out into the streets, Carnival was born.[76] The festival came to serve as a secularization of what was once a deeply spiritual practice. Carnival, as Mikhail Bakhtin observed, should not be confused with mere holidays or other state-sanctioned festivals, since its origins are in the people themselves. Carnival started from the ground up and stemmed "from a force that pre-exists priests and kings and to whose superior power they are actually deferring when they appear to sanction carnival."[77] With its masks, hierarchical inversions, celebration of joy, and classless ethos, Carnival served to ease social tensions and to prevent political hierarchies from becoming overly rigid—functions previously served by ecstatic rites.

Carnival also served, and continues to do so in many parts of the world, as a vehicle of the celebration of the repressed bodily other. As I previously noted, ecstatic states are sometimes intimately related to the body and the senses. Carnival, with its privileging of what Bakhtin calls the *grotesque*, celebrates "the lower stratum of the body, the life of the belly and the reproductive organs."[78] Grotesque literary forms are thus concerned with "acts of defecation and copulation, conception, pregnancy and birth."[79] Carnival, with its foregrounding of the lower bodily stratum, served as a healing balm for the mind/body split that occurred when the West largely turned its back on ecstatic experience. In all of its grotesque forms, Carnival carried with it the theme of madness, the virtue of which, as Bakhtin observed, was that it enabled people to look at the world with different eyes. Such madness, with its "gay parody of official reason, of the narrowness of official truth," allowed people to extend beyond the confines of self in a communal, celebratory setting.[80] For Bakhtin, as for the followers of the Dionysian and Orphic Mysteries, madness functions eudaimonically by facilitating ecstasy and thus offering a release from the confines of a self too-narrowly defined. However sad it may be, since the advent of Carnival, there have been literally thousands of acts of legislation passed throughout Europe to ban or to curtail its festivities.[81]

A more recent example of the cultural manifestation of the psychological need for ecstasy is found in the modern "rave" scene, itself a variant of the Carnival. Ecstasy needs are met so poorly in the West—usually through the euphoria of shopping, the thrill of the sports contest, the joys of eating, or the pleasures of alcohol—that young people in the 1980s began to have parties that on the surface seemed like the celebratory folly of youth but on closer inspection proved to be a resurfacing of a primeval practice—the ecstatic rite. Rave culture, a more recent version of the ecstatic hippie scene, consists of groups of people ingesting a mind-altering, mildly hallucinogenic drug not coincidentally called "ecstasy," dancing to the hypnotic rhythms of music classified in the genre of "trance-dance," and losing themselves in the joys of *ekstasis* through sexual and platonic bonding with other ravers.[82] In another era the rave would be considered a highly sacred practice and given a prominent position in the priorities of society. In the contemporary West, however, it is deemed an embarrassing subcultural activity or dismissed as a youthful decent into sex, drugs, and music. Regardless, the need exists in the human psyche and will be met in one way or another.

The recent rise of alternative religions in the West is yet another attempt at meeting ecstasy needs. In the last forty years millions of people in America and other parts of the Western world, dissatisfied with exoteric forms of monotheism, have turned to other religions in order explore, through *ekstasis*, the depths of the psyche. Finding traditional religious forms and rituals devoid of actual experience, they have turned, since the sixties, to various inner spiritualties such as Hinduism, Buddhism, Jainism, Kabbalah, and many others. As an antidote to exoteric legalism, several new, ecstatic religions have also sprouted and flourished, attracting thousands of adherents. One example is Eckankar, which was founded in 1965 but offers an ancient form of spirituality that helps people to cultivate ecstatic experiences through contemplative spiritual exercises. While some people might hastily dismiss such religions as being illegitimate, it is important to remember that all of the major, historical religions were labeled as such in their beginnings. More to the point, Eckankar offers a type of direct, participatory spirituality with ancient roots. A vehicle for helping people experience the ecstasy of God, it is the oldest kind of religion on the planet. Eckankar gratifies ecstasy needs.

Any unmet psychological need will result in neurosis and disease if denied gratification for too long. Foucault's observation about the rise of the madman and madness as central concerns in the European renaissance thus speaks to the West's denial of ecstasy needs, the effects of which returned in the early modern period after a centuries-long neglect in the form of uneasiness over and a neurotic preoccupation with madness. With our hyper-rationalism and extreme self-consciousness, we in the West will continue to be haunted by the specter of unmet ecstatic needs perhaps until we learn to recognize the inherent value of ecstasy and begin to foster social and institutional structures that will facilitate its realization. It is a sore that still festers.

11. Literary Implications:
A Problematic Rapture

The mixed reception of ecstasy in Western society and religion is mirrored in the field of literary studies, the myriad theories of which generally do not enable a literary critic to assess the eudaimonic, Dionysian aspects of the human psyche as they appear in various works. There are psychological theories that enable critics to brilliantly tease out a text's underlying neuroses by revealing that a given character, speaker, or author exhibits oedipal psychodynamics or desires to fill his lack by serving as a surrogate for his mother's phallus. There are also linguistic theories that enable a scholar to show that love in a work is not really what it appears to be, or that any expression of emotion, whether negative or positive, linguistically undermines itself by signifying in self-defeating ways. Many of these approaches are immeasurably valuable. As a professor who teaches critical theory, I also employ myriad theoretical ideas in my courses and in my scholarship.

Nevertheless, such theories, with notable exceptions,[1] are almost always put in the service of shedding light on ill-being or its mitigation, whether in the form of psychodynamics, social problems, or objectionable ideology. Where is the theory that affirmatively acknowledges ecstasy and sheds productive light on its eudaimonic implications? While a new theoretical framework has emerged in the post-theory moment, a point I will explore more fully in the final chapter, there are significant reasons why ecstatic poetics and aesthetics have been largely ignored, rejected, or trivialized in literary studies. These include a pathologizing tendency, a problematic orientation toward eudaimonic values, the neglect of affect and its corollary—the privileging of language—and the embrace of dissociative *ekstasis* over eudaimonic ecstasy. Let us explore each of these barriers.

The Pathologizing Tendency

Just as the focus on ill-being and its mitigation has, until the last decade, captured the attention of the majority of psychologists, this tendency to pathologize the human experience is also found ubiquitously in literary studies. No doubt, scholars do focus on some salutogenic aspects of human life in their studies. By and large, however, critical attention for several decades has been fixated on suffering, despair, alienation, ennui, violence, absurdity, injustice, and tragedy.

It is possible to tease out this tendency by looking at the characteristic ways in which critics in several theoretical schools might respond to Words-worth's famous sonnet, "Composed upon Westminster Bridge, September 3, 1802," which configures a eudaimonic state of being, or something like an aesthetic peak experience, that is, an ecstasy:

> Earth hath not anything to show more fair:
> Dull would he be of soul who could pass by
> A sight so touching in its majesty:
> This City now doth, like a garment, wear
> The beauty of the morning; silent, bare,
> Ships, towers, domes, theatres and temples lie
> Open unto the fields, and to the sky;
> All bright and glittering in the smokeless air.
>
> Never did sun more beautifully steep
> In his first splendor, valley, rock, or hill;
> Ne'er saw I, never felt, a calm so deep!
> The river glideth at his own sweet will:
> Dear God! The very houses seem asleep;
> And all that mighty heart is lying still![2]

A Freudian critic, for instance, might read the speaker's perceptions in terms of the psychodynamics of projection and repression. After all, it is curi-ous that he imagines "that mighty heart lying still," for a heart not beating is a dead heart and belongs to a corpse. His choice of words here signifies that he wants to disavow the object of his perception—a projection of undesirable contents of the unconscious. Whatever such disagreeable contents are, they make the speaker uncomfortable, and he wishes them to be gone from con-sciousness, to be dead or lying still.[3]

A Lacanian critic might view the poem as a quintessential example of the illusion of unity one experiences at the "mirror stage" of identity formation. The speaker looks out onto the city of London and sees in projection a mirror of his own inner state. In this moment he experiences a false sense of wholeness and unity, both of which are seen principally in the last line but implied throughout. In reality, however, his subjectivity is one of fragmentation and lack, and the beautiful moment on the bridge is actually a *meconnaissance*, a term Lacan used to designate a refusal to accept the truth. The speaker will spend the rest of his days yearning to fill his lack and overcome his sense of insufficiency through essentially futile attempts at achieving an imaginary sense of wholeness.

A deconstructive critic, working from any number of vantage points, might also pay attention to how the poem undermines itself but by appealing to language instead of psychology. The speaker seems drawn to London's silence, majestic beauty, openness, calmness, and unity, but he undermines himself with his own diction. The unity is violated by the river Thames, which "glideth at *his own sweet will*." The sense of oneness is interrupted by an autonomous entity, the river, which subverts and renders impossible his monistic fantasy. The implication here is that in imposing unity on disunity, he is telling himself a "lie," a word he actually uses in line six. The association of the word "lie" with "temples" ("temples lie") indicates that his perception of unity is an illusory fantasy, the likes of which are promulgated by the Church. This misspeaking suggests the language of the poem subverts itself and thus deconstructs into textual meaninglessness, rendering impossible the speaker's attempt at communicative utterance and self-expression.

Other critics, whose focus is on the identity politics of various marginalized groups, might be less concerned with psychology and language and more attuned to the poem's unspoken social implications. Postcolonial and anti-racism theorists, for instance, might be concerned with the symbolism of the city itself, because, at the time of composition, London was the capital of an empire involved in the slave trade and the oppression of darker skinned peoples in its various colonial enterprises around the globe. For a poet to elide such evils and aestheticize what is in fact ugly about London—its centrality in the politics of oppression—is a callous insensitivity and woeful injustice to those whom the British were exploiting at the time. The speaker's beautiful moment is thus enjoyed at the expense of the darker skinned slaves and colonial subjects who made British wealth possible. The reality of the poem is that its beauty is only possible as a result of an unspoken, unnamed ugliness—human suffering.

A Marxist would have similar concerns but perhaps with the suffering of London's lower classes, who find no direct representation in the poem but who exist nevertheless as a kind of silent other. In 1802 London was in the throes of change as a result of the industrial revolution, and the exploitation of workers by the newly emerging, capitalist class was rising to a feverish pitch that reached its zenith later in the century. The bourgeois speaker looks over London as though none of this is taking place. His view from the bridge yields a "sight so touching in its majesty," but it belies the social realities below, where a woefully unequal distribution of wealth has resulted in a swarm of criminals, prostitutes, underfed children, and disenfranchised, alienated workers who labor incessantly but receive little for their toil. The speaker's position on the bridge is a privileged one, available only to those who have the wealth necessary to enable such aesthetic perceptions of beauty and unity.

A feminist might similarly take exception to the speaker's privilege but in terms of gender rather than class. Because Romantic aesthetics called for an identification of the speaker with the poet, it is safe to conclude that the speaker is male. His perception of the city, therefore, is an assertion of male dominance—the intimidating gaze of the oppressor used against the oppressed. The gendering of the river as male reflects the poet's desire to project his maleness beyond himself. His sense of unity is a reflection of a patriarchal value system that locates its security in order, reason, and domination. The silence and stillness in which he takes such delight are, in fact, the muting of women, whose oppression the poem symbolically reenacts through its constructions.

To be sure, the foregoing readings of Wordsworth's sonnet are simplified and condensed, but I have encountered all of them in various forms as critical reactions to poems that configure eudaimonic emotions or ecstatic states. In my years of research on ecstatic and mystical verse, I have learned that many theoretical frameworks result in a pathologizing of what is, in fact, a salutogenic experience. Such perspectives, at least as they have been generally used in critical discourse, cannot seem to enable an account of the poem's ecstatic and eudaimonic dimensions. They cannot account for the speaker's peak state of wonder that climaxes into ecstasy, the results of which are that he sees the city more holistically and responds with joy, gratitude, and serenity. Such a moment enables him, as the poem suggests, to discern connections in disparate entities, to become more closely connected with nature, and to appreciate beauty more deeply. All of these eudaimonic elements, however, are overlooked or pathologized in approaches underpinned by suspicion.

I mean no disrespect to scholars using such theories, and I am highly sympathetic to the theoretical positions cited above, having made significant use of them in my courses and in my scholarly work. Still, when I read poems by Wordsworth or Rumi or Dickinson through such suspicious lenses, I am left feeling as though something went wrong, as though the critical perspective is unsuited to the poem and can only reveal a grotesquely distorted picture. The problem lies in the expectations such reading strategies call upon us to adopt. In so many cases literary theories seem to prompt a pathogenic view, even when the subject being viewed is salutogenic. The analogical equivalent here is to interpret a child's expression of joy by consulting the *DSM*, a diagnostic manual used by psychiatrists and psychotherapists for identifying various psychological disorders. There is no entry for joy in the *DSM*, so the only way to make sense of it in such a framework is to read it as a symptom of some underlying dysfunction such as a mood disorder, a manic episode, the grandiosity of a borderline personality, or a characteristic of narcissism.

Literary theory so often, but by no means exclusively, tends to move in this direction because it is *generally* focused on the absence of eudaimonia, the rectification of social ills, and the mitigation of ill-being. When confronted with an ecstatic or eudaimonic state, it often falls short. To be sure, the pathologizing focus can be productive by yielding interesting insights and flushing undesirable ideologies to the textual surface. In other cases, however, pathologizing a savored moment of tranquility or an expression of ecstatic joy or gratitude points out the limitations of theory so conceived. To focus only on negative circumstances, psychological disease, problematic ideology, and social ills is to ignore the complexities of the other half of human experience that literary works configure: developmental growth, eudaimonic states of being, a sense of meaning and purpose, fulfilling relationships, and constructive social structures. These, too, are important and need an appropriate interpretive framework, which I hope this study has helped to begin to build.

The Problem of Values

To be sure, such a statement represents a value position. In a postmodern age in which many scholars remain dubious of all valuation and adopt the stance that there are no universal ideals and values, it is problematic to endorse a value position. As the foregoing study indicates, however, ecstatic poetry is worth reading not only for its aesthetic delights but also for what it can teach us about eudaimonia. This may sound like an antiquated view, and in some ways it is reminiscent of outdated conceptions of literature, particularly the liberal humanist position, which viewed the function of literature as "the enhancement of life and the propagation of humane values,"[4] not in a propagandistic way but certainly for the betterment—the well-being—of humanity. Many literary scholars today, however, would likely experience discomfort at publicly endorsing such a conception of literature. The hermeneutics of suspicion, as it is currently conceived, has caused many scholars to interpret the "propagation of humane values" as a covert way to maintain the hegemony of capitalist ideology, to dominate darker-skinned peoples, to foster patriarchal attitudes, and to condemn alternative sexualities. In so many cases our greatest writers indeed have been compellingly shown to be complicit in various undesirable ideologies and less-than-ideal psychodynamics, but by no means does this complicity equate to "guilt." To the contrary, it merely points out one of theory's greatest insights—that writers are influenced by inescapable cultural and psychological forces.

The problem with the liberal humanist assertion that literature enhances life and propagates humane values is not so much with the truth of the statement but with the question of whose lives are enhanced and whose values are propagated. Critical theory has immensely enriched the discipline in terms of calling for considerably more rigor and offering a rich number of perspectives from which to explore a highly complex subject matter. Theory's legacy, however, is also that its political force has balkanized the study of literature and created a value vacuum. During the 1970s and 1980s, the values that came under attack were *Western* values that belonged to the dead, white, heterosexist males who wrote the texts in the canon under scrutiny. It soon became apparent, however, that all of the various groups involved in identity politics each had a value agenda. In many cases such values pitted each group not only against the establishment but also against one another. In the U.K. this politicization of literature actually began in the 1950s, when the radical left lost touch with its base in labor politics and turned to culture as a site of the contestation of values.[5] In America during the 1970s, radicals similarly turned to culture, particularly literary texts, after the political right under Nixon quelled the uprisings in the streets. In both cases, cultural theory became like war, "the continuation of politics by other means," as Terry Eagleton has observed.[6] Literature became one of the battlefields on which the cultural values war was fought.

The value of literature, nevertheless, survived the political storm. Although the anti-traditionalists in some ways won the culture war[7]—and justifiably so, since older conceptions of the canon were indeed complicit in promoting the work of dead, white males while marginalizing other perspectives—the prevailing tide of opinion seems to have fallen on the side of the liberal humanist position regarding the *function* of literature. Some literary scholars would probably consciously disagree with this last statement, but the survival of literature as a discipline—albeit in a considerably altered form—beyond the values fracas of the late twentieth century strongly suggests that most people in the field still see, whether consciously or not, immense value and insight in literary works, even those produced by dead, white males. To be sure, there still exists in the field a "school of resentment," as Harold Bloom famously called it.[8] Nevertheless, such people are the exception to the rule, and most scholars in the discipline do still have some kind of love for the subject. Before his untimely death, even Derrida weighed in on the issue, siding with the Western canon, however ideologically problematic it might be. "As soon as one examines my texts," he wrote, "not only mine but the texts of many people close to me, one sees that respect for the great texts, for the texts of the Greeks and others, too, is the condition of our work."[9] No doubt, Derrida felt British and American scholars had used his own deconstruction of Western texts in ways he did not intend, that is, expressly for political purposes to advance the causes of identity politics.

Despite Derrida's positive declaration, the common tendency among so many literary scholars has been to question *all* values, approaching literature with an intense suspicion of grand ideals such as the beauty of art, historical progress, and Western liberal democracy. Such scholars often express disillusionment with grand narratives such as the Bible, psychoanalysis, Marxism, and the Enlightenment with its notions of individual autonomy, reason, truth, certainty, and the like. Postmodernism, informed as it is by many poststructuralist ideas, has particularly cast an "irredeemable slur upon value,"[10] which many of its adherents claim is entirely contingent. Postmodernism, as Niall Lucy describes it, represents a loss of faith in a previously sustaining concept or ideal of literature, which is seen now only as having perpetuated certain myths of universal value and human nature based on a myth of 'good writing.'"[11] In their insistence on the contingency of all values, many postmodernists flatly reject the liberal humanist understanding of literature as enhancing life and propagating humane values. My reading of ecstatic poetry, by necessity, opposes this view. To assert the eudaimonic value of ecstatic verse represents a clear endorsement of a value system that privileges well-being and suggests the mitigation of ill-being is not the same as eudaimonia.

This problematic stance toward values on the part of postmodernists might be overhasty. Simply because all values are informed by cultural and ideological forces and serve the interests of those who advance them does not mean human beings can ever be value-free. Even Nietzsche, a master of suspicion and iconoclasm, asserted values. Although he denounced the "false values and delusive words" of priests in *Thus Spake Zarathustra*,[12] he recognized the virtues of cultivating innate potentials. His work is a dithyramb to human well-being and an attempt to convince his readers to reject all belief systems and values that hinder one's self-realization. It is important to stress that he did not make the ridiculous move to toss away all values but simply those that hinder the realization of the *Übermensch*. Though Nietzsche is often misinterpreted as a nihilist and embraced as such, he did advance a value system that one can feel forcefully asserting itself in the pages of his greatest work.

Jean-Francois Lyotard, a central figure in postmodernity, also did not seem to reject valuation, as many of his followers have done. To be sure, he has characterized postmodernism as "incredulity toward metanarratives"[13] because all such interpretive stories are value laden. In his own attempt at clarifying postmodernism, however, Lyotard described its predecessor, avant-garde painting, as a "highly responsible investigation of the presuppositions implied in modernity."[14] He saw immense value in avant-garde painting, which he likened to *anamnesis*, the retrieval of unconscious contents that takes place in psychoanalytic work, and he warned that if the responsibility to do the same is ignored, postmodernism would suffer from the same "neurosis, the Western schizophrenia, paranoia..."[15] that characterized so much of modernism. The "post" in postmodernism, according to Lyotard, is thus a process of "*ana*-lysing, *ana*-mnesing, of reflecting."[16] This ethical charge is clearly a value position, and it flies in the face of those who have exiled value because of a fear that endorsing values implicates one in the tyranny of a grand narrative.

Some scholars have begun to recognize the fallacy. As Cathy Burgass argues, to exist is to evaluate, the essence of which is a kind of "law of human nature."[17] It is not possible to be a human being and disregard values, for to make any decision is to be guided by a value of some kind, regardless of whether one is conscious of such underlying motivation of choices. To be deprived of these is to suffer from a paralysis of action, or neurosis, which is precisely the criticism that some scholars level against values-suspicious literary theorists. "The postmodern prejudice against norms, unities, and consensuses," writes Terry Eagleton, "is a politically catastrophic one. It is also remarkably dim-witted."[18] For any movement to assert itself, even postmodernism, there must be common, underlying values that inform and govern decisions. "What is a left without a commons?" asks Todd Gitlin. "If there is no people, but only peoples, there is no left."[19] The point is compelling.

By the end of the twentieth century, many scholars began talking about the previously ignored question of value.[20] However, the desire to "retrieve value from the black hole of infinite regress," as Burgass calls it,[21] has not resulted in any kind of positive assertions on the part of many literary critics, in part because of the postmodern legacy. As she notes, "the readmission of positive value judgment to a postmodern critical practice represents an objective not yet achieved."[22] Values, nevertheless, are inescapable, and we in literary studies must acknowledge their necessity if we are to remain a relevant voice in twenty-first century discourse.

The literary value vacuum is not only a denial of what most people intuitively believe—that there are common species-wide, human values such as love, well-being, and others and that they matter—but it also contradicts compelling work being conducted in other disciplines. Studies of brain-injured people, for instance, clearly show the importance of values in daily living. Individuals who suffer damage to the orbitofrontal cortex, a part of the brain responsible for processing emotions, cannot make decisions. Because they do not feel emotions, a fact confirmed by measurements of their autonomic nervous systems, they consequently do not know what they value. Such people "find themselves unable to make simple decisions or to set goals, and their lives fall apart."[23] Even though they exhibit perfectly intact intelligence, as measured on standard IQ tests, people with such brain damage can see a myriad of possibilities when confronted with a decision but exhibit a kind of affective paralysis because they fail to recognize which choice is more preferable. Clearly, values matter, and to reject them all as being complicit in some tyrannical grand narrative is deeply problematic and unproductive.

The foregoing study, by necessity, points to the opposite: the global ubiquity of ecstatic poetry strongly implies a universal valuation of ecstasy as a vital state of being that offers eudaimonic transformation. Ecstasy seems to matter to many cultures past and present. As I showed in chapters 3 and 4, it has been seen in many traditions as an important means of achieving well-being. Ecstasy is of significant value.

The Neglect of Affect and the Privileging of Language

Affective experiences, however, are often approached with suspicion in literary studies because there is a tacit but pervasive distrust of emotions in the discipline. In different ways Janice Radway[24] and Jane Thrailkill[25] have both analyzed this problem, demonstrating the widespread neglect of affective concerns in critical discourse. Philip Fisher's *The Vehement Passions* is an interesting account of why such distrust exists and also an indictment of the Western privileging of "dispassionate knowledge," an epistemological construct that proves lacking, because the passions do significantly inform the reasoning process.[26] Poetic rapture, which many poets, particularly those operating in a poetics of ecstasy, hoped to induce in their auditors and readers, has proven problematic in literary discourse from the time of Plato to the present. To be sure, such a statement is a generalization, and there are exceptions, particularly in the Romantic and Victorian periods. By and large, however, scholars have preferred to minimalize or marginalize affect, a practice that reached its zenith in the last three decades of the twentieth century.

The problem persists particularly in neo–Marxist, cultural materialist, and new historicist theory. Bakhtin's ideas best capture these perspectives. Despite his positive endorsement of Carnival and its ecstatic elements, Bakhtin was deeply distrustful of the principal literary genre in which affect is foregrounded—the lyric. He faulted the writing of non-narrative poetry "because the process closes itself off to the palimpsest of the external; it denies history and its heteroglossic superfluity of meaning." In his view, poetry is "in flight from history and the real."[27] The form, he argued, "is defined by a willful and permanent forgetting, an active refusal to allow the whole to be seen, and that part of the whole which is lost is the interaction of the world and the object over time, which has produced layers of supplementary or contradictory meaning."[28] No doubt, there are critics who champion the value of the lyric; for instance, Ryan Cull[29] and Nouri Gana,[30] among others, have both recently defended it on ethical grounds. The point is that the dominant tendency in the last forty years has been to denigrate the form, along with its foregrounding of affect, because of its ahistorical, atemporal nature.

Another reason for this marginalization of affect is the privileging of language in literary studies. It is in some ways understandable that literary scholars would focus on linguistic matters, particularly when the object of inquiry—textuality—is constituted by language itself. The preoccupation with language, however, has become something of an unhealthy obsession, a kind of neurosis in which affect is often reduced to the language in which it is configured. On this point, many literary scholars have taken their cue from Roland Barthes' proclamation of "the death of the author." According to such a theory, when a writer seeks to express emotion, he is deluding himself. His only real power "is to mix writings" because the inner emotional thing "he seeks to 'translate' is itself only a ready formed dictionary, its words only explainable through other words, and so on indefinitely." Instead of "writer," Barthes favored the bloodless term "scriptor," who no longer "bears within him passions, humours, feelings, impressions, but rather this immense dictionary from which he draws a writing that can know no halt...."[31] Tender emotion is here sacrificed on the bloody altar of words.

The death of the author has, in effect, amounted to the death of affect, the result of which has been the birth of a schizoid subjectivity in which language and emotion are divorced, the former given full privilege and the latter exiled. In some ways this split is quintessentially Western. The first attempt at shattering the privileging of reason over emotion came with the advent of Romanticism and its foregrounding of the unconscious, the irrational, the imagination, and the affective. It gained further impetus in modernism in the many brilliant experiments that took place in the arts, and continues in postmodern art in the widespread mistrust of reason. Despite such work in literature itself, many literary theorists have neglected emotion because of their focus on language.

This privileging of language over affect is also the result of the widespread misinterpretation of Derrida's famous dictum, "there is nothing outside of the text." Many scholars have taken Derrida's ideas to mean that language constructs reality, the hasty conclusion of which is that no perception or emotion is possible outside of mediating linguistic structures, which, in fact, represent the only reality human beings can know. According to such thinking, all experience is textual or linguistic. Recognizing this problem, Derrida later qualified his statement. In *Limited Incorporated* he averred: "The phrase which for some has become a sort of slogan, in general so badly understood, of deconstruction ('there is nothing outside the text') means ... there is nothing outside *context*."[32] The difference between "text" as it was misunderstood and "context" is slight, however, and the idea is still problematic. Although Derrida may have been attempting to rectify what he felt was a faulty reading of his work on the part of American and British postmodernists and deconstructors, his philosophy still did not bode well for affect, since it reduced all human reality to the differential freeplay of language, that is, to *différance*. The only thing outside of *différance* is *différance* itself, which he problematically exempted from objective status and located in an obscure realm mysteriously outside of the signifying chain. As he wrote, "[*différance*] is literally neither a word nor a concept."[33] Despite this refutation, which implies a tacit acknowledgement of the inescapability of the metaphysics of presence, there is still a pervasive focus on linguistic matters in literary studies, as well as a widespread neglect of affect.

The one area of literary studies in which scholars have focused on affect is the relatively unknown form of reader response criticism known as affective stylistics. A challenge to Wimsatt and Beardsley's extremely influential objection to the "affective fallacy," or confusing the supposedly objective text with the emotions it arouses in a subjective reader, affective stylistics enables a critic to account for works of literature in terms of a complex interaction between the words on the page and the affects they arouse in the responding reader. Notwithstanding its own complicity with deconstruction and its emotion denying ideas about textually, affective stylistics represents one possibility, among many, of a critical approach that gives human emotions as they appear in literary texts their full due.

Outside of literary studies there is in the twenty-first century a widespread recognition of the importance of emotions. No doubt, there is still some resistance among certain psychologists to the idea that emotions are central to cognition and adaptive behavior, but many others in the field have accepted the compelling claims coming from researchers who point out that without emotion, human beings make very bad value decisions.[34]

Equally compelling is the discourse on what has come to be called "emotional intelligence" (EQ). Howard Gardner, in his landmark study *Frames of Mind*, refuted the conception of intelligence as traditionally measure by IQ tests, arguing for not one but six variants of intelligence: verbal, mathematical, spatial, kinesthetic, musical, and personal (which includes interpersonal, or social abilities, and intra-psychic intelligence, or emotional self-awareness).[35] Gardner's conception of "personal" intelligence opened a door for the work of two brilliant researchers, Peter Salovey and John Mayer, who have articulated in a number of works an elaborate theory of emotional intelligence. In this expanded conception of intelligence, EQ is defined according to five characteristics: knowing one's emotions, managing emotions, motivating oneself, recognizing emotions in others, and handling relationships.[36] The concept of emotional intelligence explains why many people with genius-level IQs of 160 work for people with average IQs of 100, as Daniel Goleman wryly observes.[37]

Intelligence as traditionally measured does not detect the presence of the emotional skills necessary for succeeding in life,[38] and a high IQ is thus by no means a guarantee of prosperity, happiness, or well-being. To the contrary, sometimes people with extremely high IQs make extremely poor decisions and value judgments, perhaps because they are lacking in emotional intelligence. Despite their neglect in literary studies, emotions factor significantly in human life, and without a refined awareness of them, people are bereft of the values that govern healthy, constructive choices.

Not only has there been a revolution in our understanding of the value of emotions and the value-driven choices they make possible; there has also been a quantum change in the last decade in how emotions are understood to function. Until nearly the end of the twentieth century, psychologists generally understood emotions in terms of "specific action tendencies," that is, they were seen as serving a survival function by forcing a narrowing of focus and triggering a specific behavioral action. Fear, for instance, is associated with the "urge to flee, anger with the urge to attack, and disgust with the urge to expel."[39] Specific action tendencies do indeed seem to characterize all of the negative emotions, and they are almost undoubtedly linked to an instinctive survival mechanism in the human species. The problem here is that they do not characterize the positive emotions, the function of which seems elusive when viewed through a negative explanatory lens.

In 1998 Barbara Fredrickson, a research psychologist at the University of Michigan, published an influential paper,[40] the thrust of which became the tipping point that influenced Martin Seligman and the whole Positive psychology movement. Fredrickson's general idea was that *positive* emotions cannot be explained in terms of specific action tendencies. No doubt, they do result in the urge to act, as in singing and dancing when we feel joy, or giving a gift or a hug when we feel gratitude or love. By and large, however, their effects are located "downstream" rather than in the immediate moment. Positive emotions, according to Fredrickson, "broaden mindsets and build resources."[41] Emotions such as gratitude, serenity, interest, hope, pride, amusement, inspiration, awe, joy, and love have been shown to be valuable over a longer time span because they open us to the creativity necessary for later challenges, and they equip us with the ability not only to survive but to be well.

An important implication, among many, in Fredrickson's "broaden and build" theory is that positive emotions do not merely represent effects of some prior cause; they are not mere *epiphenomena* but causal agents whose impact is highly beneficial. Positivity, as Fredrickson argues, "doesn't simply *reflect* success and health, it can also *produce* success and health."[42] Positive emotions in several compelling studies have been shown to result in sharpened mental resources, deeper mindfulness and the ability to savor experiences, greater self-acceptance, a heightened sense of purpose, deeper and more trusting relationships with others, and more vibrant physical health. In general such positivity is associated with what researchers have called "upward spirals" of psychological, intellectual, social, and physical well-being.[43] George Vaillant, a professor of psychiatry at Harvard, claims that positive emotions and EQ in general are the most significant determinants and predictors of well-being—more than social class, religious denomination, and conventional conceptions of IQ.[44]

Such recent discussions call into question the relative neglect of affect in literary studies, for they demonstrate that emotion and, by implication, positive affective experiences such as ecstasy are of vital importance. All of the various theoretical schools involved in identity politics might do well to clear a space in their respective discourses for ecstasy and other aspects of eudaimonic experience, since they are at heart all ultimately concerned with the well-being of the individuals whose interests they represent. In one sense this can already be seen in the focus in identity politics discourse on the question of agency, which is itself tied to an aspect of eudaimonia—character strength. Positive emotion, however, has not received as much attention, even though it is one of the most crucial elements in human adaptation, as Vaillant claims.[45] Positive affect makes possible the signature strengths that Peterson and Seligman describe as being valued across widely different cultures.[46] Positive affect is the vital element in successful relationships of all varieties, as Fredrickson has compellingly shown.[47] Positive affect is central to the success of organizations of all kinds, whether these be families, schools, insurance companies, baseball teams, rock bands, or governments. It thus needs a discourse in literary studies.

Despite this compelling recognition of the importance of emotion, particularly positive affect, the intellectual climate in Western literary studies, by contrast, has caused many professors to be embarrassed by their own love of the arts and the imagination because the form of affect these often arouse— a rapturous, mystified response to beauty—is seen as being uncritical and unsophisticated. To experience lofty emotions as a result of reading ecstatic poetry is now seen as an antiquated, perhaps even Victorian, way of reading. I once occupied an office next to a fellow professor of English—a radical, post-structuralist scholar who told me quite seriously on several occasions that he "hates literature" and that the professor of literature is a "dying paradigm." An untenured, junior faculty member, I would often say nothing but inwardly laugh and cringe at the same time. When forced by the institution to teach a common-core literature course, he told me he intended to "rip apart" the various texts he was required to teach. An ideal response to a work of literature for such people has now become one that refuses the call to rapturous mystification and reads the text against its grain. No doubt, reading against the grain can be an interesting and valuable means of literary analysis, but it also has its limits. Some scholars read *only* against the grain and never let themselves be mystified and awed by texts. Such critics only know how to demystify literary works by arguing that they are merely coded assertions of power and thus patriarchal illusions, or examples of complicity with capitalist values and thus rooted in socio-economic conditions, or neurotic psychological defense mechanisms, or historical artifacts entirely derivative of the culture in which they were produced, or purely linguistic constructions that undermine themselves and unravel in the face of close, intellectual scrutiny. Do such disenchanted approaches that dismiss awe and wonder do full justice to the complexities of literature? I suggest they do not.

Maslow observed that one of the characteristics of his peakers is that they see the world with a sense of awe and wonder, that is, they let go and recognize that life's fundamental mysteries cannot be mastered and must be accepted and even heartily embraced. Without this ecstatic response, he claimed, human beings become disenchanted and neurotic. He went as far as to say that disenchantment can represent a defense mechanism designed to protect a fragile ego, for if one is disenchanted, he or she will never be disappointed.[48] The corollary to this last statement is that the disenchanted will never be able to self-transcend, to experience the joys and benefits of ecstasy. No doubt, literary critics must read texts critically against the grain, and they must teach their students to do the same. If this is all they do, however, and if they never learn to let go and savor the rapture that certain kinds of literature affords, they will miss the chance of experiencing the peak states that characterize the optimally functioning human psyche, a complex entity consisting of multiple parts, a point to which we now turn.

Dissociative ekstasis

Freud's "discovery" of the unconscious and his *ekstatic* decentering of the ego were downright brilliant developments in human understanding. The idea that consciousness does not represent the totality of energies in the psyche has been widely accepted by scholars in a number of disciplines. It has also been demonstrated in many ways, particularly in studies in which people report conscious disapproval of various sexual acts they are shown in video clips but then respond with exceedingly high levels of sexual arousal. Freud would have particularly loved that one! This kind of unconsciousness is also compellingly demonstrated in priming studies in which people, both black and white, who claim not to be racist or prejudiced are subliminally shown pictures of black people and demonstrate a physiological response of anxiety. The theory that we are not all of a piece is irrefutable and points to the immense complexity of human subjectivity, or rather human subjectiv*ies*. We are deep and mysterious.

Freud did not seem to cast this idea, however, in a eudaimonic light. In twenty-four brilliant volumes of theorizing about psychopathology, he managed almost completely to ignore joy, as Vaillant points out.[49] His neurotic avoidance of the eudaimonic aspects of human experience can be seen in a number of ways: (1) his crude interpretation of oceanic experiences as regressive narcissism, which I have previously discussed; (2) his insistence that psychoanalysis be conducted with no eye contact, a practice still widely used by psychoanalysts; (3) his reduction of love to libido, which transmutes what is perhaps the most important experience in human life into a simple animal drive; (4) his pessimistic refusal to see beyond neurosis and accept that genuine happiness is possible; and (5) his wholesale dismissal of religion and spirituality, which psychologists in the twenty first century are beginning to acknowledge are valuable not for their dogma, doctrines, and untestable metaphysical assumptions but as conducive frameworks for the cultivation of eudaimonia. Freud's ideas about psychopathology have exerted a direct and profound influence in literary studies.

This diseased conception of the fragmented psyche has impacted the discipline through the filters of Lacanian and Derridean theories. Scholars who use such approaches typically tease out of texts configurations of neuroses and lacks, or they locate the emptiness of subjectivity in the inessential, differential freeplay of language. The postmodern loss of faith in autonomy, innocence, and psychological interiors, as well as the widespread privileging of fragmentation and surfaces over wholeness and depth in literary discussions, represent additional endorsements of Freud's dissociative *ekstasis*. Very few literary scholars have interpreted such ideas about human identity in eudaimonic ways. To the contrary, most have continued, albeit often brilliantly, in Freud's tradition of pathologizing the fragmented subject.

For instance, Jean Baudrillard, the influential, French philosopher, has analyzed the postmodern condition in such terms. For him, the postmodern subject is characterized not by the isolation of modernism but from its opposite—the schizophrenia caused by an "ecstasy of communication" in the contemporary age. Constantly bombarded by words, images, data, and facts, the postmodern subject is a fragmented self whose identity is hopelessly lost in a hub of multiple, intersecting networks of information. In this "ecstasy" of information the whole subject becomes a shattered, fragmented object, and loneliness is replaced by an obscene instantaneousness with all things.[50] Published in 1988 but presciently anticipating the rise of the digital age and the world wide web, Baudrillard's work is an insightful meditation on the dehumanizing dangers of technology. Yet, while his analysis of postmodern subjectivity might be accurate in many aspects, it has led some scholars to believe that the multiplicity of subjectivity is entirely a pathological phenomenon, when, in fact, this is only one of the ways in which *ekstasis* registers. Baudrillard's ecstasy, then, by no means represents the full complexities of ecstasy, for there is an *ekstatic* form of madness that causes temporary dissociation but ultimately results in well-being. Ecstasy, as I have discussed it in this study, is not the "ecstasy of communication" that characterizes postmodernity. While the latter is a diseased form of *ekstasis*, the former carries eudaimonic potentials.

This pathological conception of selfhood, which is found in so much literary theory, is not only strikingly jaundiced but quite similar to post-traumatic stress disorder (PTSD). A coping mechanism that people unconsciously and defensively adopt in response to a traumatic event, PTSD is characterized by dissociation and a disruption in the usually *integrative* function of the psyche. People suffering from such a disorder "describe states of depersonalization and derealization as if a dimmer switch were increasing or decreasing lighting on a theatrical stage set, alternating extremes of overly bright intense lighting with degrees of hazy darkness in which it [is] difficult to discern people, faces, situations, and events."[51]

Dissociation is in some ways a normal, natural response to a given trauma and by no means always represents psychopathology. In *The Posttraumatic Self*, John Wilson describes it as an "organismic reaction to threats to the entire set of basic human needs, especially those which are normatively prepotent early in childhood development," such as "physiological, safety, love and belongingness, and esteem needs."[52] The psyche seems to have an *ekstatic* protective mechanism that forces the dissociation of vulnerable psychic components when an external agent threatens to damage them in some way. The problem here is not with dissociation per se but the issue of how to stop it from occurring inappropriately in later situations that do not warrant it, that is, how to prevent it from transmuting into a pathological force. A woman who survived unspeakable horrors in one of Mengele's cruel "medical" experiments, for instance, later found herself dissociating while in the hospital for innocuous leg surgery, after which she reported being able to "see around her private hospital room from all angles, floor to ceiling."[53] Often reported among those who suffer torture, this kind of dissociative out-of-body experience is a relatively common response to extreme stressors. Dissociation in the face of immediate trauma might be an effective coping mechanism, but if this kind of psychic disintegration becomes chronic, its salutogenic properties become diseased.

The point in mentioning this concept is that the concern among postmodern and other literary theorists with decentered subjectivity and multiple selves, therefore, does not need to be restricted to forms of ill-being. To the contrary, it can also represent the *ekstatic* possibility of a polyphonic but ultimately "unified" human subject. In musical polyphony several tones or melodic parts contrapuntally play against each other but serve a unified effect by existing as contrasting parts in one composition. The tension created by the contrasting parts contributes to a beautiful whole. There seems to be a dawning awareness about the issue, particularly in the preoccupation among postmodern artists and theorists with the problem of representing the "unpresentable,"[54] which began in Romanticism as an attempt to illustrate the disconnection of reason and emotion. The ubiquitous desire among such artists and theorists to deal with the problem of the limits of language might also suggest a desire, whether conscious or otherwise, to heal from a fragmented subjectivity and to move on to ecstatic wholeness. The attempt in postmodern art at "the liberation of the human mind from limiting structures, customs, categories, [and] truths,"[55] a feature it shares in common with Romanticism, is commendable and signals the possibility of a shift—a new, twenty-first century approach that recovers the whole-but-complex subject without returning to the simple, separate self of liberal humanism.

Ecstatic Wholeness

Well-being thus results from a unitive and *complex* psyche. For Csikszentmihalyi, the psychodynamics at work here are "differentiation and integration."[56] Csikszentmihalyi explains the two terms as being seemingly contradictory but actually complimentary. While differentiation "implies a movement toward uniqueness, toward separating oneself from others," integration refers to "a union with other people, with ideas and entities beyond the self." A complex sense of self, he claims, "is one that succeeds in combining these opposite tendencies."[57]

Jung's concept of *individuation* is similar to Csikszentmihalyi's in that it represents a recognition of the need to distinguish oneself and the need to connect with others as primary forces in human development. Deeply influenced by Freud, however, Jung also discusses the idea as it figures in an *ekstatic* engagement with one's own unconscious depths. To do "inner work" in Jungian therapy necessarily entails coming to consciousness of one's many unconscious "others" and relinquishing control to such energies on appropriate occasions. Jung's ideas call for self-transcendence, since ego must step aside to make room for other psychic energies. At times these forces will dissolve or expand the ego, while at others they will be so threatening that the ego will resist them and, nevertheless, find itself transformed through a productive opposition that results in the expansion of consciousness. Unlike Freud's decentered subject, which implies fragmentation and lack, there are other forms of *ekstasis* that can lead to a unified subjectivity in which a multiplicity of psychic energies all share space in one psyche in the same way that symphonies and poems can consist of contradictory or contrasting elements but still function as a gestalt.

Regardless of whether one accepts the insights of Freudian/Jungian depth psychology, John Wilson's recent work on posttraumatic stress supports the value of a unitive psyche. There is ample psychological research, he observes, to support the idea that "unity in personality facilitates organismic striving towards optimal adaptation in the environment."[58] Researchers have termed such unitive phenomena in various ways: "self-actualization, self-realization, optimal states, effectance motivation, fully functioning personality, and psychological health."[59] Disunity in personality, by contrast, has been described by researchers as "fragmentation, the loss of self-coherence, and self-pathology in which there is deintegration of self-capacities and behavior."[60] No doubt, ecstatic experiences are often dissociative and decentering, and they can leave people speechless with fear and trembling. Their consequences, however, are characteristically unitive. In the complex reorganization of the psyche they facilitate, a stronger sense of selfhood typically emerges, even if such a sense is informed by perceptions of the illusoriness of the ego. In *Quantum Change* Miller and C'de Baca characterize *ekstatic* "epiphanies and insights" as highly beneficial experiences that facilitate release from chronic, negative emotional patterns and foster a benevolent and enduring personal transformation.[61] Ecstatic experiences are entirely healthy, provided one can return from them. To glimpse the other self can be decentering but also yield productive insights about one's psychic life. Not to return from such an experience can be destructively decentering and lead to negative, life-stifling dissociation. In such cases it is probably appropriate to deem *ekstasis* a pathogenic phenomenon and treat it as such.

The key to whether an experience proves to be pathogenic or salutogenic lies in part in one's capacity to deal with a decentered ego. Miller and C'de Baca stress the importance of integrating the experience if one is to benefit from its salutogenic effects. According to Jung, the integration of unconscious elements can only occur "if [one's] conscious mind possesses the intellectual categories and moral feelings necessary for their assimilation."[62] In other words, it is not enough to have the experience; one must also make room for it in consciousness. Usually, integration of this kind is possible after an ecstatic experience, but there are cases in which a person becomes destabilized by the decentering of the ego and cannot accommodate the new possibilities, adapting to them neurotically rather than optimally.

In his interesting book on William James, James Pawelski discusses the concept in terms of religious experience. Using James's term, he calls those who skillfully accommodate epiphanies "religious geniuses."[63] Like encounters with the unconscious, epiphanies are *ekstatic* glimpses of unstructured wholeness and must be accommodated through "appropriation," or a process of "spiritual digestion" in which the "wholeness of an epiphany enters into the structure of our mundane lives."[64] Pawelski uses the oxymoronic image of "structured wholeness"[65] to characterize the optimal state of having experienced and then appropriated an epiphany. He also discusses inappropriate responses to epiphanic experiences, such as rejecting the mundane and wholly embracing the boundlessness that often accompanies epiphanies, or stoically rejecting epiphanies and privileging the mundane. Neither strategy can serve to facilitate growth, as both refuse to recognize that mundanity and epiphany, configured as complimentary opposites, offer potential to enrich the psyche. "In contrast to these pathological responses," argues Pawelski, "structured wholeness works toward health through integration," because "the alternation between epiphany and mundanity is not one of violent opposition" but of synergy.[66] One without the other renders each meaningless.

While religionists perhaps have overzealously rejected mundanity, some literary scholars have adopted the stoical response by privileging mundanity and thus failing to see the eudaimonic potentials in ecstasy. To be sure, Freudian and Lacanian theories of fragmented subjectivity are sophisticated, interesting, and productive when they are put in the service of teasing out psychological disease or demonstrating the inherent emptiness of subjectivity. Such theories deserve credit for their immense value and undeniable legacy. There does, however, seem to be the need for a reassessment of using, in nonpathological contexts, reading strategies designed to sniff out disease. Sometimes dissociative *ekstasis* can be a symptom of neurosis or a reaction to circumstances that have resulted in a form of ill-being. When *ekstasis* is accompanied by a brief dissociation and positive emotions and later results in a more complex integration of psychological components, the need for a different interpretive strategy becomes particularly acute.

Literary studies is thus characterized by a number of elements that, when combined, result in a climate that proves somewhat inhospitable to the study of ecstasy in its eudaimonic form. As I have discussed, several factors are responsible for such an intellectual environment: (1) a tendency to psychopathologize all aspects of human experience and thus to dismiss or overlook eudaimonia; (2) a focus on the mitigation or elimination of ill-being, which is by no means tantamount to directly studying well-being; (3) a postmodern suspicion of values, particularly the resistance to the idea that there are universal, species-wide values, despite that the historical record seems to show that the gratification of ecstasy needs seems to be a universal phenomenon (a point I will discuss further in the next chapter); (4) a logocentric neglect of affect and affective states; (5) a reduction of complex emotional experiences to the means by which they are linguistically communicated; (6) a discomfort among scholars to be moved to rapture, a response often equated with being simple-minded; and (7) the widespread embrace of Freud's diseased form of dissociative *ekstasis* over ecstatic wholeness.

For all of this, I do not mean to suggest that literary studies is an entirely hostile or incompatible ground for the discussion of eudaimonic experiences such as ecstasy. To the contrary, the discipline has already begun to show signs of a eudaimonic turn, the nature of which is enriching the discipline with new hermeneutics and enabling a direct focus on the complex question of well-being. The atmosphere is thus changing and becoming quite conducive to the study of ecstatic experience. Let us explore the point more fully.

12. Ecstasy and the Eudaimonic Turn

In the last three decades of the twentieth century, the most influential voices in the discipline adopted a hermeneutics of suspicion, a term originally coined by Paul Ricoer, who cited Freud, Nietzsche, and Marx as the masters of suspicion.[1] In such an interpretive framework scholars assume either complicity in objectionable discourses or locate positive affect in psychological disease and then affirm these when they are found. Suspicious reading has proven fecund, resulting as it has in the rich legacy of critical theory. The question remains, however, whether its inherent negativity bias can help us to understand the profundities of ecstatic states and other markers of well-being. Suspicion is generally inappropriate for reading eudaimonic experience because in such an interpretive framework well-being is pathologized or dismissed as a manifestation of an undesirable political or psychological condition, as I discussed in the previous chapter in relation to Wordsworth's sonnet and how various critical schools might interpret it.

The hermeneutics of suspicion, as Ricouer himself argued, is but one possible reading strategy and thus proves to be of restricted value, especially if one uses it to interpret eudaimonic experience. Its negativity bias results in an elision of the complex dimensions of ecstasies and other eudaimonic, affective experiences, often prompting critics to interpret well-being in diseased terms. To be sure, this is not a call for a dismissal of suspicion, which has been put to some rather interesting and productive uses; rather, it is a call to turn the hermeneutics of suspicion against itself, that is, to be suspicious of suspicion as a totalizing notion and to embrace what Ricouer himself called a "hermeneutics of affirmation."[2] Although suspicion proves to be of value in *some* domains of interpretation, it fails as a totalizing narrative because it can engender an inquisitorial spirit designed to sniff out ideological heresies and psychological disease in domains where they do not exist.

The New Turn

Alongside such suspicious critical tendencies there also exists today in literary studies a growing number of critics who have begun to reject, challenge, or modify suspicion by adopting alternative reading strategies. Pawelski and I call this tendency "the eudaimonic turn" in an eponymously titled volume.[3] Beginning at the end of the twentieth century and rising to a critical mass in the last decade, the eudaimonic turn has manifested in several ways, not least of which is a growing dissatisfaction with suspicious critique. Eve Sedgwick,[4] Bruno Latour,[5] and Rita Felski[6] have all astutely analyzed this rejection of critique as it was understood in the last decades of the twentieth century. In becoming disenchanted with disenchantment, many critics have sought out alternative hermeneutics that enable one to read affirmatively, sometimes even with the grain, but also in a sophisticated manner.

The eudaimonic turn has also manifested as a more direct engagement with aspects of well-being. A clear example is an excellent monograph by the late Robert Barth, *Romanticism and Transcendence: Wordsworth, Coleridge, and the Religious Imagination*, which is representative of such recent eudaimonic readings. Barth takes Wordsworth at his word and sees immense value in the privileging of the imagination, which, he argues, "is not merely an artistic faculty" but also "the faculty that permits the person to give meaning to the world and to his or her life."[7] According to Barth, there is eudaimonic value in following the thread of the imagination out of reason's labyrinthine corridors, as it leads to "an encounter with the divine,"[8] which, he argues, is itself a highly valuable experience. Another example is Philip Fisher's interesting study, *Wonder, the Rainbow and the Aesthetics of Rare Experiences*. Fisher's work is a fascinating critical inquiry into wonder, awe, and sublimity, all of which he discusses within a framework he calls an "aesthetics of surprise" and a "poetics of wonder."[9] Still another example is Charles Altieri's complex work, *The Particulars of Rapture: An Aesthetics of the Affects*. An aesthetics of the affects, as Altieri claims, "becomes a means of elaborating how there may be profoundly incommensurable perspectives on values that are nonetheless all necessary if we are to realize various aspects of our human potential."[10] Because there are far too many works in this new turn, I cite only a few representative examples here and refer the reader to *The Eudaimonic Turn: Well-Being in Literary Studies* for further citations and a more complete discussion.

Despite the challenges it poses to the older form of critique, the eudaimonic turn seems to carry the potential to *enrich*, not detract from, critical theory. It has bolstered various theoretical frameworks in at least two ways: (1) not by ignoring oppression, injustice, and psychological disease but by focusing on how such negatives may be explored in light of discussions of well-being; and (2) by analyzing previously unexamined, eudaimonic aspects of human experience. In other words, it has enriched current discussions of ill-being and also facilitated new explorations of well-being. The eudaimonic and pathological dimensions of human experience are equally complex and thus call for complex theoretical explorations. The eudaimonic turn in literary studies, then, has augmented the hermeneutics of suspicion with a hermeneutics of affirmation. It likely will never entirely supplant suspicion, as this would result in the same one-sided imbalance that eudaimonia-minded critics seek to correct. To the contrary, it will enable theoretical explorations rendered impossible by an exclusive focus on the discovery and critique of undesirable ideologies or diseased psychodynamics. The foregoing study of the ecstatic tradition thus rides on the crest of this new hermeneutics of affirmation.

Narcissism, Pubic Hair, and the Importance of Studying Ecstatic Experience

Some scholars might argue that to study the ecstasy of poets is yet another example of Western narcissism, a shameful diversion from what really matters—rectifying social inequities, eradicating prejudices, solving the problem of hunger, and addressing the survival challenges of half of the world's human beings, most of whom lack appropriate sanitation and live on less than two dollars per day. Terry Eagleton laments that some scholars in cultural studies have abandoned the whole issue of class inequities in favor of writing histories of pubic hair and the like.[11] Unlike Eagleton, I find the history of how people manicure their genitalia quite a fascinating topic, but I admit that it is by no means an answer to world hunger. The question remains whether studying ecstasy and other aspects of eudaimonia can help to better humankind. I suggest it can do so.

To support this assertion, I appeal to Positive psychologists, who have similarly had to justify their focus on well-being when there is still so much to learn about psychopathology. "The study of people who are happy, healthy, and talented," argues Peterson, "may be seen as a guilty luxury that diverts resources from the goals of problem-focused psychology" and other human discourses, but conducting research on those who are well will enable scholars to shed light on problems that will "help all people, troubled or not."[12] The more we can learn about being well, according to the argument, the more we can help people to achieve well-being. As Jorgensen and Nafstad similarly claim, "to fight inequality, dehumanization, and a difficult life with ... the predominant medical-oriented model focusing on sickness, weaknesses, and diagnostic categories is an endeavor bound to fail."[13] Only a value system informed by a disease model of human life would deem the study of eudaimonic experience to be narcissistic. To the contrary, it is highly fruitful and can serve as an instructive guide to a fuller, richer, more rewarding life for everyone.

Underpinning the dismissal of the study of ecstatic states as irrelevant is a kind of misguided cynicism that renders all eudaimonic experience as naïve self-deception. What in part underpins this view is the legacy of twentieth-century modernism, the all-pervading assumptions of which have resulted in a cynical orientation towards eudaimonia. In *The Story of Joy* Potkay brilliantly demonstrates the negative reception the construct of joy underwent in the last century. While post–WWI modernists set the tone with their eschewal of happiness, the rest of the century followed suit. By the 1970s, "happiness was considered embarrassing, a mark of shallowness." Potkay adds that to experience or express joy in twentieth century academic discourse was "a sign that you're not paying attention."[14] However sad it may be, we literary scholars have internalized the unsupportable modernist assumption that the eudaimonic is tantamount to the superficial and ill-informed. Pawelski and I have noted, however, that literary studies is changing and thus becoming far more receptive to eudaimonic experiences. The drive to be well is a universal concern, and its study is thus of paramount importance.

The Daimonic Essence

The persistence of the ecstatic tradition across cultures, even those with no cultural contact, clearly suggests that the gratification of ecstatic needs is essential to human development and occupies a central position in eudaimonia. The implication here is that the need for ecstasy is a kind of universal human essence—an assertion that warrants some qualifications.

Many literary scholars might take exception to such an idea because of the anti-essentialist spirit that informs so many critical discussions. Many critics, in their refutation of liberal humanism, have flatly rejected the notion of human essence, favoring the anti-essentialist idea that subjectivity is entirely constituted by socio-political, material, historical, and/or linguistic forces. Many of the dominant schools of literary criticism, or at least the dominant voices in most schools, with notable exceptions, root human subjectivity in such external determinants and thus deny the notion that people are born with innate traits or drives. In doing so they have clearly taken a stance on the timeless nature/nurture debate, siding with the latter and positioning their ideas against the former.

In one sense it is understandable that modern literary scholars would embrace the *tabula rasa* theory in their attempts to refute the notion of the transcendent subject who stands beyond his or her culture and language as though he or she is independent of both. The genius of modern literary theory is that it has demonstrated how thoroughly embedded human beings are in linguistic and cultural matrixes, both of which are major determinants of subjectivity. What were once considered natural differences among genders, races, classes, sexual orientations, and ethnicities have now been exposed as being not essential at all but culturally constructed and artificial. Too often in the past, such differences were used as a means of exploitation and oppression. With their admirable attention to the details of language, modern literary scholars have become highly proficient in demonstrating the artificiality of such differences, exposing them as social constructions rooted not in nature but in the ideology and values of those whose interests they serve.

To drive the idea to the absolute, however, as some literary scholars do, is to overstate the concept and render it untenable. In other ways human beings are essentially the same. We are a single species with species-wide characteristics, many of which have now come to be seen (even in literary studies) as serving evolutionary advantages. Even Terry Eagleton agrees. A Marxist who attributes to culture and ideology a primary role in shaping subjectivity, Eagleton nevertheless acknowledges the limits of the social construction theory, which, he admits, breaks down when we are discussing "grief, compassion, [or] right-angled triangles." "There are a lot of things we do," he claims, "because we are the kind of animals we are, not because we are nuns or Macedonians."[15] Cultural contingency may be an appropriate way to describe subjectivity when looked at strictly from the sociological perspective, but there are other ways of viewing human beings. The whole notion of subjectivity, moreover, resists the objectification implied by the theory of the human-as-socially-constructed-object. We are large, we contain multitudes, as Whitman said. I am not championing the pre-theory, liberal humanist position on the transcendence of the subject but simply pointing out that human beings are *partly* constructed by culture but *also* constituted by a biological design that remains largely independent of and sometimes at odds with social forces. Human beings, as Susan Rowland has said of art, are "indivisible from the social and historical contexts but never reducible to them."[16]

Modern ethologists, or biologists who study animals in their natural habitats, have endorsed the kind of "interactionism" implied in Rowland's observation. In their investigations of various species, ethologists have observed the existence of inborn traits, or "innate releasing mechanisms," that require some kind of environmental trigger as a stimulus for expression. Every animal is born with a genetically inscribed repertoire of behaviors, many of which require an external "priming" agent for their release. During mating season, the green head of a mallard drake, for instance, will elicit an amorous response in mallard ducks and thus foster courtship, copulation, and (ideally) reproduction.[17] If the priming agent is not present, however, the behavior is never exhibited.

It is by no means a stretch to say that nature has equipped every species that exists with an innate releasing mechanism that compels it to seek out the means by which it can flourish. The urge to be well—the eudaimonic essence— is thus likely rooted in our biology, our *nature*. Like other IRMs, however, it is not a simple program or an instinctive drive but rather a potential that requires a priming agent such as a conducive social environment for its actualization. Although the debate over human nature still occupies a prominent position in psychological studies,[18] many psychologists, particularly those in Positive psychology, have begun to adopt the ethological view. The prevailing stance among such researchers is that "there is a constructive developmental tendency within human nature, and ... this tendency, when given appropriate expression, leads to the well-being of both the individual and the wider community and society."[19] What is necessary for the appropriate expression of this tendency is the right environment, without which the ecstatic, innate releasing mechanism would never be primed. This would account in part for why certain people languish while others flourish, and also why there are Pol Pots and Mother Theresas in the world. When social construction theorists insist on the *tabula rasa* theory, they are ignoring the animal design and accompanying "innate releasing mechanisms" of every human body. The complex interaction between biology and culture results in the construction of the self, not just society alone.

As Maslow believed, and as I have tried to demonstrate throughout this study, the gratification of ecstasy needs is inextricably connected to the question of being well in the fullest sense. If there is a eudaimonic essence, there is also an ecstatic essence. Yet, such a statement is true only inasmuch as one's environment provides the necessary stimuli. This study thus supports the idea of interactionism. Ecstasy needs seem to be inherent in the human psyche, but they are also historically conditioned and are never gratified outside of cultural and temporal contexts. Like Nussbaum's universals, the need for ecstasy represents a kind of vague essence that crosses cultures and epochs but finds specific expression when it is gratified by (and thus finds expression in) temporal and cultural forces. The ecstatic poetic tradition is the record— indeed the history—of such a phenomenon.

The gratification of the need for ecstatic experience is a kind of "single, ultimate value," as Maslow called the drive towards self-actualization.[20] The good life is thus not complete without ecstasy. It is possible to be well—that is, to experience on a regular basis all of the positive emotions, to exercise functional capabilities in Nussbaum's domains, and to cultivate multiple character strengths—but still not *fully* be well. As Maslow has shown in his brilliant work, human beings achieve peak potential when they experience transformative peak moments, or ecstasies, the results of which represent myriad eudaimonic implications: therapeutic removal of neuroses; reorientation away from self-centeredness towards altruistic concern for others; enhancement of creativity; an intensified sense of meaning and purpose; a feeling of psychic integration (wholeness); the ability to connect with other people and with the natural world; a heightened sense of agency and autonomy; greater spontaneity and playfulness; enhanced capacity for gratitude and unconditional love[21]; and the embrace of "Being-values" such as justice, goodness, beauty, simplicity, and meaningfulness among many others.[22] The ecstatic experience is the catalyst that can trigger an alchemical transformation from either a less-than-desirable or even decent life to a full one. Ecstasy, as I hope the foregoing discuss shows, is the apotheosis of human well-being.

Chapter Notes

Chapter 1

1. Willis Barnstone, *The Poetics of Ecstasy: Varieties of Ekstasis from Sappho to Borges* (New York: Holmes & Meier, 1983).

Chapter 2

1. Much of this chapter is taken from the introduction to *Wild Poets of Ecstasy: An Anthology of Ecstatic Verse*, ed. D. J. Moores (Nevada City, CA: Pelican Pond, 2011), 3–18.

2. Walt Whitman, *Leaves of Grass and Other Writings*, ed. Michael Moon (New York: Norton, 2002).

3. Cited with permission.

4. Cited with permission.

5. *General Social Survey* (Chicago: National Opinion Research Center, 1989).

6. Marghanita Laski, *Ecstasy in Secular and Religious Experiences* (Los Angeles: Tarcher, 1961), 26.

7. Cited with permission.

8. Cited in Laski, 51.

9. Cited in Evelyn Elsaesser Valarino, *On the Other Side of Life: Exploring the Phenomenon of the Near-Death Experience*, trans. Michelle Herzig Escobar (New York: Plenum, 1997), 32.

10. Cited in Dan Merkur, *The Ecstatic Imagination: Psychedelic Experiences and the Psychoanalysis of Self-Actualization* (Albany, NY: SUNY Press, 1998), 114.

11. Cited in Stanislav Grof, *The Holotropic Mind* (New York: HarperCollins, 1990), 98.

12. Cited in Merkur, *The Ecstatic Imagination: Psychedelic Experiences and the Psychoanalysis of Self-Actualization*, 108.

13. Cited in F.C. Happold, *Mysticism: A Study and an Anthology* (New York: Penguin, 1990), 54.

14. *Ibid.*, 130.

15. Cited in John G. Neihardt, *Black Elk Speaks* (Lincoln: University of Nebraska Press, 1979), 43.

16. Abraham Maslow, *The Farther Reaches of Human Nature* (New York: Penguin, 1976), 285.

17. Emile Durkheim, *The Elementary Forms of the Religious Life* (New York: Free Press, 1915), 249.

18. Victor Turner, *The Ritual Process: Structure and Anti-Structure* (Ithaca, NY: Cornell University Press, 1966), 7.

19. For a more thorough discussion, see Albert Hoffman, *LSD: My Problem Child* (Sarasota, FL: MAPS, 2005).

20. Merkur, *The Ecstatic Imagination: Psychedelic Experiences and the Psychoanalysis of Self-Actualization*, 91.

21. *Ibid.*, 94.

22. William Wordsworth, *The Prelude: 1799, 1805, 1850*, eds. Jonathan Wordsworth, M.H. Abrams, and Stephen Gill (New York: Norton, 1979).

23. For a considerably more thorough treatment of this issue, see Martin Heidegger, *Basic Writings*, trans. Joan Stambaugh (New York: HarperCollins, 1993).

24. C.G. Jung, *The Collected Works of C.G. Jung*. 20 vols, ed. William McGuire, trans. R.F.C. Hull (Princeton, NJ: Princeton University Press, 1983), 12:60.

25. Laski, *Ecstasy in Secular and Religious Experiences*, 26.

26. *Ibid.*, 176.

27. Mihalyi Csikszentmihalyi, *Flow: The Psychology of Optimal Experience* (New York: Harper & Row, 1990), 2.

28. *Ibid.*, 49.

29. *Ibid.*, 50.

30. *Ibid.*, 49.

31. Adam Potkay, *The Story of Joy: From the Bible to Late Romanticism* (New York: Cambridge University Press, 2007), 2.

32. *Ibid.*, 20.

33. *Ibid.*, 27.

34. See Rosemarie Taylor-Perry, *The God Who Comes: Dionysian Mysteries Revisited* (New York: Algora, 2003).

35. *Ibid.*, 3.

36. Jonathan Haidt, "Elevation and the Positive Psychology of Morality," in *Flourishing: Positive Psychology and the Life Well-Lived*, ed. Corey Keyes and Jonathan Haidt (Washington, DC: American Psychological Association, 2003), 276.

37. *Ibid.*, 282.

38. Sara Algoe and Jonathan Haidt, "Witnessing Excellence in Action: The 'Other-Praising' Emotions of Elevation, Gratitude, and Admiration," *The Journal of Positive Psychology* 4.2 (2009): 110.

39. *Ibid.*, 105.

40. Haidt, "Elevation and the Positive Psychology of Morality," 282.

41. Algoe and Haidt, "Witnessing Excellence in Action," 123.

42. Haidt, "Elevation and the Positive Psychology of Morality," 286.

43. *Ibid.*, 286.

44. Paul Pearsall, *Awe: The Delights and Dangers of Our Eleventh Emotion* (Deerfield Beach, FL: Health Communications, 2007), 35–36.

45. *Ibid.*, 19.

46. James Twitchell, *Romantic Horizons: Aspects of the Sublime in English Poetry and Painting, 1770–1850* (Columbia: University of Missouri Press, 1983), 3.

Chapter 3

1. Solomon Gandz, "The Dawn of Prolegomena to a History of Unwritten Literature," *Osiris* 7 (1939): 261.

2. M.L. West, *Indo-European Poetry and Myth* (New York: Oxford University Press, 2007), 29.

3. *Ibid.*, 29.

4. *Ibid.*, 29.

5. *Ibid.*, 29.

6. Theodore M. Ludwig, *The Sacred Paths of the East* (Upper Saddle River, NJ: Prentice Hall, 2001), 37.

7. George L. Hart, *The Poems of Ancient Tamil: Their Milieu and Their Sanskrit Counterparts* (Berkeley: University of California Press, 1975), 7.

8. Kamil V. Zvelebil, *Literary Conventions in Akam Poetry* (Madras, India: Institute of Asian Studies, 1986), iv.

9. Hart, *The Poems of Ancient Tamil: Their Milieu and Their Sanskrit Counterparts*, 9.

10. *Ibid.*, 10.

11. Zvelebil, *Literary Conventions in Akam Poetry*, iii.

12. *Ibid.*, v.

13. *Ibid.*, v.

14. *Ibid.*, v.

15. Quoted in Zvelebil, *Literary Conventions in Akam Poetry*, xi.

16. *Ibid.*, viii.

17. Ludwig, *The Sacred Paths of the East*, 45.

18. Vidya Dehejia, *Antal and Her Path of Love* (Albany, NY: SUNY Press, 1990), 2.

19. *Ibid.*, 18.

20. *Ibid.*, 17.

21. A.K. Ramanujan, introduction to *Speaking of Shiva* (New York: Penguin, 1973), 39.

22. *Ibid.*, 38.

23. *Ibid.*, 20.

24. *Ibid.*, 30.

25. *Ibid.*, 11.

26. Jane Hirshfield, introduction to *Mirabai: Ecstatic Poems* (Boston: Beacon Press, 2004), 14.

27. John Stratton Hawley, afterword to *Mirabai: Ecstatic Poems* (Boston: Beacon, 2004), 90.

28. Krishna Dutta and Andrew Robinson, *Rabindranath Tagore: The Myriad-Minded Man* (London: Bloomsbury, 2009), 28.

29. *Ibid.*, 30.

30. Quoted in Dutta and Robinson, *Rabindranath Tagore: The Myriad-Minded Man*, 30.

31. *Ibid.*, 41.

32. *Ibid.*, 42.

33. *Ibid.*, 169.

34. Quoted in Dutta and Robinson, *Rabindranath Tagore: The Myriad-Minded Man*, 361.

35. Ludwig, *The Sacred Paths of the East*, 91.

36. Andrew Schelling, introduction to *The Wisdom Anthology of North American Buddhist Poetry* (Boston: Wisdom, 2005), 1.

37. *Ibid.*, 1.

38. *Ibid.*, 13.

39. *Ibid.*, 13.

40. Ludwig, *The Sacred Paths of the East*, 98.

41. Lucien Stryk, preface to *Zen Poetry* (New York: Grove, 1995), xxxvii.

42. Robert Hass, introduction to *The Essential Haiku* (Hopewell, NJ: Ecco, 1994), 14.

43. Roland Barthes, *Empire of Signs* (New York: Hill and Wang, 1982), 72.

44. Hass, *The Essential Haiku*, 15.

45. Stryk, *Zen Poetry*, xxxviii.

46. Ludwig, *The Sacred Paths of the East*, 99.

47. Lama Kunga Rinpoche and Brian Cutillo, introduction to *Drinking the Mountain Stream: Songs of Tibet's Beloved Saint, Milarepa* (Boston: Wisdom, 1995), 38.

48. Humphrey Clark, preface to *Songs of Milarepa* (New York: Dover, 2003), xi.

49. "Poem #2," in *Songs of Milarepa* (New York: Dover, 2003), 3.

50. Mircea Eliade, *Shamanism: Archaic Techniques of Ecstasy* (Princeton, NJ: Princeton University Press, 1964), 378.

51. Larry Alderink, "Creation and Salvation in Ancient Orphism," *American Classical Studies* 8 (1981): 15.

52. Michael Schmidt, *The First Poets: Lives of the Ancient Greek Poets* (London: Weidenfeld & Nicholson, 2004), 31.

53. Charles Segal, *Orpheus: The Myth of the Poet* (Baltimore, MD: Johns Hopkins University Press, 1989), 34.

54. Bruno Gentili, *Poetry and Its Public in Ancient Greece: From Homer to the Fifth Century* (Baltimore, MD: Johns Hopkins University Press, 1988), 3.

55. Segal, *Orpheus: The Myth of the Poet*, 11.

56. *Ibid.*, 15.

57. *Ibid.*, 15.

58. A.P. David, *The Dance of the Muses* (New York: Oxford University Press, 2006), 9.

59. *Ibid.*, 9.

60. *Ibid.*, 8–9.

61. Arthur Pickard-Cambridge, *Dithyramb: Tragedy and Comedy* (Oxford: Claredon, 1962), 33.

62. Rosemarie Taylor-Perry, *The God Who Comes: Dionysian Mysteries Revisited*, 13.

63. *Ibid.*, 81.

64. G.M. Sifarkis, "Organization of Festivals and the Dionysiac Guilds," *The Classical Quarterly* 15.2 (1965): 208.

65. Felix Budelmann, "Introducing Greek Lyric," in *The Cambridge Companion to Greek Lyric* (New York: Cambridge University Press, 2009), 12.

66. Susan Stewart, "Lyric Possession," *Critical Inquiry* 22.1 (1995): 47.

67. *Ibid.*, 40.

68. C.O. Pavese, "The Rhapsodic Epic Poems as Oral and Independent Poems," *Harvard Studies in Classical Philology* 98 (1998): 64.

69. Richard Hunter and Ian Rutherford, introduction to *Wandering Poets in Ancient Greek Culture* (New York: Cambridge University Press, 2009), 11.

70. Donald Hargis, "The Rhapsode," *Quarterly Journal of Speech* 56.4 (1970): 390.

71. Budelmann, "Introducing Greek Lyric," 14.

72. Pickard-Cambridge, *Dithyramb: Tragedy and Comedy*, 32.

73. Susan Stewart, "Lyric Possession," 47.

74. Penelope Murray, "Poetic Inspiration in Early Greece," *The Journal of Hellenic Studies* 101 (1981): 100.

75. Jennifer Wise, *Dionysus Writes: The Invention of Theatre in Ancient Greece* (Ithaca, NY: Cornell University Press, 1998), 2.

76. Amos Kidder Fiske, *The Great Epic of Israel: The Web of Myth, Legend, History, Law, Oracle, Wisdom and Poetry of the Ancient Hebrews* (New York: Sturgis, 1911), 17.

77. Frank Moore Cross and David Freedman, *Studies in Ancient Yahwistic Poetry* (Missoula, MT: Scholars Press, 1975), 3.

78. *Ibid.*, 3.

79. Sigmund Mowinckel, *The Spirit and the Word: Prophesy and Tradition in Ancient Israel* (Minneapolis, MN: Fortress Press, 2002), 112.

80. *Ibid.* 108.

81. *Ibid.*, 108.

82. Niek Veldhuis, "Mesopotamian Canons," in *Homer, the Bible and Beyond: Literary and Religious Canons in the Ancient World* (Boston: Brill, 2003), 27.

83. R.B. Parkinson, *Poetry and Culture in Middle Kingdom Egypt* (New York: Continuum, 2002), 7.

84. Mowinckel, *The Spirit and the Word: Prophesy and Tradition in Ancient Israel*, 108.

85. Anthony Podlecki, *The Early Greek Poets and Their Times* (Vancouver: University of British Columbia Press, 1984) 24.

86. Radin, "The Kid and Its Mother's Milk," *American Journal of Semitic Languages & Literatures* 40, no. 3 (1984): 12.

87. Happold, *Mysticism: A Study and an Anthology*, 18.

88. Sabina Flanagan, introduction to *Secrets of God: Writings of Hildegard of Bingen* (Boston: Shambhala, 1996), 3.

89. Taken from *Secrets of God: Writings of Hildegard of Bingen*, 120–122.

90. Flanagan, introduction to *Secrets of God: Writings of Hildegard of Bingen*, 4.

91. *Ibid.*, 5.

92. *Ibid.*, 2.

93. *Ibid.*, 4.

94. "Hymn to the Holy Ghost," *Secrets of God: Writings of Hildegard of Bingen*, 120.

95. Kieran Kavanaugh and Otilio Rodriguez, introduction to *The Collected Works of St. John of the Cross* (Washington, DC: ICS Publications, 1991), 42.

96. *Ibid.*, 16.

97. *Ibid.*, 27.

98. *Ibid.*, 27.

99. *Ibid.*, 23.

100. Taken from *The Collected Works of St. John of the Cross*, 50–52.

101. Kavanaugh and Rodriguez, introduc-

tion to *The Collected Works of St. John of the Cross*, 41.

102. John Matthews, "The Story of the Bards," in *The Bardic Sourcebook: Inspirational Legacy and Teachings of the Ancient Celts* (London: Blandford, 1998), 15.

103. *Ibid.*, 13.

104. Daniel Corkery, "The Bardic Schools," in *The Bardic Sourcebook: Inspirational Legacy and Teachings of the Ancient Celts*, 30.

105. *Ibid.*, 27.

106. *Ibid.*, 30.

107. *Ibid.*, 27.

108. Matthews, "The Story of the Bards," in *The Bardic Sourcebook: Inspirational Legacy and Teachings of the Ancient Celts*, 18.

109. *Ibid.*, 14.

110. *Ibid.*, 14.

111. Margaret Clunies Ross, *A History of Old Norse Poetry and Poetics* (Rochester, NY: D.S. Brewer, 2005), 2.

112. *Ibid.*, 83.

113. *Ibid.*, 92.

114. Kimberley Christine Patton, *Religion of the Gods: Ritual, Paradox, and Reflexivity* (New York: Oxford University Press, 2009), 131.

115. Ross also notes that many scholars believe the other (later) god of Norse poetry, Bragi, was an actual person, Bragi Boddason, a brilliant skaldic poet who was deified after his death. See Ross, *A History of Old Norse Poetry and Poetics*, 105.

116. Peter Salus and Paul Taylor, introduction to *The Elder Edda: A Selection*, trans. Paul B. Taylor and W.H. Auden (New York: Random House, 1969), 25.

Chapter 4

1. Ernst, *Sufism*, 8–19.

2. *Ibid.*, 152.

3. *Ibid.*, 153.

4. *Ibid.*, 152.

5. *Ibid.*, 160.

6. *Ibid.*, 166.

7. Jawid Mojaddedi, introduction to *The Masnawi: Book One* by Rumi, ed. and trans. Jawid Mojaddedi (Oxford: Oxford University Press, 2008), xx.

8. *Ibid.*, xxii.

9. Irene Nicholson, *A Guide to Mexican Poetry, Ancient and Modern* (Los Angeles: Minutiae Mexicana, 1968), 13–14.

10. *Ibid.*, 14.

11. *Ibid.*, 7, 10.

12. *Ibid.*, 10.

13. *Ibid.*, 8.

14. *Ibid.*, 25.

15. David Pollack, "Japanese 'Wild Poetry,'" *The Journal of Asian Studies* 38.3 (1979): 501.

16. Henry Wells, introduction to *Ancient Poetry from China, Japan & India* (Columbia: University of South Carolina Press, 1968), 9.

17. Isidore Okpewho, introduction to *The Heritage of African Poetry* (New York: Longman, 1985), 5.

18. Marcel Granet, *Chinese Civilization* (New York: Barnes & Noble, 1957), 170.

19. Okpewho, introduction to *The Heritage of African Poetry*, 9.

20. Evan Zuesse, *Ritual Cosmos: The Sanctification of Life in African Religions* (Athens: Ohio University Press, 1985), 183.

21. Richard Hunter and Ian Rutherford, introduction to *Wandering Poets in Ancient Greek Culture* (New York: Cambridge University Press, 2009), 15.

22. Jerome Rothenberg, preface to *Technicians of the Sacred* (Berkeley: University of California Press, 1985) xxx..

23. Friedrich Nietzsche, *The Birth of Tragedy* (New York: Cambridge University Press, 1999), 111.

24. Gentili, *Poetry and Its Public in Ancient Greece: From Homer to the Fifth Century*, 8.

25. Quoted in Gentili, *Poetry and Its Public in Ancient Greece: From Homer to the Fifth Century*, 11.

26. *Ibid.*, 11.

27. *Ibid.*, 13.

28. James Twitchell, *Romantic Horizons: Aspects of the Sublime in English Poetry and Painting, 1770–1850* (Columbia: University of Missouri Press, 1983), 3.

29. D. J. Moores, *The Dark Enlightenment: Jung, Romanticism and the Repressed Other* (Madison, NJ: Fairleigh Dickinson University Press, 2010).

30. D.J. Moores, ed., *Wild Poets of Ecstasy: An Anthology of Ecstatic Verse* (Nevada City, CA: Pelican Pond Press, 2011).

31. Willis Barnstone, *The Poetics of Ecstasy: Varieties of Ekstasis from Sappho to Borges* (New York: Holmes & Meier, 1983).

32. D.J. Moores, *Mystical Discourse in Wordsworth and Whitman: A Transatlantic Bridge* (Dudley, MA: Peeters, 2006).

33. James Miller, Karl Shapiro and Bernice Slote, *Start with the Sun: Studies in the Whitman Tradition* (Lincoln: University of Nebraska Press, 1960), 3.

34. *Ibid.*, 3.

35. *Ibid.*, 4.

36. *Ibid.*, 4.

37. Susanne Evertsen Lundquist, *Native American Literatures: An Introduction* (New York: Continuum, 2004), 6.

38. Leslie Fiedler, "Is There a Majority Literature?" *The College English Association Critic* 36 (1974): 4.

Chapter 5

1. Nevit Ergin and Will Johnson, introduction to *The Rubais of Rumi: Insane with Love*, by Rumi, trans. Nevit Ergin and Will Johnson (Rochester, VT: Inner Traditions, 2007), 18.

2. Franklin Lewis, *Rumi: Past and Present, East and West: The Life, Teachings and Poetry of Jalal al–Din Rumi* (Oxford: Oneworld, 2008), 168.

3. *Ibid.*, 314.

4. Amira El-Zein, "Spiritual Consumption in the United States," *Islam & Christian-Muslim Relations* 11.1 (2000): 73.

5. Hulya Kucuk, "A Brief History of Western Sufism," *Asian Journal of Social Science* 36.2 (2008): 310.

6. Thierry Zarcone, "Readings and Transformations of Sufism in the West," *Diogenes* 47.3 (1999): 112.

7. Hazrat Inayat Khan, *The Inner Life* (Boston: Shambhala, 1997), 38–29.

8. Taken from William Blake, *Blakes's Poetry and Designs,* eds. Mary Lynn Johnson and John E. Grant (New York: Norton, 1979), 183.

9. Annemarie Schimmel, *As Through a Veil: Mystical Poetry in Islam* (Oxford: Oneworld, 2001), 36.

10. Dick Davis, "Sufism and Poetry: A Marriage of Convenience," *Edebiyat: Journal of Middle Eastern Literatures* 10.2 (1999): 283.

11. *Ibid.*, 291.

12. *Ibid.*, 284.

13. Khan, *The Inner Life*, 95.

14. This and all subsequent citations from the text are taken from Rumi, *The Masnavi: Book One,* trans. Jawid Mojaddedi (Oxford: Oxford University Press, 2004). Used by permission of Oxford University Press. The citations refer to the book and couplet number, not the lines.

15. Annemarie Schimmel, *Mystical Dimensions of Islam* (Chapel Hill: University of North Carolina Press, 1975), 140.

16. Interestingly, Dante's decision to have his character guided by reason only up to a point was likely influenced by his reading of Sufi literature, with which scholars know he was at least partially familiar; see Kucuk, "A Brief History of Western Sufism," 292–93.

17. Dick Davis, "Narrative and Doctrine in the First Story of Rumi's Mathnawi," *Journal of Semitic Studies* 12 (2000): 104.

18. Farooq Hamid, "Storytelling Techniques in the Masnavi-yi Ma'navi of Mowlana Jalal Al-Din Rumi: Wayward Narrative or Logical Progression?" *Iranian Studies* 32.1 (1999): 28.

19. Fromm, *The Art of Loving,* 19.

20. Freud, *Civilzation & Its Discontents,* 13.

21. Fredrickson, *Positivity,* 47.

22. *Ibid.*, 47.

23. Fromm, *The Art of Loving,* 17.

24. *Ibid.*, 17.

25. *Ibid.*, 17.

26. Vaillant, *Spiritual Evolution,* 92.

27. *Ibid.*, 99.

28. Lewis, *Rumi: Past and Present, East and West: The Life, Teachings and Poetry of Jalal al–Din Rumi,* 327.

29. For a fuller discussion, see Khaled El-Rouayheb, "Heresy and Sufism in the Arab-Islamic World, 1550–1750: Some Preliminary Observations," *Bulletin of the School of Oriental & African Studies* 73.3 (2010): 357–380.

30. Llewellyn Vaughan-Lee, *Sufism: The Transformation of the Heart* (Inverness, CA: Golden Sufi Center, 2002), 13.

31. El-Rouayheb, "Heresy and Sufism in the Arab-Islamic World, 1550–1750: Some Preliminary Observations," 380.

32. Qtd. in Vaughan-Lee, *Sufism: The Transformation of the Heart,* 14.

33. This reference is taken from Franklin Lewis's translations of a limited selection of Rumi's lyrics, which are found in *Rumi: Past and Present, East and West* (Oxford: Oneworld, 2000), 345–93. The parenthetical citations refer to line numbers in the poems.

34. All references to this poem are taken from Mahmood Jamal, ed. and trans. *Islamic Mystical Poetry: Sufi Verse from the Early Mystics to Rumi* (New York: Penguin, 2009), 140–41. Rumi did not title his poems, so the one I have cited is provided by Jamal and does not appear in the original.

35. Taken from Franklin Lewis, *Rumi: Past and Present, East and West,* 345.

36. Taken from Franklin Lewis, *Rumi: Past and Present, East and West,* 381–83.

37. Based on Lewis's footnote, 381–82.

38. Ahmad Jalali, "Jalaluddin Rumi's Religious Understanding: A Prelude to Dialogue in the Realm of Religious Thought," *Diogenes* 50.4 (2003): 132.

39. Brannon Ingram, "Sufis, Scholars, and Scapegoats: Rashid Ahmad Gangohi (d. 1905) and Deobandi Critique of Sufism," *Muslim World* 99.3 (2009): 479.

40. Gabriel Warburg, "From Sufism to Fundamentalism: The Mahdiyya and the Wahhabiyya," *Middle Eastern Studies* 45.4 (2009): 664.

41. Saladdin Ahmad, "What Is Sufism?" *Forum Philosophicum* 13.2 (2008): 242.

42. Meir Hatina, "Where East Meets West: Sufism, Cultural Rapprochement, and Politics," *International Journal of Middle East Studies* 39 (2007): 404.

43. El-Zein, "Spiritual Consumption in the United States," 76.

44. Omaima Abu-Bakr, "Abrogation of the Mind in the Poetry of Jalal al–Din Rumi,"*Alif: Journal of Comparative Poetics* 14 (1994): 38.

45. Taken from Mahmood Jamal, ed. *Islamic Mystical Poetry: Sufi Verse from the Early Mystics to Rumi,* 154.

46. Jerome W. Clinton, "Rumi in America," *Edebiyat* 10 (1999): 150.

47. Schimmel, *Mystical Dimensions of Islam,* 18.

Chapter 6

1. Qtd. in Jonathan Bate, *Romantic Ecology: Wordsworth and the Environmental Tradition* (New York: Routledge, 1991), 44.

2. *Ibid.,* 14.

3. Emma Mason, *The Cambridge Introduction to William Wordsworth* (New York: Cambridge University Press, 2010), 98–110.

4. Christopher Miller, "Wordsworth's Anatomies of Surprise," *Studies in Romanticism* 46.4 (2007): 409.

5. *Ibid.,* 410.

6. This and all subsequent references to the poem are taken from *Wordsworth: Complete Poetical Works,* ed. Thomas Hutchinson (New York: Oxford University Press, 1936). The citations refer to line numbers.

7. Abraham Maslow, *Religions, Values and Peak Experiences,* 112.

8. James Twitchell, *Romantic Horizons: Aspects of the Sublime in English Poetry and Painting, 1770–1850* (Columbia: University of Missouri Press, 1983), 3.

9. *Ibid.,* 42.

10. Tim Milnes and Kerry Sinanan, introduction to *Romanticism, Sincerity and Authenticity,* (New York: Palgrave Macmillan, 2010), 4.

11. James Philips, "Wordsworth and the Fraternity of Joy," *New Literary History* 41.3 (2010): 628–29.

12. Christopher Peterson and Martin Seligman, *Character Strengths and Virtues: A Handbook and Classification* (New York: Oxford University Press, 2004), 326.

13. Gerard Huther, *The Compassionate Brain* (Boston: Shambhala, 2006), 114.

14. R.A. Foakes, "Beyond the Visible World: Wordsworth and Coleridge in Lyrical Ballads," *Romanticism* 5.1 (1999): 31.

15. See John Wilson, "Trauma, Optimal Experiences, and Integrative Psychological States," in *The Posttraumatic Self: Restoring Meaning and Wholeness to Personality,* ed. John Wilson (New York: Routledge, 2006), 211–253.

16. For a more complete discussion, see D.J. Moores, *The Dark Enlightenment: Jung, Romanticism and the Repressed Other* (Madison, NJ: Fairleigh Dickinson University Press, 2010).

17. For a more complete discussion, see D.J. Moores, *Mystical Discourse in Wordsworth and Whitman: A Transatlantic Bridge* (Dudley, MA: Peeters, 2006).

18. Onno Oerlemans, *Romanticism and the Materiality of Nature* (Buffalo, NY: University of Toronto Press, 2002), 4.

19. Jonathan Bate, Romantic Ecology: Wordsworth and the Environmental Tradition (New York: Routledge, 1991), 33.

20. Adam Potkay, *The Story of Joy: From the Bible to Late Romanticism* (New York: Cambridge University Press), 122.

21. *Ibid.,* 122.

22. Qtd. in Lawrence Beull, *The Environmental Imagination: Thoreau, Nature Writing, and the Formation of American Culture* (Cambridge, MA: Belknap Press of Harvard University Press, 1995), 11–12.

23. Greg Garrard, *Ecocriticism* (New York: Routledge, 2008), 43.

24. M.H. Abrams, *Natural Supernaturalism* (New York: Norton, 1971), 295.

25. Barbara Fredrickson, *Positivity* (New York: Three Rivers Press, 2009), 41.

26. Robert Emmons and Michael McCullough, introduction to *The Psychology of Gratitude* (New York: Oxford University Press, 2004), 9.

27. Barbara Fredrickson, "Gratitude, Like Other Positive Emotions, Broadens and Builds," in *The Psychology of Gratitude,* ed. Robert Emmons and Michael McCullough (New York: Oxford University Press, 2004), 145.

28. *Ibid.,* 153.

29. Robert Fuller, *Wonder: From Emotion to Spirituality* (Chapel Hill: University of North Carolina Press, 2006), 15.

30. *Ibid.,* viii.

31. *Ibid.,* 2.

32. *Ibid.,* 2.

33. *William Wordsworth: Selected Poems,* ed. John O. Hayden (New York: Penguin, 1994), 435.

34. Joseph Viscomi, "Wordsworth, Gilpin, and the Vacant Mind," *Wordsworth Circle* 38.1–2 (2007): 47.

35. Potkay, *The Story of Joy*, 123.

36. *Ibid.*, 220–36.

37. Stephen Gill, *William Wordsworth: A Life* (New York: Oxford University Press, 1990).

38. Stephen Gill, "Wordsworth's 'Never Failing Principle of Joy,'" *English Language History* 34.2 (1967): 216.

39. Richard Gravil, *Wordsworth's Bardic Vocation, 1787–1842* (New York: Palgrave Macmillan, 2003), 8.

40. Ian Dennis, "Romantic Joy," *Anthropoetics: The Journal of Generative Anthropology* 16.1 (2010): 27.

41. Bate, *Romantic Ecology*, 4.

Chapter 7

1. See Michael Robertson, *Worshipping Walt: The Whitman Disciples* (Princeton, NJ: Princeton University Press), 2010.

2. David S. Reynolds, *Walt Whitman's America: A Cultural Biography* (New York: Vintage, 1996), 260.

3. Paul Gilmore, "Romantic Electricity, or the Materiality of Aesthetics," *American Literature* 76.3 (2004): 473.

4. L.S. Klatt, "The Electric Whitman," *Southern Review* 44.2 (2008): 322.

5. Gilmore, "Romantic Electricity, or the Materiality of Aesthetics," 478.

6. Unless otherwise noted, all citations to Whitman's poetry are taken from *Leaves of Grass and Other Writings*, ed. Michael Moon (New York: Norton, 2002).

7. James Miller, *Leaves of Grass: America's Lyric-Epic of Self and Democracy* (New York: Twayne, 1992), 53.

8. Isaiah Berlin, *The Roots of Romanticism* (Princeton, NJ: Princeton University Press, 1999), 27.

9. Mark Maslan, *Whitman Possessed: Poetry, Sexuality, and Popular Authority* (Baltimore, MD: Johns Hopkins University Press, 2001), 2.

10. *Ibid.*, 4, 12.

11. Richard Shusterman, *Body Consciousness: A Philosophy of Mindfulness and Somaesthetics* (New York: Cambridge University Press, 2008), 21.

12. Andrew Lawson, "'Spending for Vast Returns': Sex, Class, and Commerce in the First *Leaves of Grass*," *American Literature* 75.2 (2003): 335–66.

13. Maslan, Whitman Possessed, 7.

14. Klatt, "The Electric Whitman," 325,

15. Harold Aspiz, *Walt Whitman and the Body Beautiful* (Chicago: University of Illinois Press, 1980), 239.

16. Richard Tayson, "The Casualties of Walt Whitman," *Virginia Quarterly Review* 81.2 (2005): 79–95.

17. *Ibid.*, 93.

18. Qtd. in Tayson, "The Casualties of Walt Whitman," 83.

19. Miller, *Leaves of Grass: America's Lyric-Epic of Self and Democracy*, 56.

20. Michael Moon, "The Twenty-Ninth Bather: Identy, Fluidity, Gender, and Sexuality in Section 11 of 'Song of Myself,'" in *Leaves of Grass and Other Writings*, ed. Michael Moon (New York: Norton, 2002), 860, 861.

21. *Criterion* (Nov. 10, 1855).

22. This and the foregoing quotations from reviews are taken from Harold Aspiz, *Walt Whitman and the Body Beautiful* (Chicago: University of Illinois Press, 1980), 240.

23. *Atlantic Monthly*, Sept. 1890.

24. *Tribune*, 1894.

25. Qtd. in Tayson, "The Casualties of Walt Whitman," 92.

26. Henry David Thoreau, "Letter to H.G.O. Blake, 19 November, 1856," in *Leaves of Grass and Other Writings*, ed. Michael Moon (New York: Norton), 801.

27. Ralph Waldo Emerson, "Emerson to Whitman, 1855," in *Leaves of Grass and Other Writings*, ed. Michael Moon (New York: Norton), 637.

28. Qtd. in *Leaves of Grass and Other Writings*, ed. Michael Moon (New York: Norton), 638–46.

29. Reynolds, *Walt Whitman's America: A Cultural Biography*, 203. 209.

30. Denise T. Askin, "Whitman's Theory of Evil: A Clue to His Use of Paradox," *Emerson Society Quarterly* 28.2 (1982): 121–32.

31. Qtd. in Tayson, "The Casualties of Walt Whitman," 83.

32. Jerome Loving, *Walt Whitman: The Song of Himself* (Berkeley: University of California Press, 1999), 252.

33. John Tessitore, "The 'Sky-Blue' Variety: William James, Walt Whitman, and the Limits of Healthy-Mindedness," *Nineteenth-Century Literature* 62.4 (2008): 493.

34. Thoreau, "Letter to H.G.O. Blake, 19 November, 1856," in *Leaves of Grass and Other Writings*, 801.

35. Jimmie Killingsworth, "'As if the Beasts Spoke": The Animal/Animist/Animated Walt Whitman," *Walt Whitman Quarterly Review* 28.1 (2010): 19.

36. Reynolds, *Walt Whitman's America: A Cultural Biography*, 209.

37. Susan Rowland, *The Ecocritical Psyche: Literature, Evolutionary Complexity and Jung* (New York: Routledge, 2012), 15.

38. Miller, *Leaves of Grass: America's Lyric-Epic of Self and Democracy*, 56.

39. Walt Whitman, *Specimen Days & Collect* (New York: Dover, 1995), 253.

40. Daniel G. Payne, "Emerson's Natural Theology: John Burroughs and the 'Church' of Latter Day Transcendentalism," *American Transcendentalist Quarterly* 21.3 (2007): 194.

41. Killingsworth, "'As if the Beasts Spoke': The Animal/Animist/Animated Walt Whitman," 20.

42. Qtd. in Lawrence Shapiro, *Embodied Cognition* (New York: Routledge, 2011), 56.

43. Shapiro, *Embodied Cognition*, 66.

44. The seminal text in the field is Francisco Varela, Evan Thompson, and Eleanor Rosch, *The Embodied Mind: Cognitive Science and Human Experience* (Boston: Massachusetts Institute of Technology Press, 1991).

45. Aldous Huxley, *The Perennial Philosophy* (New York: Harper, 1944), 18.

46. *Leaves of Grass and Other Writings*, 783.

47. Karen Sanchez-Eppler, "To Stand Between: Walt Whitman's Poetics of Merger and Embodiment," in *Leave of Grass and Other Writings*, ed. Michael Moon (New York: Norton, 2002), 852.

48. Mary Timothy Prokes, *Toward a Theology of the Body* (Grand Rapids, MI: William B. Eerdmans, 1996), 3–4.

49. *Ibid.*, 3.

50. John Irwin, "Whitman: Hieroglyphic Bibles and Phallic Songs," in *Leaves of Grass and Other Writings*, ed. Michael Moon (New York: Norton, 2002), 865.

51. Reynolds, *Walt Whitman's America: A Cultural Biography*, 235.

52. *Ibid.*, 236.

53. Qtd. in Reynolds, *Walt Whitman's America: A Cultural Biography*, 268.

54. Robert Fuller, *Spirituality in the Flesh: Bodily Sources of Religion* (Oxford: Oxford University Press, 2008), 100.

55. William James, *The Varieties of Religious Experience* (New York: Penguin, 1985), 90.

56. Leslie Jamison, "'A Thousand Willing Forms': The Evolution of Whitman's Wounded Bodies," *Studies in American Fiction* 35.1 (2007): 23.

57. See Doxey Hatch, "'I Tramp a Perpetual Journey': Walt Whitman's Insights for Psychology," *Journal of Humanistic Psychology* 51.1 (2011): 7–27.

58. Qtd. in Reynolds, *Walt Whitman's America: A Cultural Biography*, 244.

59. Aspiz, *Walt Whitman and the Body Beautiful*, 17.

60. Perrin Elisha, *The Conscious Body: A Psychoanalytic Exploration of the Body in Therapy* (Washington, DC: American Psychological Association, 2011), 9.

61. Harry F. Harlow and Stephen J. Suomi, "Social Recovery by Isolation-Reared Monkeys," *Proceedings of the National Academy of Science of the United States of America* 68.7 (1971): 1534–1538.

62. Thomas Lewis, Fari Amini, and Richard Lannon, *A General Theory of Love* (New York: Random House, 2000), 143.

63. Klatt, "The Electric Whitman," 322.

64. Qtd. in Loving, *Walt Whitman: The Song of Himself*, 175.

65. Janice Trecker, "The Ecstatic Epistemology of 'Song of Myself,'" *Midwest Quarterly* 53.1 (2011): 19.

66. George B. Hutchinson, *The Ecstatic Whitman* (Columbus: Ohio State University Press, 1986), 112.

67. Qtd. in Hutchinson, *The Ecstatic Whitman*, 46.

68. Killingsworth, "'As if the Beasts Spoke': The Animal/Animist/Animated Walt Whitman," 30.

69. Klatt, "The Electric Whitman," 300.

70. Qtd. in Hutchinson, *The Ecstatic Whitman*, 47.

71. See Edward Whitely, "'The First White Aboriginal': Walt Whitman and John Rollin Ridge," *Emerson Society Quarterly* 52.1–2 (2006): 105–139.

72. Hutchinson, *The Ecstatic Whitman*, 123.

73. Sanchez-Eppler, "To Stand Between: Walt Whitman's Poetics of Merger and Embodiment," 851.

74. Reynolds, *Walt Whitman's America: A Cultural Biography*, 251.

75. Aspiz, *Walt Whitman and the Body Beautiful*, 10, 243.

76. Whitman, *Specimen Days & Collect*, 248.

77. For a more complete discussion of the concept, see George Lakoff and Mark Johnson, *Metaphors We Live By* (Chicago: University of Chicago Press, 1980).

Chapter 8

1. Norbert Hirshhorn and Polly Longworth, "'Medicine Posthumous': A New Look at Emily Dickinson's Medical Conditions," *The New England Quarterly* 69.2 (1996): 312.

2. Roger Lundin, *Emily Dickinson and the Art of Belief* (Grand Rapids, MI: William B. Eerdmans, 1998), 187.

3. Qtd. in William Cooney, "The Death Poetry of Emily Dickinson," *Omega* 37.3 (1998): 243.

4. John F. McDermott, "Emily Dickinson Revisited: A Study of Periodicity in Her Work," *American Journal of Psychiatry* 158:5 (2001): 686.

5. S. Winhusen, "Emily Dickinson and Schizotypy," *Emily Dickinson Journal* 13 (2004): 77–96.

6. Christopher Ramey and Robert Weisberg, "The 'Poetical Activity' of Emily Dickinson: A Further Test of the Hypothesis That Affective Disorders Foster Creativity," *Creativity Research Journal* 16.2–3 (2004): 175.

7. John Cody, *After Great Pain: The Inner Life of Emily Dickinson* (Cambridge, MA: Harvard University Press, 1971), 130.

8. Daniel Pinchbeck, *Breaking Open the Head: A Psychedelic Journey into the Heart of Contemporary Shamanism*, 2.

9. Qtd. in William Cooney, "The Death Poetry of Emily Dickinson," 243.

10. This and all subsequent citations to the poems are taken from *The Poems of Emily Dickinson*, ed. Thomas H. Johnson (Cambridge, MA: The Belknap Press of Harvard University Press, Copyright © 1951, 1955, 1979, 1983 by the President and Fellows of Harvard College). All parenthetical citations refer to poems in Johnson's edition.

11. R.D. Laing, *The Divided Self* (New York: Penguin, 1990), 27.

12. *Ibid.*, 31.

13. Neil Scheurich, "Suffering and Spirituality in the Poetry of Emily Dickinson," *Pastoral Psychology* 56 (2007): 194.

14. See Richard G. Tedeschi and Lawrence G. Calhoun, "A Clinical Approach to Posttraumatic Growth," in *Positive Psychology in Practice*, ed. P. Alex Linley and Stephen Joseph (Hoboken, NJ: Wiley, 2004), 405–419.

15. Scheurich, "Suffering and Spirituality in the Poetry of Emily Dickinson," 195.

16. See Nina Baym, *American Women of Letters and the Nineteenth-Century Sciences: Styles of Affiliation* (New Brunswick, NJ: Rutgers University Press, 2002).

17. Lundin, *Emily Dickinson and the Art of Belief*, 220.

18. *Ibid.*, 13.

19. *Ibid.*, 220.

20. *Ibid.*, 200–201.

21. *Ibid.*, 13.

22. Magdalena Zapadowska, "Wrestling with Silence: Emily Dickinson's Calvinist God," *American Transcendentalist Quarterly* 20.1 (2006): 381.

23. Daniel L. Manheim, "'Have We Not a Hymn?' Dickinson and the Rhetoric of New England Revivalism," *The New England Quarterly* 78.3 (2005): 406.

24. Lorrie Smith, "Some See God and Live: Dickinson's Later Mysticism," *American Transcendentalist Quarterly* 1.4 (1987): 302.

25. *Ibid.*, xii.

26. Steve Carter, "Emily Dickinson and Mysticism," *Emerson Society Quarterly* 24.2 (1978): 84.

27. Angela Conrad, *The Wayward Nun of Amherst: Emily Dickinson and Medieval Mystical Women* (New York: Garland, 2000), xii.

28. Aliki Barnstone, *Changing Rapture: Emily Dickinson's Poetic Development* (Hanover, NH: University Press of New England, 2006), 103.

29. Qtd. in William Franke, "'The Missing All': Emily Dickinson's Apophatic Poetics," *Christianity and Literature* 58.1 (2008): 65.

30. Qtd. in Duncan Wu, ed. *Romanticism: An Anthology* (New York: Blackwell, 2005), 1351.

31. Maurice Lee, "Dickinson's Superb Surprise," *Raritan* 28.1 (2008): 46.

32. Christopher Ramey and Robert Weisberg, "The 'Poetical Activity' of Emily Dickinson: A Further Test of the Hypothesis That Affective Disorders Foster Creativity," 178.

33. Shira Wolosky, "Emily Dickinson: Reclusion against Itself," *Common Knowledge* 12.3 (2006): 446.

34. *Ibid.*, 446.

35. *Ibid.*, 446.

36. Sarah Emsley, "Is Emily Dickinson a Metaphysical Poet?" *Canadian Review of American Studies* 33.3 (2003): 262.

37. Maria Magdalena Farland, "'That Tritest/Brightest Truth': Emily Dickinson's Anti-Sentimentality," *Nineteenth-Century Literature* 53.3 (1998): 367.

38. James Matthew Wilson, "Representing the Limits of Judgment: Yvor Winters, Emily Dickinson, and Religious Experience," *Christianity and Literature* 56.3 (2007): 401.

39. Joanne Feit Diehl, "The Poetics of Loss: Erotic Melancholia in Agamben and Dickinson," *American Imago* 66.3 (2009): 370.

40. Qtd. in Thomas H. Johnson, *Emily Dickinson: An Interpretive Biography* (Cambridge, MA: Harvard University Press, 1955), 50–51.

41. Wilson, "Representing the Limits of Judgment: Yvor Winters, Emily Dickinson, and Religious Experience," 403.

Chapter 9

1. Rosinka Chaudhuri, "The Flute, Gerontion, and Subalternist Misreadings of Tagore," *Social Text* 22.1 (2004): 120.

2. Michael Collins, "History and the Postcolonial: Rabindranath Tagore's Reception in London, 1912–1913," *International Journal of the Humanities* 4.9 (2007): 74.

3. Kalyan Sircar, *Imagining Tagore: Rabindranath and the British Press, 1912–1941* (Calcutta: Shishu Sahitya Samsad, 2000), 112.

4. Qtd. in Krishna Dutta and Andrew Robinson, *Rabindranath Tagore: The Myriad-Minded Man* (London: Bloomsbury, 2009), 42.

5. Yeats, W.B. Introduction to *Gitanjali* by Rabindranath Tagore, ed. W.B. Yeats (New York: Scribner, 1997), 7.

6. *Ibid.*, 10.

7. Qtd. in Collins, "History and the Postcolonial: Rabindranath Tagore's Reception in London, 1912–1913," 74.

8. May Sinclair, "The 'Gitanjali': Or Song-Offerings of Rabindra Nath Tagore," *The North American Review* 690 (1913): 659.

9. Krishna Dutta and Andrew Robinson, *Rabindranath Tagore: The Myriad-Minded Man*, 169.

10. W.B. Yeats, introduction to *Gitanjali* by Rabindranath Tagore, 11.

11. Collins, "History and the Postcolonial: Rabindranath Tagore's Reception in London, 1912–1913," 82.

12. Qtd. in Ranajit Guha, *History at the Limit of World-History* (New York: Columbia University Press, 2002), 95–99.

13. Rabindranth Tagore, *The English Writings of Rabindranath Tagore*, ed. Sisir Kumar Das (Delhi: Sahitya Akademi, 1996), 79.

14. Qtd. in C.N. Sastry, *Walt Whitman and Rabindranath Tagore: A Study in Comparison* (Delhi: B.R. Publishing, 1992), 19.

15. Qtd. in Krishna Dutta and Andrew Robinson, *Rabindranath Tagore: The Myriad-Minded Man*, 148.

16. Qtd. in Andre Dommergues, "Rabindranath Tagore's Aesthetics," *Commonwealth Essays & Studies* 7.2 (1985): 3.

17. S.K. Nandi, *Art and Aesthetics of Rabindra Nath Tagore* (Calcutta: The Asiatic Society, 1999), 5.

18. *Ibid.*, 5.

19. This and all subsequent citations to Tagore's poems are taken from *Gitanjali*, ed. W.B. Yeats (New York: Scribner, 1997). The numbers are references to lines.

20. Valliant, *Spiritual Evolution: A Scientific Defense of Faith*, 134.

21. Sastry, *Walt Whitman and Rabindranath Tagore: A Study in Comparison*, 7.

22. Kalyan Sen Gupta, *The Philosophy of Rabindranath Tagore* (London: Ashgate, 2005), 88–89.

23. *Ibid.*, 89.

24. *Ibid.*, 91.

25. Qtd. in Gupta, *The Philosophy of Rabindranath Tagore*, 93.

26. Dommergues, "Rabindranath Tagore's Aesthetics," 2.

27. Dutta and Robinson, *Rabindranath Tagore: The Myriad-Minded Man*, 14.

28. Anupam Nagar, "Tagore's Mysticisim: Resisting the Myth of Finality," *Poetcrit* 19.2 (2006): 7.

29. Harendra Prasad Sinha, *Religious Philosophy of Tagore and Radhakrishnan* (Delhi: Montilal Banarsidass, 1993), 1.

30. Dutta and Robinson, *Rabindranath Tagore: The Myriad-Minded Man*, 13.

31. William Radice, "Never Not an Educator: Tagore as Poet-Teacher," *Asiatic* 4.1 (2010): 47.

32. Sinha, *Religious Philosophy of Tagore and Radhakrishnan*, 2.

33. John Stratton Hawley, *Three Bhakti Voices: Mirabai, Surdas, and Kabir in Their Time and Ours* (New York: Oxford University Press, 2005), 1.

34. Donald Tuck, "The Religious Motif in the Poetry of Rabindranath Tagore," *Numen* 21.2 (1974): 102.

35. Nagar, "Tagore's Mysticisim: Resisting the Myth of Finality," 11.

36. Rudolph Otto, *The Idea of the Holy*, trans. John W. Harvey (New York: Oxford University Press, 1958).

37. Kaiser Haq, "The Philosophy of Rabindranth Tagore," *Asiatic* 4.1 (2010): 28.

38. *Ibid.*, 29.

39. Qtd. in Dutta and Robinson, *Rabindranath Tagore: The Myriad-Minded Man*, 170.

40. Sudhir Kakar, *The Inner World: A Psycho-Analytic Study of Childhood and Society in India* (New York: Oxford University Press, 1981), 128.

41. Valliant, *Spiritual Evolution: A Scientific Defense of Faith*, 3.

42. For a complete discussion of humility see Christopher Peterson and Martin Seligman, *Character Strengths and Virtues: A Handbook and Classification* (New York: Oxford University Press, 2004).

43. Qtd. in Chaudhuri, "The Flute, Gerontion, and Subalternist Misreadings of Tagore," 107.

44. *Ibid.*, 108.

45. Dommergues, "Rabindranath Tagore's Aesthetics," 2.

46. Qtd. in Dommergues, "Rabindranath Tagore's Aesthetics," 3.

47. Susan Wolfson, *Formal Charges: The Shaping of Poetry in British Romanticism* (Stanford, CA: Stanford University Press, 1997), 1.

48. Lalita Pandit, "The Psychology and Aesthetics of Love: Sringara, Bhavana, and Rasadhvani in Gora," in *Rabindranath Tagore: Universality and Tradition*, ed. Patrick Colm Hogan and Lalita Pandit (Madison, NJ: Fairleigh Dickinson University Press, 2003), 141.

49. Sailaza Pal, "Dramatic Aesthetics/Ascetics: The Bhakti Poetry," *Rutgers Journal of Comparative Literature* 3.3–4 (1995–96): 124.

50. *Ibid.*, 127.

51. *Ibid.*, 137.

52. Gupta, *The Philosophy of Rabindranath Tagore*, 78.

53. Qtd. in Gupta, *The Philosophy of Rabindranath Tagore*, 82.

54. Nandi, *Art and Aesthetics of Rabindra Nath Tagore*, 18.

55. Radice, "Never Not an Educator: Tagore as Poet-Teacher," 79.

56. Martha Nussbaum, "Social Justice and Universalism: In Defense of an Aristotelian Account of Human Functioning," *Modern Philology* 90 (1993): 55–57.

57. *Ibid.*, 59.

58. *Ibid.*, 58–59.

59. *Ibid.*, 57.

60. *Ibid.*, 64.

61. See Nussbaum, "Social Justice and Universalism: In Defense of an Aristotelian Account of Human Functioning," *Modern Philology* 90 (1993): 46–73.

Chapter 10

1. Much of this chapter is taken from the introduction to *Wild Poets of Ecstasy*, 18–48.

2. Elisabeth Kübler-Ross, *The Tunnel and the Light* (New York: Avalon, 1999), 57.

3. Allan Kellehear, *Experiences Near Death: Beyond Medicine and Religion* (New York: Oxford University Press, 1996), 62.

4. Alderink, Larry, "Creation and Salvation in Ancient Orphism," *American Classical Studies* 8 (1981): 23.

5. Barbara Ehrenreich, *Dancing in the Streets* (New York: Henry Holt, 2006) 150–151.

6. Andrew Newberg, *Born to Believe: God, Science, and the Origin of Ordinary and Extraordinary Beliefs* (New York: Simon & Schuster, 2006), 200.

7. *Ibid.*, 75.

8. *Ibid.*, 187.

9. T.W. Kjaer et al., "The Neural Basis of the Complex Tasks of Meditation: Neurotransmitter and Neurochemical Considerations," *Brain Research: Cognitive Brain Research* 13 no.2 (2002): 255.

10. Thomas Lewis, Fari Amini, and Richard Lannon, *A General Theory of Love* (New York: Random House, 2000), 90.

11. Ljubomir Aftanas and Semen Golosheykin, "Impact of Regular Meditation Practice on EEG Activity at Rest and During Evoked Negative Emotions," *Neuroscience* 115 (2005): 894.

12. *Ibid.*, 902.

13. *Ibid.*, 894.

14. Belinda Ivanovski and Gin S. Malhi, "The Psychological and Neurophysiological Concomitants of Mindfulness Forms of Meditation," *Acta Neuropsychiatrica* 19 (2007): 76, 81.

15. *Ibid.*, 83.

16. Thomas Lewis, Fari Amini, and Richard Lannon, *A General Theory of Love*, 56.

17. *Ibid.*, 69–81.

18. Gerard Huther, *The Compassionate Brain* (Boston: Shambhala, 2006), 114.

19. *Ibid.*, 114.

20. Abraham Maslow, *Toward a Psychology of Being* (New York: D. Van Nostrand, 1968), 112.

21. Abraham Maslow, *The Farther Reaches of Human Nature*, 101.

22. Abraham Maslow, *Religions, Values and Peak Experiences*, 71.

23. Martin Seligman, *Authentic Happiness* (New York: Simon & Schuster, 2002), 31.

24. *Ibid.*, 35.

25. Sigmund Freud, *Civilzation & Its Discontents*, trans. James Strachey (New York: Norton, 1989), 12–13.

26. Mircea Eliade, *Shamanism: Archaic Techniques of Ecstasy*, trans. Willard R. Trask (Princeton, NJ: Princeton University Press, 1964), 44.

27. Ronald Hayman, *A Life of Jung* (New York: Norton, 1999), 174.

28. Trish Hall, "Seeking a Focus on Joy in the Field of Psychology," *New York Times*, April 28, 1998.

29. Christopher Peterson, *A Primer in Positive Psychology* (New York: Oxford University Press, 2006), 6.

30. William James, *The Varieties of Religious Experience* (New York: Penguin, 1985), 90.

31. *Ibid.*, 79–80.

32. For a more complete discussion see the following works by Victor Frankl: *Man's Search for Ultimate Meaning* (New York: Basic, 2000) and *Man's Search for Meaning* (New York: Simon & Schuster, 1984).

33. Numinous: relating to the spiritual or supernatural, the experience of which is beyond rational comprehension.

34. Pistis: faith.

35. C.G. Jung, *Psychology and Religion* (New Haven, CT: Yale University Press, 1938), 113.

36. Erich Fromm, *The Art of Loving* (New York: Continuum, 1956), 8.

37. *Ibid.*, 4.

38. Mihalyi Csikszentmihalyi, *Flow: The Psychology of Optimal Experience* (New York: Harper & Row, 1990), 30.

39. Ehrenreich, *Dancing in the Streets*, 11.

40. *Ibid.*, 11.

41. *Ibid.*, 27.

42. Evan Zuesse, *Ritual Cosmos: The Sanctification of Life in African Religions* (Athens: Ohio University Press, 1985), 186.

43. *Ibid.*, 189.

44. I. M. Richards, *Ecstatic Religion: An Anthropological Study of Spirit Possession and Shamanism* (New York: Penguin, 1971).

45. Daniel Pinchbeck, *Breaking Open the Head: A Psychedelic Journey into the Heart of Contemporary Shamanism* (New York: Random House, 2002), 37–38.

46. Maslow, *The Farther Reaches of Human Nature*, 103–04.

47. Timothy Leary, *The Politics of Ecstasy*, 87.

48. Ehrenreich, *Dancing in the Streets*, 37.

49. Jung, *Collected Works*, 11:285.

50. Maslow, *The Farther Reaches of Human Nature*, 279.

51. Michel Foucault, *Madness and Civilization: A History of Insanity in the Age of Reason*, trans. Richard Howard (New York: Vintage, 1965), 13.

52. *Ibid.*, 4.

53. Carlo Ginzburg, *Ecstasies: Deciphering the Witches' Sabbatth*, trans. Raymond Rosenthal (Chicago: University of Chicago Press, 1991), 76.

54. Sylvia Brinton Perera, *The Scapegoat Complex* (Toronto: Inner City, 1986), 15.

55. Robert Johnson, *Ecstasy: Understanding the Psychology of Joy* (San Francisco: HarperCollins, 1997), 48.

56. Cited in Bruce C. Daniels, *Puritans at Play: Leisure and Recreation in Colonial New England* (New York: St. Martin's, 1995), 3.

57. Marcel Granet, *Chinese Civilization* (New York: Barnes & Noble, 1957), 170.

58. Gregory Possehl, *The Indus Civilization: A Contemporary Perspective* (Walnut Creek, CA: Altimira Press, 2002), 113.

59. For a more thorough discussion, consult the following: Alain Danielou, *Gods of Love and Ecstasy* (Rochester, VT: Inner Traditions, 1992);

Wolf-Dieter Storl, *Shiva: The Wild God of Power and Ecstasy* (Rochester, VT: Inner Traditions, 2004).

60. Cited in Ehrenreich, *Dancing in the Streets*, 126.

61. David Leeming, *Jealous Gods, Chosen People: The Mythology of the Middle East* (New York: Oxford University Press, 2004), 125.

62. Huston Smith, *The World's Religions* (San Francisco: Harper, 1991), 289.

63. Steven Harris and Gloria Platzner, *Classical Mythology* (New York: McGraw-Hill, 2008), 265.

64. Ehrenreich, *Dancing in the Streets*, 63.

65. Max Radin, "The Kid and Its Mother's Milk," 212.

66. Johnson, *Ecstasy*, 44.

67. Carl W. Ernst, *Sufism* (Boston: Shambhala, 1997), 13.

68. *Ibid.*, 80.

69. *Ibid.*, 11.

70. *Ibid.*, 79.

71. Elaine Pagels, *Beyond Belief: The Secret Gospel of Thomas* (New York: Vintage, 2003), 30.

72. Ehrenreich, *Dancing in the Streets*, 71.

73. *Ibid.*, 75.

74. Rosemarie Taylor-Perry, *The God Who Comes: Dionysian Mysteries Revisited*, 115.

75. Ehrenreich, *Dancing in the Streets*, 81.

76. Ibid.

77. Mikhail Bakhtin, *Rabelais and His World*, trans. Helene Iswolsky (Bloomington: Indiana University Press, 1984), xviii.

78. *Ibid.*, 21.

79. *Ibid.*, 4.

80. *Ibid.*, 39.

81. Ehrenreich, *Dancing in the Streets*, 117.

82. Tim Pilcher, *E: The Incredibly Strange History of Ecstasy* (London: Running Press, 2008), 29.

Chapter 11

1. Just as there were psychologists in the twentieth century who focused on positive states, so have there been literary critics who have offered accounts of such states. One example, among many, is Jack Heitner's *At the Edge of Consciousness: Transpersonal Psychology and Literature* (Edina, MD: Alpha, 1986), which uses an expressly transpersonal theoretical lens.

2. Taken from William Wordsworth, *Selected Poetry of William Wordsworth*, ed. Mark Van Doren (New York: Modern Library, 2002), 152.

3. I could supply citations for all of these

examples, but I will not do so. My purpose is not to shame my fine colleagues but simply to demonstrate the negativity bias in many critical approaches.

4. Peter Barry, *Beginning Theory: An Introduction to Literary and Cultural Theory* (Manchester: Manchester University Press, 1995), 19.

5. David Ayers, *Literary Theory: A Reintroduction* (Malden, MA: Blackwell, 2008), 82.

6. Eagleton, *After Theory*, 29.

7. Eugene Goodheart, *Does Literary Studies Have a Future?* (Madison: University of Wisconsin Press, 1999), 4.

8. Harold Bloom, *The Western Canon* (New York: Riverhead, 1994), 24.

9. Cited in Tony Hilfer, *The New Hegemony in Literary Studies* (Evanston, IL: Northwestern University Press, 2003), 5.

10. Catherine Burgass, "Postmodern Value," in *Postmodern Literary Theory: An Anthology*, ed. Niall Lucy (Malden, MA: Blackwell, 2000), 347.

11. Niall Lucy, introduction to *Postmodern Literary Theory: An Anthology*, 4.

12. Friedrich Nietzsche, *Thus Spoke Zarathustra*, trans. Walter Kaufmann (New York: Modern Library, 1995), 91.

13. Jean-Francois Lyotard, *The Postmodern Condition: A Report on Knowledge*, trans. Geoff Bennington and Brian Massumi (Manchester: Manchester University Press, 1984), xxiv.

14. Jean-Francois Lyotard, "Defining the Postmodern," in *Postmodernism: ICA Documents*, ed. Lisa Appignanesi (New York: Free Association Books, 1989), 9.

15. *Ibid.*, 9.

16. *Ibid.*, 9.

17. Burgass, "Postmodern Value," 354.

18. Eagleton, *After Theory*, 16.

19. Cited in Goodheart, *Does Literary Studies Have a Future?* 13.

20. Marjorie Garber, *Academic Instincts* (Princeton, NJ: Princeton University Press, 2001), 42.

21. Burgass, "Postmodern Value," 354.

22. *Ibid.*, 357.

23. Jonathan Haidt, *The Happiness Hypothesis: Finding Modern Truth in Ancient Happiness* (New York: Basic Books, 2006), 12.

24. Janice Radway, *A Feeling for Books: The Book-of-the-Month Club, Literary Taste, and Middle-Class Desire* (Chapel Hill: University of North Carolina Press, 1997).

25. Jane F. Thrailkill, *Affecting Fictions* (Cambridge, MA: Harvard University Press, 2007).

26. Philip Fisher, *The Vehement Passions* (Princeton, NJ: Princeton University Press, 2002).

27. M.M. Bakhtin and P.N. Medvedev, *The Formal Method in Literary Scholarship*, trans. A.J. Wehrle (Baltimore, MD: Johns Hopkins University Press, 1978), 37.

28. *Ibid.*, 38.

29. Ryan Cull, "Beyond the Cheated Eye: Dickinson's Lyric Sociality," *Nineteenth-Century Literature* 65 (2010): 38–64.

30. Nouri Gana, "War, Poetry, Mourning: Darwish, Adonis, Iraq," *Public Culture* 22 (2010): 33–65.

31. Roland Barthes, "The Death of the Author," in *Twentieth-Century Literary Theory*, trans. Stephen Heath and ed. K.M. Newton (New York: St. Martin's, 1997), 122.

32. Jacques Derrida, *Limited Incorporated*, trans. Jeffrey Mehlman and Samuel Weber (Evanston, IL: Northwestern University Press, 1988), 6.

33. Jacques Derrida, *Speech and Phenomena, and Other Essays on Husserl's Theory of Signs* (Evanston, IL: Northwestern University Press, 1973), 266.

34. Peter Salovey, David Caruso, and John D. Mayer, "Emotional Intelligence in Practice," in *Positive Psychology in Practice*, ed. P. Alex Linley and Stephen Joseph (Hobkoen, NJ: Wiley, 2004), 447.

35. Howard Gardner, *Frames of Mind: The Theory of Multiple Intelligences* (New York: Basic Books, 1993), 55.

36. Daniel Goleman, *Emotional Intelligence* (New York: Bantam Books, 1995), 43.

37. *Ibid.*, 41.

38. *Ibid.*, 36.

39. Barbara Fredrickson, *Positivity* (New York: Three Rivers Press, 2009), 19.

40. Barbara Fredrickson, "What Good Are Positive Emotions?" *Review of General Psychology* 2 (1998): 300–319.

41. Fredrickson, *Positivity*, 24.

42. *Ibid.*, 18.

43. *Ibid.*, 90.

44. George Valliant, *Spiritual Evolution: A Scientific Defense of Faith* (New York: Broadway Books, 2008), 12.

45. Valliant, *Spiritual Evolution*, 12.

46. For a complete discussion, see Christopher Peterson and Martin Seligman, *Character Strengths and Virtues: A Handbook and Classification* (New York: Oxford University Press, 2004).

47. Barbara Fredrickson, "Gratitude, Like Other Positive Emotions, Broadens and Builds," in *The Psychology of Gratitude*, ed. Robert Emmons and Michael McCullough (New York: Oxford University Press, 2004), 152.

48. Maslow, The Farther Reaches of Human Nature, 74.

49. Valliant, *Spiritual Evolution*, 123.

50. Jean Baudrillard, *The Ecstasy of Communication*, ed. Sylvere Lotringer, trans. B. Schutze and C.Schutze (Paris: Editions Galilee, 1988).

51. John Wilson, "Trauma, Optimal Experiences, and Integrative Psychological States," in *The Posttraumatic Self: Restoring Meaning and Wholeness to Personality*, ed. John Wilson (New York: Routledge, 2006), 224.

52. *Ibid.*, 232.

53. *Ibid.*, 234.

54. Lucy, introduction to *Postmodern Literary Theory: An Anthology*, 7.

55. Marjean D. Purinton, "Postmodern Romanticism: the Recuperation of Conceptual Romanticism in Jeanette Winterson's Postmodern Novel The Passion," in *Romanticism Across the Disciplines*, ed. Larry H. Peer (Lanham, MD: University Press of America, 1998), 68.

56. *Ibid.*, 41.

57. *Ibid.*, 41.

58. *Ibid.*, 212.

59. *Ibid.*, 212.

60. *Ibid.*, 212.

61. Miller and C'de Baca, *Quantum Change*, 14.

62. *Collected Works*, 11:285.

63. James Pawelski, *The Dynamic Individualism of William James* (Albany, NY: SUNY Press, 2007), 3.

64. *Ibid.*, 152.

65. *Ibid.*, 152.

66. *Ibid.*, 157.

Chapter 12

1. See Paul Ricoeur, *Freud and Philosophy: An Essay on Interpretation* (New Haven, CT: Yale University Press, 1970).

2. *Ibid.*, 40.

3. James Pawelski and D. J. Moores, eds., *The Eudaimonic Turn: Well-Being in Literary Studies* (Madison, NJ: Fairleigh Dickinson University Press, 2013).

4. Eve Kosofsky Sedgwick, "Paranoid Reading and Reparative Reading: or, You're so Paranoid, You Probably Think This Introduction Is About You," in *Novel Gazing: Queer Readings in Fiction*, ed. Eve Kosofsky Sedgwick, 1–37 (Durham, NC: Duke University Press, 1997), 7.

5. Bruno Latour, "Why Has Critique Run Out of Steam? From Matters of Fact to Matters of Concern," *Critical Inquiry* 30.2 (2004): 225–48.

6. See "After Suspicion," *Profession* (2009): 28–35, and also "Suspicious Minds," *Poetics Today* 32.2 (2010): 215–34.

7. Robert Barth, *Romanticism and Transcendence: Wordsworth, Coleridge and the Religious Imagination* (Columbia: University of Missouri Press, 2003), 4.

8. *Ibid.*, 59.

9. Philip Fisher, *Wonder, the Rainbow, and the Aesthetics of Rare Experiences* (Cambridge, MA: Harvard University Press, 1998), 1, 8.

10. Charles Altieri, *The Particulars of Rapture: An Aesthetics of the Affects* (Ithaca, NY: Cornell University Press, 2003), 5.

11. Eagleton, *After Theory*, 6.

12. Peterson, *A Primer in Positive Psychology*, 12.

13. Ingvild Jorgensen, and Hilde Eileen Nafstad, "Positive Psychology: Historical, Philosophical, and Epistemological Perspectives," in *Positive Psychology in Practice*, ed. P. Alex Linley and Stephen Joseph (Hoboken, NJ: Wiley, 2004), 25.

14. Adam Potkay, *The Story of Joy: From the Bible to Late Romanticism* (New York: Cambridge University Press, 2007), 226.

15. Terry Eagleton, *After Theory* (New York: Basic Books, 2003), 56.

16. Susan Rowland, introduction to *Psyche and the Arts: Jungian Approaches to Architecture, Literature, Film, and Painting* (New York: Routledge, 2008), 2.

17. Anthony Stevens, *Jung: A Very Short Introduction* (New York: Oxford University Press, 1994), 52.

18. Jorgensen, Ingvild and Hilde Eileen Nafstad, "Positive Psychology: Historical, Philosophical, and Epistemological Perspectives," in *Positive Psychology in Practice*, ed. P. Alex Linley and Stephen Joseph (Hoboken, NJ: Wiley, 2004), 15.

19. P. Alex Linley and Stephen Joseph, "Toward a Theoretical Foundation for Positive Psychology in Practice," in *Positive Psychology in Practice*, 715.

20. Maslow, *Toward a Psychology of Being*, 153.

21. *Ibid.*, 101–114.

22. Maslow, *The Farther Reaches of Human Nature*, 308.

Bibliography

Abrams, M.H. *Natural Supernaturalism*. New York: Norton, 1971.

Abu-Bakr, Omaima. "Abrogation of the Mind in the Poetry of Jalal al–Din Rumi." *Alif: Journal of Comparative Poetics* 14 (1994): 37–63.

Aftanas, Ljubomir, and Semen Golosheykin. "Impact of Regular Meditation Practice on EEG Activity at Rest and During Evoked Negative Emotions." *Neuroscience* 115 (2005): 893–909.

Ahmad, Saladdin. "What Is Sufism?" *Forum Philosophicum* 13.2 (2008): 233–51.

Alderink, Larry. "Creation and Salvation in Ancient Orphism." *American Classical Studies* 8 (1981): 1–96.

Algoe, Sara, and Jonathan Haidt. "Witnessing Excellence in Action: The 'Other-Praising' Emotions of Elevation, Gratitude, and Admiration." *The Journal of Positive Psychology* 4.2 (2009): 105–127.

Alighieri, Dante. *The Divine Comedy*. Ed. John Ciardi. New York: New American Library, 2003.

Altieri, Charles. *The Particulars of Rapture: An Aesthetics of the Affects*. Ithaca, NY: Cornell University Press, 2003.

_____. *Postmodernisms Now: Essays on Contemporaneity in the Arts*. University Park: Pennsylvania University Press, 1998.

Antal. *Antal and Her Path of Love*. Trans. Vidya Dehejia. Albany, NY: SUNY Press, 1990.

Aristotle. *The Nicomachean Ethics*. Ed. J.L. Ackrill and J.O. Urmson, trans. David Ross. New York: Oxford University Press, 1998.

Askin, Denise T. "Whitman's Theory of Evil: A Clue to His Use of Paradox." *Emerson Society Quarterly* 28.2 (1982): 121–32.

Aspiz, Harold. *Walt Whitman and the Body Beautiful*. Chicago: University of Illinois Press, 1980.

Asselineau, Roger. *The Evolution of Walt Whitman*. Iowa City: Iowa University Press, 1999.

Ayers, David. *Literary Theory: A Reintroduction*. Malden, MA: Blackwell, 2008.

Bakhtin, Mikhail. *Rabelais and His World*. Trans. Helene Iswolsky. Bloomington: Indiana University Press, 1984.

_____, and P.N. Medvedev, *The Formal Method in Literary Scholarship*. Trans. A.J. Wehrle. Baltimore, MD: Johns Hopkins University Press, 1978.

Barnstone, Aliki. *Changing Rapture: Emily Dickinson's Poetic Development*. Hanover, NH: University Press of New England, 2006.

Barnstone, Willis. *The Poetics of Ecstasy: Varieties of Ekstasis from Sappho to Borges*. New York: Holmes & Meier, 1983.

Barry, Peter. *Beginning Theory: An Introduction to Literary and Cultural Theory*. Manchester: Manchester University Press, 1995.

Barth, Robert. *Romanticism and Transcendence: Wordsworth, Coleridge and the Religious Imagination*. Columbia: University of Missouri Press, 2003.

Barthes, Roland. "The Death of the Author." In *Twentieth-Century Literary Theory*, trans. Stephen Heath, ed. K.M. Newton, 120–123. New York: St. Martin's, 1997.

_____. *Empire of Signs*. Trans. Richard Howard. New York: Hill and Wang, 1982.

Bate, Jonathan. *Romantic Ecology: Wordsworth and the Environmental Tradition*. New York: Routledge, 1991.

Baudrillard, Jean. *The Ecstasy of Communication*. Ed. Sylvere Lotringer, trans. B. Schutze and C. Schutze. Paris: Editions Galilee, 1988.

Baym, Nina. *American Women of Letters and the Nineteenth-Century Sciences: Styles of Affiliation*. New Brunswick, NJ: Rutgers University Press, 2002.

Benvenuto, Bice, and Roger Kennedy. *The*

Works of Jacques Lacan: An Introduction. London: Free Association Books, 1986.

Berlin, Isaiah. *The Roots of Romanticism.* Princeton, NJ: Princeton University Press, 1999.

Beull, Lawrence. *The Environmental Imagination: Thoreau, Nature Writing, and the Formation of American Culture.* Cambridge, MA: Belknap Press of Harvard University Press, 1995.

Blake, William. *Blakes's Poetry and Designs.* Ed. Mary Lynn Johnson and John E. Grant. New York: Norton, 1979.

Bloom, Harold. *The Western Canon.* New York: Riverhead, 1994.

Budelmann, Felix. "Introducing Greek Lyric." In *The Cambridge Companion to Greek Lyric,* ed. Felix Budelmann, 5–23. New York: Cambridge University Press, 2009.

Burgass, Catherine. "Postmodern Value." In *Postmodern Literary Theory: An Anthology,* edited by Niall Lucy, 347–359. Malden, MA: Blackwell, 2000.

Carter, Steve. "Emily Dickinson and Mysticism." *Emerson Society Quarterly* 24.2 (1978): 83–95.

Chari, V.K. "Whitman Criticism in the Light of Indian Poetics." In *Walt Whitman: The Centennial Essays,* ed. Ed Folsom, 240–50. Iowa City: University of Iowa Press, 1994.

Chaudhuri, Rosinka. "The Flute, Gerontion, and Subalternist Misreadings of Tagore." *Social Text* 22.1 (2004): 103–22.

Clark, Humphrey. Preface to *Songs of Milarepa,* xi–xv, ed. and trans. Humphrey Clark. New York: Dover, 2003.

Clinton, Jerome W. "Rumi in America." *Edebiyat* 10 (1999): 149–54.

Cody, John. *After Great Pain: The Inner Life of Emily Dickinson.* Cambridge, MA: Harvard University Press, 1971.

Collins, Michael. "History and the Postcolonial: Rabindranath Tagore's Reception in London, 1912–1913." *International Journal of the Humanities* 4.9 (2007): 71–83.

Conrad, Angela. *The Wayward Nun of Amherst: Emily Dickinson and Medieval Mystical Women.* New York: Garland, 2000.

Conrad, Joseph. *Heart of Darkness & The Secret Sharer.* New York: Bantam, 1969.

Cooney, William. "The Death Poetry of Emily Dickinson." *Omega* 37.3 (1998): 241–49.

Corkery, Daniel. "The Bardic Schools." In *The Bardic Sourcebook: Inspirational Legacy and Teachings of the Ancient Celts,* 26–42, ed. John Matthews. London: Blandford, 1998.

Csikszentmihalyi, Mihalyi. *Flow: The Psychology of Optimal Experience.* New York: Harper & Row, 1990.

Cross, Frank Moore, and David Freedman. *Studies in Ancient Yahwistic Poetry.* Missoula, MT: Scholars Press, 1975.

Cull, Ryan. "Beyond the Cheated Eye: Dickinson's Lyric Sociality." *Nineteenth-Century Literature* 65 (2010): 38–64.

Damasio, Antonio. *Looking for Spinoza: Joy, Sorrow, and the Feeling Brain.* New York: Harvest, 2003.

Danielou, Alain. *Gods of Love and Ecstasy.* Rochester, VT: Inner Traditions, 1992.

Daniels, Bruce C. *Puritans at Play: Leisure and Recreation in Colonial New England.* New York: St. Martin's, 1995.

David, A.P. *The Dance of the Muses.* New York: Oxford University Press, 2006.

Davis, Dick. "Narrative and Doctrine in the First Story of Rumi's Mathnawi." *Journal of Semitic Studies* 12 (2000): 93–104.

_____. "Sufism and Poetry: A Marriage of Convenience." *Edebiyat: Journal of Middle Eastern Literatures* 10.2 (1999): 279–92.

Dehejia, Vidya. *Antal and Her Path of Love.* Albany, NY: SUNY Press, 1990.

Delacroix, Henri. *Etudes d'historie et de psychologie du mysticism: les grandes mystiques Chretiens.* Paris: Felix Alcan, 1908.

Dennis, Ian. "Romantic Joy." *Anthropoetics: The Journal of Generative Anthropology* 16.1 (2010): 19–28.

Derrida, Jacques. *Limited Incorporated.* Ed. Gerald Graff, trans. Jeffrey Mehlman and Samuel Weber. Evanston, IL: Northwestern University Press, 1988.

_____. *Speech and Phenomena, and Other Essays on Husserl's Theory of Signs.* Evanston, IL: Northwestern University Press, 1973.

Diagnostic and Statistical Manual of Mental Disorders—DSM-IV-TR. Washington, DC: American Psychiatric Association, 2000.

Dickinson, Emily. *The Poems of Emily Dickinson.* Ed. Thomas H. Johnson, Cambridge, MA: The Belknap Press of Harvard University Press, Copyright © 1951, 1955, 1979, 1983 by the President and Fellows of Harvard College.

Diehl, Joanne Feit. "The Poetics of Loss: Erotic Melancholia in Agamben and Dickinson." *American Imago* 66.3 (2009): 369–81.

Dommergues, Andre. "Rabindranath Tagore's Aesthetics." *Commonwealth Essays & Studies* 7.2 (1985): 1–10.

Durkheim, Emile. *The Elementary Forms of the Religious Life.* New York: Free Press, 1915.

Dutta, Krishna, and Andrew Robinson. *Ra-*

bindranath Tagore: The Myriad-Minded Man. London: Bloomsbury, 2009.

Eagleton, Terry. *After Theory*. New York: Basic Books, 2003.

_____. *The Ideology of the Aesthetic*. Cambridge, MA: Basil Blackwell, 1990.

Ehrenreich, Barbara. *Bright-Sided: How the Relentless Promotion of Positive Thinking Has Undermined America*. New York: Metropolitan, 2009.

_____. *Dancing in the Streets*. New York: Henry Holt, 2006.

Eliade, Mircea. *Shamanism: Archaic Techniques of Ecstasy*. Trans. Willard R. Trask. Princeton, NJ: Princeton University Press, 1964.

Eliot, J., ed. *Interdisciplinary Perspectives on Hope*. New York: Nova Science, 2005.

Elisha, Perrin. *The Conscious Body: A Psychoanalytic Exploration of the Body in Therapy*. Washington, DC: American Psychological Association, 2011.

Ellis, John. "The Relevant Context of a Literary Text." In *Twentieth-Century Literary Theory*, ed. K.M. Newton, 34–37. New York: St. Martin's, 1997.

El-Rouayheb, Khaled. "Heresy and Sufism in the Arab-Islamic World, 1550–1750: Some Preliminary Observations." *Bulletin of the School of Oriental & African Studies* 73.3 (2010): 357–380.

El-Zein, Amira. "Spiritual Consumption in the United States." *Islam & Christian-Muslim Relations* 11.1 (2000): 71–85.

Emmons, Robert, and Michael McCullough, eds. *The Psychology of Gratitude*. New York: Oxford University Press, 2004.

Emsley, Sarah. "Is Emily Dickinson a Metaphysical Poet?" *Canadian Review of American Studies* 33.3 (2003): 249–65.

Ergin, Nevit, and Will Johnson. Introduction to *The Rubais of Rumi: Insane with Love*, by Rumi. Trans. Nevit Ergin and Will Johnson. 5–20. Rochester, VT: Inner Traditions, 2007.

Ernst, Carl W. *Sufism*. Boston, Shambhala, 1997.

Farland, Maria Magdalena. "'That Tritest/ Brightest Truth': Emily Dickinson's Anti-Sentimentality." *Nineteenth-Century Literature* 53.3 (1998): 364–89.

Felski, Rita. "After Suspicion." *Profession* (2009): 28–35.

_____. "Suspicious Minds." *Poetics Today* 32.2 (2010): 215–34.

Ferreter, Luke. *Towards a Christian Literary Theory*. New York: Palgrave, 2003.

Fiedler, Leslie. "Is There a Majority Literature?" *The College English Association Critic* 36 (1974): 3–8.

Fisher, Philip. *Wonder, the Rainbow, and the Aesthetics of Rare Experiences*. Cambridge, MA: Harvard University Press, 1998.

Fiske, Amos Kidder. *The Great Epic of Israel: The Web of Myth, Legend, History, Law, Oracle, Wisdom and Poetry of the Ancient Hebrews*. New York: Sturgis, 1911.

Flanagan, Owen. *The Really Hard Problem: Meaning in a Material World*. Cambridge, MA: MIT Press, 2007.

Flanagan, Sabina. Introduction to *Secrets of God: Writings of Hildegard of Bingen*, 1–7, ed. and trans. Sabina Flanagan. Boston: Shambhala, 1996.

Foakes, R.A. "Beyond the Visible World: Wordsworth and Coleridge in Lyrical Ballads." *Romanticism* 5.1 (1999): 23–32.

Foucault, Michel. *Madness and Civilization: A History of Insanity in the Age of Reason*. Trans. Richard Howard. New York: Vintage, 1965.

Franke, William. "'The Missing All': Emily Dickinson's Apophatic Poetics." *Christianity and Literature* 58.1 (2008): 61–80.

Frankl, Victor. *Man's Search for Meaning*. New York: Simon & Schuster, 1984.

Fredrickson, Barbara. "Gratitude, Like Other Positive Emotions, Broadens and Builds." In *The Psychology of Gratitude*, ed. Robert Emmons and Michael McCullough, 145–166. New York: Oxford University Press, 2004.

_____. *Positivity*. New York: Three Rivers Press, 2009.

_____. "What Good Are Positive Emotions?" *Review of General Psychology* 2 (1998): 300–319.

Freud, Sigmund. *Civilzation & Its Discontents*. Trans. James Strachey. New York: Norton, 1989.

Fromm, Erich. *The Art of Loving*. New York: Continuum, 1956.

Fuller, Robert. *Spirituality in the Flesh: Bodily Sources of Religion*. Oxford: Oxford University Press, 2008.

_____. *Wonder: from Emotion to Spirituality*. Chapel Hill: University of North Carolina Press, 2006.

Gana, Nouri. "War, Poetry, Mourning: Darwish, Adonis, Iraq." *Public Culture* 22 (2010): 33–65.

Gandz, Solomon. "The Dawn of Prolegomena to a History of Unwritten Literature." *Osiris* 7 (1939): 261–522.

Garber, Marjorie. *Academic Instincts*. Princeton: Princeton University Press, 2001.

Gardner, Howard. *Frames of Mind: The Theory of Multiple Intelligences.* New York: Basic Books, 1993.

Garrard, Greg. *Ecocriticism.* New York: Routledge, 2008.

General Social Survey. Chicago: National Opinion Research Center, 1989.

Gentili, Bruno. *Poetry and Its Public in Ancient Greece: From Homer to the Fifth Century.* Trans. A. Thomas Cole. Baltimore, MD: Johns Hopkins University Press, 1988.

Gill, Stephen. *William Wordsworth: A Life.* New York: Oxford University Press, 1990.

_____. "Wordsworth's 'Never Failing Principle of Joy.'" *English Language History* 34.2 (1967): 208–24.

Gilmore, Paul. "Romantic Electricity, or the Materiality of Aesthetics." *American Literature* 76.3 (2004): 467–94.

Ginzburg, Carlo. *Ecstasies: Deciphering the Witches' Sabbath.* Trans. Raymond Rosenthal. Chicago: University of Chicago Press, 1991.

Goleman, Daniel. *Emotional Intelligence.* New York: Bantam Books, 1995.

Goodheart, Eugene. *Does Literary Studies Have a Future?* Madison: University of Wisconsin Press, 1999.

Granet, Marcel. *Chinese Civilization.* New York: Barnes & Noble, 1957.

Gravil, Richard. *Wordsworth's Bardic Vocation, 1787–1842.* New York: Palgrave Macmillan, 2003.

Grof, Stanislav. *The Holotropic Mind.* New York: HarperCollins, 1990.

Guha, Ranajit. *History at the Limit of World-History.* New York: Columbia University Press, 2002.

Gupta, Kalyan Sen. *The Philosophy of Rabindranath Tagore.* London: Ashgate, 2005.

Haidt, Jonathan. "Elevation and the Positive Psychology of Morality." In *Flourishing: Positive Psychology and the Life Well-Lived,* eds. Corey Keyes and Jonathan Haidt, 275–289. Washington, DC: American Psychological Association, 2003.

_____. *The Happiness Hypothesis: Finding Modern Truth in Ancient Happiness.* New York: Basic Books, 2006.

Hall, Trish. "Seeking a Focus on Joy in the Field of Psychology." *New York Times,* April 28, 1998.

Hamid, Farooq. "Storytelling Techniques in the Masnavi-yi Ma'navi of Mowlana Jalal Al-Din Rumi: Wayward Narrative or Logical Progression?" *Iranian Studies* 32.1 (1999): 27–49.

Happold, F.C. *Mysticism: A Study and an Anthology.* New York: Penguin, 1990.

Haq, Kaiser. "The Philosophy of Rabindranth Tagore." *Asiatic* 4.1 (2010): 27–40.

Hargis, Donald. "The Rhapsode." *Quarterly Journal of Speech* 56.4 (1970): 388–397.

Harlow, Harry F., and Stephen J. Suomi. "Social Recovery by Isolation-Reared Monkeys." *Proceedings of the National Academy of Science of the United States of America* 68.7 (1971): 1534–1538.

Harris, Steven, and Gloria Platzner. *Classical Mythology.* 5th ed. New York: McGraw-Hill, 2008.

Hart, George L. *The Poems of Ancient Tamil: Their Milieu and Their Sanskrit Counterparts.* Berkeley: University of California Press, 1975.

Hass, Robert. Introduction to *The Essential Haiku,* ed. and trans. Robert Hass, ix–xvi. Hopewell, NJ: Ecco, 1994.

Hatch, Doxey. "'I Tramp a Perpetual Journey': Walt Whitman's Insights for Psychology." *Journal of Humanistic Psychology* 51.1 (2011): 7–27.

Hatina, Meir. "Where East Meets West: Sufism, Cultural Rapprochement, and Politics." *International Journal of Middle East Studies* 39 (2007): 389–409.

Hawley, John Stratton. Afterword to *Mirabai: Ecstatic Poems,* 67–95, trans. Robert Bly and Jane Hirshfield. Boston: Beacon, 2004.

_____. *Three Bhakti Voices: Mirabai, Surdas, and Kabir in Their Time and Ours.* New York: Oxford University Press, 2005.

Hayman, Ronald. *A Life of Jung.* New York: Norton, 1999.

Heidegger, Martin. *Basic Writings.* Trans. Joan Stambaugh. Ed. David Farrell Krell. 1962. New York: HarperCollins, 1993.

Heitner, Jack. *At the Edge of Consciousness: Transpersonal Psychology and Literature.* Edina, MD: Alpha, 1986.

Hilfer, Tony. *The New Hegemony in Literary Studies.* Evanston, IL: Northwestern University Press, 2003.

Hirshfield, Jane. Introduction to *Mirabai: Ecstatic Poems,* xiii–xvi, trans. Robert Bly and Jane Hirshfield. Boston: Beacon Press, 2004.

Hirshhorn, Norbert, and Polly Longworth. "'Medicine Posthumous': A New Look at Emily Dickinson's Medical Conditions." *The New England Quarterly* 69.2 (1996): 299–316.

Hitchcock, John. *Healing Our Worldview.* West Chester, PA: Chrysalis, 1999.

Hollenback, Jess Byron. *Mysticism: Experience,*

Response, and Empowerment. University Park: Penn State University Press, 1996.

Hoffman, Albert. *LSD: My Problem Child*. Sarasota, FL: MAPS, 2005.

Holland, Norman N. *Literature and the Brain*. Gainesville, FL: PsyArt Foundation, 2009.

Hunter, Richard, and Ian Rutherford. Introduction to *Wandering Poets in Ancient Greek Culture*, eds. Richard Hunter and Ian Rutherford, 1–22. New York: Cambridge University Press, 2009.

Hutchinson, George B. *The Ecstatic Whitman*. Columbus: Ohio State University Press, 1986.

Huther, Gerard. *The Compassionate Brain*. Boston: Shambhala, 2006.

Huxley, Aldous. *The Perennial Philosophy*. New York: Harper, 1944.

Ingram, Brannon. "Sufis, Scholars, and Scapegoats: Rashid Ahmad Gangohi (d. 1905) and Deobandi Critique of Sufism." *Muslim World* 99.3 (2009): 478–501.

Irwin, John. "Whitman: Hieroglyphic Bibles and Phallic Songs." In *Leaves of Grass and Other Writings*, ed. Michael Moon, 863–72. New York: Norton, 2002.

Iser, Wolfgang. *The Act of Reading: A Theory of Aesthetic Response*. Baltimore, MD: Johns Hopkins University Press, 1978.

Ivanovski, Belinda, and Gin S. Malhi. "The Psychological and Neurophysiological Concomitants of Mindfulness Forms of Meditation." *Acta Neuropsychiatrica* 19 (2007): 76–91.

Jalali, Ahmad. "Jalaluddin Rumi's Religious Understanding: A Prelude to Dialogue in the Realm of Religious Thought." *Diogenes* 50.4 (2003): 127–134.

James, William. *The Varieties of Religious Experience*. New York: Penguin, 1985.

Jamison, Leslie. "'A Thousand Willing Forms': The Evolution of Whitman's Wounded Bodies." *Studies in American Fiction* 35.1 (2007): 21–42.

Johnson, Robert. *Ecstasy: Understanding the Psychology of Joy*. San Francisco: Harper-Collins, 1997.

Johnson, Thomas H. *Emily Dickinson: An Interpretive Biography*. Cambridge, MA: Harvard University Press, 1955.

Jorgensen, Ingvild, and Hilde Eileen Nafstad. "Positive Psychology: Historical, Philosophical, and Epistemological Perspectives." In *Positive Psychology in Practice*, eds. P. Alex Linley and Stephen Joseph, 15–34. Hoboken, NJ: Wiley, 2004.

Juan de la Cruz. *The Dark Night of the Soul*.

Trans. Fr. Benedict Zimmerman. London: Thomas Baker, 1916.

Jung, C.G. *The Collected Works of C.G. Jung*. 20 vols. Ed. William McGuire. Trans. R.F.C. Hull. Princeton, NJ: Princeton University Press, 1983.

_____. *Psychology and Religion*. New Haven, CT: Yale University Press, 1938.

Kabir. *Songs of Kabir*. Translated by Rabindranath Tagore. New York: Macmillan, 1916.

Kakar, Sudhir. *The Inner World: A Psychoanalytic Study of Childhood and Society in India*. New York: Oxford University Press, 1981.

Katz, Steven T. *Mysticism and Religious Traditions*. New York: Oxford University Press, 1983.

Kavanaugh, Kieran, and Otilio Rodriguez. Introduction to *The Collected Works of St. John of the Cross*, ed. and trans. Kieran Kavanaugh and Otilio Rodriguez, 9–43. Washington, DC: ICS Publications, 1991.

Kellehear, Allan. *Experiences Near Death: Beyond Medicine and Religion*. New York: Oxford University Press, 1996.

Khan, Hazrat Inayat. *The Inner Life*. Boston: Shambhala, 1997.

Killingsworth, Jimmie. "'As if the Beasts Spoke': The Animal/Animist/Animated Walt Whitman." *Walt Whitman Quarterly Review* 28.1 (2010): 19–35.

Kjaer, T.W., et al. "The Neural Basis of the Complex Tasks of Meditation: Neurotransmitter and Neurochemical Considerations." *Brain Research: Cognitive BrainResearch* 13, no. 2 (2002): 255–59.

Klatt, L.S. "The Electric Whitman." *Southern Review* 44.2 (2008): 321–31.

Kübler-Ross, Elisabeth. *The Tunnel and the Light*. New York: Avalon, 1999.

Kucuk, Hulya. "A Brief History of Western Sufism." *Asian Journal of Social Science* 36.2 (2008): 292–320.

Laing, R.D. *The Divided Self*. New York: Penguin, 1990.

Lakoff, George, and Mark Johnson. *Metaphors We Live by*. Chicago: University of Chicago Press, 1980.

Laski, Marghanita. *Ecstasy in Secular and Religious Experiences*. Los Angeles: Tarcher, 1961.

Latour, Bruno. "Why Has Critique Run Out of Steam? From Matters of Fact to Matters of Concern." *Critical Inquiry* 30.2 (2004): 225–48.

Lawson, Andrew. "'Spending for Vast Returns':

Sex, Class, and Commerce in the First *Leaves of Grass*." *American Literature* 75.2 (2003): 335–66.

Leary, Timothy. *The Politics of Ecstasy*. Oakland, CA: Ronin, 1998.

Lee, Maurice. "Dickinson's Superb Surprise." *Raritan* 28.1 (2008): 45–67.

Leeming, David. *Jealous Gods, Chosen People: The Mythology of the Middle East*. New York: Oxford University Press, 2004.

Lewis, Franklin. *Rumi: Past and Present, East and West: The Life, Teachings and Poetry of Jalal al-Din Rumi*. Oxford: Oneworld, 2008.

Lewis, I.M. *Ecstatic Religion: An Anthropological Study of Spirit Possession and Shamanism*. New York: Penguin, 1971.

Lewis, Thomas, Fari Amini, and Richard Lannon. *A General Theory of Love*. New York: Random House, 2000.

Linley, P. Alex, and Stephen Joseph. "Toward a Theoretical Foundation for Positive Psychology in Practice." In *Positive Psychology in Practice*, eds. P. Alex Linley and Stephen Joseph, 713–731. Hoboken, NJ: Wiley, 2004.

Loving, Jerome. *Walt Whitman: The Song of Himself*. Berkeley: University Press of California, 1999.

Lucy, Niall. Introduction to *Postmodern Literary Theory: An Anthology*, ed. Niall Lucy, 1–39. Malden, MA: Blackwell, 2000.

Ludwig, Theodore M. *The Sacred Paths of the East*. Upper Saddle River, NJ: Prentice Hall, 2001.

Lundin, Roger. *Emily Dickinson and the Art of Belief*. Grand Rapids, MI: William B. Eerdmans, 1998.

Lundquist, Susanne Evertsen. *Native American Literatures: An Introduction*. New York: Continuum, 2004.

Lyotard, Jean-Francois. "Defining the Postmodern." In *Postmodernism: ICA Documents*, ed. Lisa Appignanesi, 7–10. New York: Free Association Books, 1989.

_____. *The Postmodern Condition: A Report on Knowledge*. Trans. Geoff Bennington and Brian Massumi. Manchester: Manchester University Press, 1984.

Manheim, Daniel L. "'Have We Not a Hymn?' Dickinson and the Rhetoric of New England Revivalism." *The New England Quarterly* 78.3 (2005): 377–406.

Maslan, Mark. *Whitman Possessed: Poetry, Sexuality, and Popular Authority*. Baltimore, MD: Johns Hopkins University Press, 2001.

Maslow, Abraham. *The Farther Reaches of Human Nature*. New York: Penguin, 1976.

_____. *Religions, Values and Peak Experiences*. New York: Penguin, 1970.

_____. *Toward a Psychology of Being*. New York: D. Van Nostrand, 1968.

Mason, Emma. *The Cambridge Introduction to William Wordsworth*. New York: Cambridge University Press, 2010.

Matthews, John. "The Story of the Bards." In *The Bardic Sourcebook: Inspirational Legacy and Teachings of the Ancient Celts*, ed. John Matthews, 11–23. London: Blandford, 1998.

May, Rollo. *Love and Will*. New York: Dell, 1969.

McDermott, John F. "Emily Dickinson Revisited: A Study of Periodicity in Her Work." *American Journal of Psychiatry* 158:5 (2001): 686–90.

Merkur, Dan. *The Ecstatic Imagination: Psychedelic Experiences and the Psychoanalysis of Self-Actualization*. Albany, NY: SUNY Press, 1998.

Milarepa, Jetsun. *The Message of Milarepa*. Trans. Humphrey Clark. London: John Murray, 1958.

Miller, Christopher. "Wordsworth's Anatomies of Surprise." *Studies in Romanticism* 46.4 (2007): 409–31.

Miller, James. *Leaves of Grass: America's Lyric-Epic of Self and Democracy*. New York: Twayne, 1992.

Miller, James, Karl Shapiro, and Bernice Slote. *Start with the Sun: Studies in the Whitman Tradition*. Lincoln: University of Nebraska Press, 1960.

Miller, William, and Janet C'de Baca. *Quantum Change*. New York: Guilford Press, 2001.

Milnes, Tim, and Kerry Sinanan. Introduction to *Romanticism, Sincerity and Authenticity*, 1–28. Eds. Tim Milnes and Kerry Sinanan. New York: Palgrave Macmillan, 2010.

Milton, John. *Paradise Lost*. Ed. Scott Elledge. 2d ed. New York: Norton, 1993.

Mirabai. *Mirabai: Saint and Singer of India*. Trans. Anath Nath Basu. London: George Allen, 1934.

Mojaddedi, Jawid. Introduction to *The Masnawi: Book One* by Rumi, ed. and trans. Jawid Mojaddedi, xi–xxx. New York: Oxford University Press, 2008.

Moon, Michael. "The Twenty-Ninth Bather: Identy, Fluidity, Gender, and Sexuality In Section 11 of 'Song of Myself.'" In *Leave of Grass and Other Writings*, ed. Michael Moon, 855–63. New York: Norton, 2002.

Moores, D.J. *The Dark Enlightenment: Jung, Romanticism and the Repressed Other*. Madison, NJ: Fairleigh Dickinson University Press, 2010.

_____. *Mystical Discourse in Wordsworth and Whitman: A Transatlantic Bridge.* Dudley, MA: Peeters, 2006.

_____, ed. *Wild Poets of Ecstasy: An Anthology of Ecstatic Verse.* Nevada City, CA: Pelican Pond Press, 2011

Morrison, Toni. *Beloved.* New York: Random House, 1987.

Mowinckel, Sigmund. *The Spirit and the Word: Prophesy and Tradition in Ancient Israel.* Minneapolis, MN: Fortress Press, 2002.

Murray, Penelope. "Poetic Inspiration in Early Greece." *The Journal of Hellenic Studies* 101 (1981): 87–100.

Nagar, Anupam. "Tagore's Mysticisim: Resisting the Myth of Finality." *Poetcrit* 19.2 (2006): 5–29.

Nandi, S.K. *Art and Aesthetics of Rabindra Nath Tagore.* Calcutta: The Asiatic Society, 1999.

Neihardt, John G. *Black Elk Speaks.* 1932. Lincoln: University Press of Nebraska, 1979.

Newberg, Andrew. *Born to Believe: God, Science, and the Origen of Ordinary and Extraordinary Beliefs.* New York: Simon & Schuster, 2006.

Nicholson, Irene. *A Guide to Mexican Poetry, Ancient and Modern.* Los Angeles: Minutiae Mexicana, 1968.

Nietzsche, Friedrich. *The Birth of Tragedy.* New York: Cambridge University Press, 1999.

_____. *Thus Spoke Zarathustra.* Trans. Walter Kaufmann. New York: Modern Library, 1995.

Nussbaum, Martha. *Sex and Social Justice.* New York: Oxford University Press, 1999.

_____. "Social Justice and Universalism: In Defense of an Aristotelian Account of Human Functioning." *Modern Philology* 90 (1993): 46–73.

Oerlemans, Onno. *Romanticism and the Materiality of Nature.* Buffalo, NY: University of Toronto Press, 2002.

Okpewho, Isidore. Introduction to *The Heritage of African Poetry*, 3–34. New York: Longman, 1985.

Otto, Rudolph. *The Idea of the Holy.* Trans. John W. Harvey. New York: Oxford University Press, 1958.

Outka, Paul. "(De)composing Whitman." *Interdisciplinary Studies in Literature & Environment* 12.1 (2005): 41–60.

Pagels, Elaine. *Beyond Belief: The Secret Gospel of Thomas.* New York: Vintage, 2003.

Pal, Sailaza. "Dramatic Aesthetics/Ascetics: The Bhakti Poetry." *Rutgers Journal of Comparative Literature* 3.3–4 (1995–96): 127–63.

Pandit, Lalita. "The Psychology and Aesthetics of Love: Sringara, Bhavana, and Rasadhvani in Gora." In *Rabindranath Tagore: Universality and Tradition*, eds. Patrick Colm Hogan and Lalita Pandit, 141–74. Madison, NJ: Fairleigh Dickinson University Press, 2003.

Parkinson, R.B. *Poetry and Culture in Middle Kingdom Egypt.* New York: Continuum, 2002.

Patnaik, Priyadarshi. *Rasa in Aesthetics.* New Delhi: D.K. Printworld, 2004.

Patton, Kimberley Christine. *Religion of the Gods: Ritual, Paradox, and Reflexivity.* New York: Oxford University Press, 2009.

Pavese, C.O. "The Rhapsodic Epic Poems as Oral and Independent Poems." *Harvard Studies in Classical Philology* 98 (1998): 63–90.

Pawelski, James. *The Dynamic Individualism of William James.* Albany, NY: SUNY Press, 2007.

Pawelski, James, and Donald Moores, eds. *The Eudaimonic Turn: Well-Being in Literary Studies.* Madison, NJ: Fairleigh Dickinson University Press, 2013.

Payne, Daniel G. "Emerson's Natural Theology: John Burroughs and the 'Church' of Latter Day Transcendentalism." *American Transcendentalist Quarterly* 21.3 (2007): 191–205.

Pearsall, Paul. *Awe: The Delights and Dangers of Our Eleventh Emotion.* Deerfield Beach, FL: Health Communications, 2007.

Perera, Sylvia Brinton. *The Scapegoat Complex.* Toronto: Inner City, 1986.

Peterson, Christopher. *A Primer in Positive Psychology.* New York: Oxford University Press, 2006.

_____, and Martin Seligman. *Character Strengths and Virtues: A Handbook and Classification.* New York: Oxford University Press, 2004.

Philips, James. "Wordsworth and the Fraternity of Joy." *New Literary History* 41.3 (2010): 613–32.

Pickard-Cambridge, Arthur. *Dithyramb: Tragedy and Comedy.* Oxford: Claredon, 1962.

Pilcher, Tim. *E: The Incredibly Strange History of Ecstasy.* London: Running Press, 2008.

Pinchbeck, Daniel. *Breaking Open the Head: A Psychedelic Journey into the Heart of Contemporary Shamanism.* New York: Random House, 2002.

Podlecki, Anthony. *The Early Greek Poets and Their Times*. Vancouver: University of British Columbia Press, 1984.

Pollack, David. "Japanese 'Wild Poetry.'" *The Journal of Asian Studies* 38.3 (1979): 499–517.

Possehl, Gregory. *The Indus Civilization: A Contemporary Perspective*. Walnut Creek, CA: AltaMira Press, 2002.

Potkay, Adam. *The Story of Joy: From the Bible to Late Romanticism*. New York: Cambridge University Press, 2007.

Prokes, Mary Timothy. *Toward a Theology of the Body*. Grand Rapids, MI: William B. Eerdmans, 1996.

Purinton, Marjean D. "Postmodern Romanticism: the Recuperation of Conceptual Romanticism in Jeanette Winterson's Postmodern Novel The Passion." In *Romanticism Across the Disciplines*, ed. Larry H. Peer, 67–98. Lanham, MD: University Press of America, 1998.

Radice, William. "Never Not an Educator: Tagore as Poet-Teacher." *Asiatic* 4.1 (2010): 41–51.

Radin, Max. "The Kid and Its Mother's Milk." *American Journal of Semitic Languages & Literatures* 40, no.3 (1984): 209–218.

Radway, Janice. *A Feeling for Books: The Book-of-the-Month Club, Literary Taste, and Middle-Class Desire*. Chapel Hill: University of North Carolina Press, 1997.

Ramanujan, A.K. Introduction to *Speaking of Shiva*, 11–54, trans. A.K. Ramanujan, New York: Penguin, 1973.

Ramey, Christopher, and Robert Weisberg. "The 'Poetical Activity' of Emily Dickinson: A Further Test of the Hypothesis that Affective Disorders Foster Creativity." *Creativity Research Journal* 16.2–3 (2004): 173–85.

Reynolds, David S. *Walt Whitman's America: A Cultural Biography*. New York: Vintage, 1996.

Ricouer, Paul. *Freud and Philosophy: An Essay on Interpretation*. Trans. Dennis Savage. New Haven, CT: Yale University Press, 1977.

Rinpoche, Lama Kunga, and Brian Cutillo. Introduction to *Drinking the Mountain Stream: Songs of Tibet's Beloved Saint, Milarepa*, eds. and trans. Lama Kunga Rinpoche and Brian Cutillo, 2–41. Boston: Wisdom, 1995.

Robertson, Michael. *Worshipping Walt: The Whitman Disciples*. Princeton, NJ: Princeton University Press, 2010.

Ross, Margaret Clunies. *A History of Old Norse Poetry and Poetics*. Rochester, NY: D.S. Brewer, 2005.

Rothenberg, Jerome. Preface to *Technicians of the Sacred*, ed. Jerome Rothenberg, vxii–xxxiv. Berkeley: University of California Press, 1985.

Rougemont, Denis de. *Love in the Western World*. Translated by Montgomery Belgion. Princeton, NJ: Princeton University Press, 1983.

Rowland, Susan. *The Ecocritical Psyche: Literature, Evolutionary Complexity and Jung*. New York: Routledge, 2012.

_____. Introduction to *Psyche and the Arts: Jungian Approaches to Architecture, Literature, Film, and Painting*, ed. Susan Rowland, 1–11. New York: Routledge, 2008.

Rumi, Jalal al-Din. *The Masnavi: Book One*. Trans. Jawid Mojaddedi. Oxford: Oxford University Press, 2008.

Ryan, Robert M. "Wordworth's Response to Darwin." *Wordsworth Circle* 41.1 (2010): 10–13.

Salovey, Peter, David Caruso, and John D. Mayer. "Emotional Intelligence in Practice." In *Positive Psychology in Practice*, eds. P. Alex Linley and Stephen Joseph, 447–463. Hoboken, NJ: Wiley, 2004.

Salus, Peter, and Paul Taylor. Introduction to *The Elder Edda: A Selection*, trans. Paul B. Taylor and W.H. Auden, 13–33. New York: Random House, 1969.

Sanchez-Eppler, Karen. "To Stand Between: Walt Whitman's Poetics of Merger and Embodiment." In *Leave of Grass and Other Writings*, ed. Michael Moon, 850–55. New York: Norton, 2002.

Sastry, C.N. *Walt Whitman and Rabindranath Tagore: A Study in Comparison*. Delhi: B.R. Publishing, 1992.

Schelling, Andrew. Introduction to *The Wisdom Anthology of North American Buddhist Poetry*, 1–25. Boston: Wisdom, 2005.

Scheurich, Neil. "Suffering and Spirituality in the Poetry of Emily Dickinson." *Pastoral Psychology* 56 (2007): 189–97.

Schimmel, Annemarie. *As Through a Veil: Mystical Poetry in Islam*. Oxford: Oneworld, 2001.

_____. *Mystical Dimensions of Islam*. Chapel Hill: University of North Carolina Press, 1975.

Schmidt, Michael. *The First Poets: Lives of the Ancient Greek Poets*. London: Weidenfeld & Nicholson, 2004.

Sedgwick, Eve Kosofsky. "Paranoid Reading and Reparative Reading: or, You're so Paranoid, You Probably Think This Introduction Is about You." In *Novel Gazing: Queer Readings in Fiction*, ed. Eve Kosofsky Sedgwick, 1–37. Durham, NC: Duke University Press, 1997, 7.

Shapiro, Lawrence. *Embodied Cognition*. New York: Routledge, 2011.

Shusterman, Richard. *Body Consciousness: A Philosophy of Mindfulness and Somaesthetics*. New York: Cambridge University Press, 2008.

Segal, Charles. *Orpheus: The Myth of the Poet*. Baltimore MD: Johns Hopkins University Press, 1989.

Seligman, Martin. *Authentic Happiness*. New York: Simon & Schuster, 2002.

_____. *Learned Optimism*. New York: Vintage Books, 1990.

Sifarkis, G.M. "Organization of Festivals and the Dionysiac Guilds." *The Classical Quarterly* 15.2 (1965): 206–214.

Sinclair, May. "The 'Gitanjali': Or Song-Offerings of Rabindra Nath Tagore." *The North American Review* 690 (1913): 659–76.

Sinha, Harendra Prasad. *Religious Philosophy of Tagore and Radhakrishnan*. Delhi: Montilal Banarsidass, 1993.

Sircar, Kalyan. *Imagining Tagore: Rabindranath and the British Press, 1912–1941*. Calcutta: Shishu Sahitya Samsad, 2000.

Smith, Huston. *The World's Religions*. San Francisco: Harper, 1991.

Smith, Lorrie. "Some See God and Live: Dickinson's Later Mysticism." *American Transcendentalist Quarterly* 1.4 (1987): 302–09.

Stevens, Anthony. *Jung: A Very Short Introduction*. New York: Oxford University Press, 1994.

Stewart, Susan. "Lyric Possession." *Critical Inquiry* 22.1 (1995): 34–63.

Storl, Wolf-Dieter. *Shiva: The Wild God of Power and Ecstasy*. Rochester, VT: Inner Traditions, 2004.

Stryk, Lucien. Preface to *Zen Poetry*, xi–xlvii, eds. and trans. Lucien Stryk and Takashi Ikemoto. New York: Grove, 1995.

Tagore, Rabindranath. *The English Writings of Rabindranath Tagore*. Ed. Sisir Kumar Das. Delhi: Sahitya Akademi, 1996.

_____. *Gitanjali*. Ed. W.B. Yeats. New York: Scribner, 1997.

Taylor-Perry, Rosemarie. *The God Who Comes: Dionysian Mysteries Revisited*. New York: Algora, 2003.

Tayson, Richard. "The Casualties of Walt Whitman." *Virginia Quarterly Review* 81.2 (2005): 79–95.

Tedeschi, Richard G., and Lawrence G. Calhoun. "A Clinical Approach to Posttraumatic Growth." In *Positive Psychology in Practice*, eds. P. Alex Linley and Stephen Joseph, 405–419. Hoboken, NJ: Wiley, 2004.

Tessitore, John. "The 'Sky-Blue' Variety: William James, Walt Whitman, and the Limits of Healthy-Mindedness." *Nineteenth-Century Literature* 62.4 (2008): 493–526.

Thrailkill, Jane F. *Affecting Fictions*. Cambridge, MA: Harvard University Press, 2007.

Tuck, Donald. "The Religious Motif in the Poetry of Rabindranath Tagore." *Numen* 21.2 (1974): 97–104.

Trecker, Janice. "The Ecstatic Epistemology of 'Song of Myself.'" *Midwest Quarterly* 53.1 (2011): 11–25.

Turner, Victor. *The Ritual Process: Structure and Anti-Structure*. Ithaca, NY: Cornell University Press, 1966.

Twitchell, James. *Romantic Horizons: Aspects of the Sublime in English Poetry and Painting, 1770–1850*. Columbia: University of Missouri Press, 1983.

Underhill, Evelyn. *Mysticism:The Nature and Development of Spiritual Consciousness*. 1911. Oxford: OneWorld, 1994.

Valarino, Evelyn Elsaesser. *On the Other Side of Life: Exploring the Phenomenon of the Near-Death Experience*. Trans. Michelle Herzig Escobar. New York: Plenum, 1997.

Valliant, George. *Spiritual Evolution: A Scientific Defense of Faith*. New York: Broadway Books, 2008.

Vaughan-Lee, Llewellyn. *Sufism: The Transformation of the Heart*. Inverness, CA: Golden Sufi Center, 2002.

Veldhuis, Niek. "Mesopotamian Canons." In *Homer, the Bible and Beyond: Literary and Religious Canons in the Ancient World*, eds. Margalit Finkelberg and Guy Stroumsa, 9–28. Boston: Brill, 2003.

Viscomi, Joseph. "Wordsworth, Gilpin, and the Vacant Mind." *Wordsworth Circle* 38.1–2 (2007): 40–49.

Warburg, Gabriel. "From Sufism to Fundamentalism: The Mahdiyya and the Wahhabiyya." *Middle Eastern Studies* 45.4 (2009): 661–72.

Weber, Max. *The Religion of China and the Spirit of Capitalism*. New York: Routledge, 1992.

Wells, Henry. Introduction to *Ancient Poetry from China, Japan & India*, ed. and trans. by Henry Wells, 8–33. Columbia: University of South Carolina Press, 1968.

West, M.L. *Indo-European Poetry and Myth*. New York: Oxford University Press, 2007.

Whitely, Edward. "'The First White Aboriginal': Walt Whitman and John Rollin Ridge." *Emerson Society Quarterly* 52.1–2 (2006): 105–139.

Wilber, Ken. *The Marriage of Sense and Soul: Integrating Science and Religion*. New York: Broadway Books, 1998.

Wilson, James Matthew. "Representing the Limits of Judgment: Yvor Winters, Emily Dickinson, and Religious Experience." *Christianity and Literature* 56.3 (2007): 397–422.

Wilson, John. Introduction to *The Posttraumatic Self: Restoring Meaning and Wholeness to Personality*, ed. John Wilson, 1–8. New York: Routledge, 2006.

_____. "Trauma, Optimal Experiences, and Integrative Psychological States." In *The Posttraumatic Self: Restoring Meaning and Wholeness to Personality*, ed. John Wilson, 211–253. New York: Routledge, 2006.

Winhusen, S. "Emily Dickinson and Schizotypy." *Emily Dickinson Journal* 13 (2004): 77–96.

Wise, Jennifer. *Dionysus Writes: The Invention of Theatre in Ancient Greece*. Ithaca, NY: Cornell University Press, 1998.

Whitman, Walt. *Leaves of Grass and Other Writings*. Ed. Michael Moon. New York: Norton, 2002.

_____. *Specimen Days & Collect*. New York: Dover, 1995.

Wolfson, Susan. *Formal Charges: The Shaping of Poetry in British Romanticism*. Stanford, CA: Stanford University Press, 1997.

Wolosky, Shira. "Emily Dickinson: Reclusion Against Itself." *Common Knowledge* 12.3 (2006): 443–59.

Wordsworth, Jonathan, M.H. Abrams, and Stephen Gill, eds. *The Prelude: 1799, 1805, 1850*. New York: Norton, 1979.

Wordsworth, William. *Selected Poetry of William Wordsworth*. Edited by Mark Van Doren. New York: Modern Library, 2002.

_____. *William Wordsworth: Selected Poems*. Ed. John O. Hayden. New York: Penguin, 1994.

_____. *Wordsworth: Poetical Works*. Eds. Thomas Hutchinson and Ernest de Selincourt. New York: Oxford University Press, 1936.

Wu, Duncan, ed. *Romanticism: An Anthology*. New York: Blackwell, 2005.

Yeats, W.B. Introduction to *Gitanjali* by Rabindranath Tagore, ed. W.B. Yeats, 7–14. New York: Scribner, 1997.

Zapadowska, Magdalena. "Wrestling with Silence: Emily Dickinson's Calvinist God." *American Transcendentalist Quarterly* 20.1 (2006): 379–98.

Zarcone, Thierry. "Readings and Transformations of Sufism in the West." *Diogenes* 47.3 (1999): 110–20.

Zuesse, Evan. *Ritual Cosmos: The Sanctification of Life in African Religions*. Athens: Ohio University Press, 1985.

Zvelebil, Kamil V. *Literary Conventions in Akam Poetry*. Madras, India: Institute of Asian Studies, 1986.

Index